Java™ 2
Just Click! Solutions

Tom Swan

Hungry Minds™

**Best-Selling Books • Digital Downloads • e-Books • Answer Networks
e-Newsletters • Branded Web Sites • e-Learning**

New York, NY • Cleveland, OH • Indianapolis, IN

Java™ 2 Just Click! Solutions

Published by
Hungry Minds, Inc.
909 Third Avenue
New York, NY 10022
www.hungryminds.com

Library of Congress Control Number: 2001089314

ISBN: 0-7645-4823-9

Printed in the United States of America

10 9 8 7 6 5 4 3 2 1

1B/RQ/QX/QR/IN

Distributed in the United States by Hungry Minds, Inc.

Distributed by CDG Books Canada Inc. for Canada; by Transworld Publishers Limited in the United Kingdom; by IDG Norge Books for Norway; by IDG Sweden Books for Sweden; by IDG Books Australia Publishing Corporation Pty. Ltd. for Australia and New Zealand; by TransQuest Publishers Pte Ltd. for Singapore, Malaysia, Thailand, Indonesia, and Hong Kong; by Gotop Information Inc. for Taiwan; by ICG Muse, Inc. for Japan; by Intersoft for South Africa; by Eyrolles for France; by International Thomson Publishing for Germany, Austria, and Switzerland; by Distribuidora Cuspide for Argentina; by LR International for Brazil; by Galileo Libros for Chile; by Ediciones ZETA S.C.R. Ltda. for Peru; by WS Computer Publishing Corporation, Inc., for the Philippines; by Contemporanea de Ediciones for Venezuela; by Express Computer Distributors for the Caribbean and West Indies; by Micronesia Media Distributor, Inc. for Micronesia; by Chips Computadoras S.A. de C.V. for Mexico; by Editorial Norma de Panama S.A. for Panama; by American Bookshops for Finland.

For general information on Hungry Minds' products and services please contact our Customer Care department within the U.S. at 800-762-2974, outside the U.S. at 317-572-3993 or fax 317-572-4002.

For sales inquiries and reseller information, including discounts, premium and bulk quantity sales, and foreign-language translations, please contact our Customer Care department at 800-434-3422, fax 317-572-4002 or write to Hungry Minds, Inc., Attn: Customer Care Department, 10475 Crosspoint Boulevard, Indianapolis, IN 46256.

For information on licensing foreign or domestic rights, please contact our Sub-Rights Customer Care department at 212-884-5000.

For information on using Hungry Minds' products and services in the classroom or for ordering examination copies, please contact our Educational Sales department at 800-434-2086 or fax 317-572-4005.

For press review copies, author interviews, or other publicity information, please contact our Public Relations department at 317-572-3168 or fax 317-572-4168.

For authorization to photocopy items for corporate, personal, or educational use, please contact Copyright Clearance Center, 222 Rosewood Drive, Danvers, MA 01923, or fax 978-750-4470.

About the Author

Tom Swan has written extensively about computer programming for more than 25 years, and his numerous books on Pascal, Delphi, C++, Windows, assembly language, and now Java 2 are popular choices among career programmers worldwide. Tom has also written and published hundreds of articles in numerous computer journals. He is a former contributing editor to *PC World* and is the originator of the popular *Dr. Dobb's Journal* column "Algorithm Alley."

When not wedded to a computer screen, Tom studies the classical guitar and pursues his passion of ocean sailing. The author lives aboard his yacht in and around Miami and Key West, Florida. Be sure to visit Tom's Web site at www.tomswan.com for updates to this book and for information about the author's other books and articles.

Credits

ACQUISITIONS EDITOR
Gregory S. Croy

PROJECT EDITOR
Erik Dafforn

TECHNICAL EDITOR
Steven Haines

EDITORIAL MANAGER
Colleen Totz

PROJECT COORDINATOR
Maridee V. Ennis

GRAPHICS AND PRODUCTION SPECIALISTS
Sean Decker
Kristen Pickett
Jill Piscitelli
Erin Zeltner

QUALITY CONTROL TECHNICIAN
Laura Albert
Andy Hollandbeck
Carl Pierce

MEDIA DEVELOPMENT MANAGER
Laura VanWinkle

MEDIA DEVELOPMENT SUPERVISOR
Rich Graves

SENIOR PERMISSIONS EDITOR
Carmen Krikorian

MEDIA DEVELOPMENT SPECIALIST
Angie Denny

MEDIA DEVELOPMENT COORDINATOR
Marisa Pearman

BOOK DESIGNER
Jim Donohue

PROOFREADING AND INDEXING
TECHBOOKS Production Services Inc.

*To David Sullivan, aboard Troika II, for friendship
and good times on and off the water*

Preface

In my 25 years of writing about programming languages, one of my primary goals has been to publish as many source code listings as possible. This book is no different – in here are well over 150 sample applets and applications that demonstrate a wide variety of Java 2 programming techniques.

I love reading and writing source code, but I've wondered: Are listings in books the best way to publish computer programs? Perhaps you remember seeing a listing that shows how to parse a string, but just try finding that example. Was it the one on page 281, or was it in another book? And so you waste precious time hunting for solutions that you know are there, if only you could find them quickly and easily.

Java 2 Just Click! Solutions solves that problem in a unique way. For selected sections of each sample listing, and using software that I developed, I've created a database of the listings' programming techniques. For example, a listing named CloneDemo.java has entries such as "Right and wrong ways to implement `clone()`" and "Implementing the `Cloneable` interface." I then sorted those records two ways, alphabetically and by subject, creating hyperlinked, knowledge-based indexes that form a valuable online Java 2 reference.

In this book is a complete introduction to Java 2 programming using the newest JDK 1.3 release, covering applet and application development, AWT and Swing GUI components, and much more. All sample listings are included on the accompanying CD-ROM along with my *Just Click! Solutions* indexes that you can load into your favorite Web browser. Simply click on any topic, and you immediately see the line in the listing that provides the exact solution you need. Copies of the online indexes are also printed in Chapters 25 and 26 for use when you don't have your computer handy.

On my Web site, www.tomswan.com, you'll find sample *Just Click! Solutions* indexes for this and, in the future, other books and collections of source code listings. Your suggestions for improving this book are always welcome. Please let me know (at tom@tomswan.com) if *Java 2 Just Click! Solutions* and its hyperlinked indexes help you to learn and use this remarkable programming language. Good luck!

Acknowledgments

Special thanks to my friend Larry Weeldryer for taking my photograph with his new digital camera, and to the Island House in Key West for providing the lush foliage in the background. Thanks also to Barry Braverman for helping to brainstorm this book's title. My undying gratitude goes to my longtime editor, Erik Dafforn, not only for making numerous suggestions and corrections but also for sewing together the many loose ends of production. Many thanks to Steven Haines for his technical review and suggestions. I also thank Greg Croy, Joe Wikert, and Richard Swadley at Hungry Minds, Inc. (formerly IDG Books) for their unwavering support over the years. Thanks are due also to Eric Newman and Colleen Totz in Editorial, Maridee Ennis in Production, and Marisa Pearman, Carmen Krikorian, and Angie Denny in Media Development.

Contents at a Glance

Contents

Part I

Introductions

Chapter 1

Introducing This Book

THIS AND THE NEXT two chapters in Part I, "Introductions," introduce *Java 2 Just Click! Solutions,* and they help you prepare for getting the most bang from your book. Read this chapter for system requirements, for conventions used in the text, and for part and chapter summaries. Chapters 2 ("Using the *Just Click! Solutions* Indexes") and 3 ("Getting Started with Java 2") explain how to download the Java 2 JDK 1.3 and runtime environments free of charge, and they suggest ways to use the CD-ROM's online hyperlinked indexes and source code listings to your best advantage.

IN THIS CHAPTER

- ◆ Java 2 system requirements
- ◆ Conventions used in this book
- ◆ Summaries of the book's parts
- ◆ Summaries of the book's chapters

How to Use This Book

Java 2 is a true cross-platform programming language and runtime system. For that reason, this book does not focus on only one type of computer or operating system. Following are general requirements for running this book's sample programs, and also a list of conventions used in the book's text.

Requirements

The Java 2 compiler, runtime environment, and miscellaneous utilities run on most modern PCs using any of the following operating systems:

- ◆ Windows 95, Windows 98, Windows NT 4.0, and Windows 2000
- ◆ Most versions of Linux and UNIX
- ◆ Systems running the Sun Solaris operating system

Hardware requirements are not particularly critical nor extreme, but PCs should have a Pentium processor running 166 MHz or faster, and about 120MB free disk space to install everything. I compiled and ran all of this book's programs on a Dell Inspiron 7500 laptop using off-the-shelf releases of Windows 98 and Mandrake Linux version 7.

To run this book's Java 2 applets, you need a Web browser such as Internet Explorer or Netscape, although you can instead use the JDK's appletviewer utility. However, you need a browser to view this book's *Just Click! Solutions* hyperlinked indexes. The accompanying CD-ROM includes Netscape and Internet Explorer for readers who do not have browsers, or who need to upgrade.

Because of Sun's licensing restrictions, the accompanying CD-ROM does not include the Java 2 runtime system and plug-in. However, these items and others are available free of charge from Sun. See Chapter 2 for downloading instructions.

Conventions

The following information describes a few conventions used in this book's text:

- ◆ File pathnames use a forward slash as the separator character. Windows users should change this to a backslash. For example, you might need to enter the path src/c04/Welcome.java as src\c04\Welcome.java.

- ◆ Items that you are to type are in `bold monospace`.

- ◆ Programming words are `monospaced`.

- ◆ New terms are introduced in *italic*.

In writing this book, I have assumed that operating system commands and file-names are case-sensitive. However, your operating system might permit you to enter some of these items in all upper- or lowercase. Even so, the Java 2 compiler, runtime system, and other programs expect you to type upper- and lowercase text exactly as printed.

Throughout this book's chapters, you'll encounter helpful tips and suggestions that look like this:

Read this book's tips for suggestions about improving performance and getting the most out of Java 2.

General notes that further explain or clarify information in the text, or that offer advice out of context of the present discussion, look like this:

 This is an example of a general-purpose note that adds an explanation or that clarifies the discussion at hand.

Part Summaries

This book's chapters are arranged in five parts, as follows:

- Part I, "Introductions" – This part provides overviews of the book's contents, instructions on downloading the Java 2 JDK 1.3, runtime system, and plug-in, and instructions on using this book's *Just Click! Solutions* hyperlinked indexes.

- Part II, "Java 2 Tutorials" – This part offers a complete tutorial of the Java 2 programming language. You need no prior programming experience to understand this information, but you should have a working knowledge of your computer and operating system.

- Part III, "Collections" – This part presents extensive discussions and examples of Java's collections class library.

- Part IV, "Applets and Applications" – This part includes advanced information about programming with Java 2. You learn how to write threaded code and how to create applets, applications, and graphical interfaces using the AWT and Swing component libraries. Chapters in this part also cover general-purpose graphics commands, plus input and output techniques.

- Part V, "Just Click! Solutions" – Refer to the chapters in this part to solve problems such as how to input a string from the command line and how to create a GUI button. The chapters in this part are copies of the online *Just Click! Solutions* indexes for use when you don't have access to your computer.

Chapter Summaries

Following are summaries that briefly describe each of this book's 26 chapters:

◆ Chapter 1, "Introducing This Book" — As you are discovering, this chapter introduces this book, lists requirements and conventions, and provides overviews of the book's parts and chapters.

◆ Chapter 2, "Using the Just Click! Solutions Indexes" — This chapter explains how to use this book's hyperlinked Just Click! Solutions indexes. Copies of the online indexes are printed in Chapters 25 and 26 for use when you don't have access to your computer.

◆ Chapter 3, "Getting Started with Java 2" — This chapter explains how to download and install the Java 2 JDK 1.3 development system, the runtime system, and the browser plug-in needed to compile and run this book's sample applets and applications. Instructions are also included for downloading other optional files such as the Java 2 documentation suite and the JDK's source code. As mentioned, Sun Microsystems does not permit redistribution of Java 2 files, and for that reason I was not able to include them on this book's CD-ROM. However, the downloaded files are free of charge.

◆ Chapter 4, "Java 2 Fundamentals" — This chapter introduces Java 2 programming and covers the language's fundamental elements.

◆ Chapter 5, "Operators and Statements" — This chapter explains how to use operators in expressions and how to write statements that perform actions at runtime.

◆ Chapter 6, "Object-Oriented Programming" — This chapter details the *class* — the object-oriented heart and soul of all Java applets and applications.

◆ Chapter 7, "Exception Handling" — This chapter shows how to use exceptions to handle error conditions gracefully using a minimum of programming.

◆ Chapter 8, "String Things" — This chapter is devoted to Java's `String` and `StringBuffer` classes, used to hold character data in memory, and to perform a variety of operations on character strings.

◆ Chapter 9, "Numeric Classes" — This chapter explains how to use Java's numeric wrapper classes to put an object-oriented face on native integer, floating point, and other data types.

◆ Chapter 10, "Arrays" — This chapter is all about Java arrays, which unlike those in many programming languages, are created at runtime and, as a result, are not fixed in size.

◆ Chapter 11, "Abstract Classes" — This chapter explains more about classes, access rules, and abstract classes for creating *polymorphic objects* that define their own actions at runtime.

- ◆ Chapter 12, "Interfaces" – This chapter introduces the all-important interface, a purely abstract construction that provides a kind of multiple inheritance not possible with classes alone.

- ◆ Chapter 13, "Packages" – This chapter shows how to organize classes into packages, and also how to import classes from the JDK's many packages.

- ◆ Chapter 14, "Introducing Collections" – This chapter introduces Java's extensive set of collection storage classes and provides illustrations and tables that document the class library's hierarchies.

- ◆ Chapter 15, "List Collections" – This chapter shows how to use the collection library's list classes for creating array and list-type storage structures.

- ◆ Chapter 16, "Set Collections" – This chapter shows how to use the collection library's set classes to create storage structures that contain unique object instances.

- ◆ Chapter 17, "Map Collections" – This chapter shows how to use the collection library's map classes for creating associative storage structures.

- ◆ Chapter 18, "Utilities and Legacy Classes" – This chapter lists and explains many of Java's utility classes, and it also details some legacy classes still available but no longer recommended for use in new code.

- ◆ Chapter 19, "Threaded Code" – This chapter introduces the concept of threads, and shows examples of the correct ways to write threaded code in which multiple processes run concurrently.

- ◆ Chapter 20, "AWT Applets and Applications" – This chapter explains how to write programs using the Abstract Windowing Toolkit for creating graphical user interfaces. The chapter also explains in detail the delegation event model introduced in the JDK 1.1 and compares AWT and the newer Swing components.

- ◆ Chapter 21, "Swing Applets and Applications" – This chapter explores the new Swing components, which are based on the AWT but greatly expand Java's GUI programming tools. Swing is now a core element in Java 2's JDK 1.3 and largely replaces the AWT.

- ◆ Chapter 22, "Swing Components" – This chapter explains more about using Swing components to create graphical interfaces, including toolbars and buttons that display icons and that use HTML-formatted text.

- ◆ Chapter 23, "Graphics Techniques" – This chapter shows numerous examples of Java's graphics classes and methods, used in both AWT and Swing applets and applications.

- ◆ Chapter 24, "Input and Output Techniques" – This chapter explains how to utilize standard input and output files and how to read and write binary and text files using stream classes in Java's I/O package.

◆ Chapter 25, "Just Click! Solutions by Name" — This chapter is a printed copy of the online *Just Click! Solutions* by-name index, arranged alphabetically. Each of the over 600 named topics directs you to one of this book's listings, showing the listing number, page number, and line number of the statements you want to find. To use this chapter's index, simply browse for key words and phrases to find the information you need.

◆ Chapter 26, "Just Click! Solutions by Subject" — This chapter is a printed copy of the online *Just Click! Solutions* by-subject index. The more than 600 entries are the same as in Chapter 25, but they are arranged and cross-referenced by over 100 subject categories. To use this chapter's index, browse the main subject categories, then look up the key word or phrase in the associated named topics.

Summary

◆ This chapter introduces *Java 2 Just Click! Solutions,* lists the book's requirements and conventions, and provides part and chapter overviews.

◆ You may use most versions of Windows, UNIX, Linux, and Sun Solaris systems to compile and run this book's Java 2 programs.

◆ The book is divided into 5 parts and 26 chapters, covering the entire Java 2 programming language, the JDK 1.3, and showing examples of many types of applets and applications.

Chapter 2

Using the Just Click! Solutions Indexes

READ THIS CHAPTER for instructions on using the book's online, hyperlinked *Just Click! Solutions* indexes. This chapter also explains how to copy the indexes and source code files from the accompanying CD-ROM to your hard drive.

 If you discover a file named Readme.txt on the CD-ROM, be sure to consult it for updates, corrections, and late-breaking installation instructions. For even more up-to-date information, browse my Web site, www.tomswan.com.

IN THIS CHAPTER

◆ The *Just Click! Solutions* philosophy

◆ Installing the indexes on your computer

◆ Browsing the listing files

◆ How to find the source code files

Need a Solution? Just Click!

As I wrote in the preface, solutions to many programming problems are available in computer books like this one, but finding the answers to specific questions isn't always easy. The book's subject index, as good as it is (and the publisher's indexers are among the best in the business), helps you find information in the text, but the subject index lacks entries for specific statements inside the listings.

That's where my *Just Click! Solutions* indexes come in. They provide online and printed references to the techniques demonstrated in the book's sample programs. In addition, you can use the online indexes to view this book's programs online while you read about them in the text. And, when you don't have access to your computer, you can refer to the copies of the indexes printed in Chapters 25, "Just Click! Solutions by Name," and 26, "Just Click! Solutions by Subject."

Installing the Indexes

The *Just Click! Solutions* indexes on the CD-ROM are ready to use. Just open the Index.html file in the outer directory. Click Listings in the menu, and you'll see the page shown here in Figure 2-1.

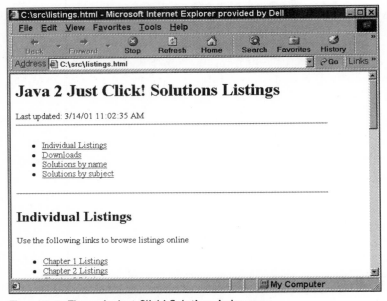

Figure 2-1: The main Just Click! Solutions index page

For faster responses, copy the indexes and sample programs to your hard drive. The exact commands for doing this differ from one system to the next. Insert the CD-ROM into your computer's drive, then follow these general steps:

1. Create a new directory or folder on your hard drive's file system. You can name the directory anything you like (I named mine j2jc, short for *Java 2 Just Click! Solutions*).

2. Copy the src directory and all subdirectories and files from the CD-ROM to the directory you created in Step 1.

3. Copy Index.html, help.html, and cover.jpg from the CD-ROM outer directory to the directory you created in Step 1.

You can now open the Index.html file in your new directory to begin using the online indexes. (You may remove the CD-ROM from your computer.) See also "Finding Source Code Files" in this chapter for help locating this book's source code files so you can compile and run the book's sample programs.

Chapter 2: Using the Just Click! Solutions Indexes 11

Copying files from a CD-ROM to a hard drive usually results in those files being marked "read-only." To make and save suggested changes to this book's source code files, you probably have to change the files' access permissions. If you are using Windows, after copying the files you want, open a DOS prompt window, and then enter the following commands (I assume you copied the files from the CD-ROM to \j2jc):

```
cd \j2jc
attrib -r *.* /S
```

The -r option removes the specified files' read-only status. The *.* option processes all files. The /S option (you must type a capital S) locates files in all sub-directories. You can now open one of the copied .java text files (use Notepad or another text editor), edit its contents, and save the results back to disk.

TIP If you use a word processor to edit a .java source code file, be sure to save it as plain or ASCII text.

Linux and UNIX users first have to mount the CD-ROM. Insert the disk into your computer and mount it by typing the following command (most Linux systems use /mnt/cdrom as the CD drive's mount point):

```
mount /mnt/cdrom
```

Next, create a new directory and copy the mounted CD-ROM files to it by typing commands such as the following (the first line changes to your user directory, but you can create the new directory elsewhere if you want):

```
cd
mkdir j2jc
cd j2jc
cp -R /mnt/cdrom/src/* .
cp /mnt/cdrom/Index.html .
```

Be sure to type a single space ahead of the periods at the ends of the last two commands. To add write-permission to all copied files, type the following command:

```
chmod -R a+w *
```

The -R option recursively "walks" the directory tree. The a+w option adds write permission. The asterisk specifies all files. You can now open, edit, and save a copied file using your favorite programming or text editor. Unmount the CD-ROM by typing the following command (on many Linux systems, the drive's eject button is disabled until the disk is unmounted):

```
umount /mnt/cdrom
```

Notice that the correct spelling of this command is umount — not *unmount*.

 If you don't want to copy all files to your hard drive, open Index.html on the CD-ROM using your Web browser, click the Listings button, and select Files to download or copy. You can then copy individual ZIP files, arranged by chapter and containing the book's source code files, to your hard drive.

Browsing the Chapter Listings

After opening Index.html, either on the CD-ROM or on your hard drive if you copied all files as suggested, click the Listings button to view the opening index page. These instructions also work for the sample indexes on my web site, www.tomswan.com, but the full indexes and files are available only on this book's CD-ROM. After opening Index.html, select one of these four main links:

◆ *Listings by chapter* — Click this link, then select a chapter to view listings online while you read the text. Listings are arranged by chapter and listing number. Just follow the links to find any listing in the book.

◆ *Files to download or copy* — If you copied the CD-ROM files to your hard drive, you can skip this link. It's needed only if you are viewing listings online or directly on the CD-ROM. Click one of these links to copy or download the book's source code files in ZIP format. After copying, unpack the file into a new directory using a utility such as WinZip. Preserve all relative pathnames when unpacking.

◆ *Solutions by name* — Click this link for a list of source code solutions arranged alphabetically. Click any entry's link to find the statement for the exact solution you need. Each of over 600 entries shows the listing name, number, line number, and page number where you'll find the listing in this book.

◆ *Solutions by subject* — Click this link for a list of source code solutions arranged by over 100 subject categories. These are the same entries as in the *Solutions by Name* index, but they are extensively cross-referenced to help you quickly locate the information you need. (Hint: Scroll to the *Listing files* subject for a list of this book's listings, arranged alphabetically by filename.)

Listings printed in the book and viewed online have line numbers added for reference purposes. The associated source code files, which you can compile and run, do not have line numbers. To find the source files, see *Finding Source Code Files* in this chapter.

The online indexes are mostly intuitive. Just click the links to browse the listings and find solutions to specific problems and topics. Following are a few additional tips to help you use the indexes more effectively:

◆ Before clicking a link to a listing, make a mental note of the listing name and line number, shown in the link. Usually, but not always, that line will appear at the top of the browser window. If not, you may have to look around a little to find it.

◆ After clicking an index link, scroll upward to find the program's file name and number, for example, Listing 4-1, Welcome.java. Click on the file name to open, download, or copy the source code file. Exactly what happens depends on your file system — if you see the file text in the browser window, use File|Save to save it to a file on your hard drive. Or, you might be prompted whether to open or download the file. In any case, you'll probably want to save the file so you can compile and run the program.

◆ Use your browser's Back button to return to the by-name or by-subject index. This way, you are returned to the location from which you left the page. Or, click `Return to top`, then click `Switch to Solutions by name page` or `Switch to Solutions by subject page` to view the index you want from the top. Click `Return to Listings page` to return to the main page.

◆ Use the browser's search command (in Internet Explorer, this is probably called Edit|Find (on This Page)...) to locate specific class names, files, and other information in any of the index and listing pages.

◆ Expand your browser to full screen, and if you have a low-resolution display, close any side windows such as Favorites in Internet Explorer. The online index entries are fairly long, and they are more easily viewed using as wide a window as possible.

To save space in the book, I cut some duplicated and irrelevant lines out of many of this book's printed listings. However, you always see the entire listing when you view it online.

Finding Source Code Files

After you read about a listing and view its text onscreen, or as printed in the book, you can compile and run the program to see how it works. To do this, you need to locate the program's source code files. Those files are not exactly the same as the printed listings, and their directories may contain supplemental files not listed in the book or on line – for example, the HTML files that load applets into a Web browser or the appletviewer utility. For reference, the printed and online listings have line numbers added, and they also eliminate miscellaneous comments at the top of each file. (I didn't think you'd appreciate seeing my copyright notice over 150 times.) The real source code files – the ones you compile and run – do not have line numbers and they include the miscellaneous headers. To run a program, you first need to locate these files.

You can locate a listing's source code files several ways, depending on how you choose to install the CD-ROM indexes. The first (and easiest) method is to copy the entire src directory from the CD-ROM to your hard drive, as suggested earlier in this chapter under "Installing the Indexes." After you have done that, following these steps to locate a source code file. I assume you have named your installation directory j2jc:

1. Find the chapter directory in the src/listings directory. For example, to locate Chapter 4's source code files, change to j2jc/src/listings/c04.

2. Find the program's name in the chapter directory. For example, to find Chapter 4's Welcome.java source code file, first change to j2jc/src/listings/c04, and then change to the Welcome subdirectory. In this book, every program is in a subdirectory named the same, minus the .java file name extension. (Hint: The subdirectory and file names are shown in the online indexes.) As mentioned, after copying a file from the CD-ROM, it may be marked read-only. Change the file's write-permission as explained earlier in this chapter in the section "Installing the Indexes."

The second way to locate a source code file is to use the online indexes on the CD-ROM. Use this method if you do not want to copy all files to your hard drive:

1. Open Index.html on the CD-ROM, click the Listings button, select `Listings by chapter`, select the chapter you want, and click on the listing's name and number.

2. You now see the numbered listing, the same as printed in the book. To find the associated source code file, scroll up if necessary to the listing number and file name. Click the file name, and if requested, elect to open the file or to download (or save) it to any directory of your choosing. If the file opens in your browser, use File|Save to save it.

3. Switch to your terminal window, and change to the directory where you copied the listing. Change the file's write-permission if necessary.

 As mentioned, some programs, and all applets, in this book have additional files that are required for running the program. The preceding steps copy *only* the listing's source code file, not any required supplemental files. However, the steps work for most single-file source code listings and are useful particularly if you are viewing the sample indexes on the Internet.

A third way to find a source code file is to download one of the chapter ZIP files, as suggested earlier under *"Installing the Indexes"*. Use this method if you don't want to copy the entire CD-ROM to your hard drive, or if you want to compile and run only the listings in selected chapters:

1. Open Index.html on the CD-ROM, click the Listings button, and select Files to download or copy. Choose the chapter ZIP file you want and copy it to a new directory. (The listings.zip file contains a copy of each chapter's ZIP files.)

2. Use a Zip utility such as WinZip to unpack the chapter's source code files. Be sure to preserve all subdirectories.

3. Using a terminal window, change to the directory where you unpacked the files, and then change to the subdirectory, named the same as the program.

Finally, you can use the "brute force" method to locate individual listing source code files. These steps may be easiest if you want to try only selected sample programs and applets:

1. Insert or mount the CD-ROM.

2. Create a directory to hold the source code files. I'll call it /j2jc/ex.

3. Change to the chapter and listing directory on the CD-ROM. For example, change to src/listings/c04/Welcome.

4. Copy all files from the current directory to the directory you created in Step 2. You might also use a file program such as Windows Explorer or, in Linux, a KDE desktop window, to copy individual files. Change the files' write-permission if necessary.

TIP See "Compiling and Running Listings" in Chapter 4 for general instructions about running this book's sample programs. Before you can do that, you need to install the JDK, the runtime system, and for applets, the Java 2 plug-in. Downloading instructions also follow in Chapter 3.

Summary

◆ This book's CD-ROM contains hyperlinked *Just Click! Solutions* indexes to all of the book's sample listings. Using the indexes, you can view listings online, you can copy and download listing files, and you can locate solutions to specific programming problems.

◆ For best results, copy the entire src directory from the CD-ROM to your hard drive. Open the Index.html file and follow the links to locate the listing you want. You may also view the indexes and listings directly on the CD-ROM if you don't want to copy files to your hard drive. You may have to change a file's write-permission before you can edit and save the file.

◆ To compile and run a program, locate its source code files on the CD-ROM, or in the copy of the src directory on your hard drive. Listings printed in the book and viewed online have line numbers added for reference. The source code files that you compile and run do not have these numbers.

Chapter 3

Getting Started with Java 2

BEFORE YOU CAN COMPILE and run Java 2 programs, you first need to obtain and install a few files, available free of charge over the Internet from Sun Microsystems. So you can get started quickly, this chapter lists files that you must download and install but also covers desired files such as the online documentation and JDK sources that you can delay installing for now.

Sun Microsystems has repeatedly denied my and the publisher's requests to provide any of Java 2 on this book's CD-ROM (and, as far as I could determine, on any other book's disc). Perhaps someday, Sun Microsystems will revise their distribution policies and make Java 2 easier to acquire. Until then, however, to make full use of this book, you must download and install the JDK 1.3 development system, a Java 2 runtime environment appropriate for your system, and the Java 2 plug-in for your Web browser. I offer my humble apologies for the inconvenience, and I request that you send any comments about this situation directly to Sun Microsystems.

IN THIS CHAPTER

- ◆ Downloading Java 2
- ◆ Installing Java 2 on Windows
- ◆ Installing Java 2 on Linux
- ◆ Installing optional Java 2 files
- ◆ Testing your installation

Where to Get Java 2

Following are suggestions and notes about how to find and download the various files needed to compile and run Java 2 applets and applications. As of this writing, Java 2's JDK release number is 1.3. If a newer release is available, by all means use it. However, many of the program's in this book require JDK 1.3, so if you already have an older Java compiler and runtime system, you should upgrade as soon as possible.

Required Elements

Java 2 contains three essential pieces that all users must download and install. The exact filenames differ depending on your platform, but the three pieces are otherwise the same for all systems. The pieces are

- ◆ The Java 2 Development Kit, or JDK, 1.3. This contains the compiler, runtime utilities, and compiled libraries needed to compile and run Java 2 applets and applications. Sun also calls this the Java 2 SDK — but they are one and the same.

- ◆ The Java 2 Runtime Environment, or JRE, Standard Edition 1.3. This enables your operating system to run Java 2 applets and applications.

- ◆ The Java 2 Plug-in for your Web browser. This piece is included with the Java 2 Runtime Environment. It enables Internet Explorer and Netscape to run Java 2 and Swing applets.

You should locate, download, and install at least those elements for your operating system. Detailed instructions follow the next section, which lists optional files that you can download and install now or later.

Desired Elements

In addition to the required elements listed in the preceding section, you may want to download and install a few other files. The following items are optional but highly recommended:

- ◆ The Java 2 Online Documentation. This is an extensive set of HTML files that document all of Java's numerous classes and methods. It's an essential tool that serious Java programmers should have. By the way, a Japanese translation is available on Sun's Web site.

- ◆ The Java 2 Source Code files. You can't recompile the JDK using these files, but they are the perfect companions to the online documentation. Reading the JDK's sources is a great way to learn Java 2 programming techniques and to gain a better understanding of the development system's classes and interfaces.

- ◆ The HTML converter utility. You need this utility only to load Swing applets into a Web browser or the appletviewer utility. If you aren't going to use Swing, you don't need this utility. The utility is offered for downloading from Sun's Java 2 Plug-in Web page.

Java 2 comes in three editions: Standard (J2SE), Enterprise (J2EE), and Micro (J2ME). I recommend that you use the standard edition with this book's sample programs. The enterprise edition is primarily for building server-side systems, and the micro edition is for embedded systems such as palm-top computers. After you finish this book, you might want to try the other editions, but stick with the standard one for now. I used J2SE to write and test all of this book's sample programs.

Downloading Java 2

The following notes explain how to navigate Sun's Web site and locate the files you need for Windows and Linux. Because those are the systems I use, they are the only ones I have tested. However, Java 2 is also available for Sun Solaris operating systems (Intel and SPARC) from the same Web pages described here.

Web pages are frequently updated, and the following information may become out of date even as I type these words. Sun's Web site is huge, and there are undoubtedly many different ways to find the necessary files, so don't be surprised if you discover alternate paths and methods. Set aside a good chunk of time, build a tall one of your favorite refreshment, and take notes in case you have to repeat a step.

Using Sun's Web Site

Regardless of your operating system, begin the same way. Log on to Sun's Web site by typing the following link exactly as shown into your Web browser's Address field:

```
http://java.sun.com/
```

Do not preface the link with the usual www. However, if you have trouble, try logging on to www.sun.com, and then click the *Java 2 SDK* button. I don't know why Sun sometimes calls the JDK the SDK (Software Development Kit), but as mentioned, there is only one development system, and it is correctly named the JDK 1.3.

Try to find the j2se page (Java 2 Standard Edition). Look for a link that takes you there, or you can try logging directly on to this slightly deeper link:

```
http://java.sun.com/j2se
```

If that doesn't work, look for a button labeled *Products and APIs* (it was on the left of the screen the last time I looked), click it, and select *Java 2 Platform, Standard Edition*. That should bring up the correct page from which you can begin downloading. You know you are on the right page if you see sections titled *Current Releases, Related Technologies,* and *Previous Releases.* You want the files in only the first two sections.

From this point, installation instructions and filenames differ depending on your operating system. Be sure to read all installation instructions for your operating system on Sun's Web site, but also read the following notes for additional suggestions and hints that I found helpful when I installed the files.

 In addition to the files listed here, you will find others available for downloading from Sun's Web site. I have documented only the files that I have used and found useful in Java 2 programming and in writing this book.

Downloading Windows Files

Following are the files that I suggest you download and install to use Java 2 on Microsoft Windows. Filenames may differ due to version number updates, but they should be similar to those listed here. Only the first two files are absolutely required:

- `j2sdk-1_3_0_02-win.exe` — This is the Java 2 JDK 1.3, and it contains the compiler and utilities needed to compile Java 2 programs. The file size is 31.2 MB.

- `j2re-1_3_0_02-win.exe` — This is the Java 2 Runtime Environment. This file includes the Java 2 Plug-in. The file size is 5.1MB.

- `j2sdk-1_3_0-update1-doc.zip` — This file contains the Java 2 online documentation. Notice that this one is a ZIP file — the others are self-extracting executables. Although the filename says "update," this is the complete file. The file size is 22.3MB. It is the same file for all supported platforms.

- `jdk1_3_0-src-win.zip` — This is the most difficult file to locate and download. For help finding it, see the notes following this section. The file size is 40.1MB.

- `htmlconv2_3.zip` — This file contains the HTML converter utility for translating <applet> tags for use with Swing applets. The file is obscurely located in the *Java 2 Plug-in* page. The file size is 149.3KB. The converter is a Java application, and therefore, the same program runs on all supported platforms.

To locate all of those files means wading through several layers of information. Most files are found using similar commands, but some use a different and confusing array of links and buttons. The following suggestions should help you navigate through the site and find what you need:

♦ Look for a section that lets you choose "One large bundle." The other choice is for downloading large files in 1.44MB pieces. Use that method only if your online connection terminates before the download is complete. In that case, follow instructions on the Web site that explain how to join the pieces and create the finished installation file. You cannot use the smaller pieces to install Java 2 from floppy disks, even though the file sizes seem to suggest that this is possible. You must install from a hard drive directory. Be sure to compare the finished and joined-together file size with the file on the Web site before proceeding.

♦ Downloading the JDK source code files requires you to register a user name and password with Sun's site. You can then "order" the source code product, for which you receive an invoice in the amount of "$0.00" and an order confirmation number. This is the most confusing file to locate and download — be sure to select the right one for your operating system. Expect trouble if your ISP's DNS numbers do not "reverse resolve" into a domain name, another subtle requirement of Sun's that, apparently, is intended to prevent downloads outside of the U.S.A. The sources are provided in different compression formats. Windows users should select a ZIP file. Linux users should select the .tar.gz formats.

♦ When you finally get to the download page for each file, you will probably find a series of FTP buttons. Select the *Default FTP* site if possible, but if you have trouble, try selecting another site nearest your location.

♦ Internet Explorer 5 users: If clicking an FTP button starts displaying text in the window, *immediately* click the browser's *Stop* and *Back* buttons. Scroll down to a button labeled *HTTP download*. Clicking that button should bring up a dialog that prompts you whether to open or save the file. Select *Save* and the download should begin.

Downloading Linux Files

Many Linux fans use Windows for Internet access because so many PCs have WinModems, none of which are compatible with Linux. If that's you, follow instructions in the preceding section, but download the Linux files listed next. You can then reboot into Linux, log on as the super user (root), and copy the files from a mounted DOS partition to a Linux directory. Despite dire warnings you may have read about this method scrambling file contents, I have successfully transferred many files between Windows and Linux this way.

Of course, if you are using Netscape in Linux, you can log on to Sun's Web site and begin downloading directly to your home or another directory. You might also be able to use the ftp utility in a terminal window, although I haven't tried this. Whatever method you decide to use, first read the preceding section for an overview of the process and tips for navigating through Sun's Web site. Linux files for Java 2 are provided in two formats:

◆ *RedHat RPM shell script* — select this format if you have the RedHat Package Manager on your system. Most Linux systems, not only RedHat's edition, have an installed copy of RPM, and therefore, most Linux users should download these files.

◆ *GNUZIP Tar shell script* — select this format if you know your way around Linux and want more control over the installation directories, or if you don't have RPM. You can probably also use these files to install Java 2 on GNU UNIX. Using these files, you can create a system-wide installation (you must have super user privileges), or you can install Java 2 in a user directory. By the way, GNU is a recursive acronym that stands for "GNU is Not UNIX."

As with Windows, you have the option for each file (except the very small ones) to download "One large bundle" or to divide the download into 1.44MB pieces. Download in pieces only if your ISP prevents you from completing the larger download. Follow instructions on Sun's Web site for joining the pieces to create the finished file. Be sure to compare the finished file size with the file on the Web site before proceeding.

Linux users who have RPM should download the following two files, both of which are required:

◆ j2sdk-1_3_0_02-linux-rpm.bin — This is the JDK 1.3 containing the compiler and utilities. The file size is 25.6MB.

◆ j2re-1_3_0_02-linux-rpm.bin — This is the Java 2 Runtime Environment, needed to run Java 2 applications and applets. The file size is 14MB.

Readers not using RPM should instead download the following two files, both of which are required. Despite differences in sizes, the files have the same contents as the preceding two; only the installation details are different:

◆ j2sdk-1_3_0_02-linux.bin — The JDK 1.3. The file size is 27.1MB.

◆ j2re-1_3_0_02-linux.bin — The Java 2 Runtime Environment. The file size is 14.4MB.

All readers may choose to download the following optional files. For serious Java 2 programming, however, you should download them all:

◆ j2sdk-1_3_0-update1-doc.zip — This contains the Java 2 online documentation in HTML format. Although the filename says "update," this is the complete file. The file size is 22.3MB. It is the same file for all supported platforms. However, at one point, it was named j2sdk...doc.tar.gz.

◆ `j2sdk1_3_0-src-linux.tar.gz` — These are the source code files for the JDK 1.3. You cannot use these files to recompile the JDK — they are intended for information only. See the notes in the preceding section on how to find this file. You will have to wade through several layers of the Web site, and you must register a user name and password with Sun before you can download this one.

◆ `htmlconv2_3.zip` — This file contains the HTML converter utility for translating `<applet>` tags for use with Swing applets. The file is obscurely located in the *Java 2 Plug-in* page. The file size is 149.3KB. The converter is a Java application, and therefore, it runs on all supported platforms.

Installing Java 2 for Windows

Sun's Web site provides complete instructions for installing Java 2 on Windows 95, Windows 98, Windows NT 4.0, and Windows 2000. Be sure to read those instructions, but also read the following notes — my suggestions differ here and there. Because I use Windows 98, the following notes are for that system only. However, the steps should be similar for most other Windows versions.

 Because this section is strictly for Microsoft Windows users, unlike elsewhere in this book, all pathnames use the correct backslash character.

Installing the JDK

First, install the JDK by running the following self-extracting program. It's easiest to use Windows Explorer to do that, but you can type the program's name into the Start menu's Run command if you prefer:

```
j2sdk-1_3_0_02-win.exe
```

Select the default directory, C:\jdk1.3. If you specify a different directory, some HTML links may be broken. After installation, open \jdk1.3\readme.html for additional notes. To uninstall, use the *Add/Remove Programs* command in the Windows control panel.

Installing the JRE

Follow a similar procedure to install the Java 2 Runtime Environment (JRE) by running this self-extracting program:

```
j2re-1_3_0_02-win.exe
```

Again, select the default directory C:\Program Files\JavaSoft\Jre\1.3. This should also install the *Java 2 Plug-in,* but to check this, run the program of that name in the Windows control panel. Make sure that *Plug-in enabled* is selected.

> After installing the JRE, open and read the Welcome.html and README.txt files in the aforementioned path. These contain deployment notes and further explanations of the runtime files and directories.

Setting Environment Variables

After installing the JDK and JRE, you are asked to reboot your system. Do *not* do that yet. First, you need to set two environment variables so you can run the javac compiler and java runtime interpreter. Do this by modifying the DOS environment variables, PATH and CLASSPATH.

Windows NT users can select Control Panel → System Properties → Environment Options to check and set the variables. In other versions of Windows, to check the variables' current settings, open a DOS prompt window if you haven't done so already. Type set to check the current environment settings. You should find a PATH setting, but there may not be one for CLASSPATH. Java 2 can use, but does not require, a CLASSPATH setting.

> Many Windows users may be unfamiliar with using a DOS prompt window. For simplicity, this book's sample programs are best compiled and run using this window, so now is a good time to configure your DOS prompt if you haven't done so before. To open a DOS prompt window, double-click the icon labeled "MS-DOS Prompt" on your desktop. If no such icon exists, create one using Windows Explorer to locate the file Command in C:\Windows. (Select the file with no extension, *not* the one named Command.com.) Right-click and drag that file to an unused space on the desktop, and select "Create shortcut(s) here" from the pop-up menu to create the shortcut icon.
>
> To configure your DOS prompt window, right-click the shortcut icon and select Properties. Or, open the DOS prompt window by double-clicking the shortcut icon, and click the button labeled with a large capital A, which of course stands for Aardvark. (The button actually opens the Properties dialog, and should probably be renamed P for Peacock.)

Use a text editor such as Notepad to edit C:\Autoexec.bat. At the bottom of that file, or after the last PATH command (if any), enter

```
SET PATH=%PATH%;C:\jdk1.3\bin
```

That makes it possible to run the Java 2 compiler and other programs from any other directory. Also add the following CLASSPATH setting:

```
SET CLASSPATH=
```

That effectively turns the CLASSPATH variable off. This is contrary to Sun's suggestion that you set this variable to a single period, which references the current directory. If the preceding doesn't work for you, try this:

```
SET CLASSPATH=.
```

 If you cannot make this change to the CLASSPATH — for example, because you are running a Java visual developer that also uses this variable — use the -classpath command-line switch with the javac compiler to compile this book's programs.

If you have read Sun's installation instructions, you are directed to run Autoexec.bat by typing autoexec at a DOS prompt. Do *not* do that — it usually causes DOS to run out of environment space, and worse, also resets the DOS prompt window to full screen text mode. If this happens to you, follow these steps to reset the window:

1. Type exit at the full-screen DOS prompt to close the prompt and return to Windows.

2. Right-click the MS-DOS Prompt icon. If you don't have this icon, create one as mentioned in an earlier note by using Windows Explorer to right-click and drag the file C:\Windows\Command to the desktop.

3. Select Properties from the pop-up menu.

4. Click the Screen tab.

5. Select Window under Usage.

6. Click OK to close the Properties window.

Save your changes to Autoexec.bat. Now you may reboot. This runs Autoexec.bat automatically and completes your installation. Turn to "Compiling and Running

Listings" in Chapter 4, or read on if you want to install Java 2's source code, documentation, and HTML converter utility.

Installing Other Files

To install the JDK's source code files, look for a file named src.jar. This might be in the C:\jdk1.3 directory, or depending on how you downloaded it, the file might be inside another compressed ZIP archive. Copy src.jar to C:\jdk1.3 if necessary, and then enter these commands at a DOS prompt:

```
cd \jdk1.3
jar xvf src.jar
```

That creates the directory src in the current directory, and unpacks the JAR (Java Archive) file. Unlike most command-line utilities, you do not have to type a hyphen ahead of the option letters xvf (meaning respectively *extract, use verbose mode,* and *open archive file*).

 The JDK source code files apparently terminate lines with line feeds, a UNIX convention. This causes Windows programs such as Notepad to display the text in one unreadable blob punctuated with little black squares. Numerous available text converters can fix the files, but I found that opening them with the Windows Wordpad utility displays the text correctly.

To install the Java 2 online documentation, copy the following file to the outer C:\ directory:

```
j2sdk-1_3_0-update1-doc.zip
```

The HTML files in that archive must be installed using the default path jdk1.3\docs and subdirectories; otherwise, the links don't work. Because the internally archived paths begin with jdk1.3\, you must copy the archive to a directory one level *higher* than where you installed the JDK. Otherwise, you may end up with an awkward, though harmless, directory structure such as \jdk1.3\jdk1.3\docs...

Use WinZip or a similar program to open the archive and extract all files, being sure to preserve the directory structures. After unpacking, open C:\jdk1.3\docs\index.html using your Web browser. You can then follow the links to all of Java 2's documentation. By the way, the documentation was produced by the javadoc utility, part of the JDK 1.3. Examine the JDK source code files to see the raw commands used to prepare the documentation. (I used my own similar, but different, system to prepare this book's *Just Click! Solutions* indexes.)

Create a shortcut to C:\jdk1.3\docs\index.html on your desktop by right-clicking and dragging that filename to an empty space on the desktop, then selecting the pop-up menu command "Create shortcut(s) here." This provides a fast way to open the documentation by double-clicking the shortcut icon. To change the icon's name, right-click it and select the pop-up menu command Rename.

Finally, if you are going to write your own Swing applets, install the HTML converter utility to translate `<applet>` tags in HTML files. Download or copy the following file to C:\jdk1.3:

```
htmlconv1_3.zip
```

Like the documentation archive, the converter must be installed using the default directories. However, unlike the documentation archive, the converter's path begins with converter\. So, this time, you *should* copy the archive to C:\jdk1.3 in order to install it in the path C:\jdk1.3\converter. (However, you may install the program elsewhere if you want.) In any case, use WinZip or a similar compression utility to extract all files and subdirectories. See Chapter 21, "Swing Applets and Applications," for more information on using the converter.

Installing Java 2 for Linux

The JDK and JRE files for Linux are bundled into shell scripts that display Sun's license agreement before installation begins. In the recent past, these files ended with .sh. Now, they end in .bin, even though they are still shell scripts. Because of this change, unless you have recently downloaded the files, you may have to alter the following instructions slightly.

Installing the JDK Using RPM

If you are using the RPM files, follow the steps in this section to install the JDK. First, copy the following file into your user directory, or to any other convenient location:

```
j2sdk-1_3_0_02-linux-rpm.bin
```

That and other Java 2 .bin files must be executable. If they aren't, make them so by entering a command such as

```
chmod +x j2sdk-1_3_0_02-linux-rpm.bin
```

TIP Experienced Linux users know that pressing Tab automatically completes long filenames. You can probably just enter the first part of the preceding command stopping at j2s and then press Tab. Windows users should be so lucky!

The location of the installation file is not important because it specifies internally the installation paths that RPM uses to install the JDK's files. You must become the super user to begin the installation. Do that by typing su and entering the root password, and then enter these commands:

```
./j2sdk-1_3_0_02-linux-rpm.bin
rpm -iv j2sdk-1_3_0_02-linux.rpm
```

The first command displays Sun's license and creates the .rpm file. The second command installs the JDK. If you receive an error message concerning glibc, this is probably because glibc was not installed using RPM on your system (and as a result it's not on the RPM installed-file list). In that case, enter the following alternate command:

```
rpm -iv --nodeps j2sdk-1_3_0_02-linux.rpm
```

If you are reinstalling over an earlier version, you may also need to use the --force option to force RPM to complete the installation.

NOTE Readers with glibc versions earlier than 2.1.2–11 may need to upgrade this critical library file. See "Upgrading glibc" in this chapter for instructions.

Installing the JRE Using RPM

Next, install the Java Runtime Environment (JRE) by locating the following RPM file:

```
j2re-1_3_0_02-linux-rpm.bin
```

As when installing the JDK, the location of that file is not critical. Copy it to any convenient directory, and if necessary, make it executable. Assuming you are still the super user (if not, enter su and the root password), and type the following two commands to install the JRE:

```
./j2re-1_3_0_02-linux-rpm.bin
rpm -iv j2re-1_3_0_02-linux.rpm
```

Once again, you may need to use the `--nodeps` and, possibly, the `--force` options if you receive an error message concerning glibc, or if you are reinstalling over an earlier release.

Installing the JDK and JRE Using Shell Scripts

If you are not using RPM, you can install Java 2 in any directory. You may choose a system-wide installation – for example, /usr/local – in which case you must log on as or become the super user. Or, you may install Java 2 into your home directory, in which case all files are under your control, and with the proper permissions set, only you may use them. Copy the following files into the directory you want to use for the installation:

```
j2sdk-1_3_0_02-linux.bin
j2re-1_3_0_02-linux.bin
```

Next, enter the following commands to install the Java 2 JDK and JRE:

```
./j2sdk-1_3_0_02-linux.bin
./j2re-1_3_0_02-linux.bin
```

In each case, you'll see Sun's license agreement and you need to answer any prompts appropriately. You can now turn to "Installing the Plug-in" to complete your Java 2 installation.

Upgrading glibc

If you need to upgrade glibc, locate the most recent release on your Linux system's Web site (for example, log onto `www.mandrake.com` and search for glibc). The library's version numbers change frequently. Locate and download the following three files (the lowercase x is a digit, and the asterisks represent one or more other characters):

```
glibc-2.x.x-xmdk.ix86.rpm
glibc-devel*.rpm
glibc-profile*.rpm
```

Log on as or become the super user again if necessary, and enter the following command for each of the preceding files in the order listed here:

```
rpm -Uv glibc...rpm
```

You should now be able to complete the JDK and JRE installations.

Installing the Linux Plug-in

See Sun's documentation for current instructions on installing the Java 2 Plug-in for Netscape, or enter the following commands. Remove the existing Plug-in by entering

```
rm -fr $HOME/.netscape/java
rm $HOME/.netscape/plugins/javaplugin.so
```

Instead of typing $HOME, you can enter ~/. If you are using Netscape 4, set the following variable by typing the command:

```
export NPX_PLUGIN_PATH=<jre>/plugin/i386/ns4
```

If you are using Netscape 6, the steps are more complex. You need to create soft links from the plug-ins directory – <netscape>/plugins – to the JRE's plug-in directory, <jre>/plugin/i386/ns600/libjavaplugin_oji.so. The exact command depends on your installation directories. Enter something like this (all on one line), replacing <jre> and <netscape> as appropriate:

```
ln -s <jre>/plugin/i386/ns600/libjavaplugin_oji.so
<netscape>/plugins/.
```

You should now be able to restart Netscape and load Java 2 applets including those that use Swing components and converted HTML <applet> tags, as explained in Chapter 21. Sun's documentation indicates that you may have to restart Netscape twice before the Plug-in is properly recognized.

Turn to "Compiling and Running Listings" in Chapter 4 or read on to install the documentation, source code files, and HTML converter.

Installing Other Files

The Java 2 documentation is the same for all supported platforms and is provided in HTML-formatted files. Locate the following file:

```
j2sdk-1_3_0-update1-doc.zip
```

Use the Linux unzip command, or another decompression utility if you have one, to unpack the files into any directory. After unpacking, open the index.html file using Netscape to view the documentation.

Installing the JDK source code files and HTML converter are simple tasks. However, the exact commands differ depending on the compression format of the files that you downloaded. If they are in ZIP format, use the unzip command to unpack them:

```
unzip htmlconv1_3.zip
```

Or, if the files are in the so-called "tarball" format, ending in .tar.gz, extract the files using commands similar to these:

```
gunzip filename.tar.gz
tar -xvf filename.tar
```

At one point, the documentation files for Linux, although they are the same for all platforms, were provided in a file named j2sdk...tar.gz. In that case, use the preceding commands to unpack and install the files.

 If you are still logged on as the super user, enter exit to become mortal again before continuing.

Testing Your Installation

After installing Java 2 and copying this book's source code files and indexes to your hard drive, test your installation by trying a few simple examples. You can then turn to the next chapter to begin learning about the Java 2 programming language.

To make sure you can run the compiler, enter one of the following commands. Windows users can simply type

```
javac
```

Linux users need to add an option:

```
javac --help
```

You'll see some messages and a list of command-line options. Linux users can find out where the compiler was installed (probably /usr/bin) by entering

```
whereis javac
```

Linux users can also verify the installed compiler version by entering the following command, but this doesn't work for some reason under Windows:

```
javac --version
```

If those commands work as expected, try compiling and running a simple example. Enter the following commands to compile and run Welcome.java from Chapter 4, "Java 2 Fundamentals":

```
cd j2jc/src/listings/c04/Welcome
javac Welcome.java
java Welcome
Welcome to Java 2 programming!
```

TIP   The directory name j2jc assumes you copied the entire src directory and its subdirectories and files from the CD-ROM to your hard drive into that base directory. Type the filenames exactly as shown — the compiler and runtime interpreters are case-sensitive, even if your file system is not. Windows users: open a DOS prompt window, and remember to change the forward slashes to backslashes.

If the program is an applet, compile its source code file the same way, but don't use the java utility to run it. Instead, load the HTML file located in the same directory into appletviewer using commands such as

```
cd j2jc/src/listings/c20/RandomColor
javac RandomColor.java
appletviewer RandomColor.html
```

Alternatively, you can use Windows Explorer, or in Linux, a KDE or Gnome desktop file system, to locate and open the HTML file. This should bring up the applet in Internet Explorer, Netscape, or another default Web browser. If you have trouble, check that the Java 2 Plug-in is properly installed.

Summary

- ◆ Before getting started with Java 2 programming, you need to download and install several files as explained in this chapter. Supported platforms include Windows 95, Windows 98, Windows NT 4.0, Windows 2000, Linux, and Sun Solaris operating systems for Intel and SPARC computers.

- ◆ Java 2 comes in three editions: Standard, Enterprise, and Micro. I recommend using the Standard edition J2SE along with this book.

◆ This chapter gives detailed instructions for navigating Sun's Web site, downloading the necessary Java 2 elements, and installing under most versions of Windows and Linux. Be sure to read Sun's documentation on their Web site in case any of this information has changed.

◆ All readers need to download and install the JDK 1.3 development kit, the JRE 1.3 runtime environment, and the Java 2 Plug-in. I also recommend installing the online documentation and the JDK source code files, but these pieces are optional.

◆ For developing Swing applets, you also need to download and install the HTML converter to translate `<applet>` tags in HTML files for use with the Java 2 Plug-in. The converter is obscurely located on the *Plug-in* download page on Sun's Web site.

Part II

Java 2 Tutorials

Chapter 4

Java 2 Fundamentals

THIS CHAPTER helps you discover what Java 2 is and how easy it is to use. If you know another programming language, such as C++, Visual Basic, or Pascal, so much the better. I assume only that you know a few basics such as what bits and bytes are, and how to create and edit text files. If you are starting from scratch, you've come to the right place to begin.

IN THIS CHAPTER

◆ An introduction to Java programming

◆ Identifiers and keywords

◆ Adding comments to programs

◆ Literal values

◆ Data types and variables

Welcome to Java Programming

A Java program consists of one or more *source code files,* which are merely text files with the filename extension .java. Most Java source code files contain plain ASCII text, also known as ISO Latin-1. Internally, Java converts plain text to Unicode, which means that if you have a Unicode editor, you can use it to prepare and edit source code files. With Unicode, you can insert special character symbols into programs. More important, in keeping with Java's international appeal, Unicode makes it possible to design program elements such as menu commands and window titles using almost any human language. However, for simplicity, all listings in this book and on the CD-ROM are in plain ASCII text.

It's your choice which editor to use for creating and modifying Java source code files. If you run Windows 95 or 98 or another version, you can use the Windows Notepad. Or, in a DOS window, use the Edit program. You can also use a word processor such as Microsoft Word, WordPad, or WordPerfect to edit Java source code files. If you do that, however, be sure to save all files as plain or Unicode text. Linux and UNIX users have many choices of editors, but the Emacs editor, found on all Linux installations, is one of the most popular.

In this section, you enter, compile, and run a simple Java program. Because I run Linux and Windows 98 on my computer, the sample commands printed here may differ if you use another operating system. If you have any trouble, turn to the installation instructions in Chapter 3, "Getting Started with Java 2," for help.

C and C++ programmers may recognize a lot of information in this and other chapters. This is because Java is similar in many respects to C and C++ (especially in their fundamental elements), but there are many key differences that you might miss if you gloss over the chapters in this part.

Tutorial Listings

The source code file in Listing 4-1, Welcome.java, shows the basic format of a Java program. Each line is numbered for reference in this book and for use with the *Just Click! Solutions* indexes on the CD-ROM, but the numbers and colons at far left are not part of the program. For practice, you might want to type in this and other listings — in that case, omit the line numbers and colons. Although Java programs may consist of multiple files, most of the sample tutorial listings in this and the other chapters in Part II are self-contained in single files.

Listing 4-1: Welcome.java

```
001: class Welcome {
002:  public static void main(String args[]) {
003:   System.out.println("Welcome to Java 2 programming!");
004:  }
005: }
```

You can find Welcome.java in the src/listings/c04/Welcome subdirectory on the accompanying CD-ROM. Remember that in Windows, at a DOS prompt, you must type a backslash as a path separator. In Linux and UNIX terminals, and in all Web browsers, type a forward slash.

As Welcome.java shows, a basic Java program consists of a class named the same as its filename minus the .java extension. The class is bracketed with opening and closing braces, inside of which are various declarations and other items that make up the program. Source code lines are typically indented to show their association, but Java ignores indentation and line separations, which simply make programs more readable and understandable. (Due to space limitations, this book's listing lines are indented in multiples of one space. It's more common, however, to indent lines by two or four spaces, or to use tab characters.)

The key element in the sample program is its *class,* a construction that encapsulates a program's data and executable elements. Other chapters in this part explain more about classes. For now, you need to know only that a Java program exists inside at least one class such as `Welcome`. Without its content, the `Welcome` class looks like this:

```
class Welcome {
  . . .
}
```

Here and elsewhere in this book, a three-dot ellipsis indicates text you are expected to supply or that is irrelevant to the topic at hand. In this example, the `Welcome` class contains a *method*, code that performs the program's activity. This method is defined inside the `Welcome` class as

```
public static void main(String args[]) {
  System.out.println("Welcome to Java 2 programming!");
}
```

A method is a named group of one or more statements and is similar to a *subroutine* or a *function* in other programming languages. In Java, however, a method is always inside a class. There are numerous elements to the method shown here, all of which you'll meet in due course. The important facts in this example are the method's name (`main`) and the statement inside the method's delimiting braces. That statement calls another method, `println()` ("print line" in English), provided by the standard output file `out` in the `System` class, which is available to all Java programs. (Chapter 24, "Input and Output Techniques," explains more about files.)

All Java programs that run in stand-alone fashion (that is, not as applets in a Web browser) must have one and only one `main()` method. The program begins running at the first statement inside `main()`. To distinguish them from other items, method names in this book are followed by a pair of parentheses.

I'll explain more about objects, classes, and methods as we go along. For now, you need to understand only that the result of running this program is the string `Welcome to Java 2 programming!` appearing on your display. The next section explains how to make this happen.

Compiling and Running Listings

There are many ways to compile and run Java programs. Some of you might be using a visual developer such as Forté, JBuilder, or Visual Café. That's okay, but for learning Java programming, it is simpler and more instructive to compile and run sample listings at a DOS command-line prompt or a Linux terminal window. From now on, I refer to this environment as the *terminal window*.

If you followed the installation instructions in Chapter 2, "Using the *Just Click! Solutions* Indexes," you have copied all of this book's listings from the CD-ROM to your hard drive. If you haven't done that, you can use the online hyperlinked indexes to copy individual files. In any case, after locating the Java listing you need, open or switch to your terminal window. Enter a *change directory* (CD) command such as

```
cd /j2jc/src/listings/c04/Welcome
```

That assumes you copied the book's listings to a fresh directory named /j2jc. Next, type the following command to compile the Welcome.java source code file:

```
javac Welcome.java
```

You must type the .java filename extension. In Java, filenames are case sensitive, and you must type the command exactly as shown. Normally, unless something goes wrong, the Java 2 compiler runs silently. For a running dialog of the compilation process, enter a -verbose option like this:

```
javac -verbose Welcome.java
```

Assuming your Java 2 compiler is properly installed, after a brief pause, you should again see the prompt in your terminal window. A directory (type dir in Windows or ls in Linux) shows a new file, Welcome.class, created by compiling the source code file. This file contains Java *byte codes,* which you can execute by feeding them to a Java *Virtual Machine,* or VM, also sometimes called an *interpreter* or *viewer.* Do that now by entering this command:

```
java Welcome
```

Again, you must type a capital W. The VM reads the byte codes in the Welcome.class file (you do not have to type the filename extension in this case) and runs the program. Here's what appeared on my screen when I did this in Windows 98 (my typing is in bold face):

```
C:\j2jc\src\listings\c04\Welcome>java Welcome
Welcome to Java 2 programming!
```

The program's output is shown here on the second line. Compile and run most sample program listings in this book using similar commands.

Identifiers and Keywords

The individual elements of a Java source code file are known as *tokens*. Tokens consist of literals, operands, operators, separators, identifiers, and reserved words.

◆ *Literals* are values such as 3.14159 or strings such as "Hi there!" that you enter into a program. Other literals are symbols such as true and false that have special meanings.

◆ An *expression* such as A + B consists of the operands A and B, and one or more operators such as +. Together, operands and operators create expressions and *statements* that perform calculations on data and perform other actions.

◆ *Separators* have special meaning in programs. A separator can be a space, a semicolon, a period, a colon, or another punctuation character. I won't list each separator character here; you can easily learn proper separator etiquette by examining this book's listings. There's one separator, however, that you must know about — the semicolon. It's the source of a lot of confusion in Java and in other programming languages. In Java, a statement *always* ends with a semicolon, as demonstrated by the output statement from Welcome.java:

```
System.out.println("Welcome to Java programming!");
```

The reason you need to terminate a statement with a semicolon is because statements might have numerous tokens, and the compiler needs you to identify the statement's end. Declarations, however, do not need semicolons because the compiler can detect their ends from the declaration's context. For example, a class declaration ends with a closing brace — a semicolon would be superfluous (and is not allowed):

```
class ClassName {
  ...
}  // No semicolon here!
```

Other Java tokens are identifiers and keywords, both of which are important enough to deserve the following separate explanations.

Identifiers

Identifiers are words that you invent to describe your program's variables, methods, and classes. For example, you might identify a data object as accountBalance or a method as switchOff().

You may use any combination of letters, digits, underscores, and dollar signs in identifiers. An identifier, however, must begin with a letter. (Technically, identifiers may begin with an underscore or a dollar sign, but these are special symbols used internally by Java. To avoid conflicts, always begin identifiers with letters.) Because spaces are not allowed in identifiers, some programmers like to use underscores to make words more readable, as in the identifier

```
speed_of_light
```

Because underscores are sometimes difficult to see on screen, I prefer to use cap-italization for a similar effect:

```
speedOfLight
```

Java source code is case sensitive, which means that the three identifiers speedOfLight, speedoflight, and SPEEDOFLIGHT are completely different words. All-uppercase identifiers are permitted, but not recommended because they might conflict with #define text macros in code linked to C and C++ libraries.

The standard Java specification states that identifiers may consist of letters a through z, and A through Z, plus Unicode characters with values greater than hexadecimal 0x00C0. (For identification purposes, hexadecimal values are preceded by 0x.) In practice, however, it's best to create readable identi-fiers using only the keys on your keyboard.

Keywords

Keywords are identifiers that Java reserves for its own purposes. You've already seen one such keyword—class. Because this word has special meaning to Java, you can't use it for anything but its intended purpose.

Following is a list of Java's reserved keywords. The keywords const and goto are reserved but not used. Some early Java compilers reserved another keyword, byvalue, not listed here. The words true, false, and null are not technically key-words—they are considered to be the same as literal values like 123—but I included them in the list because you cannot use these words for your own identifiers.

abstract	boolean	break	byte
case	catch	char	class
const*	continue	default	do
double	else	extends	false†
final	finally	float	for
goto*	if	implements	import
instanceof	int	interface	long
native	new	null†	package
private	protected	public	return
short	static	strictfp	super

switch	synchronized	this	threadsafe
throw	throws	transient	true†
try	void	volatile	while

*reserved but not used
†literal value; not a keyword

Comments About Comments

While writing this book, I made many notes on the side to remind me to expand a thought, research a fact, or insert a program listing in the text. Comments in a program are exactly like these notes. They are private messages that document a program. The Java compiler completely ignores comments. Java has three styles of comments, as explained in the next sections.

C-Style Comments

A standard Java comment, also recognized in C and C++, is delimited with the two-character symbols /* and */. All text between and including these symbols is ignored. You can use this style to create single- or multiple-line comments. For example, you might enter a header like the following one at the beginning of a program file:

```
/* Title: MyProgram.java by Tom Duck */
/* Revision 2.0 -- all bugs converted to features */
/* Copyright (c) 2001 by Ugly Duckling Software, Inc. */
```

The advantage of this type of comment style is that it may extend for two or more lines. For example, the preceding text could also be written this way:

```
/* Title: MyProgram.java by Tom Duck
   Revision 2.0 -- all bugs converted to features
   Copyright (c) 2001 by Ugly Duckling Software, Inc. */
```

C++-Style Comments

For single-line comments, or for those at the ends of lines, begin the text with a double slash. For example, the compiler ignores the following line:

```
// The compiler ignores this comment.
```

This style, resurrected in C++ from an earlier language called BCPL (and also recognized by other languages such as Delphi's Object Pascal), starts with the double slash and extends to the end of the line. This makes the double-slash comment style ideal for adding a note to the end of a statement or declaration such as

```
char ch;   // Input character variable
```

The preceding comment documents the use of the character variable ch. In a large program with hundreds of declarations, good comments are essential for creating understandable source code.

TIP   Good code should be readable on its own. Don't rely on comments by themselves to make your intentions clear. For instance, a variable named wdisp is not as clear as widthOfDisplay. Good comments *clarify* self-documenting code; they don't take the place of it.

Documentation Comments

A third type of comment is sometimes used in Java to create automatic documentation. This *documentation comment* is a C-style comment with an extra asterisk. For example, the following text documents a method named MakeItHappen():

```
/** This makes it happen */
public static void MakeItHappen() {
  ...
}
```

The second asterisk identifies the comment as documentation for a following declaration, in this case, the MakeItHappen() method. Using the javadoc utility, provided with the JDK, you can create documentation HTML files that you can view using any Web browser such as Netscape or Internet Explorer.

NOTE   The Java 2 online documentation was created using documentation comments embedded in the JDK's source code files. See Chapter 3, "Getting Started with Java 2," for instructions on downloading and installing the online documentation and JDK source code.

Listing 4-2, NoComment.java, demonstrates Java's three comment styles.

Listing 4–2: NoComment.java

```
001: /* This paragraph shows that C-style comments
002:    may extend for
```

```
003:    several lines. */
004:
005: /** The NoComment class demonstrates comment styles */
006: /** This and the last line are "Java Documentation Comments" */
007: class NoComment {
008:  public static void main(String args[]) {
009:   // This comment is not displayed
010:   System.out.println("This string is displayed");
011:   System.out.println( /* Embedded comment is not displayed */
012:    "This string is also displayed");
013:   /* This single-line C-style comment is not displayed */
014:  }
015: }
```

If you open the listing source code file or view it online, you'll see a few additional C++ style comments that identify the filename and list my copyright notice. These lines look like this:

```
//===============================================================
// NoComment.java - Demonstrates Java comment styles
// Copyright (c) 2001 by Tom Swan. All rights reserved.
//===============================================================
```

All listings on the CD-ROM begin similarly, but to save space, this extra header information is deleted from the printed listings. Following the header is a three-line comment that uses the C-style double-character brackets. Documentation comments precede the program's class, NoComment. Inside the listing are several other C and C++ style comments.

 Despite my copyright notice in each listing, as in all of my books, you are free to incorporate any or all of the programming in this book into your own code.

Debugging with Comments

You might use an embedded comment to temporarily disable some items for debugging purposes. Just surround the text with comment brackets as in this example:

```
System.out.println(/*"Original string"*/ "test string");
```

In that statement, the original string is *commented out* and a second string is entered for test purposes. You might also disable entire statements this way, and then run the program to observe what happens:

```
/*
System.out.println("some text"); // Display some text
System.out.println("more text");
*/
```

Both of the disabled `println()` statements are easily restored by deleting the comment brackets. I usually place the brackets on separate lines to make them easy to find. Notice that the double-slash comment appears to be nested inside the C-style comment. However, no logical nesting takes place — the compiler simply treats all of the text between the symbols /* and */, including the C++ style comment, as one big comment.

Literal Values

A *literal value* is a number, a character, a string of characters, or a symbolic name such as `true` or `false` that you type directly into a program. You might use a literal value to initialize an object to hold that value — assigning 10, for example, to an integer variable:

```
int i = 10;  // Assign literal 10 to variable i
```

The following sections briefly describe literal values just to introduce their formats. The next section, "Data Types and Variables," gives more complete examples of each value type.

Numeric Literals

Numeric literals are either integers (whole numbers) or floating point values (fractions). Integers may be expressed in decimal (base 10), hexadecimal (base 16), or octal (base 8). Following are examples of each type of integer literal:

```
int i = 123;      // Assign decimal 123 to integer i
int j = 0x10F9;   // Assign hexadecimal 10F9 to integer j
int k = 0123;     // Assign octal 123 to integer k
```

To identify a value's number base, or *radix,* begin decimal values with the digits 1 through 9, hexadecimal values with 0x, and octal values with 0. Floating point numbers include a decimal point or are expressed in scientific notation — a whole number followed by the letter e or E and a positive or negative exponent. Here are some examples:

```
double f1 = 123.45;    // Assign 123.45 to floating point f1
double f2 = 4.257e-3;  // Assign 0.004257 to floating point f2
double f3 = 4.257e2;   // Assign 425.7 to floating point f3
```

The reserved word `double` is a type of floating point variable. Unless specified otherwise, literal floating point numbers are of this type. Any numeric literal number can be made negative by preceding it with a minus sign:

```
int q = -45;          // Assign -45 to integer q
double p = -67.8;     // Assign -67.8 to floating point p
double r = -3.41e-4;  // Assign -0.000341 to floating point r
```

Character and String Literals

Enclose single characters in single quotes. Enclose strings of zero or more characters in double quotes. Following are some examples:

```
char ch = 'X';        // Assign X to character ch
char atSign = '@';   // Assign @ to character atSign
String s = "Multiple characters";  // Assign string to s
String emptyString = "";  // Assign empty string
```

TIP When entering characters and strings, don't type opening and closing quote marks as you might in a word processing document. Type all quotes using the apostrophe/quote key (I call them *straight quotes*) to the left of the Enter key on most PC keyboards. If you are using a word processor to edit source code files, be sure to turn off any feature that replaces straight quotes with opening and closing (also known as "smart" or "curly") quote marks.

Boolean Literals

In addition to numeric, character, and string literals, a Java program may have *symbolic literal values*. Most common are the predefined values `true` and `false`, spelled in lowercase. These are *boolean* values, used in programs to determine the truth or falsehood of various expressions. The following statement, for example, sets a `boolean` variable named `debugging` to `true`:

```
boolean debugging = true;  // Assign true to debugging
```

Another statement might inspect this variable to decide whether to display a value for test purposes:

```
if (debugging)
 System.out.println("Reached this part of program");
```

When that statement executes, if `debugging` is `true`, the program displays a message, which indicates the part of the program that is running at this time. To remove the effect of the statement, but leave it in place for future testing, simply set the `debugging` variable to `false`.

Data Types and Variables

Variables are typed identifiers that can change value over the course of a program. For example, the `debugging` variable in the preceding section is of type `boolean`, and the program can change its value to `true` or `false` as many times as necessary. Another way to think of variables is to consider them to be named places in memory that can store data. A variable can hold only one value at a time of its particular type, but its value can change as many times as needed.

The key to using variables correctly is to learn as much as you can about Java's data types. When you create a variable, you must specify its type, and any operations on that variable must conform to that type. It makes no sense, for example, to multiply two strings. It also makes no sense to assign a character to a floating point variable. As you will learn, there are ways to convert values to different types — for example, translating a string into a floating point value — but you can't indiscriminately mix values of any types.

In this section, you learn more about Java's data types and how to use them to create variables in programs. First, however, we need to agree on a few terms.

A Few Good Terms

The following definitions are not rigorous (I'll leave such concerns to compiler documenters), but I find them helpful in using data in programs:

◆ A *data type* is literally the amount of memory space that can hold a value of a specific type. Declaring a variable of a data type reserves one or more bytes of memory for this kind of value. Most important is to realize that it can take a different amount of space to hold different types of values: A `double` value, for example, takes 8 bytes, while an `int` value uses only 4.

◆ A *variable* is an *instance* of a specific data type. It is called a variable because the program can change the instance's value, either by assigning to it a literal value or the value of another variable, or by performing some operation on the variable — adding 10 to an integer variable, for example.

◆ An *object* in this book is an instance of a class — but more on that in Chapter 6, "Object-Oriented Programming." In some other books, you might see the word *object* used to describe all kinds of variables. Here, an object is always an instance of a class.

◆ A *value* refers to the contents of a variable or object. Values can also be literal. A value is not necessarily numeric. For example, 123 is a value, but the string "Cockadoodledo" is also correctly called a value.

◆ A *simple data type* is an integer, floating point, boolean, or character type. You may also come across the equivalent terms *built-in type* or *native type* to describe Java's simple data types. Simple variables occupy a fixed amount of space.

◆ A *composite* or *complex* data type is an array, a class, or an interface (you'll meet that term in Chapter 12, "Interfaces"). In some cases, composite types occupy variable amounts of space — for example, not all strings are the same length. Many complex data types have associated methods that perform operations such as searching a string for sub-strings. I explain many such methods throughout this book.

Declaring Variables

To store a value of a specific type, you declare a variable of that type. As with all other Java programming elements, variables are always declared inside a class. Listing 4-3, VarDemo.java, demonstrates how to declare and assign a value to a variable.

Listing 4-3: VarDemo.java

```
001: class VarDemo {
002:   public static void main(String args[]) {
003:     int count;    // Declare a variable
004:     count = 10;   // Assign value to variable
005:     System.out.println("Count = " + count);
006:   }
007: }
```

Inside method main(), the program declares an integer variable, count, of the data type int. Next, the program assigns to count the value 10. Finally, it displays count's value. When you compile and run the program, it displays

```
Count = 10
```

Notice how a plus sign appends the value of count to a string in the println() statement. Actually, this *converts* count to a string, which is appended to the literal string. You can use a similar technique to display most kinds of values, as long as Java can convert them to strings.

In place of lines 3 and 4 in the listing, you can declare and assign a value to a variable with one statement:

```
int count = 10;
```

This declares `count` as an `int` variable and assigns it the initial value 10. If you don't initialize a variable, it is automatically assigned a value of zero. Depending on the variable's type, this might set the variable to `false` (if it's `boolean`), or for a `char`, the Unicode value `'\u0000'`. You can declare multiple variables on separate lines:

```
int i;  // Declare int variable i
int j;  // Declare int variable j
int k;  // Declare int variable k
```

Or, you can declare multiple variables of the same type by separating them with commas. The following declares three `int` variables:

```
int i, j, k;  // Declare int variables i, j, and k
```

Integer Variables

Java defines the memory sizes of its simple data types, and these sizes are guaranteed to be the same on any computer that can run Java byte codes. This fact gives Java a tremendous advantage over other computer languages such as C, in which the sizes of data types are left to the particular implementation. With Java, an `int` is always 32-bits long and can represent values in decimal ranging from −2,147,483,648 to 2,147,483,647.

Commas in numbers are for readability in this book. In a program's source code, numeric values never have commas.

Java supports several different types of integers with different memory sizes and corresponding minimum and maximum value ranges. Table 4-1 lists Java's integer data types, their sizes in bytes and bits, and their minimum and maximum ranges. All integer types are signed (that is, they can hold negative and positive values).

TABLE 4-1 INTEGER DATA TYPES

Type	Bytes	Bits	Minimum	Maximum
byte	1	8	−128	127
short	2	16	−32,768	32,767

Type	Bytes	Bits	Minimum	Maximum
int	4	32	−2,147,483,648	2,147,483,647
long	8	64	−9,223,372,036,854,775,808	9,223,372,036,854,775,807

You may specify integer values of any type in decimal, hexadecimal, or octal. Decimal values cannot begin with zero. As mentioned, hexadecimal values are preceded with 0x or 0X (that's a zero, not a capital O). Octal values must begin with zero. Here are some sample declarations using each format and showing the equivalent values in decimal:

```
int decimalCount = 123; // decimal 123
int hexCount = 0xF89C; // decimal 63644
int octalCount = 037; // decimal 31
```

Literal values are by default considered to be of the int data type. As long as the values are in the proper range, Java can convert them to the appropriate size. Literal 255, for example, can be converted automatically to a 2-byte short value. When a program executes a statement such as

```
short shortCount = 255;
```

Java first interprets 255 as an int value, which is then downsized to the short data type for assigning to shortCount. The following, however, does not compile:

```
byte byteCount = 255; // ???
```

That doesn't work because 255 is higher than the maximum value that a byte variable can hold, which is 127.

 In this book, the comment // ??? indicates a construction that either doesn't compile or that might produce faulty results.

Because literal numbers are of type int by default, you must append L to numbers larger than 2,147,483,647. This is true even when specifying values in hexadecimal. (You may use a lowercase l, but this isn't recommended because it looks too much like the digit 1.) For example, the following declares a long variable, bigNumber, and assigns it the maximum possible positive value:

```
long bigNumber = 0x7FFFFFFFFFFFFFFFL;
```

Listing 4-4, IntDemo.java, demonstrates various integer values. From now on, I won't list similar programs for every single example statement, so don't wait for me to suggest running the code examples in this book. Insert them into a program and try them out!

Listing 4–4: IntDemo.java

```
001: class IntDemo {
002:  public static void main(String args[]) {
003:
004:    // Values in decimal, hex, and octal
005:    int decimalCount = 123; // decimal 123
006:    int hexCount = 0xF89C;  // decimal 63644
007:    int octalCount = 037;   // decimal 31
008:
009:    // Display preceding variables
010:    System.out.println("decimalCount = " + decimalCount);
011:    System.out.println("hexCount     = " + hexCount);
012:    System.out.println("octalCount   = " + octalCount);
013:
014:    // Variables of each integer data type
015:    byte byteCount = 0x0F;
016:    short shortCount = 32767;
017:    int intCount = 99999;
018:    long bigNumber = 0x7FFFFFFFFFFFFFFFL;  // Note final L
019:
020:    // Display preceding variables
021:    System.out.println("byteCount    = " + byteCount);
022:    System.out.println("shortCount   = " + shortCount);
023:    System.out.println("intCount     = " + intCount);
024:    System.out.println("bigNumber    = " + bigNumber);
025:  }
026: }
```

Compiling and running IntDemo.java produces the following output on screen, showing each assigned value in decimal:

```
decimalCount = 123
hexCount     = 63644
octalCount   = 31
byteCount    = 15
shortCount   = 32767
intCount     = 99999
bigNumber    = 9223372036854775807
```

Floating Point Variables

Java has two floating point data types, float and double. A float variable represents *single-precision* values. A double variable represents *double-precision* values. Table 4-2 shows Java's floating point data types, their sizes, and their value ranges. Because float and double variables can hold very small and very large values, the table expresses minimum and maximum values using scientific notation.

TABLE 4-2 FLOATING POINT DATA TYPES

Type	Bits	Minimum	Maximum
float	32	1.4013e–045	3.40282e+038
double	64	2.22507e–308	1.79769e+308

When using floating point variables, keep in mind that their values may be approximate. Mathematical operations on floating point values might be rounded internally, and it is a mistake to expect the results to be perfectly exact. (This is true of most computer languages, by the way, not only Java.)

 Java supports strict and non-strict floating point operations. With strict floating point in effect, Java evaluates floating point expressions identically on all platforms. With non-strict floating point, the local system's floating point library is used for computations, and this might produce small variations in expression evaluations. See "Strict Floating Point" in Chapter 6 for more information on this topic. Floating point evaluations are non-strict by default.

You can specify a literal floating point value to be of the float or double data types. Append F to a literal value to specify it as a float type. Append D to specify the double type. You may do this using decimal or scientific notation. You may also use lowercase letters f and d. Generally, Java chooses the correct data type to represent literal floating point values, but you can use this technique for extra safety. Consider these declarations:

```
double d1 = 1.55000009e-100D;  // Force double type
double d2 = 1.55000009e-100F;  // Force float type
double d3 = 1.55000009e-100;   // ??? but probably okay
```

The first assignment forces the literal value to be of type `double`. The second assignment forces the value to be of type `float`. Because that type is less precise than `double`, d2 may not be exactly equal to d1. The third assignment is probably okay, provided the Java interpreter is correctly programmed. For safety, however, appending a `D` to the literal value as in the first assignment ensures that the correct type is used.

You can't use the preceding technique to force an inappropriately large or small value to fit into a smaller space. For example, the following statements do not produce the expected results:

```
float doubleTrouble = 1.556701e-050F;  // ???
System.out.println("doubleTrouble = " + doubleTrouble);
```

Early Java versions allowed this to compile, although the results were wrong because the literal value is outside the allowable range for the `float` data type. Now, Java 2 reports the following error message:

```
X.java:8: floating point number too small
float doubleTrouble = 1.556701e-050F;  // ???
1 error
```

Boolean Variables

A `boolean` variable can have only one of two values, `true` or `false`. Unlike in some programming languages, Java's `boolean` is an actual data type, and equivalent integer values for `true` and `false` are not defined. This means you cannot mix integer and `boolean` values in expressions, as you can, for example, in C and C++.

Variables of type `boolean` and related expressions become more important when you examine flow control statements in Chapter 5, "Operators and Statements," so the following statements have no practical purpose. However, if you want to run them, you can insert the statements into a `main()` method (use any of the sample listings presented so far):

```
boolean positive = true;   // Assign true to positive variable
boolean negative = false;  // Assign false to negative variable
System.out.println("positive = " + positive);
System.out.println("negative = " + negative);
```

The keyword `boolean` is lowercase (as are all Java keywords). So are the values `true` and `false`. As the output statements show, you can display the values of `boolean` variables such as `positive` and `negative`. When you compile and run the preceding code, it displays these lines on screen:

```
positive = true
negative = false
```

Character Variables

A character variable holds one 16-bit Unicode value that can potentially represent any character in any written language. Declare a character variable using the char data type. Try these statements in a main() method:

```
char ch = '#';
System.out.println("ch = " + ch);
```

As you probably suspect, that displays the pound-sign character, #. Internally, characters are represented as Unicode values, so you can also assign integers to char variables. Change the first line to

```
ch = 123;
```

and the program now displays an opening brace, {, the character having the Unicode value 123. You may specify any value from 0 to 65535. The following two examples use this method to assign equivalent values to ch (notice that Unicode integer values are unsigned):

```
ch = 65000;    // Assign integer Unicode value to ch
ch = 0xFDE8;   // Same as above but in hexadecimal
```

When you assign an integer value to a char variable, you are assigning it a *bit pattern*. This is not necessarily equivalent to a Unicode character's value. Consider these three declarations:

```
ch = '\037';   // Octal
ch = '\37';    // Octal
ch = '\u0037'; // Unicode 0037
```

The first two assignments are equivalent because digits following a backslash in a literal character or string are always in octal. Use the \u prefix to specify a Unicode value, which must have four digits and is expressed in hexadecimal, but without the usual 0x prefix. The Unicode character associated with \u0037 is the digit character '7'. To verify this, try the following two lines in a main() method. The statements display the digit 7:

```
char ch = '\u0037';  // Unicode 0037
System.out.println("ch = " + ch);
```

Specify control codes by using the backslash symbols in Table 4-3. These special codes, also called *nonprinting characters,* represent characters that have no display symbols, or that don't appear on most keyboards. Because a backslash indicates the following character is a control code, type "\\" to insert a single backslash into a string. Also, because quotes delimit characters and strings, you must use the back-slash symbols \' and \" to designate single and double quote marks respectively. All nonprinting characters may be used as literal characters and inserted into strings.

TABLE 4-3 NONPRINTING CHARACTERS

Name	Example	Result
New line	'\n'	Start new output line
Tab	'\t'	Insert tab
Backspace	'\b'	Backspace
Return	'\r'	Carriage return
Form feed	'\f'	Eject page (form feed)
Backslash	'\\'	Insert backslash
Single quote	'\''	Insert single quote
Double quote	'\"'	Insert double quote
Unicode hex value	'\u0037'	Unicode digit 7
Unicode octal value	'\37'	Unicode octal 037

String Variables

I won't say much about strings here because we'll get into them in detail in Chapter 8, "String Things." All strings in Java are actually objects of the String or StringBuffer classes, and because you haven't learned much about classes at this point, I'll merely mention strings for now.

You already know that strings are delimited with double quotes. Although they may appear to be arrays of characters, internally they are sophisticated objects with a wide variety of associated methods.

Like characters, strings may include any of the nonprinting symbols in Table 4-3. One useful trick is to insert new-line codes, \n, to display blank lines. The following displays the value of count with an extra blank line above and below. This is often simpler and more efficient than using multiple println() statements:

```
int count = 123;
System.out.println("\nCount = " + count + '\n');
```

Summary

◆ A Java program consists of one or more source code files, which are merely text files that end with the filename extension, .java. Source code files may contain Unicode characters or plain ASCII text. Internally, Java processes plain text as Unicode.

◆ Using javac to compile a Java source code file ending with the filename extension .java produces byte codes in a new file named the same but ending with .class. To run the byte codes, you load them into the Java Virtual Machine, for example, by running the java interpreter.

◆ The individual elements of a Java source code file are known as tokens. These include literals, operands, operators, separators, identifiers, and keywords.

◆ Java has three comment styles. Text bracketed with /* and */ is ignored. Text beginning with // is ignored to the end of the line. You may also use Java's documentation comment, /** ... */ along with the javadoc utility.

◆ Declare variables using Java's many data types. There are several kinds of integer, floating point, character, and string types from which to choose.

Chapter 5

Operators and Statements

NOW THAT YOU KNOW about data types and how to declare variables, you're ready to begin performing actions on data. To do that, as this chapter explains, you write expressions and statements using a wide variety of operators.

IN THIS CHAPTER

- ◆ Understanding expressions and operators
- ◆ Evaluating floating point expressions
- ◆ Type casting
- ◆ Programming with flow-control statements

Understanding Expressions

A key element of all computer programming languages is the concept of an expression. This is any combination of variables, literals, and operators that the program can evaluate, or reduce, to a value that might be assigned to a variable, or used to determine the future course of the program. To understand how to use expressions, you first need to learn Java's operators.

Introducing Operators

An operator is a symbol that performs some kind of action on data. For example, the plus sign + is an operator that adds two numbers or joins two strings. Java's operators include some additional separation characters such as commas for listing multiple items and periods for specifying related objects, as in this statement:

```
balance = account - charges;
```

That assumes the three items — balance, account, and charges — are variables of some compatible data type. When the program runs, the statement evaluates the expression account - charges, and then it assigns that result to balance. The order in which expression elements are evaluated depends on operator precedence, as shown in Table 5-1. Operators higher in the table take precedence over those on lower lines. Operators on the same row have equal precedence.

TABLE 5-1 OPERATOR PRECEDENCE

( )	.	[ ]			
++	- -	+	-	!	~
new					
*	/	%			
+	-				
<<	>>	>>>			
<	>	<=	>=	instanceof	
==	!=				
&					
^					
&&					
||					
?:					
=	op=				
,					

The plus and minus signs on line two are unary operators. The same symbols on line five are binary operators.

In expressions, operators with higher precedence are evaluated before those with lower precedence. Otherwise, expressions are evaluated from left to right. For example, the expression to the right of the equal sign in the following statement multiplies c and d and then adds that product to b before assigning the total to a:

```
a = b + c * d;
```

The expression works this way because the times operator (*) has a higher precedence than +. To force a different evaluation order, use parentheses:

```
a = (b + c) * d;
```

You may also use extra parentheses to make an expression clear — encasing the entire expression ((b + c) * d), for example. Regardless of precedence, operations inside parentheses are always completed before those outside.

Notice that the equal sign is Java's *assignment operator*. In the statement

```
a = b + c + d;
```

the result of adding b, c, and d is assigned to a. I am purposely not declaring the data types of these variables — they might be integers, or they could be floating point values. As a general rule, the destination should be as large as the largest operand. For example, if b and d are type int and c is type long, then variable a must be long to hold the result of the expression. In the next several sections, I'll explain more about different types of expressions.

 One way to remember mathematical operator precedence is to memorize the child's phrase, "My Dear Aunt Sally." The first letters of each word are the same as in "Multiply, Divide, Add, Subtract," the precedence order of the operators *, /, +, and -.

Unary Integer Expressions

Unary integer expressions are so called because they have only one operator. The statement

```
a = -b;  // Assign negation of b to a
```

assigns the negation of b to a. This does not change b's value. To do that, you would have to write

```
b = -b;  // Negate b
```

Use the tilde (~) to perform a bitwise negation, turning all binary ones to zeros and vice versa:

```
a = ~b;  // Assign bitwise negation of b to a
```

Use the double character operators ++ and -- to increment and decrement operands. Unlike unary - and ~, the operators ++ and -- change the values of their operands. The expression

```
count++;
```

increments the value of count by one, and has the same result as

```
count = count + 1;
```

That's not necessarily as efficient, however, because most computers have low-level increment and decrement instructions. (There's no guarantee, however, that a specific Java interpreter will use those instructions.) Consider some more examples:

```
i = i + 1;   // Add 1 to i
i++;         // Same as above
j = j - 1;   // Subtract 1 from j
j--;         // Same as above
```

One concept that confuses many programmers on first meeting is that an expression such as i++ performs an action (incrementing i) but also has a value. In fact, all expressions have values, so this isn't a special rule. It is important here, however, because the placement of ++ and -- affects the expression's result. The statements

```
++i;   // Prefix notation
i++;   // Postfix notation
```

each increment the value of i. The first expression, however, equals i's incremented value because ++ comes *before* its operand. The second expression equals the value of i before it is incremented because ++ comes *after* its operand. The two different placements are called prefix and postfix notation. A few more examples will help make this concept clear. First, declare variables i and j and assign 100 to i:

```
int j, i = 100;
```

Next, increment i and assign the result to j:

```
j = i++;   // j = 100, i = 101
```

The comment shows the resulting values of i and j. Because postfix notation is used in the expression i++, the value of i is assigned to j *before* i is incremented. Using prefix notation produces a different result. The following reassigns 100 to i and then increments i with ++, but this time with the operator before its operand:

```
i = 100;   // Reassign 100 to i
j = ++i;   // j = 101, i = 101
```

Because prefix ++ is applied to its operand before the expression is evaluated, the second statement sets j to 101. The same prefix and postfix rules apply to the -- operator. Try these statements in a program:

```
int i, j;   // Declare integer variable i and j
i = 100;    // Initialize i to 100
```

```
j = i--;    // j = 100, i = 99
j = --i;    // j = 98, i = 98
```

Here's a hint: To display the variable values, insert the following statement at strategic locations in the program. Notice how the + operator is used multiple times to form an output string.

```
System.out.println("j = " + j + ", i = " + i);
```

Binary Integer Expressions

Binary integer expressions — a + b, for example — are so called because they require two operands. You may mix any types of integers — byte, short, int, and long — in a binary integer expression. Because Unicode characters are represented as 16-bit unsigned integers, you may also mix char values in binary integer expressions.

If any value, whether literal or variable, in a binary integer expression is of type long, then the results are long, even if the value of that result might fit in a smaller space. In all other cases, the results of binary integer expressions are type int, which holds true even if all operands are of shorter types.

Ignoring that fact will cause you no end of grief! For example, the following statements do not compile:

```
byte b1 = 1, b2 = 2, b3;
b3 = b1 + b2;    // ???
System.out.println("b3 = " + b3);
```

You cannot declare three byte variables, add two of them, and assign the result to the third because the data type of the expression b1 + b2 is int, not byte, and you cannot assign larger int values to smaller bytes. (By larger and smaller, I mean the space these values occupy in memory, not their integer values.) The solution is to use a *type-cast expression,* which is merely the intended type in parentheses ahead of a variable or expression:

```
b3 = (byte)(b1 + b2);
```

The program now compiles because the type-cast expression tells the compiler to downsize the result of the expression to an 8-bit byte. It is your responsibility, however, to ensure that the resulting value can be represented by a byte. Otherwise, a loss of information might occur. For example, consider these statements:

```
int a, b = 1;
int c = 2147483647;
a = b + c;
System.out.println("a = " + a);
```

The resulting value of a might surprise you. Because c equals the maximum integer value that can fit in 16 bits, that value plus 1 actually equals –2,147,483,648, an effect known as *wrap around*. To compute the correct result, you can change variables a and b to type long. This now sets a to one greater than c:

```
long a;
long b = 1;
int c = 2147483647;
a = b + c;
```

Shorthand Operators

When the result of an expression is to be reassigned to one of its operands, you can often use shorthand operator expressions to save some typing, and perhaps improve the program's efficiency. For example, rather than write

```
count = count + k;
```

use the shorthand equivalent:

```
count += k;   // Assign count + k back to count
```

Both statements do the same thing. They add count to k and assign the result back to count. The += characters form a single operator, which might seem a bit cryptic but permits you to write count only once. This might improve runtime performance because the interpreter needs to find where count is in memory only once.

Table 5-2 lists Java's binary integer operators and shows their shorthand assignment forms.

TABLE 5-2 BINARY INTEGER OPERATORS

Operator	Description	Assignment Shorthand
*	Multiply	*=
/	Divide	/=
+	Add	+=
–	Subtract	–=
%	Modulo	%=
&	Bitwise AND	&=

Operator	Description	Assignment Shorthand
|	Bitwise OR	|=
^	Bitwise XOR	^=
<<	Left shift	<<=
>>	Right shift	>>=
>>>	Shift in 0 at right	>>>=

The modulo operator returns the remainder of an integer division, any fraction of which is truncated. Given the declarations

```
int a = 7, b = 2, c = 0;
```

this sets c to 3 (a divided by b):

```
c = a / b;   // c = 3
```

This sets c to 1 (the remainder of a divided by b):

```
c = a % b;   // c = 1
```

Use the bitwise logical operators, & (AND), | (OR), and ^ (XOR) to perform those operations on the binary digits in integer values. If result is an int variable, the statement

```
result = result ^ 0xFFFFFFFF;
```

applies an XOR (exclusive OR) operation with each bit in result and 1, resulting in a value with all 1 bits changed to 0 and all 0 bits changed to 1. Repeating this same operation sets result back to its original value. Rather than write result twice, you may use this shorthand notation:

```
result ^= 0xFFFFFFFF;
```

Use shift operators to shift the bits in an integer variable left:

```
result = result << 3;   // Shift result left 3 bits
```

Or, using the alternative shorthand, shift the bits to the right:

```
result >>= 4;   // Shift result right 4 bits
```

Shift operations are signed, which might cause results to be different from what you expect (especially if you are used to thinking in binary). Use the zero-fill-shift operator to perform unsigned right shifts. For example, try these statements:

```
int result = 0x80000001;
result >>= 4;     // result = 0xF8000000
```

The hexadecimal value assigned to `result` equals the negative decimal value –2,147,483,647. Shifting this value right four bits fills `result` with 1 bits from the left. The resulting value in hexadecimal, 0xF8000000, or –134,217,728 in decimal, remains negative. Using the zero-fill-shift operator produces a different result:

```
int result = 0x80000001;
result >>>= 4;     // result = 0x08000000
```

This time, the resulting value in hexadecimal, 0x08000000, equals 134,217,728 in decimal. Because zeros are shifted in at left, the negative integer becomes positive.

Floating Point Expressions

You can use arithmetic operators – *, /, +, and – – in floating point expressions. You can also combine floating point and integer values, but the result is always either `float` or `double`. If all values are of type `float` or any integer type, the result is `float`; if any value is `double`, the result is `double`. Here's an example:

```
double d1, d2;
d1 = 3.14159;
int q = 3;
d2 = d1 * q;   // d2 = 9.42477
```

The final line multiplies `double` d1 by integer q and assigns the `double` result to d2. You may also use shorthand assignment operators like this:

```
d2 *= d1;
```

That's equivalent to

```
d2 = d2 * d1;
```

Unlike in some programming languages, modulo, increment, and decrement operators are defined for floating point values. The following declares three `double` variables and applies the modulo operator:

```
double result;
double a = 3.14159, b = 3;
result = a % b;   // result = 0.14159 (rounded)
```

The final line sets `result` to approximately `0.14159` (rounded), which is the remainder of dividing 3.14159 by 3.0. (The exact result may differ slightly on different systems.)

You can also use increment ++ and decrement -- operators as you do in integer expressions. They increase and decrease the integer part of a floating point value. Examine these statements:

```
double result = 3.14159;
result++;   // result = 4.14159
++result;   // result = 5.14159
result--;   // result = 4.14159
--result;   // result = 3.14159
```

As with integer expressions, prefix notation increments or decrements its operand before evaluation; postfix increments or decrements after evaluation. If `count` is type `double`, the statement

```
result = count++;
```

sets `result` equal to `count`, and then increments `count` by one. The following statement increments `count`, and then sets `result` equal to `count`'s new value:

```
result = ++count;
```

Floating Point Errors

Three types of errors might occur with floating point expressions. These are

- ◆ **Overflow** — Result is too large for data type
- ◆ **Underflow** — Result is too small for data type
- ◆ **Divide by zero** — Attempt to divide by zero

Overflow sets the result to a special value named `Infinity`. Underflow sets the result to `0`. Dividing a floating point value by zero sets the result to `Infinity`, but unlike with many programming languages, it does not halt the program with an error message. For example, the following simply displays `result = Infinity`:

```
double result = 3.14159;
result = result / 0.0;
System.out.println("result = " + result);
```

An invalid floating point expression results in another special value, NaN, short for "Not a Number." For example, dividing Infinity by Infinity equals NaN.

Type Casting

As mentioned, type casting is often required to assign a value of one type to a variable of another type. Some type-casting operations are safe; others may or may not cause a loss of information. For example, it is always safe to assign an int value to a long variable because the value is guaranteed to be within the long data type's defined minimum and maximum boundaries.

Safe type casts occur automatically. These statements

```
long result;
int a = 10;
result = a;
```

assign an int variable to a long. Trying to make this assignment in the other direction is like using a shoe horn to put sneakers on a buffalo:

```
a = result;  // ???
```

That doesn't even compile because the int data type is smaller in size than long. If the *value* in result is small enough to fit in an int variable, you can force the compiler to accept the statement (ignore the choking sound you hear during compilation) by using a type-cast expression:

```
a = (int)result;
```

It is now your responsibility to ensure that the value can safely fit inside a. If not, bits are lost and the resulting value may not be what you expected.

Table 5-3 shows the allowable type casts that do not potentially lose information and are automatically handled. Others such as assigning an int value to a byte variable require an explicit type-cast expression prefaced with the target data type in parentheses.

TABLE 5-3 SAFE TYPE CASTS

Value of Type	Can Be Safely Assigned To
byte	short, char, int, long, float, double
short	char, int, long, float, double
char	int, long, float, double

Value of Type	Can Be Safely Assigned To
int	long, float, double
long	float, double
float	double
double	double

When casting floating point values to integer variables, the results are truncated — they are not rounded. For example, the following program fragment sets the integer `result` equal to 4:

```
int result;
double v = 4.999999;
result = (int)v;  // Use type cast to assign v to result
```

 One exception to Java's type-casting rules is `boolean`. A `boolean` value cannot be cast to any other type.

Flow-Control Statements

With what you know so far about Java data types, variables, and expressions, you can begin writing simple programs that perform useful actions. To do this, you need to use *flow-control statements,* which affect the order in which the program's statements are executed.

Flow-control statements can select actions based on the values of variables, they can perform loops, and they can do other useful work. In most cases, one or more *relational expressions* provide the fuel for a flow-control statement, so let's start there.

Relational Expressions

Relational operators create `boolean` expressions that have `true` or `false` values. Don't confuse them with integer operators, a common mistake. For example, the statement

```
a = b;
```

assigns the value of b to a, but the statement

```
a == b;
```

is a `boolean` expression that equals `true` only if a equals b. You might use such an expression in an `if` flow-control statement, which selects among two actions, depending on whether its relational expression is `true`:

```
if (a == b)
 System.out.println("a equals b");
```

If the value of a equals b, the program displays a message; otherwise, it skips the `println()` statement. A common mistake I've probably made as many times as I've gotten up in the morning is to write = in place of ==. If you mistakenly type

```
if (a = b)  // ???
 System.out.println("a equals b");
```

Java reports an error that tells you the compiler expected a `boolean` expression but found an `int`. This differs from C and C++ in which `boolean` and integer expressions are interchangeable. In Java, they are not.

In addition to their use in flow-control statements, relational expressions can be assigned to `boolean` variables. For example, the following fragment sets a `boolean` variable, `result`, to `true`:

```
boolean result;
int a = 1, b = 1;
result = (a == b);
if (result == true)
   System.out.println("result is true!");
```

The third line evaluates the expression (a == b), producing a `true` or `false` result, which is assigned to the `result` variable. Notice how the `if` statement compares the value of `result` with `true`. Because `result` is already of type `boolean`, this isn't necessary, and you can more simply write

```
if (result)
 System.out.println("result is true!");
```

Table 5-4 lists Java's relational operators, which give `boolean` results when used in expressions. You'll see examples of these operations in the next several sections.

TABLE 5-4 RELATIONAL OPERATORS

Operator	Description	Example
<	Less than	(a < b)
>	Greater than	(a > b)
<=	Less than or equal	(a <= b)
>=	Greater than or equal	(a >= b)
==	Equal	(a == b)
!=	Not equal	(a != b)
&&	And	(a <= b) && (b <= c)
||	Or	(a <= b) || (b >= c)

if–else Statements

Use if, optionally followed by else, to conditionally execute code. For example, the following fragment tests whether an integer is less than another and displays an appropriate message:

```
int a = 10, b = 20;
if (a < b)
 System.out.println("a < b");
else
 System.out.println("a >= b");
```

An else statement is optional and can be followed by another if statement to create multipath conditionals:

```
if (a < b)
 System.out.println("a < b");
else if (a == b)
 System.out.println("a = b");
else
 System.out.println("a > b");
```

Only one of the println() statements executes, depending on the values of the compared integers. To execute more than one statement, create a *statement block* delimited by braces:

```
if (a < b) {
 System.out.println("a < b");
 System.out.println("That's all folks!");
}
```

switch Statements

A switch statement selects statements to execute based on the value of a condition. It is a kind of shorthand for a complex if-else statement, also known as a *multiway decision tree*, which looks like this:

```
if (a == 1)
  // statement for a == 1
else if (a == 2)
  // statement for a == 2
else if (a == 3)
  // statement for a == 3
else
  // statement for all other values
```

For clearer and possibly more efficient code, use a switch statement to do the same job. Listing 5-1, Switcher.java, demonstrates how to create a switch statement as a multiway decision tree.

Listing 5-1: Switcher.java

```
001: class Switcher {
002:  public static void main(String args[]) {
003:   int a = 2;
004:   switch (a) {
005:    case 1:
006:     System.out.println("Case 1");
007:     break;
008:    case 2:
009:     System.out.println("Case 2");
010:     System.out.println("Final statement in case 2");
011:     break;
012:    case 3:
013:     System.out.println("Case 3");
014:     break;
015:    default:
016:     System.out.println("All other cases");
017:   }
018:  }
019: }
```

Remember, to compile sample listings in this book, type `javac Switcher.java`. To run the compiled program, type `java Switcher`. These commands are case sensitive. From now on, I'll assume you know how to compile and run programs, so I won't repeat these instructions again.

The control expression in parentheses after the keyword `switch` may be any expression or variable that can be compared to a literal integer or character. Follow the `switch` keyword and control expression with the word `case`, a value to compare to the control, and a colon. If the control expression matches the `case` value, the statements following that case are executed.

Use `break` statements in each `case` to exit the `switch` statement. If you forget to insert `break`, execution continues with the next case (in other words, the program "falls through" the current case to the next one). This is often a mistake, but it might be useful in rare circumstances. Try taking out the `break` from case 2 in the sample listing and run the program modified like this:

```
case 2:
 System.out.println("Case 2");
 System.out.println("Final statement in case 2");
// falls through to next case
case 3:
 System.out.println("Case 3");
 break;
```

If the control expression equals 2, the program prints the two statements for that case, but also falls through to print the statement for case 3.

You may follow a `switch` statement with an optional `default` statement, which is executed if no case matches the control expression. You do not have to supply a `default` case, but if you do, it must be last. You don't need to insert a `break` in the `default` statements, but doing so is not an error:

```
switch (c) {
...
  default:
    // statements for default case
    break;  // okay but not required
}
```

while Statements

A `while` statement performs an operation as long as its control expression is true. Presumably, something in the `while` statement eventually causes the expression to become false; otherwise, the `while` loops endlessly. (Actually, this can be a useful technique – but I'll avoid the subject of endless loops until we examine threads in Chapter 19, "Threaded Code.") The program WhileCount.java in Listing 5-2 displays the values 1 through 10.

Listing 5-2: WhileCount.java

```
001: class WhileCount {
002:  public static void main(String args[]) {
003:   int count = 0;
004:   while (count < 10) {
005:    count++;
006:    System.out.println("Count = " + count);
007:   }
008:  }
009: }
```

When the control expression (count < 10) becomes false as a result of the program incrementing count, the loop ends. In this case, so does the program because no other statement follows the while loop.

do-while Statements

You might never use a do-while statement, but they are handy on rare occasions. It's similar to a plain while, but the control expression comes at the end instead of at the beginning. For comparison, Listing 5-3, DoWhileCount.java, counts from 1 to 10 using a do-while loop.

Listing 5-3: DoWhileCount.java

```
001: class DoWhileCount {
002:  public static void main(String args[]) {
003:   int count = 0;
004:   do {
005:    count++;
006:    System.out.println("Count = " + count);
007:   } while (count < 10);
008:  }
009: }
```

The key to selecting between while and do-while is to remember that a while loop does not execute its statements at all if the controlling expression is initially false. A do-while loop, however, always executes its statements at least once because its controlling expression is evaluated at the end of the loop.

for Statements

A `for` statement is as versatile as a hammer, and you'll use it in many circumstances. It is usually preferred over `while` or `do-while` when you or the program can determine in advance how many loops to execute. A `for` statement has these elements:

◆ The keyword `for`

◆ A three-part expression in parentheses

◆ A statement or block to execute

The design of a `for` loop is easiest to learn in schematic form. It uses this layout:

```
for (statement; expression1; expression2) {
 // statement or block to execute
}
```

The braces are required only if the block to execute contains two or more statements, but you can use braces anyway for clarity. Listing 5-4 uses a `for` loop to count from 1 to 10.

Listing 5-4: ForCount.java

```
001: class ForCount {
002:  public static void main(String args[]) {
003:   int count;
004:   for (count = 1; count <= 10; count++) {
005:    System.out.println("Count = " + count);
006:   }
007:  }
008: }
```

Rather than declare the integer `count` variable separately, as done in the sample listing, you may declare the control variable inside the `for` statement:

```
for (int count = 1; count <= 10; count++) {
 System.out.println("Count = " + count);
}
```

When you declare a `for` statement's control variable that way, it exists only for the loop's statements. In this case, `count` is available for use only in statements executed by `for` — this also means that another statement can declare another variable named `count` with no conflict.

This example loop initially sets `count` to 1. It executes the loop's statement or statement block *while* the controlling expression, `count <= 10`, is `true`. After executing the loop's statement or block, it executes the final expression, which in this case increments count by one. As with other loops, it is usually important that this expression perform some action that eventually causes the control expression to become false so that the loop ends.

label, break, and continue Statements

These three types of flow-control statements are easily misused, and are best put into play only when absolutely necessary. A label marks any statement in a program. A break or continue statement halts a while, do-while, or for loop, and starts execution at the labeled position.

An example helps make these concepts clear and also shows the subtle difference between break and continue. Listing 5-5 shows the correct way to use these statements, but as this listing also demonstrates, the results can be messy. To make the sample program easier to follow, I commented the closing braces, showing the flow-control statement to which each belongs.

Listing 5-5: LabelDemo.java

```
001: class LabelDemo  {
002:  public static void main(String args[]) {
003:    int i, j;
004: OuterLoop:
005:    for (i = 1; i < 100; i++) {
006:      System.out.println("\nOuter loop # " + i);
007: InnerLoop:
008:      for (j = 1; j < 10; j++) {
009:        if (j % 2 == 0)
010:          continue InnerLoop;  // Skip even j values
011:        if (i > 4)
012:          break OuterLoop;     // Abort if i > 4
013:        System.out.println("j = " + j);
014:      } // end of inner for statement
015:    }   // end of outer for statement
016:    System.out.println("Program exiting at OuterLoop:");
017:  }     // end of main() method
018: }       // end of class declaration
```

A label is any unused identifier followed by a colon, for example, OuterLoop: at line 004. The sample program executes two for loops, one inside the other. Two labels — OuterLoop: and InnerLoop: — mark the position above each loop.

Inside a while, do-while, or for statement, a continue statement causes an immediate jump to the designated position. Use continue to continue executing the loop from a specific point when you do not want to execute any other statements from that point on. This might be easier to fathom in schematic form:

```
L1:
for (...) {
  // statements to always execute
  if (condition)
    continue L1; // Do another loop skipping all that follows
  // statements to conditionally execute
}
```

If the condition is true, the `if` statement executes `continue`, beginning another loop (unless the `for` is finished) but skipping the rest of the statements.

A `break` statement is similar to `continue`, but completely exits the loop. Again, this might be easier to understand in schematic form:

```
L2:
for (...) {
  // statements to always execute
  if (condition)
    break L2; // exit loop completely
  // statements to conditionally execute
}
```

The difference is that, if the condition is `true`, the `break` statement halts execution of the loop, and the program continues after the `for` statement's closing brace. Despite appearances, the `for` statement does not begin anew. A good use for `break` is to get out of a nested flow-control statement because of an error or other condition.

 Unlike C, C++, and many other programming languages, Java does not support an unconditional `goto` statement. This is no deficiency — any task that a `goto` can do, a more structured flow-control statement can accomplish as well but with clearer results. However, Java reserves the `goto` keyword.

Summary

♦ Expressions are constructions that Java can evaluate, or reduce, to a single value. Expressions can be simple — for example, the name of a variable is an expression that equals its value. They can also be complex and involve operators that combine two or more values.

♦ Operators perform actions on data values. Java supports numerous mathematical, logical, and bitwise operators that you can use to create expressions for manipulating data. Operators with higher precedence are evaluated before operators with lower precedence; otherwise, expressions are evaluated from left to right. Use parentheses to force a different expression evaluation order.

◆ Flow-control statements conditionally select among a program's statements and perform other jobs such as creating loops. Java has `if`, `switch`, `while`, `do-while`, and `for` statements. Java also supports labeled statements for use with `break` and `continue`, which are occasionally useful for ending deeply nested `while` and `for` loops.

Chapter 6

Object-Oriented Programming

JAVA IS COMPLETELY object-oriented. This means that every piece of data and every action in a Java program exists or takes place in the context of a class. As you will learn in this chapter, the class is Java's basic building block. You can use classes to perform all sorts of operations such as input and output, and you can also create your own classes.

Because classes have extensive features, it is impractical to cover everything about classes and objects in one chapter. This chapter introduces classes and the concepts of object-oriented programming with Java. We'll return to these topics again and again in future chapters.

 Although Java and C++ classes resemble each other, their likeness is only skin deep. There are many differences, some subtle, between Java and C++ classes, so even if you know C++, don't skip this chapter.

IN THIS CHAPTER

- ◆ Introducing classes and objects
- ◆ Class methods
- ◆ Input and output methods
- ◆ Objects and garbage collection

Introduction to Classes and Objects

The primary purpose of a class is to encapsulate data and the methods that operate on that data. Keeping data and methods together helps you create well-organized programs and also prevents pitfalls that are common in conventional programming languages, such as passing the wrong data to subroutines.

Declaring Classes

A class begins with the `class` keyword followed by braces that delimit the class's contents:

```
class AnyClass {
 ...
}
```

Most classes have one or more methods, such as `main()`, which is found in all stand-alone Java applications:

```
class AnyClass {
 public static void main(String args[]) {
  // statements inside main()
 }
}
```

The method is declared to be `public` so that it can be referred to from outside of the class. As you have seen, statements inside `main()` perform the program's actions. You can also create other methods and call them from `main()` and from other places:

```
class AnyClass {
 public static void hiThere() {
  System.out.println("Hi there!");
 }
 public static void main(String args[]) {
  HiThere();  // Call HiThere() method
 }
}
```

This class has two methods, `hiThere()` and `main()`. The statement in `main()` calls the `hiThere()` method, which displays a string. (If you enter this program, save it in a file named `AnyClass.java`.)

Class names are usually capitalized. Variables and methods begin with lowercase letters. These conventions are not requirements, but help make programs clearer to read and understand.

As you know, you can declare variables inside functions. You also can declare variables in a class:

```
class AnyClass {
 static int i;  // Declare class variable
 public static void hiThere() {
  for (i = 0; i < 4; i++)
   System.out.println("Hi there!");
 }
 ...
}
```

The static int i declaration creates an integer variable that any method in the class can use. You might wonder (rightly) at this point why I am using the word static in every variable and method declaration. This is because the sample programs have so far used classes in only a rudimentary way — as shell-like constructions that specify data and code. But classes are more than simply shells; they are schematics for creating *objects*.

Declaring Objects

An *object* is also sometimes called an *instance* of a class. An object is a variable, just like integers, characters, and those of other data types. An object occupies space in memory, and it must be initialized. You may create objects of most any class, and you may create as many objects of a specific class as you need. Listing 6-1, DateObject.java, shows the basics of creating classes and objects.

Listing 6-1: DateObject.java

```
001: // Declare DateClass
002: class DateClass {
003:  int month;
004:  int day;
005:  int year;
006:  public DateClass(int m, int d, int y) {
007:   month = m;
008:   day = d;
009:   year = y;
010:   // year = y + 1900;
011:  }
012:  public void display() {
013:   System.out.println(month + "/" + day + "/" + year);
014:  }
015: }
016:
017: // Declare main program class
018: class DateObject {
019:  public static void main(String args[]) {
020:   // Create and display a DateClass object
```

```
021:    DateClass birthday = new DateClass(7, 18, 64);
022:    birthday.display();
023:    // Create and display another DateClass object
024:    DateClass future = new DateClass(1, 1, 01);
025: //  DateClass future = new DateClass(1, 1, 101);
026:    future.display();
027:    }
028: }
```

The sample application declares two classes. DateClass stores a date using three integer *instance variables,* month, day, and year. A *constructor* method, named the same as the class (see line 006), initializes the instance variables by assigning its parameters (m, d, and y). The class also declares a method, display() (line 012), that shows the date in m/d/y format. Some Java texts call constructors *creation methods*. They are used to initialize newly created objects.

To use the class, the main program creates an object by using Java's new operator. This tells the interpreter to *instantiate* the class — in other words, to create an object of the class:

```
DateClass birthday = new DateClass(7, 18, 64);
```

The object is named birthday, and it is initialized by a new instance of the DateClass constructor. The integer arguments in parentheses are passed to the class constructor's parameters, which as mentioned, are saved in the object's instance variables. After creating an object, a program typically calls methods in reference to it. For example, this calls the class's display() method for the birthday object:

```
birthday.display();
```

It's useful to think of this statement as giving the birthday object a command to display itself. In object-oriented programming, it's common to perform actions this way by calling class methods. For example, you might tell a graphics object to display itself or to change its colors.

The sample program also shows how to create multiple objects of the same class. The following statement, for instance, constructs another object, named future, of DateClass, to the date 4/10/2005:

```
DateClass future = new DateClass(4, 10, 05);
```

As mentioned earlier, a class is a schematic for creating objects. A class is a data type, in much the same way of other built-in types such as integers. Compare the preceding statement to one that creates an integer variable:

```
int count = 10;
```

The only difference is that, to create class objects, you use the new operator and you typically (but not always) pass values to the class constructor to initialize instance variables. You can also declare class objects in one place and initialize them at another:

```
DateClass d1;  // Declare d1 object
...
d1 = new DateClass(5, 6, 70);  // Initialize d1
```

The first line declares a DateClass object, after which the program performs some other tasks (indicated by the ellipsis). When ready, the program initializes d1 using new. You may also reinitialize an object to give it other values. For example, the preceding fragment could be followed by

```
d1 = new DateClass(8, 9, 10);  // Reinitialize d1
d1.display();  // Display new object
```

which reinitializes the object and displays its value. You do not have to delete or dispose of the objects you create. When the program no longer refers to an object, Java automatically deletes it from memory, a process called *garbage collection.*

 Objects such as those demonstrated here are actually references to the real object data stored somewhere in memory. This has important benefits such as when passing an object to a method, because what's actually passed is merely a reference (the memory address) of the real object, not the object's data. Usually, it's safe to consider an object simply to be itself. But tuck this fact in the back of your mind: *Objects are actually references.*

Modifying Classes

One of the key benefits of object-oriented programming is that classes control access to their data and methods. You'll learn more about this subject throughout this book, but for a simple demonstration, consider how you might improve the DateClass in the DateObject.java sample program (refer back to Listing 6-1). A problem with that program is that it displays dates such as January 15, 2001 as

```
1/15/1
```

It would be better if the year were displayed in full, and to make that change we can arbitrarily specify that the DateClass store years minus 1900. Accordingly, the year value 50 equals 1950; the year value 105 equals 2005, and so on. To make this change, modify the statement `year = y;` to the following (delete line 009 and enable line 010 by removing the comment symbol):

```
year = y + 1900;
```

Also modify the following statement in the main program class (change the year 01 to 101 by deleting line 024 and enabling line 025):

```
DateClass future = new DateClass(1, 1, 101);
```

When compiled and run, the program now displays dates such as

```
7/18/1964
1/1/2001
```

Another improvement might be to change the integer instance variables to smaller data types. There's hardly any good reason to waste space by storing month and day values as 32-bit integers! You can reduce the size of DateClass by declaring month and day as type byte:

```
class DateClass {
 byte month;
 byte day;
 int year;
 public DateClass(int m, int d, int y) {
  month = (byte)m;
  day = (byte)d;
  year = y;
 }
 ...
}
```

This change also requires using type-cast expressions in the assignments to month and day in the DateClass() constructor, since the program still passes the parameters as integers (they could also be changed to bytes).

Significantly, none of these changes affect the use of the class. The main program remains unchanged even though the storage format of the DateClass has been altered. This is another benefit of object-oriented programming. In general, you may make changes to well-designed classes without affecting their use in other parts of the program.

Importing Classes

Our DateClass class is merely a demonstration model — a real date class needs more sophisticated programming such as the ability to get the current date from the operating system, and to perform calculations on dates. One great benefit of Java is that it comes loaded with a rich class library of *packages* that provide ready-to-use classes for a variety of purposes. Instead of writing new classes, try to use Java's packaged classes whenever possible. They save you time, and they reduce the size of your programs. Also, because Java's classes are debugged, they help you create robust code.

For example, Java already has a date class named `java.util.Date`. The class name is `Date`; it is declared as part of the `java.util` package, which provides other classes. (You learn more about packages in Chapter 13, "Packages.") To use a Java class library package, you *import* it into your program. Do this with an `import` statement such as

```
import java.util.Date;
```

Generally, this and other `import` statements should be at the top of your program's source file. You may also use a wild-card asterisk to import multiple classes. The statement

```
import java.util.*;
```

imports all classes declared in the `java.util` package. The following statement imports all `java` package classes:

```
import java.*;
```

Java's language classes, collected in the java.lang package, are automatically imported into all applications. You do not have to import the `System` class in order to write statements such as `System.out.println();`.

Listing 6-2, `DateDemo.java`, shows how to import a class and use it in a program.

Listing 6-2: DateDemo.java

```
001: import java.util.Date;  // Import the Date class
002:
003: // Use the imported Date class
004: class DateDemo {
005:   public static void main(String args[]) {
006:     Date today = new Date();
007:     System.out.println(today.toString());
008:   }
009: }
```

Use Java's classes the same way you do your own. First, import the class with an `import` declaration as shown in the sample program, and then use the `new` operator to create one or more objects of the imported class. For example, the sample application constructs a `Date` object with the statement:

```
Date today = new Date();
```

That creates an initialized object, `today`, set to the current date and time. Java's `Date` class also provides ways to extract the object's information. For example, call the `toString()` method to get a string representation of the date and time:

```
System.out.println(today.toString());
```

When I ran the program, that statement printed the following line on my screen:

```
Mon May 21 11:10:36 EST 2001
```

Although you can use the `Date` class as shown here, Java 2 adds better date support in its `DateFormat`, `TimeZone`, and `Calendar` classes. Look them up in Java's online documentation. Some class features, such as the ability to construct `Date` class objects from strings and integer values, have been deprecated in Java 2.

Inheriting Classes

When a class doesn't do exactly what you want, you can build a new class based on it. Your class *inherits* the original class's methods and instance variables, to which you can add your own code and data. Inheriting classes is a great way to reuse existing code. The term *code reuse* does not refer to a text editor's cut and paste commands. Developing reusable code means writing and debugging classes, and then building new classes from them. You can get a lot of work done in a relatively short time by using as many existing classes as possible — either those of your own design, or those from Java's rich class library.

To demonstrate how to inherit and build on an existing class, Listing 6-3, `DateShow.java`, adds a `display()` method to Java's `Date` class.

Listing 6-3: DateShow.java

```
001: import java.util.Date;  // Import the Date class
002:
003: // Extend the imported Date class
004: class NewDate extends Date {
005:   public void display() {
```

```
006:    System.out.println(toString());
007:    }
008: }
009:
010: // Use the NewDate class
011: class DateShow {
012:   public static void main(String args[]) {
013:     NewDate today = new NewDate();  // Construct NewDate object
014:     today.display();  // Call the new display() method
015:   }
016: }
```

The sample program imports the Date class as before. It then extends Date by declaring a new class like this:

```
class NewDate extends Date {
   ...
}
```

The NewDate class inherits all members (instance variables and methods) from Date. However, the extended class does not inherit any constructors. To its inheritance, NewDate adds a display() method, which uses the println() method to display the object's date in string form. Take a close look at the statement that makes this happen (see line 006):

```
System.out.println(toString());
```

In past examples, you called methods such as toString() in reference to an object such as today. Because this statement is in the NewDate class, and because that class inherits Date's members, the statement can call the inherited toString() method directly.

To create and use an instance of the extended class, the sample program's main() method constructs a NewDate object and then calls the display() method in reference to that object:

```
NewDate today = new NewDate();
today.display();
```

Because constructors are not inherited, the first line must now refer to the extended class name, NewDate, to construct the object. NewDate() is known as a *default constructor*, which is implicitly created by Java if the program itself does not declare one. The second statement calls our new display() method, which in turn calls the inherited toString() method for the today object, thus printing today's date and time.

An extended class efficiently reuses its inherited members. Only one copy of any method ever exists in memory, no matter how many classes extend other classes and no matter how many objects you construct. Each object has its own copies of any instance variables, but all objects of a class share the class's code. Objects don't *contain* code — they *associate* code with their instance variables.

Subclass and Superclass

An extended class such as NewDate in the preceding sample program is called a *subclass*. The class from which it is extended is called the *superclass*. Other object-oriented languages such as C++ and Object Pascal use the terms *ancestor* and *descendent* to describe class relationships — and you might also come across the term *base class,* which is analogous to a *superclass* in Java.

Any subclass can be used as a superclass, and there is no practical limit to the number of subclasses you can create for any class. You can import a class, extend it, import the resulting subclass, extend it again, and so on. In fact, most classes you import into a program are already extended from several other classes. All Java classes, including those that you create, are extended from a superclass called Object. All classes, and all objects, are therefore related through the Object class. Among other members, the Object class declares a method, toString(), that you may call for any object.

Class Methods

Class methods, as you have seen in the sample programs presented so far, execute statements. They are analogous to subroutines in conventional programming languages such as BASIC. Methods can declare *local variables* and they can call other methods. As you know, every stand-alone Java application must have a main() method in a class named the same as the program's source code file.

Programming with Methods

A method can be a *function* that returns a value. Declare the return-value's data type before the method's name, and list any parameters and their types in parentheses. Here's a sample method that declares three integer parameters and returns an integer value:

```
int sum(int a, int b, int c) {
  return a + b + c;
} // <-- no semicolon here!
```

In the method, a *return statement* passes back the `sum()` function's integer result – the sum of the three `int` parameters, a, b, and c, which are separated by commas in the method's declaration. Notice that there is no semicolon after the method's closing brace. Another statement might call `sum()` like this:

```
int k = sum(x, y, 25);   // k = x + y + 25;
```

If a method returns no value, declare it as type `void`. This is typically done for methods that perform some action rather than calculate a value. For example, the following function returns no value and requires no parameter arguments:

```
void doSomething();
```

Call the method simply by writing its name in statements such as

```
doSomething();      // Call method
o.doSomething();   // Call method for an object
```

Reminder: In this text, empty parentheses indicate a function name. You know that `sum()` is a function, but `count` is probably a variable.

Listing 6-4, `Methods.java`, demonstrates how to declare and use methods in a program.

Listing 6-4: Methods.java

```
001: // Method demonstration class
002: class MethodClass {
003:   int sum(int a, int b, int c) {
004:     return a + b + c;
005:   }
006:   double product(double x, double y) {
007:     return x * y;
008:   }
009:   void showErrorMessage(int code) {
010:     switch (code) {
011:     case 1:
012:       System.out.println("Error 1: Deep trouble!");
013:       break;
014:     case 2:
015:       System.out.println("Error 2: Deeper trouble!");
016:       break;
```

```
017:   default:
018:    System.out.println("Unknown code: Situation hopeless");
019:   }
020:   }
021: }
022:
023: // Main program class
024: class Methods {
025:   public static void main(String args[]) {
026:    // Create demo object of the MethodClass class
027:    MethodClass demo = new MethodClass();
028:
029:    // Call demo object's sum() method
030:    int k = demo.sum(10, 25, 16);
031:    System.out.println("sum = " + k);
032:
033:    // Call demo object's product() method
034:    double f = demo.product(3.14159, 4.5);
035:    System.out.println("product = " + f);
036:
037:    // Call demo object's showErrorMessage() method
038:    demo.showErrorMessage(1);
039:    demo.showErrorMessage(2);
040:   }
041: }
```

The sample program's MethodClass declares three methods: sum(), product(), and showErrorMessage(). The first two methods return int and double values respectively. The third returns void — that is, no value. To call the methods, the program first constructs an object, demo:

```
MethodClass demo = new MethodClass();
```

Next, the program calls each method in reference to the object. A period (sometimes called *dot notation)* shows the association with the object and the class method names:

```
int k = demo.sum(10, 25, 16);
double f = demo.product(3.14159, 4.5);
demo.showErrorMessage(1);
```

Static Methods

Methods may be called in reference to a class, rather than to an object, in which case the method declaration is prefaced with the key word static. For example, the `main()` method is `static` so it can be called without having to construct an object of its class:

```
public static void main(String args[]) { ...
```

The `main()` method is also declared `public`, which makes it available to other classes. (I'll cover this topic along with other *access rules* in Chapter 11, "Abstract Classes.") Static methods are of limited use. Because they are not called in reference to objects, they may not access instance variables in the class. For example, the following statements illustrate a common mistake:

```
class DontDoThis {
 int i;  // instance variable
 public static void main(String args[]) {
  i = 10;  // ???
...
}
```

These statements do not compile because `static` methods may not use instance variables — there is no instance of the `DontDoThis` class, and therefore, the instance variable `i` is not available to the `static` method.

Serializing Objects

Like methods, data members in a class can also be `static`. One good use for this is to create serialized objects, which automatically assign themselves unique values that might be used for identification purposes. Listing 6-5, Serial.java, demonstrates how to create such a class.

Listing 6-5: Serial.java

```
001: class Serialized {
002:   static private int nextSerialNum;  // Initialized to 0
003:   private int serialNum;
004:   // Construct a Serialized object
005:   Serialized() {
006:   // Increment and assign serial number to an object
007:     serialNum = ++nextSerialNum;
008:   }
009:   // Show the object's serial number
010:   public void showSerialNumber(String name) {
011:     System.out.println(name + "'s serial number = " + serialNum);
012:   }
013: }
014:
015: class Serial {
```

```
016:   public static void main(String args[]) {
017:     Serialized obj1 = new Serialized();
018:     Serialized obj2 = new Serialized();
019:     Serialized obj3 = new Serialized();
020:     obj1.showSerialNumber("Object 1");
021:     obj2.showSerialNumber("Object 2");
022:     obj3.showSerialNumber("Object 3");
023:   }
024: }
```

The `Serialized` class declares two data items at lines 002 and 003. Both are `private` to the class and therefore can be used only by the class's methods (but see "Packages and Access Rules" in Chapter 13, "Packages," for an exception to this rule). The first, `nextSerialNum`, is also declared to be `static`, and it is therefore used in reference to the class. Every object of the class has its own copy of the non-static instance of the `serialNum` integer; but no object contains a `nextSerialNum` variable.

In the class constructor (see lines 005–008), each new object's `serialNum` instance variable is given the next increment of the class's static `nextSerialNum` value. In this way, each object is given successive serial numbers, as demonstrated by the program's output, produced by creating three `Serialized` objects and calling the `showSerialNumber()` method:

```
Object 1's serial number = 1
Object 2's serial number = 2
Object 3's serial number = 3
```

Overloaded Methods

A class may declare more than one method using the same name as long as each declaration differs by at least one parameter. This technique is called *overloading*, and it is useful for creating sensible code that can accept a variety of arguments. It's a handy tool particularly for creating methods that are named the same but can operate on different types of data.

Listing 6-6, `Overload.java`, demonstrates how to declare, implement, and use overloaded methods.

Listing 6-6: Overload.java

```
001: class DemoClass {
002:   // Method #1
003:   void show(int x) {
004:     System.out.println("int x = " + x);
005:   }
006:   // Method #2
007:   void show(double x) {
```

```
008:    System.out.println("double x = " + x);
009:    }
010:    // Method #3
011:    void show(char x) {
012:      System.out.println("char x = " + x);
013:    }
014: }
015:
016: class Overload {
017:   public static void main(String args[]) {
018:     DemoClass myObj = new DemoClass();  // Create object
019:     myObj.show(123);        // Call show() #1
020:     myObj.show(3.14159);    // Call show() #2
021:     myObj.show('Q');        // Call show() #3
022:   }
023: }
```

DemoClass declares three methods, all named show(). The methods differ only in the types of parameters. As the sample program's main() method demonstrates, Java decides which method to call based on the type of argument passed to the method's int, double, or char parameters. Running the program displays

```
int x = 123
double x = 3.14159
char x = Q
```

To be properly overloaded, the methods must be named the same and must differ in at least one parameter's data type (not its name; its type). As long as they are properly overloaded, the methods may return different types, but the return type alone cannot be changed without also changing the type of at least one parameter.

Understanding Scope

Variables declared in a method are available only to that method. This concept is called *scope*. Variables declared in a class are available to all methods in the class. Any *local variables* declared in methods, however, take precedence over any variables of the same names in the class. For example, consider this class:

```
class AnyClass {
 int k = 20;
 void anyMethod() {
  int k = 10;  // Local variable k hides instance variable k
  System.out.println(k);  // Displays 10
 }
}
```

AnyClass declares an instance variable, k. Because anyMethod() also declares k, the output statement prints 10. If you delete the declaration of the local variable, the program displays 20 because anyMethod() then refers to the variable in the outer (class) scope.

It's useful to think of scope as a series of nested rooms with one-way mirrors. Inside any room, you can see out to other rooms, but outside you can't peer in through the windows. Consequently, one method's local variables do not conflict with another method's. For example, two methods may declare integer variables named i without conflict:

```
class AnyClass {
 public static void f1() {
  int i = 10;  // Belongs to scope of f1()
 }
 public static void f2() {
  int i = 20;  // Belongs to scope of f2()
 }
...
}
```

TIP Choosing good identifiers helps prevent bugs caused by accidentally hiding variable names declared in an outer scope. In general, to avoid this kind of trouble, it's best to use simple names such as i, j, and k only as local variables in methods; use more descriptive names such as accountBalance for class instance variables.

Strict Floating Point

You can perform floating point arithmetic in Java in two ways — strict and non-strict. The default is non-strict, which is generally faster because it uses the local operating system's floating point hardware or, perhaps, a software library. However, since not every computer system is identical in its floating point implementations, the results of non-strict arithmetic may differ slightly.

Usually, such differences are insignificant and can be safely ignored. However, if you need to ensure that your floating point calculations are identical on all systems that execute your Java programs, you can specify that system to use strict floating point. This will cost your program some performance points, so don't do this unless you really must.

To enable strict floating point, a class, interface, or method may be declared using the modifier strictfp. (Interfaces are introduced in Chapter 12, "Interfaces.") You may declare an entire class or interface to use strict floating point:

```
strictfp class Strictly {
...
}
```

Or, you may similarly declare a method using the same modifier:

```
public static strictfp void DoStrictMath() {
  double f = 3.14159 * 0.000002;
  System.out.println("Strict output = " + f);
}
```

Input and Output Methods

Although the purpose of this chapter is to introduce classes and object-oriented programming, it's useful to discuss the topics of input and output here. In order to begin presenting more useful sample programs, we need techniques to get data into and out of applications. Actually, output is simpler, so I'll cover that first.

Output Statements

You've already seen how to display text and other values using the println() method in statements such as

```
System.out.println("\nValue of k = " + k);
```

This displays a string and the value of k. The special character \n precedes the string with a new line. In general, a variable such as k may be of any data type because Java can convert most kinds of values to strings, which you can join using plus signs as shown here.

Calling println() this way, however, isn't always convenient, especially for displaying multiple values. It's often better, and probably faster, to construct a string and then display it using one output statement. Chapter 8, "String Things," discusses strings in more detail, but Listing 6-7, OutputDemo.java, demonstrates the basic technique of using a string for displaying relatively complex output.

Listing 6-7: OutputDemo.java

```
001: class OutputDemo {
002:   public static void main(String args[]) {
003:     StringBuffer s = new StringBuffer();
004:     for (char c = 'A'; c <= 'Z'; c++) {
005:       s.append(c);
006:     }
007:     System.out.println(s);  // Displays the alphabet
008:   }
009: }
```

The sample program constructs a StringBuffer object, using the statement at line 003. This creates an object, s, called a *mutable string,* to which the program can append characters. In this program, a for loop appends the letters A through Z to s by calling the StringBuffer class's append() method. After constructing the string, the program displays it with a single println() statement, which displays the alphabet:

ABCDEFGHIJKLMNOPQRSTUVWXYZ

 Objects of Java's String class are fixed in size and cannot be changed (they are often called *immutable strings*). When a string expands or is expected to be changed frequently, the StringBuffer class is the better choice. Again, I'll get back to this subject in Chapter 8.

Input Statements

To input characters and strings from the keyboard, a program can call the System.in.read() method, as Listing 6-8, InputDemo.java, demonstrates.

Listing 6-8: InputDemo.java

```
001: import java.io.IOException;
002:
003: class InputDemo {
004:  public static void main(String args[]) {
005:   try {
006:    // Input a single character
007:    System.out.println("Type a character:");
008:    char ch = (char)System.in.read();
009:    System.out.println("You entered: " + ch);
010:    // Throw out new line
011:    while (ch != '\n')
012:     ch = (char)System.in.read();
013:    // Input a string
014:    System.out.println("Type a string:");
015:    StringBuffer s = new StringBuffer();
016:    while ((ch = (char)System.in.read()) != '\n')
017:     s.append(ch);
018:    System.out.println("You entered: " + s);
019:   } catch (IOException e) {
020:    System.out.println("Input error detected");
021:   }
022:  }
023: }
```

The sample program inputs a class named IOException and uses *exception handling* to trap any input errors that might occur. I'll cover exceptions in the next chapter, but they are necessary here because Java requires input statements to handle their own errors.

Use the following statement to read a single character from the keyboard:

```
char ch = (char)System.in.read();
```

Because the user must press Enter after typing the character, follow this statement with a similar one to throw out the '\n' new line character:

```
while (ch != '\n')
  ch = (char)System.in.read();
```

To read a string, you can use a StringBuffer object and a while loop such as the following, which builds a string from characters typed at the keyboard:

```
StringBuffer s = new StringBuffer();
while ((ch = (char)System.in.read()) != '\n')
 s.append(ch);
```

The foregoing techniques provide only simple input and output, adequate only for reading and writing text in simple programs. Chapter 24, "Input and Output Techniques," covers more sophisticated methods for input, output, and file handling.

Cleaning Up Class Objects

Java automatically *garbage collects* objects when they are no longer in use. For example, when a method ends, any objects that it created are eventually destroyed, and their memory space is freed. This keeps memory free of unused objects and helps make available as much free memory as possible for creating other objects. You don't need to perform any special actions to use Java's garbage collection—it is fully automatic and runs in a background thread that does not interfere with your program.

Sometimes, however, it is necessary to perform one or more actions just before an object is deleted. To perform such cleanup activities, create a finalize() method:

```
protected void finalize() {
...
}
```

However, `finalize()` is *not* a good place to perform tasks such as saving data in a file. A `finalize()` method is never required in Java, and most important, is not guaranteed to be called. It will be called *only* if an object of its class is deleted, and this will occur only if Java needs to garbage collect objects to free up some memory. As Listing 6-9, `FinalDemo.java`, demonstrates, you can therefore never rely on your `finalize()` methods being called.

Listing 6-9: FinalDemo.java

```
001: class AnyClass {
002:   AnyClass() {
003:     System.out.println("Inside AnyClass() constructor");
004:   }
005:   protected void finalize() {
006:     System.out.println("Inside AnyClass() finalize method");
007:   }
008: }
009:
010: class FinalDemo {
011:   public static void f() {
012:     System.out.println("Start method f()");
013:     AnyClass obj1 = new AnyClass();
014:     System.out.println("End method f()");
015:   }
016:   public static void main(String args[]) {
017:     System.out.println("Start method main()");
018:     f();
019:     AnyClass obj2 = new AnyClass();
020:     System.out.println("End method main()");
021:   }
022: }
```

The sample program also shows the difference between a class constructor and `finalize()`. The constructor at line 002 is named the same as the class and has no return type, not even `void`. It is called when an object of the class is created with a statement such as

```
AnyClass obj1 = new AnyClass();
```

The `finalize()` method at line 005 has the return type `void` (it returns nothing) and is typically made `protected` (see Chapter 11), because it is never called by a program statement. Running the program shows that, despite this declaration, `finalize()` is never called:

```
Start method main()
Start method f()
Inside AnyClass() constructor
End method f()
Inside AnyClass() constructor
End method main()
```

This happens because in such a simple program, plenty of memory is available, and the program runs for only a short time. When function `f()` (see line 011) ends, the `AnyClass obj1` object (line 013) is no longer in use, and it is subject to garbage collection. However, that action is unlikely to occur in this simple program, and therefore, `finalize()` is never called.

 C++ programmers and those who know other object-oriented languages such as Object Pascal should be careful not to equate Java's `finalize()` method with a destructor. In C++, for example, class destructors are guaranteed to be called when objects are deleted. In Java, because objects are never explicitly deleted, but are garbage collected automatically, destructors are not needed.

Summary

- Java is completely object-oriented. Every piece of data and every action take place in the context of one or more classes.

- A class encapsulates data (instance variables) and code (methods). Programming with classes encourages the reuse of debugged code, which potentially simplifies software development.

- A class constructor is a method named the same as the class but with no return type. Constructors initialize objects of classes. A class may declare a cleanup method named `finalize()`, which Java calls if it garbage collects an object of the class. This, however, is not guaranteed to happen.

- To use a class, it is usually instantiated with the `new` operator. This creates an object of the class. You may create as many objects of a class as you need. Each object has separate copies of any non-static instance variables declared in the class. All objects of a class, however, share the class's methods.

- A source code module can import classes from Java's packages using `import` statements. There are numerous classes such as `Date` in the `java.util` package from which to choose. You can create your own classes, but always check whether an existing class is available before reinventing the wheel.

◆ Classes may extend other classes. The original class is called the super-class. Its extension is called the subclass. Any subclass may be used as a superclass that may be further extended. All classes have the `Object` class as their most distantly related superclass.

◆ Methods are declared and implemented in a class. They may return a value of any type or `void` (no value). Methods may be called in reference to an object of a class. Static methods, however, may be called in reference to the class itself, but static methods may not use any of the class's instance variables because there is no instance, or object, of the class in this case.

◆ Classes may also declare static data, for example, to create serialized objects.

Chapter 7

Exception Handling

ONE OF THE KEYS to writing robust code is to catch errors caused by all possible exceptional conditions. In conventional programming, satisfying that requirement can be extremely difficult, and programmers tend to either put off writing error handling code, do it badly, or ignore the subject altogether.

Java is different. It provides *exceptions* for adding error handling to a program as you write the code. As you learn in this chapter, an *exception* is an object that is *thrown* to indicate an extreme event such as a file not found or incorrect user input. Programs *catch* exception objects so they can respond gracefully to unplanned events. The result is battle-tested code that handles all possible errors.

IN THIS CHAPTER

- ◆ Exception terminology
- ◆ An introduction to exceptions
- ◆ Programming with exceptions
- ◆ Class library exceptions

A Few Good Terms

Java exceptions come with their own terminology and concepts. Following are some overviews that will help you to read and understand this chapter:

- ◆ An *exception* is just that — an *exceptional condition* that requires special handling. Exceptions are best used to handle errors that might naturally be expected to occur. For example, Java's `RandomAccessFile` class throws `FileNotFoundException` to indicate an attempt to open a file that doesn't exist, perhaps because the user mistyped the filename.

- ◆ *Checked exceptions* are so named because the Java compiler checks whether methods throw only exceptions that are listed for those methods. Most of the exceptions you deal with in writing Java applications and applets are checked exceptions.

- ◆ *Unchecked exceptions* are those that are thrown due to unexpected programming errors. For example, accessing an array with an out-of-bounds

101

index value causes Java to throw an `IllegalArgumentException`. Unchecked exceptions should be handled by fixing the source code so the problem never occurs in the first place.

◆ To create an exception, a statement *throws* an object that describes the nature of the exceptional condition. The object must be a subclass of the `Throwable` class or, preferably, it should extend a class such as `Exception` or `RuntimeException`.

◆ To handle an exception, a statement *catches* an exception object that another statement *throws*. Any method may throw one or more exceptions to indicate various exceptional conditions.

◆ Programs prepare to catch exceptions by *trying* one or more statements that are known to throw exceptions for specific types of errors. In general, to use exceptions, you simply *try* one or more methods and you *catch* any exceptions those methods *throw*.

◆ Java programs run in *threads,* a subject for Chapter 19, "Threaded Code." Unhandled exceptions terminate the current thread, but beforehand, the thread's `ThreadGroup` gets one final crack at dealing with the problem, or at least reporting it to the user. In most cases, unhandled exceptions cause the program to end abruptly, indicating a serious problem that needs immediate attention.

Introducing Exceptions

The basic mechanism for handling exceptions is the *try block*. This is a brace-delimited block of one or more statements preceded with the keyword `try`. The following template shows the format of a `try` block:

```
try {
 // statements that might throw an exception
} catch(exceptionClass exObject) {
 // handle the exception
}
```

A `try` block is always followed by at least one `catch` block, which dictates the program's response. It can also be followed by a `finally` block, but more on that later (see "Programming with Exceptions"). Inside the `try` block, the program can call methods or execute statements that might throw one or more exception objects. The `catch` block lists these exception objects, and the code in that block is expected to take whatever evasive action is necessary to deal with the problem.

A single `try` block may catch multiple types of exceptions. For example, the following incomplete code fragment catches three types of exception objects:

```
try {
  // statements that might throw an exception
} catch (EOFException e) {
  // handle end-of-file exception
} catch (FileNotFoundException e) {
  // handle file-not-found exception
} catch (IOException e) {
  // handle all other I/O exceptions
}
```

The EOFException and FileNotFoundException classes are each subclasses of IOException. The preceding code tries one or more statements that might throw these types of exceptions. After the try block, catch blocks handle the first two specific types of I/O exceptions. The last catch block handles all other IOException class errors.

Handling All Exceptions

Although it's possible, it is not usually a good idea to attempt catching all possible types of exception objects. For example, the following incomplete code fragment catches all exception objects of the Throwable class:

```
try {
 // Call method(s) which might throw an exception
} catch (Throwable e) {   // ???
 System.out.println(e.getMessage());
}
```

Because all exception objects are of classes that extend Throwable, the program catches every possible exceptional condition. This includes, however, any unchecked exceptions that indicate a programming error such as an out-of-bounds array index. For this reason, the preceding technique, while technically acceptable, is not recommended.

Rather than catch Throwable objects, to handle most exceptions, you can catch Exception class objects, which are direct descendants of Throwable and are intended for application use. For example, the code

```
try {
 // Call method(s) which might throw an exception
} catch (Exception e) {
 System.out.println(e.getMessage());
}
```

catches most types of exceptions, but permits other more sensitive types of the Throwable and Error classes (another Throwable subclass) to pass on to the Java virtual machine for proper handling.

In most cases, however, rather than attempt to catch all exceptions (except, perhaps, in small test programs), it is almost always best to catch objects of specific classes descended from Exception. Each Java method, including your own, specifies the types of checked exceptions it might throw. Your code needs to respond to those and only those types of exceptions. Likewise, your own code should specify the exceptions it might throw so that users of that code can catch all possible boundary conditions and errors.

 The Java compiler is able to detect that your code, or the virtual machine, handles exceptions that might be thrown. You will receive errors from the compiler if it determines that a possible exception is not handled. For example, if you call a method that might throw a specific kind of exception, the compiler will complain, "Exception X not caught or declared by Y," where X is the exception class name and Y is your method that calls the exception-throwing method. When you see this error, you can insert the method call in a try block and provide a catch block that handles the reported exception. Alternatively, you can declare your own method as one that throws an exception of this type. This pushes, but does not eliminate, responsibility for handling the exception onto the caller of your method.

Using Exceptions

When a statement in a try block causes an exception to be thrown, the rest of the statements in that try block do not execute. Instead, the program jumps immediately to a catch block statement that either matches the declared exception class exactly or matches a superclass of the thrown exception object. Take a look at an example.

```
try {
  method1();  // always executes
  method2();  // does not execute if m1 throws exception
  method3();  // does not execute if m1 or m2 throw an exception
} catch (Exception e) {
  System.out.println(e.getMessage());
}
```

If method1() throws an exception, then method2() and method3() are not called, and the program immediately jumps to the catch block statement, which in this example calls the Exception class getMessage() method and (we hope) prints an intelligent message about what happened. Similarly, method3() does not execute if method1() or method2() throws an exception. If no exceptions are thrown, the catch block statement does not execute.

In addition to these rules, if the `try` block ends abnormally — that is, if an associated `catch` block does not handle the exception object — then the method containing this `try` block immediately returns. Any return value is uninitialized. In that event, the exception stays alive, and it must eventually be handled, or the thread (and most likely the program) terminates. If the `try` block ends normally — that is, if no exceptions occur or if any are handled by a `catch` statement — then the program continues running after the last `catch` block associated with this `try`.

It is also possible for a `catch` block to handle an exception and then *rethrow* the object to pass it upward in the chain of method calls that led to a problem. Rethrowing an exception is an important technique that allows a program to indicate a problem but pass responsibility for handling that problem to a higher authority. For example, the following fragment catches most checked exceptions since these are all descended from the `Exception` class:

```
try {
  // call method(s) which might throw an exception
} catch (Exception e) {
 System.out.println("Trouble in paradise!");
 throw e;  // Rethrow the exception
}
```

As mentioned, it is generally not a good idea to catch all exceptions this way. However, because the `throw` statement rethrows the exception, this code does not prevent another exception handler from dealing with a specific problem.

Programming with Exceptions

In addition to catching exceptions thrown by Java's class library methods, you can also create your own exception classes and objects. It's a good idea to do this as you develop your programs — don't put off error-handling until the last moment! It's also good to use exception handling for *all* errors and exceptional conditions rather than attempt to create your own error protocols such as returning special values from methods.

To demonstrate how to create your own exception classes and objects, Listing 7-1, ExceptDemo.java, implements a `power()` method that can raise any `double` value to any `double` exponent value. Although the `Math` class already provides a similar method, `pow()`, that method does not generate exceptions for illegal values such as a zero base and a negative exponent, or a negative base and a fractional exponent (trying to raise –4, for example, by a power of 1.5). The sample program adds exception handling to a `power()` method that calls `Math.pow()` to do most of the hard work of the calculation.

Listing 7-1: ExceptDemo.java

```
001: class NewMathException extends Exception {
002:   // Constructor
```

```
003:  public NewMathException(double b, double e) {
004:   super("Domain error: base = " + b + " exp = " + e);
005:  }
006: }
007:
008: final class NewMath {
009:  // Prevent instantiation of class
010:  private NewMath() { }
011:  // Return b raised to the power of e
012:  public static double power(double b, double e)
013:  throws NewMathException {
014:   NewMathException error = new NewMathException(b, e);
015:   if (b > 0.0) return Math.pow(b, e);
016:   if (b < 0.0) {
017:    Double d = new Double(e);
018:    double ipart = d.intValue();
019:    double fpart = e - ipart;
020:    if (fpart == 0) {
021:     if ((ipart % 2) != 0)  // i.e. ipart is odd
022:      return -Math.pow(-b, e);
023:     else
024:      return Math.pow(-b, e);
025:    } else
026:     throw error;
027:   } else {
028:    if (e == 0.0) return 1.0;
029:    if (e < 1.0) throw error;
030:    return 0.0;
031:   }
032:  }
033: }
034:
035: class ExceptDemo {
036:  public static void main(String args[]) {
037:   if (args.length < 2) {
038:    System.out.println("Specify value and exponent");
039:    System.out.println("ex. java ExceptDemo -4 1.5");
040:   }
041:   else
042:   try {
043:    double base = new Double(args[0]).doubleValue();
044:    double exponent = new Double(args[1]).doubleValue();
045:    double result = NewMath.power(base, exponent);
046:    System.out.println("Result = " + result);
```

```
047:    } catch (NewMathException e) {
048:      System.out.println(e.getMessage());
049:    }
050:  }
051: }
```

Through the use of exceptions, running the program with illegal values causes it to display an error message showing the values that caused the problem:

```
java ExceptDemo -4 1.5
Domain error: base = -4.0 exp = 1.5
```

The sample listing begins with a class declaration (lines 001 to 006) that creates a new exception type, extended from Java's Exception class. When creating your own exceptions, you'll often want to declare a similar class to report special conditions and their associated values. For instance, in this case, we want to report not only that an error occurred, but also what values caused a problem. To do that, the program extend the Exception class with the declaration

```
class NewMathException extends Exception {...
```

In the NewMathException class, a constructor takes as arguments two double values:

```
public NewMathException(double b, double e) {...
```

To use the new exception class, the program's NewMath class declares the power() method and informs the world that this method might throw an object of the NewMathException type (see lines 012 and 013):

```
public static double power(double b, double e)
 throws NewMathException {...
```

Because power() states that it might throw a NewMathException object, any statements that call power() must be in a try block, or they must themselves exist in a method that also throws NewMathException. This is a good example of a checked exception — one that the compiler checks is thrown and caught properly. Because the method explicitly declares an exception class, attempts to execute statements such as

```
double x = NewMath.power(1.2, 1.3);  // ???
```

cause the compiler to complain that the NewMathException is neither declared nor caught. Compiling the preceding statement produces this output:

```
ExceptDemo.java:49: unreported exception
 NewMathException; must be caught or declared to be thrown
double x = NewMath.power(1.2, 1.3);  // ???
                ^
```

By the way, notice how the caret character on the last line points to the place in the source code where the error occurs. To fix the problem, rather than call power() in a try block, a method could declare this same exception, and in this way pass any thrown objects back up the method-call chain that led to the exception. For example, you could write a method f() as follows:

```
public void f() throws NewMathException {
 double x = NewMath.power(1.2, 1.3);
 ...
}
```

Now it is okay to call NewMath.power() without using a try block because f() explicitly states that it might throw a NewMathException object. If power() throws an exception, f() immediately returns to its caller and passes responsibility for handling the exception to that caller. That code might be written like this:

```
try {
 f();
} catch (NewMathException e) {
   System.out.println(e.getMessage());
}
```

A method may state that it throws more than one type of exception class object. Separate multiple exception-class names with commas after the throws key word. For example, this declaration of a method named test() states that it might throw one of three types of exceptions:

```
public void test()
 throws NewMathException,
        BadEntryException,
        IncompleteException {
 ...
}
```

I just made up the last two exception names to show the format. Try always to declare your methods this way along with all the exceptions they throw. This will help incorporate error handling into your code and also help the compiler ensure that all exceptions are properly handled.

There are two more important points to remember about try blocks and exceptions:

◆ If any statement in the `try` block throws an exception, none of the subsequent statements in that block are executed.

◆ If any statement in the `try` block throws an exception and that exception is not caught, the method that executed the `try` block immediately returns to its caller.

The second point might cause a method to skip critical code that must execute regardless of whether an exception is thrown. The next section explains how to write this type of critical code using a `finally` block.

Finally Block

As I just mentioned, if a `try` block detects an exception and that exception is not handled, the method that executed the `try` block immediately returns. Technically speaking, this happens because the `try` block ends abnormally, which causes the block that executes the `try` also to end. To deal with situations that require executing statements regardless of whether an exception is thrown or caught, insert a *finally block* after the `try` and any `catch` statements.

Listing 7-2, `FinallyDemo.java`, demonstrates the purpose and effect of a `finally` block following a `try` block. The sample program tests three situations: throwing no exceptions, throwing an exception of a predefined Java class, and throwing an object of a class defined in the program itself. Running the program shows what you can expect from a `finally` block and also shows what happens to any unhandled exceptions.

Listing 7-2: FinallyDemo.java

```
001: // Exception class
002: class ThrowMe extends Exception {
003:   ThrowMe() { }
004:   ThrowMe(String s) {
005:     super(s);
006:   }
007: }
008:
009: class FinallyDemo {
010:   // Test method -- pass 0, 1, or 2 for different exceptions
011:   static void testMethod(int n) throws Exception, ThrowMe {
012:     switch (n) {
013:     case 1:
014:       throw new Exception("Unhandled exception");
015:     case 2:
016:       throw new ThrowMe("To the wolves");
017:     default:
018:       return;
019:   }
```

```
020:  }
021:  // Main program
022:  public static void main(String args[])
023:    throws Exception {
024:    int argument = 0;
025:    if (args.length > 0)
026:      argument = Integer.parseInt(args[0]);
027:    try {
028:      testMethod(argument);
029:    } catch (ThrowMe e) {
030:      System.out.println("ThrowMe: " + e.getMessage());
031:    } finally {
032:      System.out.println("Finally statement");
033:    }
034:    System.out.println("Statement after try block");
035:  }
036: }
```

After compiling the program, run it three times by typing the following commands:

```
java FinallyDemo
java FinallyDemo 1
java FinallyDemo 2
```

The first command shows what happens when no exceptions are thrown. On screen, the text shows that, in the absence of any exceptions, the main() method's finally block executes as does the statement at line 035 following the try block:

```
Finally statement
Statement after try block
```

This last statement is significant because its execution proves that the preceding try block ended normally. Because of this, we know that main() did not return prematurely due to an exception. The second test, which causes testMethod() at lines 011-020 to throw an Exception object, displays these results:

```
Finally statement
Exception in thread "main" java.lang.Exception: Unhandled exception
  at FinallyDemo.testMethod(FinallyDemo.java:20)
  at FinallyDemo.main(FinallyDemo.java:35)
```

The output shows what happens when the program fails to catch an exception. Even so, the finally block, indicated by the first line, is executed, ensuring that any critical code runs regardless of even this serious problem.

You should normally not throw objects of the Exception class, as done for demonstration purposes in FinallyDemo.java. Normally, programs should extend Exception to create new exception classes. I used Exception in this unusual way to force an unhandled exception condition — and it is to Java's credit that this is difficult to do!

The third and final experiment shows what happens when an exception is thrown and caught in a normal fashion. On screen you see

```
ThrowMe: To the wolves
Finally statement
Statement after try block
```

The first line indicates that the ThrowMe class object is caught and handled properly (see line 029). Again, because the exception was handled, the try block ends normally and main() does not end prematurely as it did with the prior test with an unhandled exception. Thus, the "Statement after try block" executed normally. In addition, the finally block is also executed, again ensuring that critical code is always run.

A finally block's statements run even if the associated try block executes a return, break, continue, or throw statement. You can really trust a finally block to run regardless of what occurs in its try block.

Nested try Blocks

You may nest try blocks inside each other to simplify some kinds of error handling. Generally speaking, however, more than two levels of nesting may be more confusing than helpful. But the technique might be necessary to respond to an exception on more than one level — an inner try block, for example, may handle a specific kind of error that is additionally handled in a more general way in an outer try block. Listing 7-3, NestedTry.java, demonstrates how to program nested try blocks that each respond to the same exception object in different ways.

Listing 7-3: NestedTry.java

```
001: class NewException extends Exception { }
002: class NewNewException extends NewException { }
003:
004: class NestedTry {
005:   public static void test() throws NewNewException {
```

```
006:    throw new NewNewException();
007:    }
008:    public static void main(String args[]) {
009:    try {
010:     try {
011:      test();
012:     } catch (NewNewException e) {
013:      System.out.println("Inner try block exception caught");
014:      throw e;  // Rethrow exception
015:     }
016:    } catch (NewException e) {
017:     System.out.println("Outer try block exception caught");
018:    }
019:    }
020: }
```

The program begins by declaring two new exception classes. NewException is the more general of the two classes. NewNewException represents a more specific kind of error. (A real world example of this technique might be a file system that reports a general file-input error but also reports the specific cause of the problem, such as a data element in the wrong place.) By the way, these two classes are examples of what I call *name-only exceptions* – they contain no new programming or instance variables. Their class names are all that indicate the type of exception and, therefore, the nature of a specific problem.

Method test() at line 005 throws the more specific type of exception. The program's main() method implements a two-level try block. In the inner block, the program calls test(), which throws the specific exception, caught by the catch statement at line 012. To handle the same exception in a more general way, line 014 rethrows the exception object. This causes the inner try block to end abnormally, also causing the outer block's catch statement at line 016 to catch NewException (the general case class). This works because the more specific NewNewException class extends NewException. Thus a NewNewException object is simply a more specific kind of NewException object. Running the program proves that the exception is caught in each case:

```
Inner try block exception caught
Outer try block exception caught
```

Tracing the Stack

Properly understanding why an exception occurred often requires knowing the order in which methods were called that led to the exception being thrown. A useful method in the Exception class can print this information for you. It's particularly effective as a debugging tool.

Listing 7-4, StackTrace.java, shows how to display the line numbers of the statements that lead to an exception. You might use a similar technique to trace the origin of an unhandled exception that unexpectedly terminates a program.

Listing 7-4: StackTrace.java

```
001: class NewException extends Exception { }
002:
003: class StackTrace {
004:  // Cause an exception to be thrown
005:  public static void test() throws NewException {
006:    throw new NewException();
007:  }
008:  // Main program--catch the thrown exception
009:  public static void main(String args[]) {
010:    try {
011:      test();
012:    } catch (NewException e) {
013:      System.out.println("NewException caught. Tracing stack:");
014:      e.printStackTrace();  // Trace exception origin
015:    }
016:  }
017: }
```

The program declares a name-only exception, NewException, extended from the Exception class. An exception of that class is thrown in a test() method (see line 006). The program's main() method calls test() in a try block and catches the thrown exception object at line 012. The last statement in catch displays a trace of the method-call stack. Running the program displays

```
NewException caught. Tracing stack:
NewException
        at StackTrace.test(StackTrace.java:12)
        at StackTrace.main(StackTrace.java:17)
```

The first line is printed by the program's output statement at line 013. The subsequent lines are printed by the Exception class's printStackTrace() method. They show the class name, the method called, and the relevant line numbers (subtract six to match them to the printed listing, and see the following note). This is obviously great information for tracing the origin of any exceptions received during a program run.

The reported line numbers do not match those in the printed listings because of extra header comments removed to save room here. As mentioned, to find the correct lines, subtract six from the stack trace line numbers. Or, view the actual source code file for this listing as explained in Chapter 2.

Class Library Exceptions

Methods in Java's packages use exceptions extensively, and programs are expected to respond to the conditions that the exceptions report. As you read through this book and Java's online documentation, you will discover notes that method so-and-so throws an exception of class such-and-such. To provide error handling, in most cases, you can simply call the method from within a try block, followed by one or more catch statements that handle the listed exception classes.

It's important, however, to also understand how Java organizes its exception classes. The following overviews will help you to use exceptions correctly and avoid some common mistakes.

Exception Class Hierarchy

All exception classes extend Throwable, a class in the java.lang package (see Figure 7-1). Throwable descends directly from Object, the lowliest of Java classes. Objects of Throwable subclasses contain at least these two items:

♦ A string that describes the exceptional condition

♦ A snapshot of the execution stack, which as mentioned, you can use to print a trace of method calls that help locate the origin of a problem

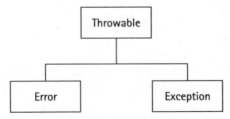

Figure 7-1: All exception classes descend from Throwable.

The diagram shows that two main classes, Error and Exception, extend Throwable. Understanding the distinction between these two subclasses is vital for properly creating exception handlers in your code.

Error and Exception Classes

Exceptions of classes that extend Error are serious in nature, usually involve a system problem such as a stack overflow, and are unchecked. Following is a list of Error's subclasses.

AbstractMethodError	ClassCircularityError
ClassFormatError	ExceptionInInitializerError
IllegalAccessError	IncompatibleClassChangeError
InstantiationError	InternalError
LinkageError	NoClassDefFoundError
NoSuchFieldError	NoSuchMethodError
OutOfMemoryError	StackOverflowError
ThreadDeath	UnknownError
UnsatisfiedLinkError	UnsupportedClassVersionError
VerifyError	VirtualMachineError

There is never any good reason for an application to extend the Error class for its own exceptions. Technically, Java permits you to extend Error, and it also permits programs to throw and catch these types of exceptions, but doing so is considered poor programming for several reasons:

◆ Error exceptions are unchecked. The compiler does not verify that methods declare unchecked exceptions, nor that they are caught in a try-catch block. By extending Error, you sidestep one of the more helpful features of the Java compiler that ensures your code properly throws and handles exceptions.

◆ Methods that throw unchecked exceptions do not need to declare them in a throws clause, and therefore there is no easy way except by reading every statement to know what exceptions the method might throw.

◆ Catching Error exceptions, while on rare occasion useful, is also not usually good programming because this may lead to system problems – such as attempting to continue running after an internal error is detected due to a bug in a Java byte-code interpreter.

Instead of attempting to extend Error, applications and applets should extend the Exception class for their own error handling. These types of exceptions are checked – in other words, methods that throw them must declare them in a throws clause, and the compiler checks that all such exceptions are caught in catch statements. By basing your exceptions on the Exception class, you create good error handling logic in your code.

> If an Error exception occurs, it usually terminates the program. Because you can't do much to prevent this unhappy occurrence, I don't describe each type of Error class here. For example, a VirtualMachineError exception indicates that the Java interpreter has a problem, and there's nothing you can do about that since your code may be executing on a computer somewhere halfway around the world. But don't be overly concerned. It is highly unlikely that your program will suffer from Error exceptions. However, there are two "exceptions" to that comment — one, an OutOfMemoryError might occur due to improper creation of too many objects that can't be garbage collected, and two, a StackOverflowError might indicate a runaway recursion of a method that calls itself repeatedly. These problems are likely caused by programming mistakes; the others listed here are extremely unlikely to occur.

RuntimeException Class

Another subclass, RuntimeException, extends the Exception class (refer back to Figure 7-1). These types of exceptions, while less serious than those of Error subclasses, typically indicate programming mistakes that need to be resolved in the source code. For example, ArrayStoreException is thrown if the program attempts to insert an object of an incorrect type into an array, perhaps by using a type-cast expression that the compiler allows but the interpreter doesn't. This type of error can't be corrected at runtime.

As with Error exceptions, those of the RuntimeException class and its subclasses are unchecked. For the same reasons mentioned for Error, applications and applets should never extend RuntimeException, nor in most cases should these types of exceptions be caught in try-catch blocks (unless, perhaps, by temporary code inserted for debugging purposes). Following is a list of the RuntimeException subclasses.

ArithmeticException	ArrayIndexOutOfBoundsException
ArrayStoreException	ClassCastException
ConcurrentModificationException	EmptyStackException
IllegalArgumentException	IllegalMonitorStateException
IllegalStateException	IllegalThreadStateException
IndexOutOfBoundsException	MissingResourceException

NegativeArraySizeException   NoSuchElementException

NullPointerException   NumberFormatException

SecurityException   StringIndexOutOfBoundsException

UndeclaredThrowableException   UnsupportedOperationException

RuntimeException Subclasses

My sailing friends and I like to say that there are two kinds of sailors: those who run aground and the fibbers who claim never to touch bottom. Likewise, there are two kinds of programmers. Those who make boneheaded programming mistakes (I speak from experience), and those who never tell anyone about their errors. Regardless of which group you belong to, just *in case* you receive one of the exceptions in the preceding list of RuntimeException subclasses, the following notes may help you pinpoint the cause. As for running aground, I wrote this book not long after spending the night at a 45-degree angle in my sailboat high and dry on a sandbar. The boat was fine but my pride suffered a little. Don't let yours do the same if you receive one of these:

◆ ArithmeticException

This exception can be reported for a variety of mathematical errors, but almost always indicates an attempt to divide an integer value by zero. Keep in mind that Java does *not* throw an exception for dividing floating point values by zero; in that case the result is set to the special value NaN (not a number) and no exception is thrown.

◆ ArrayIndexOutOfBoundsException

This is a special extension of the more general IndexOutOfBoundsException. If you receive this error, the most likely cause is a for or other loop that performs one too many iterations on an array. Remember that array indexes begin with 0, and therefore the highest legal index value is one *less* than the number of elements in the array. Programmers often refer to this common mistake as an "off by one error."

◆ ArrayStoreException

An object of this type is thrown if a statement attempts to store the wrong type of object in an array. Usually, the compiler catches this type of mistake, but it might occur if you are using a type-cast expression to attempt to convert one type of object or value to another.

◆ ClassCastException

Java throws an object of this class if a statement attempts to subclass an object to an inappropriate class. The Java compiler is much better now at detecting this type of mistake, so you are unlikely to see this exception. However, if you do, it probably is the result of a type-cast expression that attempts to convert an object of one type into another.

◆ ConcurrentModificationException

An object was modified concurrently by two processes. Improper synchronization in threaded code could be the cause.

◆ EmptyStackException

The Stack class throws this exception to indicate that an attempt was made to pop a value from an empty stack.

◆ IllegalArgumentException

Various methods throw this exception to indicate that an argument value passed to a method is illegal. Two further subclasses of this class are IllegalThreadStateException and NumberFormatException.

◆ IllegalMonitorStateException

This exception class does *not* indicate a problem with your CRT, but rather that a thread has attempted to wait on an unowned object's *monitor* — a term and technique that applies to threaded code.

◆ IllegalStateException

The state of the program or object does not permit this operation. You are attempting to perform a task that cannot be completed.

◆ IllegalThreadStateException

The current thread cannot fulfill a request such as attempting to start a thread that is already running.

◆ IndexOutOfBoundsException

You will probably catch and throw one of two subclasses of IndexOutOfBoundsException rather than use objects of this super class. See ArrayIndexOutOfBoundsException and StringIndexOutOfBoundsException.

◆ MissingResourceException

A specified resource bundle could not be found. The cause is probably in the program's internationalizations. For more information, look up that topic and the abstract ResourceBundle class in Java's online documentation.

◆ NegativeArraySizeException

Java throws an object of this class if a statement attempts to construct an array using a negative size argument, which might happen when using a variable to specify the array's size. The usual cause is in an expression that computes the array's size, especially with multidimensional arrays that contain variable-sized components.

◆ NoSuchElementException

An object of this class is thrown to indicate that there are no more elements in an Enumeration. This type of error is common when using Java's collection classes and is a rare example of a RuntimeException that might be reasonably nabbed by a catch statement.

◆ NullPointerException

Java throws an object of this class to indicate that a statement has attempted to use an uninitialized object. Such an object, for example, might be declared but not constructed using the new operator. The typical cause is a method that returns a class object but that in some cases might return null if the method cannot construct the requested object. Statements that call that method must check whether the return result is null, or they may suffer this exception. Two suggestions: one, rewrite the method to return an object that can be safely used by the method's caller but that has no actual effect or data, or two (better), have the method throw an exception to report the unusual condition.

◆ NumberFormatException

Typically thrown to indicate an attempt to convert a badly formatted string to a value – for example, trying to convert an alphabetic string to an integer. This is another rare example of a RuntimeException that can be safely caught, perhaps to deal with improper input.

◆ SecurityException

The java.lang.SecurityManager class throws an exception of this type to indicate a security violation or a potential security-related problem. An application's security policy, for instance, might require verification before attempting a critical operation. For example, the checkPackageAccess() method in the SecurityManager class throws a SecurityAccess exception if the user does not have access to the package. By implementing a security policy, it's possible to safely restrict the use of a package or class – after a trial period has expired, for example, in a shareware collection of programming tools.

◆ StringIndexOutOfBoundsException

This exception is a more general case of the IndexOutOfBoundsException class. It indicates an out of bounds index value, similar to that explained for ArrayIndexOutOfBoundsException, but for a string object.

◆ UndeclaredThrowableException

This exception is thrown to indicate that a proxy class's invoke() method has thrown an exception of a class not listed in the real method's throws clause. Using proxy classes is an advanced technique beyond the scope of this book, but in general it is a way of creating classes for existing objects to add new runtime features such as tracing method calls or performing other debugging chores. Applications rarely need proxy classes, and you are unlikely to experience this exception. If you do, however, the mistake is undoubtedly in your proxy class's invoke() method.

◆ UnsupportedOperationException

Java's collection classes might throw this exception if an attempt is used to access an object in a collection in an illegal way.

Summary

◆ An *exception* is an exceptional condition that requires special handling. Checked exceptions are those that the compiler can verify from a method's throws clause and that are caught by a catch statement. Unchecked exceptions are not similarly verifiable and generally indicate a system problem or a bug in the source code.

◆ To use exceptions, programs call methods and execute statements in a try block. Any exceptions thrown by those methods or statements are handled in one or more catch blocks.

◆ If an exception is not handled by a catch block, the try block ends abnormally, causing the method in which it exists to immediately return to its caller. In the case of unchecked exceptions, this might cause the current thread or program to terminate.

◆ To ensure that critical code is executed, insert statements in a finally block. A finally block's statements are always executed, regardless of whether an exception is thrown in a try block.

◆ All exception classes are subclasses of Throwable. There are two basic kinds. Error exceptions indicate serious system problems and are rarely caught explicitly by applications. Exception classes are those that a program can catch and typically deal with at runtime — such as a file not found error.

◆ The RuntimeException class extends Exception to provide another set of unchecked exceptions. These are generally less serious than Errors but indicate a problem in the source code — a loop, for example, that attempts to access an array element beyond its last index.

Chapter 8

String Things

STRINGS ARE PROBABLY THE MOST COMMON and widely used type of data in computer programming. In this chapter, you learn about Java's two string classes, and also how to use individual characters.

IN THIS CHAPTER

- ◆ Declaring and using strings
- ◆ Declaring and using characters
- ◆ `String` and `Stringbuffer` classes
- ◆ The `Character` class
- ◆ Getting user input

Declaring and Using Strings

Java supports Unicode characters, each 16 bits long, and capable of representing most if not all written human languages in the world. Because the first 127 of these characters are equivalent to the ASCII character set, Java programs can be written using just about any text editor. However, if you have a Unicode editor, you can use it to prepare Java source code. This means you can use Unicode for your program's identifiers, class names, variables, as well as for characters and strings.

As you have already seen in many of this book's sample listings, a literal string is written as zero or more characters delimited with double quotes. Probably the most common use for a literal string is as a label or greeting. For example, this statement displays a literal string:

```
System.out.println("A string is a wonderful thing!");
```

Similarly, you can declare a string variable, and assign it a literal value:

```
String s = "I am a string!";
```

In this chapter, you learn several other ways to create strings, and you learn about many of the methods you can call for the `String` and `StringBuffer` classes.

This chapter also covers individual characters of type char, as well as the Character wrapper class.

Concatenating Strings

You may use the + and += operators to *concatenate,* or join, strings. You may also create strings from other types of data by attaching them to another string. The following statements display a string composed of three parts — two literal strings and the value of distance:

```
double distance = 45.5;
System.out.println("Distance = " + distance + " miles");
```

Programmers who know other languages may think that the value of distance is somehow passed to println(). It isn't. Because of the plus signs and the presence of a literal string label, Java converts distance to a string, appends it to the two literal strings, and then passes that result to println(). Java attempts to convert most data types this way to strings, which makes it easy to display values of most types. If you run those two statements, you see on screen

```
Distance = 45.5 miles
```

Strings as Objects

Internally, all strings are represented as objects of the String or StringBuffer classes. It's important to understand, however, that when you use a string in a program, it is represented as an object, not as an array of characters as in other languages such as C. (However, you can create arrays of characters if you want — see "Character Arrays" in this chapter.)

You can create String objects for creating and storing string data, which is often more convenient than passing literal strings to methods such as println(). For example, these three statements display the same results as in the preceding section:

```
double distance = 45.5;
String s = "Distance = " + distance + " miles";
System.out.println(s);
```

This time, however, the program constructs a String object, s, and then displays it using a println() statement. Again, Java converts distance to a string, concatenates it to the two literal strings, and assigns the result to the string object. Having strings as objects opens all sorts of possibilities for programs. You can, for example, find the length of a string by calling the String class's length() method as in this statement:

```
System.out.println("Length = " + s.length() + " character(s)");
```

Attached to the preceding fragment, the statement displays

```
Length = 21 character(s)
```

One significant characteristic of a String object is that it may have a length of zero. If you create and assign a string as follows, the program displays empty's length as zero:

```
String empty = "";
System.out.println("Length = " + empty.length());
```

Strings created as objects of the String class are immutable — once constructed, their values cannot be changed. To create string objects that can be changed at runtime, you may instead use the StringBuffer class. But first, let's look at another related type, the char.

Declaring and Using Characters

Java programs may declare and use individual char variables. The char data type is native to Java. It is 2 bytes long, and it holds an unsigned integer value. Literal characters are represented as any character you can type, delimited by single quotes. For example, this statement creates a char variable, dollarSign, and assigns it the dollar sign character:

```
char dollarSign = '$';
```

The literal character value is typed using single quotes (apostrophes on most PC keyboards). You may create literal characters this way using any symbol that you can type. To enter Unicode symbols that you can't type on the keyboard, you can use the escape sequence \uxxxx to specify a character in hexadecimal:

```
char c = '\u0a76';
System.out.println("Char = " + c);
```

The Unicode escape sequence may appear anywhere in a literal string or character. The actual character displayed, however, depends on whether your output terminal supports Unicode characters. If not, you see a default value for the character — a question mark, for example, in a Windows DOS prompt window. Type two backslashes to represent one:

```
System.out.println("C:\\Windows\\Command");
```

That displays the Windows path C:\Windows\Command.

TIP   One significant difference between strings and characters is that a `char` variable can never have a length of zero.

Mixing Characters and Strings

You may mix characters and strings in several ways. For example, use the + operator to concatenate a character and a string:

```
char ch = 'Q';
System.out.println("Char = " + ch);
```

You can also use the += operator to construct `String` objects out of characters. The following fragment creates a `String` object, s, containing the lowercase alphabet characters 'a' through 'z'.

```
String s = "";
for (char ch = 'a'; ch <= 'z'; ch++)
 s += ch;
System.out.println(s);
```

In addition to its native `char` data type, Java also provides a `Character` *wrapper class*. Later in this chapter, I'll explain more about how to use this class.

TIP   Wrapper classes provide an object-oriented interface to a native data type such as `char` or `double`. Chapter 9, "Numeric Classes," covers more about wrapper classes.

Character Arrays

Although in Java strings are represented as `String` or `StringBuffer` objects, you may construct arrays of `char` values for a variety of purposes. For example, you might store arrays of characters for simplicity when you don't need a full string object.

You haven't learned about arrays yet (more about them in Chapter 10, "Arrays"), but they differ from arrays in other languages. In Java, arrays are constructed at runtime using the `new` operator. For example, this statement defines an array of 26 `char` values:

```
char letters[] = new char[26];
```

The empty square brackets state that `letters` is an array. The `new` operator constructs an array of 26 `char` values, assigned to the `letters` identifier. Each character in the array is initialized to the value zero. By the way, you may place the empty square brackets after the data type or the identifier. You can write the preceding statement as follows:

```
char[] letters = new char[26];
```

I mention this only in case you come across code that uses this alternate style. The former style is recommended. You may also declare and define a `char` array using separate statements such as

```
char letters[];
...
letters = new char[26];
```

The first line declares that `letters` is an array of `char` values. Elsewhere in the program, the last line constructs the actual array and assigns its reference to `letters`. Because the array is constructed at runtime, you may use a variable to specify its size — one great advantage in Java over C and C++. Here's yet another way to create the `letters` array:

```
char letters[];
int k = 26;
letters = new char[k];
```

At runtime, the final statement creates the `letters` array capable of storing a number of `char` values equal to k.

String Classes

Now, let's get back to Java's string classes. There are two kinds:

- ◆ `String`: Use this one for fixed length strings that will not change at runtime. A `String` object is *immutable*.

- ◆ `StringBuffer`: Use this class for variable-length strings that might change at runtime. A `StringBuffer` object is *mutable*.

You may be surprised to learn that these two classes are each extended from the `Object` superclass but are not otherwise related to each other. The next sections explain how to use each of Java's two string classes.

The String Class

Java's String class provides numerous public constructors and methods, so to make them easier to learn, I divided their declarations into reference listings ending with the file extension .txt. These and similar listings in this chapter are stored in .txt files on the CD-ROM. They contain no code and cannot be compiled.

STRING CONSTRUCTORS

Listing 8-1 shows the String class constructors, which give you nine different ways to construct String objects. In addition to these, Java 2 still provides but deprecates the following two constructors, which were intended to convert byte arrays to strings but are unreliable. Use the constructors in Listing 8-1 instead of these two:

```
//deprecated String constructors
public String(byte ascii[], int hibyte, int offset, int count);
public String(byte ascii[], int hibyte);
```

Listing 8-1: StringConstructors.txt

```
001: public String();
002: public String(String value);
003: public String(char value[]);
004: public String(char value[], int offset, int count);
005: public String(byte bytes[], int offset,
        int length, String enc);
006: public String(byte bytes[], String enc);
007: public String(byte bytes[], int offset, int length);
008: public String(byte bytes[]);
009: public String(StringBuffer buffer);
```

The String class overloads nine constructors that give you a variety of ways to create String objects. The default, no-parameter, constructor is used when you construct a string like this:

```
String s = new String();
```

The resulting object, s, has zero length, and because a String object is immutable, you won't usually create strings this way. However, the technique is often valuable to avoid a NullPointerException, as Listing 8-2, NullString.java, demonstrates.

Listing 8-2: NullString.java

```
001: class NullString {
002:  // Return a null string reference
003:  public static String badString() {
```

```
004:    String s = null;
005:    return s;
006:  }
007:  // Return a zero-length string
008:  public static String goodString() {
009:    String s = new String();
010:    return s;
011:  }
012:  // Try the preceding two methods
013:  // The NullPointerException is intentional
014:  public static void main(String args[]) {
015:    String s;
016:    s = badString();  // Change to goodString() and rerun
017:    System.out.println("Length(s) = " + s.length());
018:  }
019: }
```

Running the program causes it to fail with a NullPointerException. On screen, you see this message from the Java runtime interpreter:

```
Exception in thread "main" java.lang.NullPointerException
        at NullString.main(NullString.java:23)
```

This happens because method badString() (see line 003) returns a null reference instead of a constructed String object. The attempt to use that reference as an object at line 017 causes the exception to be thrown. Because String s is null, the expression s.length() is not allowed. The situation is common with many methods that return class objects. One possible fix is to test the method's return value for null:

```
s = BadString();
if (s != null)
  // use s safely
```

But this is tedious in programs that call the method in many different places. A better solution is to return an empty string, as demonstrated by method goodString() (see lines 008 and 009). To fix the program, change badString() at line 016 to goodString().

Getting back to String's constructors, there are two common ways to initialize a String object using a literal string:

```
String s1 = "Literal construction";
String s2 = new String("Alternate method");
```

Either technique is correct and produces similar results (but see "The Internal String Pool" in this chapter). Assigning a literal string to a String object actually calls the String constructor that declares a String parameter (see Listing 8-1, line 002).

It is also occasionally useful to create String objects using char arrays, perhaps read from a file or constructed in code. Listing 8-3, CharArray.java, shows how.

Listing 8-3: CharArray.java

```
001: class CharArray {
002:   public static void main(String args[]) {
003:   String s;
004:   char array[] = new char[26];
005:   for (char c = 'a'; c <= 'z'; c++)
006:    array[c - 'a'] = c;
007:   s = new String(array);
008:   System.out.println(s);
009:   }
010: }
```

The program declares a String variable, and also an array of 26 char values. A for loop fills array with the lowercase letters 'a' through 'z'. Line 007 shows how to construct the String object by passing the array to the class constructor. Alternatively, you can pass a starting index and count to construct the string using only a portion of the char array. For example, given the array in the listing, the following constructs a String object equal to "efghijklmn":

```
s = new String(array, 4, 10);
```

When constructing strings from arrays, a NullPointerException is thrown if the array is null, so you may want to place the statement in a try-catch block. However, this isn't necessary here since we know that array is not null.

Be aware that, when converting an array of char to a string, the array contains characters in 16-bit Unicode format. C and C++ programmers are especially likely to assume incorrectly that Java's char data type is 8-bit ASCII. It isn't. When you need to convert an 8-bit array of ASCII characters, you must instead use a byte array and pass it to one of the four String constructors that begin with the parameter byte bytes[] (see Listing 8-1 lines 005-008).

TIP   As mentioned, the String class provides two deprecated constructors for converting byte arrays to strings. To do this, use only one of the four constructors shown in Listing 8-1.

You might need to convert ASCII character arrays in cases where your Java programs calls a C or C++ library function, or receives the data from some other source. Starting with a `byte` array declared and initialized as follows:

```
byte byteArray[] = new byte[26];
for (int i = 0; i < 26; i++)
 byteArray[i] = (byte)(i + 'a');
```

The type-cast expression in the last line is necessary because Java evaluates the expression `i + 'a'` as type `int`. To convert the resulting `byte` array to a `String` object, use a statement such as

```
s = new String(byteArray);
```

As with `char` arrays, you can additionally specify offset and length values to create a string using only a portion of the array:

```
s = new String(byteArray, 2, 5);
```

If `byteArray` holds the lowercase alphabet, that statement creates a `String` object equal to `"cdefg"`.

Two other constructors (see Listing 8-1, lines 005–006) perform similar conversions of `byte` arrays to strings, but also take an additional parameter `String` parameter named `enc` for *encoding*. This string specifies the platform character encoding used on the target system to convert ASCII characters to Unicode. The exact encoding to use depends on the system, but all systems support the encodings in Table 8-1.

TABLE 8-1 CHARACTER ENCODINGS

Encoding	Description
ISO-8859-1	Same as ISO-Latin-1 on many systems
US-ASCII	Standard 7-bit ASCII
UTF-16	16-bit Unicode, byte-order marked
UTF-16BE	16-bit Unicode, big endian byte order
UTF-16LE	16-bit Unicode, little endian byte order
UTF-8	8-bit Unicode

Listing 8-4, CharEncoding.java, demonstrates how to construct a String object from an array of 8-bit bytes (that is, standard ASCII values), to an encoded Unicode string. You may replace the encoding literal string in line 011 with any of the values in Table 8-1. You may also try other encodings, but be prepared to receive an UnsupportedEncodingException if the encoding is not supported on your system. Also, some of the encodings may not produce visible results — for example, an MS-DOS Prompt window supports only the US-ASCII and UTF-8 encodings.

Listing 8-4: CharEncoding.java

```
001: import java.io.UnsupportedEncodingException;
002:
003: class CharEncoding {
004:   public static void main(String args[]) {
005:     String s;
006:     byte byteArray[] = new byte[26];
007:     for (int i = 0; i < 26; i++)
008:      byteArray[i] = (byte)(i + 'a');
009: // Convert byte array to a String using an encoding
010:     try {
011:      s = new String(byteArray, "UTF-8");
012:      System.out.println(s);
013:     } catch (UnsupportedEncodingException e) {
014:      System.out.println(e.getMessage());
015:     }
016:   }
017: }
```

As you can with arrays of char, you can also specify index and length values. For example, if you replace line 011 with the following statement, the resulting string equals "klmnopqr":

```
s = new String(byteArray, 10, 8, "UTF-8");
```

Finally, you may construct a String using a StringBuffer object — but more on that in this chapter's discussion of the StringBuffer class.

STRING METHODS

Listing 8-5, StringMethods.txt, shows most of the methods available in the String class. Refer to this listing while reading the sample code and discussions in the following sections.

Listing 8–5: StringMethods.txt

```
001: // String class inspection methods
002: public int length();
003: public char charAt(int index);
004: public void getChars(int srcBegin, int srcEnd,
       char dst[], int dstBegin);
005: public byte[] getBytes(String enc);
006: public byte[] getBytes();
007: public int hashCode();
008:
009: // String class comparison methods
010: public boolean equals(Object anObject);
011: public boolean equalsIgnoreCase(String anotherString);
012: public int compareTo(String anotherString);
013: public int compareTo(Object o);
014: public int compareToIgnoreCase(String str);
015: public boolean regionMatches(int toffset, String other,
       int ooffset, int len);
016: public boolean regionMatches(boolean ignoreCase,
       int toffset, String other, int ooffset, int len);
017: public boolean startsWith(String prefix, int toffset);
018: public boolean startsWith(String prefix);
019: public boolean endsWith(String suffix);
020:
021: // String class index methods
022: public int indexOf(int ch);
023: public int indexOf(int ch, int fromIndex);
024: public int lastIndexOf(int ch);
025: public int lastIndexOf(int ch, int fromIndex);
026: public int indexOf(String str);
027: public int indexOf(String str, int fromIndex);
028: public int lastIndexOf(String str);
029: public int lastIndexOf(String str, int fromIndex);
030:
031: // String class conversion methods
032: public String substring(int beginIndex);
033: public String substring(int beginIndex, int endIndex);
034: public String concat(String str);
035: public String replace(char oldChar, char newChar);
036: public String toLowerCase(Locale locale);
037: public String toLowerCase();
038: public String toUpperCase(Locale locale);
```

```
039: public String toUpperCase();
040: public String trim();
041: public char[] toCharArray();
042: public native String intern();
```

Unnumbered lines in Listing 8-5 are continuations of the preceding lines, broken here to fit on the page. If you are using a Web browser to view the listing, the text appears on one line.

SEARCHING STRINGS FOR CHARACTERS

To determine which character is at a certain index position in a string, call the charAt() method, which returns char. It's a good idea to verify that the target string length is greater than the specified index, as this fragment demonstrates:

```
String s = "abcdefg";
if (s.length() >= 5) {
 char ch = s.charAt(4);
 System.out.println("Char at 4 = " + ch);
}
```

That sets ch equal to 'e', the character at the fourth index position in the test string. The first index position is zero, so the fourth is the fifth character.

If you call charAt() with an argument that is greater than or equal to the string length, Java throws StringIndexOutOfBoundsException.

To perform the reverse operation — finding the integer index of a specific character — call one of several indexOf() methods, possibly followed by a call to substring() to extract a portion of a string. The following fragment searches a string for the letter k:

```
String s = "abcdefghijklmnop";
int index = s.indexOf('k');
if (index >= 0) {
 String sub = s.substring(index);
 System.out.println(sub);
}
```

If index is zero or greater, the program creates another string, sub, to which it assigns the string "klmnop" — the value from the reported index to the end of the original string. If indexOf() returns -1, the requested character was not found. Another form of substring() takes a second integer argument, representing the final index of the string to extract. Given the preceding code, this statement sets sub to "klm":

```
String sub = s.substring(index, index + 3);
 System.out.println(sub);
```

STRINGS AND SUBSTRINGS

Other forms of indexOf accept additional parameters. For example, you can specify an index to begin searching a string from a position other than the beginning. Listing 8-6, MonthNames.java, shows how to use indexOf() to parse a string composed of variable-length substrings and separator characters ('#').

Listing 8-6: MonthNames.java

```
001: class MonthNames {
002:  public static void main(String args[]) {
003:   String s = "#January#February#March#April" +
004: "#May#June#July#August#September#October" +
005: "#November#December#";
006:   int i = 0, j;
007:   while (i++ >= 0) {
008:    j = s.indexOf('#', i);  // i = starting index
009:    if (j >= 0) {
010:     String month = s.substring(i, j);
011:     System.out.println(month);
012:    }
013:    i = j;
014:   }
015:  }
016: }
```

 To write a long literal string on multiple lines, use the concatenation operator + as shown in Listing 8-6, lines 003-005. Early versions of Java allowed ending strings with a backslash and then continuing the string on the next line, but Java 2 no longer supports nor needs this *line continuation character*.

The sample program extracts the month names from the original string, using two integer index values and the indexOf() method to hop from separator to separator.

Other forms of indexOf() accept a string argument, which is useful for finding substrings, as in the fragment:

```
String s = "Passwords.txt";
int index = s.indexOf(".txt");
if (index >= 0)
 System.out.println(s + " is a text file");
```

The statements search a filename string for the extension, .txt. A potentially easier technique uses the endsWith() method, which returns a boolean true or false value:

```
String s = "LoveLetters.txt";
if (s.endsWith(".txt"))
 System.out.println(s + " is a text file");
```

Conversely, use startsWith() to find out if a string begins with a certain substring:

```
String s = "Accounts1.txt";
if (s.startsWith("Accounts"))
 System.out.println(s + " is an Accounts file");
```

COMPARING STRINGS

To compare two strings, call compareTo(), which returns an integer value. Listing 8-7, Compare.java, demonstrates this method.

Listing 8-7: Compare.java

```
001: class Compare {
002:  public static void main(String args[]) {
003:   String s1 = "abcdefg";
004:   String s2 = "ABCDEFG";
005:   int result = s1.compareTo(s2);
006:   if (result == 0)
007:    System.out.println("s1 = s2");
008:   else if (result < 0)
009:    System.out.println("s1 < s2");
010:   else // if (result > 0)
011:    System.out.println("s1 > s2");
012:  }
013: }
```

The compareTo() method returns −1 if its string object is alphabetically less than the argument passed to the method. It returns 0 if the two strings are exactly equal. It returns +1 if the object is alphabetically greater than its argument.

You can also compare one string with another using the `equals()` method, as in

```
if (s1.equals(s2))
  System.out.println("s1 = s2");
```

Don't, however, attempt to compare strings using the `==` or `!=` operators. Remember that string variables are actually references to real string objects that exist somewhere in memory. Java permits you to write a statement such as

```
if (s1 == s2)        // ???
  DoSomething();
```

That compares whether the references `s1` and `s2` are to the same *object*, not whether the two strings have the same *content*. This is not necessarily incorrect — but be sure it's what you want to do; otherwise, use a method such as `equals()` to compare strings.

 TIP Because `equals()` is inherited from `Object`, the method can compare *any* two objects, not only strings.

To compare strings ignoring case, call `equalsIgnoreCase()` like this:

```
if (s1.equalsIgnoreCase(s2))
  System.out.println("s1 = s2");
```

Compare substrings by calling one of two `regionMatches()` methods. The two methods differ only in having an initial `boolean` parameter, which you can set to `true` to ignore case; otherwise, or if this parameter is `false`, the comparison is case sensitive. The full method is defined as

```
public boolean regionMatches(boolean ignoreCase, int toffset,
  String other, int ooffset, int len);
```

The overloaded method is the same, but it lacks the `ignoreCase` parameter. Following are descriptions of this method's somewhat cryptic parameters:

- ◆ `boolean ignoreCase` — Set to `true` to ignore case for the comparison. Omit this argument, or set it to `false`, for a case-sensitive comparison.

- ◆ `int toffset` — The offset index to begin the comparison of the string object for which you call `regionMatches()`.

- ◆ `String other` — The second string to compare with the string object for which the method was called.

- ◆ `int ooffset` — The offset index to begin the comparison of the other string object parameter, `other`. The spelling with two initial o's is intentional.

- ◆ `int len` — The number of characters to compare in both strings.

The following code shows how to use `regionMatches()` to determine whether a substring is part of another string.

```
String s = "Haste makes waste";
String sub = "waste";
if (s.regionMatches(true, 12, sub, 0, sub.length()))
 System.out.println("sub string found in s");
```

OTHER USEFUL STRING METHODS

The `String` class has several other useful methods. Call `toLowerCase()` and `toUpperCase()` to return a string with all lower- or uppercase characters. The methods do not alter the original string; to do that, reassign the results back to the object. Examine this fragment:

```
String s = "Haste makes waste";
System.out.println(s.toUpperCase());
System.out.println("s = " + s);
s = s.toUpperCase();
System.out.println("s = " + s);
```

The statements display a string in uppercase, then convert it to uppercase and display the result. Conversions such as this might require different actions depending on where the program is run. To conform to the current *locale,* import the `Locale` class and use it in the string conversion. Listing 8-8, StringLocale.java, shows how.

Listing 8-8: StringLocale.java

```
001: import java.util.Locale;
002:
003: class StringLocale {
004:   public static void main(String args[]) {
005:   String s = "ABCDEFGHIJKLMNOPQRSTUVWXYZ";
006:   System.out.println("Before : " + s);
007:   s = s.toLowerCase(Locale.CANADA);
008:   System.out.println("After  : " + s);
009:   }
010: }
```

The first line imports Locale, which supports several default localization objects. Line 007 specifies the CANADA Locale. The French-Canadian object is named CANADA_FRENCH. Locales might specify country names with and without languages. Or, they might specify a language. For example, other commonly used locales include ENGLISH, FRENCH, GERMAN, ITALIAN, JAPANESE, CHINESE, and TRADITIONAL_CHINESE. There are many others — see the source code for the Locale class for a complete list.

To concatenate *and save* string objects, use the concat() method. Because this method does not alter the original string, to actually append strings you must reassign the results of the method back to the original object. For example, Listing 8-9, Concat.java, builds the string, "Testing One Two Three", in the test String object.

Listing 8-9: Concat.java

```
001: class Concat {
002:   public static void main(String args[]) {
003:     String s1 = " One";
004:     String s2 = " Two";
005:     String s3 = " Three";
006:     String test = "Testing";
007:     test = test.concat(s1);
008:     test = test.concat(s2);
009:     test = test.concat(s3);
010:     System.out.println(test);
011:   }
012: }
```

Rather than call concat(), however, you can use the string concatenation operator (+) to do the same job. This is a little neater and can replace lines 007-009:

```
test = test + s1 + s2 + s3;
```

Call replace() to replace all occurrences of a specific character with another character. The fragment

```
String s = "#January#February#March#April#May#";
System.out.println(s.replace('#', '@'));
```

changes the '#' separators to '@' characters in String s. The method does not alter the original string. Again, to do that, you must assign the results back to the object:

```
s = s.replace('#', '@');
```

Several String methods are available for converting between char and byte arrays and String objects. You might do this to create 8-bit ASCII data for use with other languages such as C and C++.

Call toCharArray() to assign any String object to an array of characters. You do not have to initialize the array—the method creates it at runtime, as this fragment demonstrates:

```
char alpha[];
String s = "abcdefghijklmnopqrstuvwxyz";
alpha = s.toCharArray();
```

The result is the alphabetic characters in a newly allocated array of char, which is assigned to the array variable, alpha. The statement effectively converts the Unicode characters in a string to 8-bit ASCII.

Another way to get character data out of a String object is to call one of two methods—getChars() or getBytes(). Use getChars() as follows to extract the Unicode characters from a String object into a char array:

```
String s = "abcdefghijklmnopqrstuvwxyz";
char alpha16[] = new char[6];  // char array
s.getChars(12, 18, alpha16, 0);
```

The results are stored in the alpha16 array passed here as the third argument to the getChars() method. A similar method, getBytes(), with similar parameters except for an array of bytes in the third position, has been deprecated in Java 2. Do not use this method:

```
//deprecated
public void getBytes(int srcBegin, int srcEnd,
 byte dst[], int dstBegin);
```

Instead, use one of two methods declared as

```
public byte[] getBytes();
public byte[] getBytes(String enc);
```

Either call getBytes() with no parameters, and assign the result to a byte array, or pass an encoding string. See "String Constructors" in this chapter for an explanation of encoding strings.

Call trim() to remove any leading and trailing blanks from a string. As with several other String methods, calling trim() does not alter the original string. If you want to do that, assign the result back to the object as Listing 8-10, StringTrimmer.java, demonstrates at line 005.

Listing 8-10: StringTrimmer.java

```
001: class StringTrimmer {
002:   public static void main(String args[]) {
003:     String s = "    blankety blank    ";
004:     System.out.println("Length before = " + s.length());
005:     s = s.trim();   // trim blanks from string
006:     System.out.println("Length after  = " + s.length());
007:   }
008: }
```

THE INTERNAL STRING POOL

Referring back to Listing 8-5 you find one more String method, intern(), at the bottom of the list. This obscure method returns a string from a pool of strings that are guaranteed to be unique. The String class automatically maintains and uses this pool, but you may access it through the intern() method. If you call that method, you get back a String object equal to the one you specify, but if that string value is in the pool, you receive that object, not a brand new one. In addition, if the string is not already in the pool, it is added. Listing 8-11, StringIntern.java, demonstrates the effect of calling intern().

Listing 8-11: StringIntern.java

```
001: class StringIntern {
002:   public static void main(String args[]) {
003:     String s1 = "Unique string";
004:     String s2 = s1.intern();
005:     if (s1 == s2)
006:       System.out.println("s1 equals s2");
007:   }
008: }
```

This is one case where it is correct to use the == operator to compare two strings (see line 005) because, after calling intern(), we want to verify whether s1 and s2 refer to the same *object*, not merely whether their character values are the same. Running the program displays s1 equals s2, proving that intern() found the literal string "Unique string" in the pool, and returned that object to be assigned to s2 at line 004.

You don't have to call intern() this way to avoid duplicating strings needlessly. Java does so automatically. For example, if you create two strings and assign them identical literal values, Java assigns the same String object to both variables:

```
String s1 = "Unique string";
String s2 = "Unique string";   // s1 == s2
```

However, the string pool is not used when you construct a String object using a statement such as:

```
String s3 = new String("Unique string");
```

In that case, the string to which s3 refers is not taken from the pool.

STRING VALUE-OF METHODS
A series of highly useful overloaded methods are all named valueOf(). They convert values of built-in Java types to strings. Listing 8-12, StringValue.txt, shows the method declarations in the String class:

Listing 8-12: StringValue.txt

```
001: public static String valueOf(Object obj);
002: public static String valueOf(char data[]);
003: public static String valueOf(char data[],
       int offset, int count);
004: public static String copyValueOf(char data[],
       int offset, int count);
005: public static String copyValueOf(char data[]);
006: public static String valueOf(boolean b);
007: public static String valueOf(char c);
008: public static String valueOf(int i);
009: public static String valueOf(long l);
010: public static String valueOf(float f);
011: public static String valueOf(double d);
```

Use the valueOf() methods to convert values to strings. For example, these statements set String s to the string "3.14159":

```
double d = 3.14159;
String s = String.valueOf(d);
```

You've seen in other sample statements another way to do a similar job. Java converts values automatically to strings in statements such as

```
String s = "Value = " + d;
```

Because of the literal string label, Java assumes you want to create a string result. The compiler calls the appropriate String class valueOf() method to perform the conversion. However, the following statement does not compile:

```
String s = d;  // ???
```

Java rejects that because the String and double data types are incompatible for assignment — the compiler does not make the logical conclusion that you want to *convert* d to a string. To do that, call valueOf() as just shown.

All `valueOf()` methods are declared `static`, which means they are normally called in reference to the `String` class. You may call them in reference to a `String` object, but I can think of no good reason to do so. The methods accept the following types of parameters (refer back to Listing 8-10):

- `boolean b` — Converts `boolean` value to string `"true"` or `"false"`.

- `char c` — Converts a character to a string.

- `char data[]` — Converts an array of characters to a string.

- `char data[], int offset, int count` — Converts an array of characters to a string using `count` characters starting with the offset index in the `data` array.

- `double d` — Converts a `double` value to a string.

- `float f` — Converts a `float` value to a string.

- `int i` — Converts an `int` value to a string.

- `long l` — Converts a `long` value to a string.

- `Object obj` — Converts any other object to a string.

 TIP To convert your own class objects to strings, override and implement the `toString()` method inherited from `Object`. You can then use your class objects in concatenation statements, or you can call `toString()` and assign the result to a `String` object.

Two related overloaded methods named `copyValueOf()` convert a `char` array to a `String` object. Call the method like this:

```
char alpha[] = new char[26];
for (char c = 'a'; c <= 'z'; c++)
  alpha[c - 'a'] = c;
String s = String.copyValueOf(alpha);
```

First, the program creates an array of `char` values equal to the alphabet. The final line calls `copyValueOf()` to convert the array to a `String` object. Because this method is static, you normally call it in reference to the `String` class as shown here. Alternatively, you may specify integer `offset` and `count` values to create a `String` object from a portion of a `char` array. Given the preceding code, the following statement creates `String s` equal to `"jklmno"`:

```
String s = String.copyValueOf(alpha, 9, 6);
```

The StringBuffer Class

As mentioned, String objects are immutable. To create string objects that you can modify at runtime, use the StringBuffer class. Listing 8-13 shows the constructors and methods for Java's StringBuffer class. Refer to this listing while reading the following sections about how to use this class.

Listing 8-13: Java's StringBuffer class

```
001: // StringBuffer class constructors
002: public StringBuffer();
003: public StringBuffer(int length);
004: public StringBuffer(String str);
005:
006: // StringBuffer class length and capacity methods
007: public int length();
008: public int capacity();
009: public synchronized void ensureCapacity(int minimumCapacity);
010: public synchronized void setLength(int newLength);
011:
012: // StringBuffer class char methods
013: public synchronized char charAt(int index);
014: public synchronized void getChars(int srcBegin, int srcEnd,
        char dst[], int dstBegin);
015: public synchronized void setCharAt(int index, char ch);
016:
017: // StringBuffer class append methods
018: public synchronized StringBuffer append(Object obj);
019: public synchronized StringBuffer append(String str);
020: public synchronized StringBuffer append(char str[]);
021: public synchronized StringBuffer append(char str[],
        int offset, int len);
022: public StringBuffer append(boolean b);
023: public synchronized StringBuffer append(char c);
024: public StringBuffer append(int i);
025: public StringBuffer append(long l);
026: public StringBuffer append(float f);
027: public StringBuffer append(double d);
028:
029: // StringBuffer class delete and replace methods
030: public synchronized StringBuffer delete(int start, int end);
031: public synchronized StringBuffer deleteCharAt(int index);
032: public synchronized StringBuffer replace(int start, int end,
        String str);
033:
034: // StringBuffer class substring methods
```

```
035: public String substring(int start);
036: public synchronized String substring(int start, int end);
037:
038: // StringBuffer class insert methods
039: public synchronized StringBuffer insert(int index,
        char str[], int offset, int len);
040: public synchronized StringBuffer insert(int offset, Object
obj);
041: public synchronized StringBuffer insert(int offset, String
str);
042: public synchronized StringBuffer insert(int offset,
        char str[]);
043: public StringBuffer insert(int offset, boolean b);
044: public synchronized StringBuffer insert(int offset, char c);
045: public StringBuffer insert(int offset, int i);
046: public StringBuffer insert(int offset, long l);
047: public StringBuffer insert(int offset, float f);
048: public StringBuffer insert(int offset, double d);
049:
050: // StringBuffer class other methods
051: public synchronized StringBuffer reverse();
052: public String toString();
053: private synchronized void readObject(
        java.io.ObjectInputStream s);
```

 Many StringBuffer methods are *synchronized,* which means they are suitable for use in threaded code. See Chapter 19, "Threaded Code," for more information.

STRINGBUFFER CONSTRUCTORS

You can construct a StringBuffer object three ways. To create one for later use, but not initialize it to any specific value or maximum size, declare the object like this:

```
StringBuffer buffer = new StringBuffer();
```

You must use the new operator to initialize all StringBuffer objects. Alternatively, however, you may delay construction of the object using two separate steps:

```
StringBuffer filler;
...
filler = new StringBuffer();
```

Specify an initial length by passing an integer value to the StringBuffer constructor. For example, the following statement constructs a StringBuffer object that can initially hold up to 80 characters:

```
StringBuffer buffer = new StringBuffer(80);
```

When you know how many characters you will assign to the object, specifying an initial length that way is more efficient than allowing the string to expand automatically. The string can still grow larger than the specified length. Because construction takes place at runtime, you may also use a variable as the StringBuffer object's size:

```
int len = 45;
StringBuffer buffer = new StringBuffer(len);
```

The third and final way to create a StringBuffer object is to initialize it using a String object. For that, Java calls the following constructor:

```
StringBuffer(String str);
```

You might use this method to convert an immutable string into a StringBuffer for modification:

```
String s = "Make me variable!";
StringBuffer canChange = new StringBuffer(s);
```

In that code fragment, String object s is immutable. The second statement converts the String object to a StringBuffer object, which can be changed by other statements. For example, you can append a new string to canChange.

STRINGBUFFER APPEND METHODS

Strings that will not change are best declared using the String class. Strings that might change during a program should be StringBuffer objects. Although it's true that the String class provides methods such as concat(), a close inspection of the method's declaration

```
public String concat(String str);
```

reveals that it returns a String object, indicating that calling concat() creates an entirely new instance of the String class. This is highly inefficient, especially when creating string variables out of multiple parts such as filenames. For example, the code

```
String name = "Account";
String extension = ".dat";
```

```
String fileName = name;
fileName = fileName.concat(extension);
```

creates the `String` object `fileName` equal to the string `"Account.dat"`. Compare this to the equivalent `StringBuffer` technique, which calls the `Append()` method using the same `name` and `extension` objects:

```
String name = "Account";
String extension = ".dat";
StringBuffer fileName = new StringBuffer(80);
fileName.append(name);
fileName.append(extension);
```

This might appear to be more work because (ignoring the first two declarations) it uses three statements instead of two. Actually, however, this is more efficient because Java needs to construct only one `fileName StringBuffer` object to which the `name` and `extension` are appended.

You may use numerous variations of `append()` to attach data in string form to `StringBuffer` objects. You may append `boolean`, `char`, `char[]` array, `double`, `float`, `int`, `long`, and `String` class values. You may also append any other object that provides a `toString()` method.

Listing 8-14, StringAppend.java, demonstrates somewhat frivolously how to use the `StringBuffer.append()` method.

Listing 8-14: StringAppend.java

```
001: class StringAppend {
002:   public static void main(String args[]) {
003:     // Declare and initialize a StringBuffer object
004:     StringBuffer buffer = new StringBuffer(80);
005:     // Declare some variables of different types
006:     boolean truth = false;
007:     long value = 1000000;
008:     char ch = '$';
009:     // Append literal strings and variables to buffer
010:     buffer.append("You won ");
011:     buffer.append(ch);
012:     buffer.append(value);
013:     buffer.append(" is a ");
014:     buffer.append(truth);
015:     buffer.append(" statement!");
016:     // Display the result
017:     System.out.println(buffer);
018:   }
019: }
```

The program declares at line 004 the variable `buffer` as a `StringBuffer` object with an initial capacity of 80 characters. Lines 006-008 create a few variables of various types, which are appended along with literal strings to the buffer. Lines 010-015 show how to call `append()`. Running the program displays

```
You won $1000000 is a false statement!
```

> Calling `append()` and other `StringBuffer` methods that modify the object's content directly affect the object. With the `String` class, to save any modifications such as extracting a substring, you have to save the result of a method in a `String` object. With many `StringBuffer` methods, you simply call them to modify the object.

For every `append()` method, there is a corresponding `insert()` method that you can use to insert data into any position in a `StringBuffer` object. This is often convenient for poking values into the middle of a string, as in this code:

```
double value = 65.7;
StringBuffer buffer =
 new StringBuffer("Value =  light years");
buffer.insert(8, value);  // Insert value at index 8
```

That fragment creates the following string in the `StringBuffer` object:

```
Value = 65.7 light years
```

Because the first index in a `StringBuffer` is zero, you can use a statement such as follows to preface a string with a label:

```
buffer.insert(0, "Preface: ");
```

STRINGBUFFER LENGTH AND CAPACITY METHODS

All `StringBuffer` objects have `length()` and `capacity()` methods. A `StringBuffer` object's *length* equals the number of characters it currently holds. The object's *capacity* is the number of characters it can hold before the object is expanded. Unless specified, a `StringBuffer` object's default initial capacity is 16 characters. The following statements display each value for the `buffer` object:

```
System.out.println("Length = " + buffer.length());
System.out.println("Capacity = " + buffer.capacity());
```

If you append more data than a StringBuffer can hold, Java allocates additional space to the object. Too many such reallocations are potentially inefficient, and you can prevent them by allocating enough space to your StringBuffer objects. For example, this creates a StringBuffer object that can initially hold up to 128 characters:

```
StringBuffer buffer = new StringBuffer(128);
```

 All characters in a StringBuffer object are significant; there is no length byte or termination null character as in C, C++, and other languages. A StringBuffer declared with a length of 80 can hold up to exactly 80 characters. Appending or inserting more characters causes the StringBuffer object to be expanded automatically.

Call setLength() to alter the length of a StringBuffer's string data. This in effect appends blanks to the end of any existing string and might be useful for creating a series of strings all of the same length for display purposes, as this code demonstrates:

```
StringBuffer buffer = new StringBuffer(40);
buffer.append("Short");
buffer.setLength(40);
```

The last statement pads buffer with blank characters to ensure its length is equal to its capacity. The setLength() method is also useful for erasing a StringBuffer object's contents. The statement

```
buffer.setLength(0);
```

clears all character data from buffer. The object's capacity, however, is not changed. To do that — and ensure that a StringBuffer object can hold a string of a certain length, for example — call ensureCapacity() like this:

```
buffer.ensureCapacity(128);
```

As long as enough memory is available, calling ensureCapacity() guarantees that buffer can hold at least 128 characters.

Regardless of its length, if a string's capacity is already greater or equal to the argument passed to ensureCapacity(), Java makes no change to the StringBuffer object's capacity.

Calling ensureCapacity() never reduces a StringBuffer object's size. To do that, you can reallocate the object by calling one of its constructors. For example, when you are finished using a StringBuffer object, you can reduce its memory size by reallocating the object with a statement such as

```
buffer = new StringBuffer();  // Reallocate buffer
```

This creates a buffer object with a length of zero and a default initial capacity of 16 characters.

EXTRACTING CHARACTERS FROM STRINGBUFFER

It is often necessary to extract string data from a StringBuffer object. There are two basic techniques. Call toString() to convert a StringBuffer object to a String object, as in the following fragment, which converts buffer to a String object s:

```
StringBuffer buffer =
 new StringBuffer("A penny saved is a penny earned");
String s = buffer.toString();
```

To extract the individual characters from a StringBuffer object, call getChars() with four arguments:

◆ int srcBegin — The index in the source StringBuffer of the first character to copy.

◆ int srcEnd — The index in the source StringBuffer where copying stops. The character at index srcEnd - 1 is the last to be copied. The character at srcEnd is *not* copied to the destination.

◆ char dst[] — The destination char array, with a length greater or equal to srcEnd - srcBegin;.

◆ int dstBegin — The starting index in the dst array to which characters should be copied.

These statements demonstrate how to use getChars() to extract a substring from a StringBuffer object:

```
StringBuffer buffer =
```

```
new StringBuffer("A stitch in time saves nine");
char chArray[] = new char[6];
buffer.getChars(2, 8, chArray, 0);
```

This fragment first constructs a buffer and a six-char array, chArray. The final statement calls getChars() to extract the string "Stitch" from buffer into chArray.

Another way to extract character data from a StringBuffer object is to call charAt() with an integer index argument. For example, the code

```
char chArray[] = new char[buffer.length()];
for (int i = 0; i < buffer.length(); i++)
 chArray[i] = buffer.charAt(i);
```

uses a for loop to extract the characters from buffer, one at a time, and deposit each character in chArray. Notice how the array is constructed to be the same size as the buffer's length. (Of course, it would be easier to call getChars() — this code merely demonstrates how to use the charAt() method.)

OTHER STRINGBUFFER METHODS

Conversely, you can change any character in a StringBuffer object by calling the setCharAt() method. For example, the following code fragment creates a 40-character StringBuffer object, sets its length to 40 (which pads it with blanks), and then calls setCharAt() to change every character in the object to an asterisk:

```
StringBuffer buffer = new StringBuffer(40);
buffer.setLength(40);
for (int i = 0; i < buffer.length(); i++)
 buffer.setCharAt(i, '*');
```

Finally, in StringBuffer is a traditional string-processing method named reverse() that reverses an object's string, end for end. The following code demonstrates the method by reversing the alphabetic characters, a through z:

```
StringBuffer buffer = new StringBuffer(26);
buffer.append("abcdefghijklmnopqrstuvwxyz");
buffer.reverse();  // Reverse alphabet in buffer
```

Character Class

To provide object-oriented methods for working with char values, Java provides a *wrapper class,* Character. You can use this class to compare characters, to determine whether they are upper- or lowercase, and to perform other operations such as determining whether a character is allowed for a Java identifier.

Listing 8-15 shows Java's Character wrapper class declaration. Remember that static methods are typically called in reference to the class, not to an object of the class. Non-static methods are always called in reference to an object.

Listing 8-15: Character.txt

```
001: // Character class constructor
002: public Character(char value);
003:
004: // Character class methods
005: public char charValue();
006: public int hashCode();
007: public boolean equals(Object obj);
008: public String toString();
009: public static char toLowerCase(char ch);
010: public static char toUpperCase(char ch);
011: public static char toTitleCase(char ch);
012: public static int digit(char ch, int radix);
013: public static int getNumericValue(char ch);
014:
015: // Character class "is" methods
016: public static boolean isLowerCase(char ch);
017: public static boolean isUpperCase(char ch);
018: public static boolean isTitleCase(char ch);
019: public static boolean isDigit(char ch);
020: public static boolean isDefined(char ch);
021: public static boolean isLetter(char ch);
022: public static boolean isLetterOrDigit(char ch);
023: public static boolean isJavaLetter(char ch);
024: public static boolean isJavaLetterOrDigit(char ch);
025: public static boolean isJavaIdentifierStart(char ch);
026: public static boolean isJavaIdentifierPart(char ch);
027: public static boolean isUnicodeIdentifierStart(char ch);
028: public static boolean isUnicodeIdentifierPart(char ch);
029: public static boolean isIdentifierIgnorable(char ch);
030: public static boolean isSpace(char ch);
031: public static boolean isWhitespace(char ch);
032: public static boolean isISOControl(char ch);
033:
034: // Character class other methods
035: public static int getType(char ch);
036: public static char forDigit(int digit, int radix);
037: public int compareTo(Character anotherCharacter);
038: public int compareTo(Object o);
```

Character Class Methods

The Character wrapper class provides only one constructor. You can use it as follows to create a class object, which can hold one character value:

```
Character chObj = new Character('Q');
```

However, this isn't a practical technique for storing character data. Instead, you'll normally use the Character class to call one of several static methods, which do not require constructing an object. For example, use one of the static "is" methods to determine what kind of character the object holds. The following statement tests whether a char variable, ch, is a lowercase alphabetic character:

```
if (Character.isLowerCase(ch))
  System.out.println("is lowercase");
```

Use other "is" methods to test for digits, spaces, uppercase characters, and so on. Call isJavaLetter() to determine whether a character is a legal first character for a Java identifier:

```
if (Character.isJavaLetter(ch))
  // okay to use for first letter of identifier
```

Call isJavaLetterOrDigit() to determine whether ch is legal for a non-initial identifier character:

```
if (Character.isJavaLetterOrDigit(ch))
  // okay to use for identifier
```

Obtain the char value of a Character class object by calling charValue(). For example, use the following technique to convert a Character object back to a char value:

```
char ch = chObj.charValue();  // Convert chObj back to char
```

Two methods determine whether a character is invisible — commonly called *white space*. This includes characters such as tabs and new line codes that are embedded in text, but are not visible, and more important for parsers, are not to be considered in processing. Call isSpace() to determine generally if a character is white space. Call isWhiteSpace() to determine whether a character is white space according to the same rules used for parsing Java source code.

Character Digits

One good use for the Character class is in code that parses strings representing values in a specified radix, for example, hexadecimal. Use the digit() method to convert a character to an integer value in a radix. For example, the following code fragment converts the hexadecimal (radix 16) character 'F' to a corresponding digit:

```
char ch = 'F';
int digit = Character.digit(ch, 16);
System.out.println(ch + " = " + digit);
```

Running the fragment displays

```
F = 15
```

To go the other way — determining what character represents a certain value in a specified radix — call forDigit(). For example, the code

```
int digit = 12;
char ch = Character.forDigit(digit, 16);
System.out.println(digit + " = " + ch);
```

sets ch to the character that represents the value 12 in radix 16 (hexadecimal). The output statement displays

```
12 = c
```

If you instead want an uppercase letter, call toUpperCase() like this:

```
int digit = 12;
char ch = Character.forDigit(digit, 16);
ch = Character.toUpperCase(ch);
System.out.println(digit + " = " + ch);
```

To ensure that radix and character values are within allowable ranges, the Character class provides the constants MIN_RADIX and MAX_RADIX. Listing 8-16, ChRadix.java, uses these constants and the digit() method to print a list of characters in the ranges '0' to '9' and 'A' to 'Z', and show whether they are used in a specific radix.

Listing 8-16: ChRadix.java

```
001: class ChRadix {
002:   public static void main(String args[]) {
003:     System.out.println("Min radix = " + Character.MIN_RADIX);
004:     System.out.println("Max radix = " + Character.MAX_RADIX);
005:
006:     int radix = 12, result;
007:     char ch = '0';
```

```
008:    if (Character.MIN_RADIX <= radix &&
009:        radix <= Character.MAX_RADIX) {
010:    while (ch <= 'Z') {
011:     result = Character.digit(ch, radix);
012:     if (result >= 0)
013:       System.out.println(
014:         ch + " in base " + radix + " = " + result);
015:     else
016:       System.out.println("Char " + ch + " undefined for radix");
017:     if (ch == '9')
018:       ch = 'A';
019:     else
020:       ch++;
021:    } // while
022:   } else
023:    System.out.println("Radix " + radix + " out of range");
024:  }
025: }
```

Change the radix value at line 006 to any value. If out of range, the program reports that fact. Otherwise, it shows the characters used for representing values in this radix. For example, for radix 12, the program displays the following table (shortened here for space):

```
Min radix = 2
Max radix = 36
0 in base 12 = 0
1 in base 12 = 1
...
A in base 12 = 10
B in base 12 = 11
Char C undefined for radix
...
Char Z undefined for radix
```

Character Types

Call the Character class getType() method to determine the type of a character. Compare the results of this function to one of the constants shown in the following list of character type constants:

COMBINING_SPACING_MARK	CONNECTOR_PUNCTUATION
CONTROL	CURRENCY_SYMBOL
DASH_PUNCTUATION	ECIMAL_DIGIT_NUMBER

ENCLOSING_MARK	END_PUNCTUATION
FORMAT	LETTER_NUMBER
LINE_SEPARATOR	LOWERCASE_LETTER
MATH_SYMBOL	MODIFIER_LETTER
MODIFIER_SYMBOL	NON_SPACING_MARK
OTHER_LETTER	OTHER_NUMBER
OTHER_PUNCTUATION	OTHER_SYMBOL
PARAGRAPH_SEPARATOR	PRIVATE_USE
SPACE_SEPARATOR	START_PUNCTUATION
SURROGATE	TITLECASE_LETTER
UNASSIGNED	UPPERCASE_LETTER

The Character class defines these constants as byte values. Reference them using an expression such as Character.MATH_SYMBOL.

Listing 8-17, ChType.java, demonstrates how to use the constants in the preceding list along with the getType() method to determine the nature of several different characters.

Listing 8-17: ChType.java

```
001: class ChType {
002:
003:   // Display type of ch (not all types listed)
004:   public static void showType(char ch) {
005:    int type = Character.getType(ch);
006:    String s;
007:    switch (type) {
008:     case Character.UPPERCASE_LETTER:
009:      s = "uppercase letter"; break;
010:     case Character.LOWERCASE_LETTER:
011:      s = "lowercase letter"; break;
012:     case Character.DECIMAL_DIGIT_NUMBER:
013:      s = "decimal digit number"; break;
014:     case Character.OTHER_PUNCTUATION:
015:      s = "punctuation symbol"; break;
016:     case Character.MATH_SYMBOL:
017:      s = "math symbol"; break;
018:     case Character.CURRENCY_SYMBOL:
019:      s = "currency symbol"; break;
020:     default:
021:      s = "unknown symbol";
```

```
022:   }
023:   System.out.println("char " + ch + " : " + s +
024:     " (" + (int)ch + ")");
025:   }
026:
027:   public static void main(String args[]) {
028:     showType('A');
029:     showType('z');
030:     showType('3');
031:     showType('!');
032:     showType('+');
033:     showType('$');
034:     showType('\u0123');
035:   }
036: }
```

Running the program displays the types of the characters shown at lines 028-034. Notice that the last of these statements passes a Unicode value in hexadecimal to the program's showType() method. On screen, the program displays

```
char A : uppercase letter (65)
char z : lowercase letter (122)
char 3 : decimal digit number (51)
char ! : punctuation symbol (33)
char + : math symbol (43)
char $ : currency symbol (36)
char ? : lowercase letter (291)
```

The values in parentheses are the Unicode values for each character. To obtain this value, the program simply uses a type-cast expression (int)ch at line 024.

Getting User Input

Now that you know how to use strings and characters, it's time to clarify an important subject that will lead to more interesting sample programs — how to get input from users. The following sections explain two basic techniques — how to prompt users to enter data at the keyboard (usually in response to a prompt), and how to extract command-line arguments entered after the program's name.

Prompting for Input

To read something a user types at the keyboard, use the technique shown in Listing 8-18, InputString.java. The program uses a StringBuffer object to hold the results of your typing. Each character is read by a call to System.in.read() (see line 010)

in a `while` loop that appends each character received until you press Enter or Return (or whatever it's called on your keyboard). The program also shows how to import and catch any `IOException` errors. This is not optional — you are required to catch `IOException` if thrown by `System.in.read()`.

Listing 8-18: InputString.java

```
001: import java.io.IOException;
002:
003: class InputString {
004:  public static void main(String args[]) {
005:    try {
006:      StringBuffer buffer = new StringBuffer(64);
007:      char ch;
008:  // Prompt for and read a string
009:      System.out.print("Type something: ");
010:      while ((ch = (char)System.in.read()) != '\n')
011:       buffer.append(ch);  // Build string using ch
012:      // Display string entered
013:      System.out.println("You entered: " + buffer);
014:    } catch (IOException e) {          // Trap exception
015:      System.out.println(e.toString());   // Display error
016:    }
017:  }
018: }
```

While certainly useful, the technique shown in Listing 8-18 is rarely needed in production Java programs. We need it here for this book's sample programs, which as you know, run at a terminal or DOS prompt. Most Java programs run either in a Web browser, or as a stand-alone window-based application — environments that provide alternative input methods (covered in Part IV, "Applets and Applications").

 Earlier versions of Java supported reading user input into an array of `byte`, but this type of code no longer compiles in Java 2.

Reading Command-Line Arguments

Users may also pass data to Java applications by entering one or more arguments after the program name. Listing 8-19, `CommandLine.java`, shows the basic techniques.

Listing 8-19: CommandLine.java

```
001: class CommandLine {
002:   public static void main(String args[]) {
003:     System.out.println("Number of arguments = " + args.length);
004:     for (int i = 0; i < args.length; i++) {
005:       System.out.println(args[i]);
006:     }
007:   }
008: }
```

After compiling the program, run it with a command such as

```
java CommandLine Arg MoreArgs LastArg
```

The program displays the number of arguments and echoes their text:

```
Number of arguments = 3
Arg
MoreArgs
LastArg
```

All command-line arguments, if any, are stored in the `args[]` String array passed to the `main()` method. Line 002 declares this parameter. The expression `args.length` (see line 004) tells you how many argument strings are in the array. If this value is zero, the user typed no arguments.

Summary

- Use the `String` class for string objects that will not change during the course of a program. `String` objects are immutable.

- Use the `StringBuffer` class for string objects that are likely to change in size or content. `StringBuffer` objects are mutable.

- The `String` and `StringBuffer` classes are not directly related to each other, although both are derived from `Object`. Both classes provide numerous methods you can call to perform many operations on string data.

- The `Character` wrapper class puts an object-oriented face on Java's native `char` data type. You will most often use the `Character` class's static methods such as `isLowerCase()` to determine the nature of characters.

◆ This chapter shows how to call `System.in.read()` to read user input into a `StringBuffer` object. Since most Java programs run in a Web browser or in a graphical window, this input technique is of limited use, although it is needed for this book's relatively simple programming examples.

◆ Another way to get user input is to use the `args[]` `String` array declared for an application's `main()` method. Use this technique to extract command-line arguments typed at the terminal or DOS prompt.

Chapter 9

Numeric Classes

JAVA'S MATH AND NUMERICAL CLASSES make even tough math chores as easy as counting on your fingers and toes. In this chapter, you take a close look at Java's mathematical classes and methods, random numbers, and numerical wrapper classes that put an object-oriented face on built-in types such as `int` and `double`.

IN THIS CHAPTER

- ◆ Using the `Math` utility class
- ◆ Using the `Random` class
- ◆ Creating random-number generators
- ◆ Programming with numerical wrapper classes

The Math Class

Java's `Math` class provides numerous methods that you can call to perform a variety of mathematical operations. Listing 9-1 shows the `Math` class's constructor, constant declarations, and methods. Refer to this listing while reading the following sections.

 The `Math` class is automatically imported into every Java application. You do not need an `import` statement to use this class.

Listing 9-1: Math.txt

```
001: // Math class constructor
002: private Math() {}
003:
004: // Math class constants
005: public static final double E = 2.7182818284590452354;
006: public static final double PI = 3.14159265358979323846;
007:
```

```
008: // Math class methods
009: public static double sin(double a);
010: public static double cos(double a);
011: public static double tan(double a);
012: public static double asin(double a);
013: public static double acos(double a);
014: public static double atan(double a);
015: public static double toRadians(double angdeg);
016: public static double toDegrees(double angrad);
017: public static double exp(double a);
018: public static double log(double a);
019: public static double sqrt(double a);
020: public static double IEEEremainder(double f1, double f2);
021: public static double ceil(double a);
022: public static double floor(double a);
023: public static double rint(double a);
024: public static double atan2(double a, double b);
025: public static double pow(double a, double b);
026: public static int round(float a);
027: public static long round(double a);
028: public static double random();
029: public static int abs(int a);
030: public static long abs(long a);
031: public static float abs(float a);
032: public static double abs(double a);
033: public static int max(int a, int b);
034: public static long max(long a, long b);
035: public static float max(float a, float b);
036: public static double max(double a, double b);
037: public static int min(int a, int b);
038: public static long min(long a, long b);
039: public static float min(float a, float b);
040: public static double min(double a, double b);
```

Math Class Constructor

The Math class constructor is declared private to the class (see Listing 9-1, line 002). This means that any attempt to create a Math class object fails to compile:

```
Math m = new Math();  // ??? Can't do this
```

It is highly unusual to declare a constructor private, but in doing so, you effectively prevent any objects of the class from being created. Because all of the Math class's constants and methods are static, they are used in reference to the class itself, and you never need to construct a Math object. This is a good technique to remember for your own classes that provide static methods, and that you don't want used to create objects.

Math Fields

The Math class declares two static fields, or constants, E and PI (see lines 005-006). The double field E represents the base of the natural logarithms. The double field PI represents the value of π. The following statements (which you can insert in a test main() method)

```
System.out.println("E = " + Math.E);
System.out.println("Pi = " + Math.PI);
```

   display these values:

```
E = 2.71828
Pi = 3.14159
```

   Internally, however, the values are more accurately represented as the double values E = 2.7182818284590452354 and PI = 3.14159265358979323846 respectively.

Math Utility Methods

The Math class provides a bunch of utility methods that perform miscellaneous mathematical operations. Some of these are overloaded so you can pass them different types of arguments. For example, there are four versions of method abs(). That's not short for abdominal muscles, but for *absolute value.*

   Use the abs() methods in formulas requiring positive values when the argument might be negative. For example, suppose an integer value is positive or negative as a result of some other operation. To ensure a positive value, perhaps for using the integer as a character, call Math.abs() as in Listing 9-2, AbsValue.java.

Listing 9-2: AbsValue.java

```
001: class AbsValue {
002:   public static void main(String args[]) {
003:     int v = -100;
004:     char ch = (char)Math.abs(v);
005:     System.out.println("char(" + Math.abs(v) + ") = " + ch);
006:   }
007: }
```

   The statement at line 004 casts the absolute value of integer v into a char and assigns it to ch. The result is the lowercase 'd' in ch. Running the program displays

```
char(100) = d
```

Other forms of abs() permit double, float, and long arguments. Similarly overloaded are the min() and max() methods, which compare double, float, int, and long values, and return the minimum or maximum of two arguments. Listing 9-3, MinMax.java, demonstrates the methods.

Listing 9-3: MinMax.java

```
001: class MinMax {
002:  public static void main(String args[]) {
003:    long v1 = 99;
004:    long v2 = v1 * 2;
005:    System.out.println("v1=" + v1 + " v2=" + v2);
006:    System.out.println("Maximum value = " + Math.max(v1, v2));
007:    System.out.println("Minimum value = " + Math.min(v1, v2));
008:  }
009: }
```

Lines 006 and 007 show how to call Math.max() and Math.min() to find the maximum and minimum of two arguments. Running the program displays

```
v1=99 v2=198
Maximum value = 198
Minimum value = 99
```

Two other utility methods find the smallest or largest integer value closest to a floating point value. Math.ceil() returns the closest integer value greater or equal to (at the ceiling of) a given floating point value. The floor() method returns the closest integer less than or equal to (at the floor of) a floating point value. Listing 9-4, CeilFloor.java, demonstrates the methods:

Listing 9-4: CeilFloor.java

```
001: class CeilFloor {
002:  public static void main(String args[]) {
003:    double d = 10.0;
004:    while (d < 11.0) {
005:      System.out.println("d=" + d + " ceil(d)=" + Math.ceil(d) +
006:       " floor(d)=" + Math.floor(d));
007:      d += 0.1;
008:    }
009:  }
010: }
```

Running the program displays the ceiling and floor values for a double variable d, ranging from 10.0 to 10.9. The program's display, shortened by several lines here, also shows that the floating point representation of d + 0.1 is close, but not exactly, what you might expect (this is not a bug, but a normal characteristic of floating point representation):

```
d=10.0 ceil(d)=10.0 floor(d)=10.0
d=10.1 ceil(d)=11.0 floor(d)=10.0
d=10.2 ceil(d)=11.0 floor(d)=10.0
d=10.299999999999999 ceil(d)=11.0 floor(d)=10.0
...
d=10.999999999999996 ceil(d)=11.0 floor(d)=10.0
```

Some other methods — which if you are mathematically inclined you will no doubt find valuable — are exp(), which returns E to the power of its double argument, and log(), which returns the natural logarithm of its double argument. Use pow() to raise any value to any exponent, as Listing 9-5, PowerDemo.java, demonstrates.

Listing 9-5: PowerDemo.java

```
001: class PowerDemo {
002:  public static void main(String args[]) {
003:   if (args.length < 2) {
004:    System.out.println("Enter two values as follows:");
005:    System.out.println("java PowerDemo 2 8");
006:   } else {
007:    try {
008:     int j = Integer.parseInt(args[0]);
009:     int k = Integer.parseInt(args[1]);
010:     System.out.println(j + " ^^ " + k + " = " + Math.pow(j, k));
011:    }
012:     catch (NumberFormatException e) {
013:     System.out.println("Error in argument " + e.getMessage());
014:    }
015:   }
016:  }
017: }
```

Compile and run the program using commands such as

```
javac PowerDemo.java
java PowerDemo 2 8
```

The second command displays the value of 2 to the 8th power:

```
2 ^^ 8 = 256.0
```

The program also shows how to pick up integer command-line arguments, parsing the strings to `int` values (see lines 008 and 009). This technique uses the `parseInt()` method in the `Integer` wrapper class, covered later in this chapter. The method throws `NumberFormatException` for an illegal argument. To see how this is handled, enter a command such as follows:

```
java PowerDemo 2 X
Error in argument X
```

Two other utility methods fall into the miscellaneous category. Use `IEEEremainder()` to compute the IEEE remainder of the division of two floating point arguments, demonstrated in Listing 9-6, Remainder.java.

Listing 9-6: Remainder.java

```
001: class Remainder {
002:   public static void main(String args[]) {
003:     double arg1 = 3.14159;
004:     double arg2 = 2;
005:     double result = Math.IEEEremainder(arg1, arg2);
006:     System.out.println(arg1 + " / " + arg2 + " = " + result);
007:   }
008: }
```

Running the program displays the following:

```
3.14159 / 2.0 = -0.8584100000000001
```

The result does not equal the modulo value of `arg1` divided by `arg2`, as you might expect. If that's what you need, use the modulo operator instead of calling the `IEEEremainder()` method:

```
double result = arg1 % arg2;
```

That displays

```
3.14159 / 2.0 = 1.1415899999999999
```

Finally in the miscellaneous utility category is a method that computes the square root of a `double` argument. This statement displays the square root of 2:

```
System.out.println("Square root of 2 = " + Math.sqrt(2));
```

Math Rounding Methods

There are three methods in the `Math` class for rounding `double` and `float` values. The first, `rint()`, returns a `double` value for a `double` argument. Two overloaded round() methods each take a floating point argument and return the equivalent rounded integer. Note the different types in the two methods:

```
public static int round(float a);
public static long round(double a);
```

The int method accepts a float argument. It can't take a double argument because overloaded methods must differ in at least one parameter data type. The long method accepts a double argument. Be sure to use appropriate data types, or the compiler may report the error "possible loss of precision." This happens if, for example, you pass a double variable to round() but assign the result to an int instead of a long. Listing 9-7, Round.java, demonstrates the three rounding methods in the Math class and also shows at line 005 how to use a type-cast expression to avoid the compilation error. Line 006, however, is preferred because it assigns the result to a long variable.

Listing 9–7: Round.java

```
001: class Round {
002:   public static void main(String args[]) {
003:     double arg = 3.14159;
004:     double doubleResult = Math.rint(arg);
005:     int    intResult    = (int)Math.round(arg);
006:     long   longResult   = Math.round(arg);
007:     System.out.println("double rint(arg) = " + doubleResult);
008:     System.out.println("(int)round(arg)  = " + intResult);
009:     System.out.println("(long)round(arg) = " + longResult);
010:   }
011: }
```

Running the program displays

```
double rint(arg) = 3.0
(int)round(arg)  = 3
(long)round(arg) = 3
```

Math Trigonometry Methods

The Math class provides the usual set of methods for computing the sine, cosine, tangent, and other trigonometry functions. Each of these takes a double argument and returns type double. The methods are simple to use, but a demonstration program shows an interesting factor in using these and all floating point methods. Listing 9-8, CosDemo.java, displays the cosine values for –1.0 through 1.0.

Listing 9-8: CosDemo.java

```
001: class CosDemo {
002:  public static void main(String args[]) {
003:   double fp, result;
004:   for (fp = -1.0; fp <= 1.0; fp += 0.1) {
005:    result = Math.cos(fp);
006:    System.out.println("fp = " + fp + ", cosine = " + result);
007:   }
008:  }
009: }
```

When you run the program, you'll see the following lines on screen (I deleted some lines to save space):

```
fp = -1.0, cosine = 0.5403023058681398
fp = -0.9, cosine = 0.6216099682706644
fp = -0.8, cosine = 0.6967067093471654
...
fp = -1.3877787807814457E-16, cosine = 1.0
...
fp = 0.8999999999999998, cosine = 0.6216099682706646
fp = 0.9999999999999998, cosine = 0.5403023058681399
```

As this shows, the value for zero (essentially computed in the sample program as -0.1 + 0.1) is not necessarily 0.0 (see the line marked in bold). The result is a very small value that is *close* to zero and will probably compare equally to 0.0 in an expression — the cosine result for zero is correct — but it is not *physically* zero (all bits set to zero) as you might reasonably assume.

TIP Remember always that floating point values might be only approximately accurate.

Math Random Method

It always interests me that, in such an orderly and methodical business as computer programming, randomness intrigues programmers like no other subject. With all the effort spent writing code to put values in order, an equal amount of time (if not more) is spent scrambling everything up — or, I should say, creating a true random sequence.

Call the Math class's random() method for the next double value between 0 and 1 in a presumed arbitrary sequence. Listing 9-9, RandomDemo.java, demonstrates how to use the method.

Listing 9-9: RandomDemo.java

```
001: class RandomDemo {
002:  public static void main(String args[]) {
003:    double doubleResult;
004:    int intResult;
005:    for (int i = 1; i < 10; i++) {
006:      doubleResult = Math.random();
007:      System.out.print(doubleResult + " \t");
008:      intResult = (int)(doubleResult * 100);
009:      System.out.println(intResult);
010:    }
011:  }
012: }
```

The sample program displays ten random floating point values. It also demonstrates a way to convert the `double` values to integers. Here's a portion of one program run:

```
Floating point values    Integer values
0.26218545605972865      26
0.41877027636959074      41
0.2099903858228669       20
0.9878354983452603       98
0.04033550145685827      4
```

`Math.random()` returns a value r such that

`0.0 <= r < 1.0`

The method produces a different sequence each time a program using it is started. To produce random integer values, multiply by an arbitrary factor and round the result, or simply cast the result to type `int` or `long` (or another integer type). For example, line 008 multiplies the `double` result by 100 and then casts that value to type `int`. Parentheses carry out the multiplication before the type conversion.

Although `Math.random()` is certainly a handy method, more exacting needs require a more sophisticated generator. See the discussion of the `Random` class in the following section if you need additional random-number capabilities.

The Random Class

Use the `Random` class when you need random-number capabilities beyond the simple floating point sequences that the `Math.random()` method produces. Each instance of the `Random` class creates a unique pseudo-random-number generator. You can also create repeatable random sequences by *seeding* a `Random` generator object—useful for testing programs based on random numbers. Listing 9-10 shows the Random class constructors and public declarations.

Listing 9-10: Random.txt

```
001: // Random class constructors
002: public Random();
003: public Random(long seed);
004:
005: // Random class methods
006: synchronized public void setSeed(long seed);
007: public void nextBytes(byte[] bytes);
008: public int nextInt();
009: public int nextInt(int n);
010: public long nextLong();
011: public float nextFloat();
012: public double nextDouble();
013: synchronized public double nextGaussian();
```

The Random class is based on an algorithm called the *linear congruential method* attributed to D. H. Lehmer and explained in Donald E. Knuth's *Art of Computer Programming,* vol. 2 (Addison-Wesley, 1997).

Constructing Random Number Generators

The Random class provides two constructors. Use them to create objects that you might think of as random-number-generator factories. First import the class from java.util using this statement near the beginning of the source code file:

```
import java.util.Random;
```

Then, inside a method such as main(), call Random's default constructor to create the generator object:

```
Random generator = new Random();
```

That seeds the generator using the current date and time in milliseconds, guaranteeing a different sequence for each new object, and each new program run. Alternatively, you may supply a seed value to the constructor:

```
Random generator = new Random(1234);
```

Constructed like that, the generator object begins the same random sequence every time the program executes this statement. As mentioned, this can be helpful when debugging programs in order to ensure the same random data on each run.

 Repeated numeric sequences can still be random, even though their values are identical, because it is the distribution of values in the sequence that determines its randomness, not the particular set of values. (Without getting too technical, in other words, a number is considered random if it cannot be predicted statistically from those numbers that are generated before.)

Random Class Methods

After constructing the `Random` object, you can call various methods to obtain numbers at random. For example, Listing 9-11, `RandGen.java`, displays a table of random floating point or integer values.

Listing 9-11: RandGen.java

```
001: import java.util.Random;
002:
003: class RandGen {
004:  public static void main(String args[]) {
005:   Random generator = new Random();
006:   int rows, cols;
007:   StringBuffer buffer;
008:   for (rows = 1; rows <= 8; rows++) {
009:    buffer = new StringBuffer(128);
010:    for (cols = 1; cols <= 3; cols++) {
011:     buffer.append(generator.nextDouble() + " \t");
012: //   buffer.append(generator.nextInt() + " \t");
013:    }
014:    System.out.println(buffer);
015:   }
016:  }
017: }
```

The program builds each row of its output by appending values and tab control characters into a `StringBuffer` object. Running the program displays a table such as the following (shortened here to save room):

```
0.8698866164685745    0.1394602179807719    0.547958400488095
0.3368385654088868    0.20612391761001359   0.42516370464157494
```

```
. . .
0.17060159546084008   0.6867922191959271   0.8405425994020024
```

To create an integer table, delete line 011 and the comment symbol in front of line 012, compile, and run. Now the table looks like this:

```
135895775     2117998577    890454722
1601399493    -684065780    -2100152423
. . .
644254617     -2111290244   2083412152
```

For the next floating point value in a random sequence, call the `nextDouble()` method as demonstrated at line 011. For the next integer value, call `nextInt()` as on the next line. Notice that positive and negative integers are generated. However, `double` values are from 0.0 up to but not including 1.0. Similar methods, `nextLong()` and `nextFloat()`, produce `long` and `float` values respectively.

Finally, you can call the rarely needed, but possibly useful, `nextBoolean()` method to get a `true` or `false` value selected randomly, perhaps in a coin toss simulation:

```
Random gen = new Random();
Boolean heads = gen.nextBoolean();
```

Random Integer Ranges

One typical problem when using random integers is how to produce a sequence from 0 up to but not including a higher value, call it `N`. Any other sequence can be extrapolated by subtracting or adding a constant to the resulting values. This might seem to be a simple modulo `N` operation, but that can skew the results and make them anything but random. The `Random` class goes to some extremes to produce a statistically random sequence within a specified integer range.

To use this method, pass an integer constant to the overloaded `nextInt()` method. For example, to assign an integer at random between 0 and 99 inclusive, use statements such as:

```
Random gen = new Random();
int k;
. . .
k = gen.nextInt(100);   // 0 .. 99
```

Random Byte Blocks

Using a `Random` class method, `nextBytes()`, you can fill an array of bytes with values chosen at random. This is sometimes helpful in creating test data. Although the code isn't hard to write, the `Random` class provides it for you, so you might as well use the method. Additionally, the class ensures that the values are evenly distributed, which might not be the case if you simply take 8 bits out of every randomly generated `int` or `long` value. Listing 9-12, RandomBytes.java, demonstrates how to use the method.

Listing 9–12: RandomBytes.java

```
001: import java.util.Random;
002:
003: class RandomBytes {
004:   static int SIZE = 64;     // Number of bytes to generate
005:   static byte byteArray[]; // The array of bytes
006:
007:   // Display byte array
008:   public static void showArray(String label) {
009:     System.out.println("\n\n" + label);
010:     for (int i = 0; i < byteArray.length; i++) {
011:       if (i % 8 == 0)
012:         System.out.println();     // Start new row
013:       else
014:         System.out.print('\t');   // Start new column
015:       System.out.print(byteArray[i]);
016:     }
017:   }
018:
019:   public static void main(String args[]) {
020:     Random generator = new Random();
021:     byteArray = new byte[SIZE];
022:     showArray("Before randomizing");
023:     generator.nextBytes(byteArray);  // Fill array
024:     showArray("After randomizing");
025:   }
026: }
```

Lines 004 and 005 declare two static values, `SIZE` equal to the number of bytes to generate, and `byteArray`, an array of `SIZE` bytes. (See Chapter 10, "Arrays," for more on arrays.) The static method at lines 008-017 displays the bytes in `byteArray` in a row and column table. Omitting some lines to save space, running the program displays the following two tables:

```
Before randomizing
0       0       0       0       0       0       0       0
...
0       0       0       0       0       0       0       0
```

```
After randomizing
-111    127     -78     26      118     -87     -41     -60
...
40      -2      121     -15     -83     86      63      58
```

The program also shows that, before filling the array, Java initializes its values to zero. Line 020 creates a random number generator object using the Random class's default constructor. Line 023 calls the nextBytes() method for that object to fill byteArray with bytes selected randomly.

Other Random Methods

Finally, in the Random class are two miscellaneous methods (refer back to Listing 9-10). Call method setSeed() with a long argument to start a new random sequence for an existing Random object. This is useful for restarting a random number sequence without constructing a new object, as Listing 9-13, RandomSeed.java, demonstrates.

Listing 9-13: RandomSeed.java

```
001: import java.util.Random;
002:
003: class RandomSeed {
004:   static long SEED = 12345;
005:   public static void main(String args[]) {
006:     Random generator = new Random(SEED);
007:     System.out.println("\nInitial sequence:");
008:     for (int i = 0; i < 32; i++)
009:       System.out.print(generator.nextInt(100) + " \t");
010:     generator.setSeed(SEED);  // Reseed the generator
011:     System.out.println("\n\nAfter reseeding generator:");
012:     for (int i = 0; i < 32; i++)
013:       System.out.print(generator.nextInt(100) + " \t");
014:   }
015: }
```

Running the program displays two tables of integer values selected at random, using for loops at lines 008 and 012. The Random object is constructed at line 006. Line 010 calls setSeed() to reset that object to start the same sequence over, using the static long SEED value initialized at line 004. On screen, you see two tables, each with the same values (I show only the first table here):

```
Initial sequence:
51  80  41  28  55  84  75  2   1   89
17  42  90  6   12  84  87  3   32  75
1   51  92  16  28  81  25  43  71  39
29  97
```

Finally in the `Random` class, you'll find the method `nextGaussian()`, which generates a random distributed value of type `double` with a mean of 0.0 and standard deviation of 1.0. The algorithm used to produce this value is defined in Donald Knuth's *Art of Computer Science* series, section 3.4.1, section C, algorithm P.

Numerical Wrapper Classes

As you learned from the discussion of the `Character` class in Chapter 8, "String Things," a *wrapper class* puts an object-oriented face on a native data type. In addition to `Character`, Java provides the wrapper classes `Boolean`, `Byte`, `Short`, `Integer`, `Long`, `Float`, and `Double` for, respectively, the `boolean`, `byte`, `short`, `int`, `long`, `float`, and `double` native data types. Except for the `Boolean` class, discussed first in this section, the wrapper classes share many of the same or similar methods, and once you know how to use one, you can easily figure out how to use the others.

 TIP Wrapper class names are capitalized; native types are not. For example, `Boolean` refers to the wrapper class for the `boolean` data type. The one exception is the `Integer` class, which represents native `int` values. There is no `Int` wrapper class.

The Boolean Wrapper Class

Listing 9-14 shows Java's `Boolean` wrapper class public declarations. As with similar listings in this chapter, the text file contains no code and cannot be compiled.

Listing 9-14: Boolean.txt

```
001: // Boolean wrapper class fields
002: public static final Boolean TRUE;
003: public static final Boolean FALSE;
004:
005: // Boolean wrapper class constructors
006: public Boolean(boolean value);
007: public Boolean(String s);
008:
009: // Boolean wrapper class methods
010: public boolean booleanValue();
011: public static Boolean valueOf(String s);
012: public String toString();
013: public int hashCode();
014: public boolean equals(Object obj);
015: public static boolean getBoolean(String name);
```

Two static fields provide the object-oriented equivalents of Java's native `true` and `false` values. The constants, TRUE and FALSE (see lines 002-003) are spelled in all uppercase. They are *objects* of the `Boolean` wrapper class; they are *not* `boolean` values.

When using the `Boolean` as well as other wrapper classes, it's important to keep straight on whether you are using objects or native values. For example, Listing 9-15, `BooleanDemo.java`, demonstrates the differences between using a wrapper object and a native `boolean` variable.

Listing 9-15: BooleanDemo.java

```
001: class BooleanDemo {
002:   public static void main(String args[]) {
003:     // Shows that TRUE and FALSE are objects
004:     Boolean boolObject = new Boolean(true);
005:     if (boolObject.equals(Boolean.TRUE))
006:       System.out.println("boolObject is true");
007:     // But that true and false are native values
008:     boolean boolValue = true;
009:     if (boolValue = Boolean.TRUE.booleanValue())
010:       System.out.println("boolValue is true");
011:   }
012: }
```

The program constructs a `Boolean` class object at line 004 using the statement

```
Boolean boolObject = new Boolean(true);
```

The class has no default constructor—you must specify an initial value such as `true`. Following this, an `if` statement tests whether the object is true:

```
if (boolObject.equals(Boolean.TRUE))...
```

You cannot simply use an equate expression. You must instead call a method such as `equals()`, and compare the *objects* with TRUE or FALSE, which are themselves objects. Contrast this with the second half of the sample program, which uses a convoluted technique to test whether a native `boolean` value is `true` or `false`:

```
if (boolValue = Boolean.TRUE.booleanValue())...
```

I'm not suggesting you actually do that, but the statement proves that TRUE is an object, and as such, it may be used to call a `Boolean` class method such as `booleanValue()`. That method returns the object's native `true` or `false` value.

Another way to construct a `Boolean` object is to pass it a string, as in this example:

```
Boolean boolObject = new Boolean("True");
```

Use this form to convert strings, either entered at the keyboard or taken from a command-line argument. For example, this statement

```
Boolean boolObject = new Boolean(args[0]);
```

constructs a `Boolean` object using a command-line argument, which you might pass to a program by typing

```
java YourProgram True
```

You must spell the word `True` in full, but case is ignored. The word `False` or any other string value is considered to be false.

One common use for the `Boolean` wrapper class is to convert a string to a `Boolean` object value. Call the static `valueOf()` method to translate a string into a `Boolean` object. The statement

```
Boolean boolObject = Boolean.valueOf(args[0]);
```

constructs `boolObject` by parsing a command-line string and calling the static `valueOf()`. To further convert a string to a native `boolean` value, call the object's `booleanValue()` method like this:

```
boolean boolValue = Boolean.valueOf(args[0]).booleanValue();
```

This might seem complex, but it simply translates a command-line argument (or any other `String` or `StringBuffer` object) to a `Boolean` object, using the `valueOf()` method. That result is then translated to a native `boolean` value by calling `booleanValue()`, which is assigned to the `boolValue` variable.

To go the other direction — converting a `Boolean` object to a string — call the `toString()` method. For example, the output statement

```
System.out.println(boolObject.toString());
```

displays `true` or `false` depending on the value of the `Boolean` class object, `boolObject`. The resulting string is all lowercase. All wrapper classes — in fact most all Java classes — provide a `toString()` method.

Finally, the `Boolean` class provides `getBoolean()` to test `boolean` system properties. The method returns true if a specified property exists, and if that property's value is the string `"true"`. All other values return `false`. Listing 9-16, GetProperty.java, demonstrates how to use the method.

Listing 9-16: GetProperty.java

```
001: class GetProperty {
002:   static String DEBUGGINGPROP = "Debugging.prop";
003:   static String NAMEPROP = "Program.name.prop";
004:   static String NAMEVALUE = "GetProperty";
005:
006:   public static void main(String args[]) {
007:     System.setProperty(DEBUGGINGPROP, "true"); // Boolean prop
008:     System.setProperty(NAMEPROP, NAMEVALUE);   // Other prop
009:
010:     boolean result;
011:     String valueStr;
012:
013:     // Get true or false value of boolean property
014:     result = Boolean.getBoolean(DEBUGGINGPROP);
015:     System.out.println(DEBUGGINGPROP + " = " + result);
016:
017:     // Get value of non-boolean property
018:     valueStr = System.getProperty(NAMEPROP);
019:     result = Boolean.getBoolean(NAMEPROP);
020:     System.out.println(NAMEPROP + " value = " + valueStr);
021:     System.out.println(NAMEPROP + " result = " + result);
022:   }
023: }
```

Lines 002-004 define a few string constants. Line 007 calls `System.setProperty()` to set `DEBUGGINGPROP` to `"true"`. Notice that this value is a string, not a `boolean` value. Line 008 sets another property and value to identify the program's name. Because the first property value is the string `"true"`, `Boolean.getBoolean()` returns `true`, and the program displays

```
Debugging.prop = true
```

To get a non-`boolean` property value, call `System.getProperty()` as in the demonstration program at line 018. For this statement, the program displays

```
Program.name.prop value = GetProperty
```

However, because the second property value is neither `"true"` nor `"false"`, `Boolean.getBoolean()` at line 019 returns false and causes the program to display

```
Program.name.prop result = false
```

The following list shows the system property strings that you can pass to `System.getProperty()` as demonstrated at line 023 in the sample program:

file.separator	java.vm.specification.vendor
java.class.path	java.vm.specification.version
java.class.version	java.vm.vendor
java.ext.dirs	java.vm.version
java.home	line.separator
java.specification.name	os.arch
java.specification.vendor	os.name
java.specification.version	os.version
java.vendor	path.separator
java.vendor.url	user.dir
java.version	user.home
java.vm.name	user.name
java.vm.specification.name	

All Java implementations are expected to recognize at least these properties, although some might not produce useable results depending on the system. For instance, the user.name under Windows 98 is simply "default."

The Integer Wrapper Class

The Integer wrapper class is representative of other integer wrappers, Byte, Short, and Long. Listing 9-17 shows the declarations that are common to all four of these classes.

Listing 9-17: IntCommon.txt

```
001: // Common to Short, Byte, Integer, and Long classes
002: public byte byteValue();
003: public short shortValue();
004: public int intValue();
005: public long longValue();
006: public float floatValue();
007: public double doubleValue();
008: public String toString();
009: public int hashCode();
010: public boolean equals(Object obj);
011: public int compareTo(Object o);
```

The methods with the word Value in them — intValue() for example — are extended from the abstract Number class, from which all numeric wrapper classes are derived. (You learn more about abstract classes in the aptly named Chapter 11, "Abstract Classes.") Java uses the value methods to convert values from one type to another. You can call them, but most often you'll simply use a type-cast expression as in the following, which converts an `int` to a `long` value:

```
int intValue = 123;
long longValue = (long)intValue;
```

To do that using a wrapper class, you can use a statement such as

```
Integer intObject = new Integer(123);
long longValue = intObject.longValue();
```

Of more practical value is the common `toString()` method (see line 008), which returns a string representation of the object's value. Again, the conversion to a string is automatic, which you've seen in this book's sample output statements such as

```
int k = 123;
System.out.println("k = " + k);
```

However, you may use an object to represent the integer value, and call `toString` for its string representation:

```
Integer intObject = new Integer(123);
System.out.println("intObject = " + intObject.toString());
```

The `hashCode()`, `equals()`, and `compareTo()` methods are also shared by all numeric wrapper classes. The chapters in Part III, "Collections," explain how to use hash codes along with collection (container) objects. The other two methods make it possible to compare a numeric object with any other object, assuming that such comparison is a reasonable operation to perform.

In addition to their shared methods, the numeric wrapper classes provide two constants—`MIN_VALUE` and `MAX_VALUE`—that indicate the range of allowable values for objects of each type. The fields are static and, as such, may be called in reference to their respective classes; you don't have to declare an object to get to the values. For example, the following statement displays the maximum allowed integer value:

```
System.out.println("Max integer = " + Integer.MAX_VALUE);
```

Replace `Integer` with `Byte`, `Short`, `Long`, `Double`, or `Float` to find those maximums. Print `MIN_VALUE` to find the minimum allowed values for any of these types.

Listing 9-18, Integer.txt, shows the public non-common methods in the Integer wrapper class.

Listing 9-18: Integer.txt

```
001: // Integer wrapper class constructors
002: public Integer(int value);
003: public Integer(String s);
004:
005: // Integer wrapper class methods
006: public static String toString(int i, int radix);
007: public static String toHexString(int i);
008: public static String toOctalString(int i);
009: public static String toBinaryString(int i);
010: public static String toString(int i);
011: public static int parseInt(String s, int radix);
012: public static int parseInt(String s);
013: public static Integer valueOf(String s, int radix);
014: public static Integer valueOf(String s);
015: public int compareTo(Integer anotherInteger);
016:
017: // Integer wrapper class property methods
018: public static Integer getInteger(String nm);
019: public static Integer getInteger(String nm, int val);
020: public static Integer getInteger(String nm, Integer val);
021: public static Integer decode(String nm);
```

The class has two constructors, one that takes an int value as an argument, and another that takes a string. The string constructor is particularly useful for converting command-line arguments to integer values:

```
Integer intObject = new Integer(args[0]);
```

Some of the most useful methods in the Integer wrapper class convert values to String objects, and also parse strings into values formatted for a specific number base — for example, octal. Listing 9-19, ConvertInt.java, demonstrates how to use these methods. You can use similar techniques with the Long wrapper class.

Listing 9-19: ConvertInt.java

```
001: class ConvertInt {
002:   public static void main(String args[]) {
003:     if (args.length < 1)
004:       System.out.println("ex. java ConvertInt 1234");
005:     else
006:       try {
007:         int intValue = Integer.parseInt(args[0]);
008:         System.out.println("Default = "
009:           + Integer.toString(intValue));
010:         System.out.println("Hex = "
```

```
011:        + Integer.toHexString(intValue));
012:      System.out.println("Octal = "
013:        + Integer.toOctalString(intValue));
014:      System.out.println("Binary = "
015:        + Integer.toBinaryString(intValue));
016:      System.out.println("base 32 = "
017:        + Integer.toString(intValue, 32));
018:    } catch (NumberFormatException e) {
019:      System.out.println(
020:       "Format error in argument " + e.getMessage());
021:    }
022:  }
023: }
```

The sample program calls `Integer` methods such as `toString()` and `toHexString()` to convert a command-line argument to various string formats. For example, running the program with the following command displays the entered value in hexadecimal, octal, binary, and base 32 formats:

```
java ConvertInt 1234
Default = 1234
Hex = 4d2
Octal = 2322
Binary = 10011010010
base 32 = 16i
```

Lines 018-020 in Listing 9-18, Integer.txt, show three overloaded `Integer` methods, `getInteger()`. These are intended for use with system property settings; those with any associated integer values. If your system defines any such properties, this method and its variations provide the means to read them.

Finally in the `Integer` class is a static method `decode()`, which parses a formatted string in decimal, hexadecimal, or octal. Because `decode()` is static, you call it in reference to the `Integer` class. You don't need to create an `Integer` object. The following statements demonstrate how to use `decode()`:

```
int k;
k = Integer.decode("1234");    // decimal
k = Integer.decode("0x1234");  // hexadecimal
k = Integer.decode("#1234");   // hexadecimal
k = Integer.decode("01234");   // octal
```

Digit characters from 1 through 9 are considered to be decimal. The prefaces `0x` and `#` indicate a value in hexadecimal. Values starting with 0 are octal.

The Long Wrapper Class

Listing 9-20 shows Java's Long wrapper class, which represents long native values in class form. The Long class is similar to Integer, and most methods are the same, except that parseInt() is named parseLong(), and method return values are type long. As with other listings in this section, the listing here shows only the public non-common methods in the wrapper class.

Listing 9-20: Java's Long wrapper class

```
001: // Long wrapper class constructors
002: public Long(long value);
003: public Long(String s);
004:
005: // Long wrapper class methods
006: public static String toString(long i, int radix);
007: public static String toHexString(long i);
008: public static String toOctalString(long i);
009: public static String toBinaryString(long i);
010: public static String toString(long i);
011: public static long parseLong(String s, int radix);
012: public static long parseLong(String s);
013: public static Long valueOf(String s, int radix);
014: public static Long valueOf(String s);
015: public static Long decode(String nm);
016: public int compareTo(Long anotherLong);
017:
018: // Long wrapper class property methods
019: public static Long getLong(String nm);
020: public static Long getLong(String nm, long val);
021: public static Long getLong(String nm, Long val);
```

The Byte Wrapper Class

Listing 9-21, Byte.txt, shows the constructors and public non-common methods for the Byte wrapper class. You can use this class in much the same ways as Integer and Long, but it doesn't support the formatted string methods for converting from hexadecimal and octal.

Listing 9-21: Byte.txt

```
001: // Byte wrapper class constructors
002: public Byte(byte value);
003: public Byte(String s);
004:
005: // Byte wrapper class methods
006: public static String toString(byte b);
```

```
007: public static byte parseByte(String s);
008: public static byte parseByte(String s, int radix);
009: public static Byte valueOf(String s, int radix);
010: public static Byte valueOf(String s);
011: public static Byte decode(String nm);
012: public int compareTo(Byte anotherByte);
```

The Short Wrapper Class

The Short wrapper is nearly identical to Byte, but specifies short integer values for method parameters and return results. Listing 9-22, Short.txt, shows the constructors and public non-common methods for the Short wrapper class.

Listing 9-22: Short.txt

```
001: // Short wrapper class constructors
002: public Short(short value);
003: public Short(String s);
004:
005: // Short wrapper class methods
006: public static String toString(short s);
007: public static short parseShort(String s);
008: public static short parseShort(String s, int radix);
009: public static Short valueOf(String s, int radix);
010: public static Short valueOf(String s);
011: public static Short decode(String nm);
012: public int compareTo(Short anotherShort);
```

The Float Wrapper Class

For working with floating point values as objects, Java provides the two wrapper classes Float and Double. Like the integer wrappers, these two classes provide the methods shown in Listing 9-17, IntCommon.txt, which are inherited from the abstract Number class. In addition, Float and Double share the declarations listed here in Listing 9-23, FloatCommon.txt

Listing 9-23: FloatCommon.txt

```
001: // Common to Float and Double classes
002: public static final double POSITIVE_INFINITY;
003: public static final double NEGATIVE_INFINITY;
004: public static final double NaN;
005: public static final double MAX_VALUE;
006: public static final double MIN_VALUE;
007: public boolean isNaN();
008: public boolean isInfinite();
```

The five static fields at lines 002-006 represent useful boundary values. As already mentioned, NaN means "not a number," and is used to represent an illegal result such as dividing a floating point value by another NaN value. Although the Float and Double classes share these same fields, they are type float in the Float class, and type double in the Double class.

The two public methods, isNan() and isInfinite(),inspect whether a Float or Double object is not a valid number, or is infinite (and therefore also invalid):

```
Float floatObject = new Float(3.14159 / Float.NaN);
if (floatObject.isNaN())
 System.out.println("object is NaN");
```

Listing 9-24 shows the constructors and public non-common methods in the Float wrapper class. Notice there are three constructors—two for constructing a Float object from a float or double value, and one for constructing the object from a string. Constructing a Float object from a double value may result in a loss of precision.

Listing 9–24: Float.txt

```
001: // Float wrapper class constructors
002: public Float(float value);
003: public Float(double value);
004: public Float(String s);
005:
006: // Float wrapper class methods
007: public static String toString(float f);
008: public static Float valueOf(String s);
009: public static float parseFloat(String s);
010: static public boolean isNaN(float v);
011: static public boolean isInfinite(float v);
012: public int compareTo(Float anotherFloat);
013:
014: // Float wrapper class bit converters
015: public static native int floatToIntBits(float value);
016: public static native float intBitsToFloat(int bits);
```

As with the Integer and Long wrappers, some of the more useful Float methods convert values between floating point and string formats. The following statements show how to convert a float variable to a String object for display:

```
float value = (float)3.14159;
String s = Float.toString(value);
System.out.println(s);
```

The type-cast expression is necessary because Java normally represents floating point values as type `double`. Also highly useful is `parseFloat()`. Use the method to parse a string into a `float` value without requiring a `Float` class object. Listing 9-25, ParseFloat.java, demonstrates.

Listing 9-25: ParseFloat.java

```
001: class ParseFloat {
002:  public static void main(String args[]) {
003:   if (args.length < 1)
004:    System.out.println("ex. java ParseFloat 3.14159");
005:   else {
006:    try {
007:     float f = Float.parseFloat(args[0]);
008:     System.out.println("Value == " + f);
009:    } catch (NumberFormatException e) {
010:     System.out.println("Error in argument " + e.getMessage());
011:    }
012:   }
013:  }
014: }
```

Line 007 shows how to call `parseFloat()` to parse a string entered at the command line. It is not necessary to construct a `Float` object; just call the method as shown in reference to the `Float` class. You must catch `NumberFormatException`, thrown if the string contains any illegal characters. The method recognizes standard and scientific notation. For example, run the program as follows:

```
java ParseFloat 8e2
Value == 800.0
```

Finally in the `Float` class are two methods that you can use to convert floating point values to and from their bit representations in IEEE 754 floating point format (see lines 015 and 016 in Listing 9-24, Float.txt). Applications developers probably have little use for these, but if you need to get at the bit representation of a `float` value, the methods provide the means.

The Double Wrapper Class

Listing 9-26 shows Java's `Double` wrapper class, which resembles `Float` but is probably more useful because `double` is Java's default floating point data type.

Listing 9-26: Double.txt

```
001: // Double wrapper class constructors
002: public Double(double value);
003: public Double(String s);
```

```
004:
005: // Double wrapper class methods
006: public static String toString(double d);
007: public static Double valueOf(String s);
008: public static double parseDouble(String s);
009: static public boolean isNaN(double v);
010: static public boolean isInfinite(double v);
011: public int compareTo(Double anotherDouble);
012:
013: // Double wrapper class bit converters
014: public static native long doubleToLongBits(double value);
015: public static native long doubleToRawLongBits(double value);
016: public static native double longBitsToDouble(long bits);
```

The Double class is nearly identical to Float, except that parameters, method return values, and some method names are of type double. For example, you can revise the ParseFloat.java program to use type double by replacing line 007 with

```
double f = Double.parseDouble(args[0]);
```

The rest of the program remains unchanged.

Last in the Double class are three methods for converting double values to and from their bit representations in IEEE 754 format. The first long method, doubleToLongBits(), converts a double value to its bit representation, with NaN equal to 0x7ff8000000000000L. The other long method converts a double value to its "raw" representation, using whatever value NaN happens to actually be in memory. Other than that, the two methods are equivalent. Use the double method, longBitsToDouble(), to reconvert a long value back to floating point.

Summary

◆ Java's numerical classes provide object-oriented interfaces for various mathematical operations.

◆ The Math class provides miscellaneous methods, and is automatically imported into every application. You cannot instantiate the Math class. Instead, you call its methods and use its constants in reference to the class itself.

◆ Objects of Java's Random class are random-number generators. Call the Random class's methods to seed the generator. Because Java carefully defines the algorithms used by the Random class, the resulting pseudo-random sequences are potentially repeatable across all conforming Java installations.

◆ Java's numerical and `Boolean` wrapper classes provide object-oriented interfaces for numeric and `boolean` data types. The wrapper class names are the same as the represented native types, but are capitalized, except for `Integer`, which represents `int` values. Java's wrapper classes are `Boolean`, `Byte`, `Short`, `Integer`, `Long`, `Float`, and `Double`. (Chapter 8 describes the `Character` wrapper class.)

Chapter 10

Arrays

WHEN YOU HAVE MULTIPLE OBJECTS or values to store in memory, an array is often the best choice of data structures. Java arrays are particularly easy to use, and they are more versatile than arrays in many other programming languages. With Java, you can create variable-size arrays at runtime instead of having to specify a size when you write the program. Also, you can create multidimensional arrays with variable-sized elements — a feature that makes creating complex structures such as triangular arrays easy in Java.

This chapter introduces Java arrays, explains how to create and manage arrays for data storage, and shows many related features.

IN THIS CHAPTER

- ◆ Introducing Java arrays
- ◆ Creating multidimensional arrays
- ◆ Programming sparse arrays
- ◆ Catching array exceptions
- ◆ Using the `Arrays` utility class
- ◆ Sorting and searching arrays

Introducing Java Arrays

In Java, arrays are object-oriented, making them safe and easy to use. Array indexes are checked, and exceptions are thrown for out-of-range boundary errors. Arrays are declared in the program code but are created at runtime; their sizes are therefore variable and can be determined by a program calculation. In addition, unlike in other object-oriented languages such as C++, the initialization rules for array elements are strictly defined and simple to understand.

Furthermore, an array is a Java type that behaves as a class object and, as such, provides features such as an instance variable `length` that you can inspect to find out the number of objects or values in an array. Unlike true classes, however, arrays cannot be extended — there is no `Array` class. However, arrays operate as though there were.

Creating Arrays

An array is literally a *composite type,* which can be made of zero or more instances of another type. If that type is another array, the array is *multidimensional.* In a Java program, an *array variable* is a reference to an element of the array's type. Use empty brackets to inform the compiler that you intend to use an identifier as a typed array. For example, to declare an array of integers, you can use a statement such as

```
int intArray[];  // Declare integer array reference
```

This declaration states only that `intArray` is capable of referring to an array that contains zero or more integer values. It does not create an array, nor does it reserve any memory for array elements. Before using the array, a program statement must allocate memory for the array. This is always done at runtime. For example, given the preceding declaration, at runtime, the following statement creates an array of 10 integer values in memory:

```
intArray = new int[10];
```

After that statement executes, `intArray` refers to the array's first element. Each element in the array is initialized according to the specific type's default value—in this case, all elements are set to zero. (An array of class objects initially holds all `null` references.) To refer to a specific array element, follow the array variable with square brackets containing an index value. For example, this statement prints the contents of the preceding array:

```
for (int i = 0; i < 10; i++)
 System.out.println(intArray[i]);
```

Assign a value to a specific array element using a statement such as

```
intArray[4] = 123;
```

That assigns the value 123 to the fifth array element. Because the first index value is zero, the index 4 references the fifth element in the array. The value assigned must be type compatible with that of the array's declared type.

You may also declare and construct an array in one easy motion using a single statement such as

```
int intArray[] = new int[10];
```

This actually performs two actions—declaring `intArray` to the compiler and, at runtime, constructing an array of 10 integer values referred to by `intArray`. The array size may be variable. For example, the following fragment declares and constructs `intArray` using the value of integer n:

```
int n;
// ... code that sets n to some positive value
int intArray[] = new int[n];
```

The value of n could be calculated by program statements, or obtained from the user. If n is zero, the array is initialized but contains no elements. If n is negative, Java throws NegativeArraySizeException, so it is often best to create variable-size arrays using a try-catch block.

As the preceding samples show, Java arrays are completely dynamic, and their sizes are determined at runtime. However, after constructing the array, the program cannot change the array's size. (See the chapters in Part III, "Collections," for array-like containers that can be resized at runtime.) To change the size of an array, you have to create a new one and copy to it the old array's elements. For convenience, the System class provides method arraycopy() that you can use for this purpose. See "Copying Arrays" in this chapter for more about this method.

Because of Java's automatic garbage collection, you can always assign a new array to an array variable. For example, if intArray already references an array of integers, the following statement creates a new array for this same variable:

```
intArray = new int[250];   // Create another array
```

The old array that intArray referenced is deleted, and its objects are disposed by Java's garbage collector if and when more memory is needed. This happens automatically.

 One good way to ensure that array elements are disposed properly is to declared the array variable in a method. When the method ends, the array and its elements are automatically put out for the garbage collector.

Because arrays are constructed at runtime, it's usually best to use the length field — available with all arrays — in loops and other statements that use array index values. For example, this statement sets intArray's values equal to their associated indexes:

```
for (int i = 0; i < intArray.length; i++)
  intArray[i] = i;
```

The expression intArray.length equals the number of array elements, and therefore the loop works correctly for all arrays regardless of size. The maximum index value allowed is always one less than the value of length.

TIP In method `main()`, command-line arguments are stored in the `args` `String` array. Use the expression `args.length` to determine how many arguments the user entered.

Using an array index value outside of the range 0 ... `length - 1` throws an `ArrayIndexOutOfBoundsException` object. To catch this error, use a `try-catch` block as demonstrated in Listing 10-1, ArrayBounds.java.

Listing 10-1: ArrayBounds.java

```
001: class ArrayBounds {
002:  public static void main(String args[]) {
003:   int intArray[] = new int[10]; // Create array
004:   try {
005:    int q = intArray[5];   // no error
006:    int p = intArray[11];  // throws exception
007:   } catch (ArrayIndexOutOfBoundsException e) {
008:    System.out.println("Array index out of bounds");
009:   }
010:  }
011: }
```

Running the program displays the error message at line 008 because the statement at line 006 attempts to reference an element in the array outside of its size. This error must be caught at runtime as shown. The exception is unchecked, and therefore you are not required to catch it. In most cases, if you receive this exception, you should rewrite the source code to prevent the error from occurring.

 TIP Keep in mind that any Java array may be empty, in which case its `length` field equals zero. Accessing a zero-length array using any index value throws `ArrayIndexOutOfBoundsException`.

Multiple Arrays

When declaring arrays, you may place the empty brackets either after the array data type or after the array identifier. For example, the declaration

```
int intArray[];
```

is syntactically identical to

```
int[] intArray;
```

Both statements declare `intArray` as a reference to an array of integer values; neither allocates any memory or actually constructs the array, which as I've explained, you must do using the `new` operator. The alternate declaration style is convenient for declaring multiple arrays of the same type. For example, the statement

```
int[] array1, array2, array3;
```

declares three integer arrays, which might be constructed at runtime of different sizes using statements such as

```
array1 = new int[10];
array2 = new int[20];
array3 = new int[30];
```

The expression `int[]` is also useful when you need to refer to an array type, as when declaring method parameters:

```
void myMethod(int[] arrayOfInt);
```

Java permits any array to be assigned to a variable of type `Object`. For example, if `array1` is an array of integers, the statement

```
Object obj = array1;
```

causes `obj` to refer to the array. You cannot, however, use `obj` as an array because it is not legal to arbitrarily apply brackets, `[]`, to a variable of type `Object`. This technique, though, might be useful for passing arrays to method `Object` parameters.

 If enough space is not available to define an array at runtime, Java throws an `OutOfMemoryError` **exception.**

Multidimensional Arrays

A multidimensional array is merely an array of arrays. For instance, a two-dimensional array is similar to a chessboard with rows and columns. In Java, however, the rows do not have to be all the same lengths as they do in many other programming languages. This is a consequence of the fact that arrays are constructed at runtime.

Declare a multidimensional array by using multiple pairs of empty brackets. The following statement declares that `trouble` is a reference to a two-dimensional array of floating point `double` values:

```
double trouble[][]
```

Define the array's memory at runtime using a statement such as the following, which creates a 10-by-10 array of `double` values:

```
trouble = new double[10][10];
```

The two sizes can be different:

```
trouble = new double[10][20];
```

This creates an array having 10 rows of 20 `double` values each. Only the first size must be specified at runtime (but it can be variable rather than literal as shown here). The preceding statement, for instance, is equivalent to the following fragment:

```
trouble = new double[10][];
for (int i = 0; i < trouble.length; i++)
 trouble[i] = new double[20];
```

The first statement defines space for a 10-element array of `double` values, and it causes `trouble` to refer to that space. A `for` loop then creates 20-element arrays, assigned to each of `trouble`'s elements. It's important to understand that those elements are arrays. Specifically, the data type of the expression `trouble[n]` is `double[]`, a reference to an array of `double` values.

Multidimensional arrays may have more than two dimensions. The following statement declares `fifthDimension` as a five-level array of `double` values:

```
double fifthDimension[][][][][];
```

This is of little practical value — it is rarely useful for an array to have more than three dimensions. However, Java places no limit on the number of dimensions you can specify.

Triangular Sparse Arrays

Using multidimensional arrays makes it possible to define variable-size structures. As an example, Listing 10-2, Triangle.java, shows how to create a *triangular array*, a structure that is easy to create in Java, but not so simple in other programming languages.

Listing 10-2: Triangle.java

```
001: class Triangle {
002:  public static void main(String args[]) {
003:   // Create a triangular array
004:   int triangular[][];
```

```
005:    triangular = new int[8][];
006:    for (int i = 0; i < triangular.length; i++)
007:      triangular[i] = new int[i + 1];
008:
009:    // Assign values at random to the array
010:    for (int i = 0; i < triangular.length; i++)
011:      for (int j = 0; j < triangular[i].length; j++)
012:        triangular[i][j] = (int)(Math.random() * 100);
013:
014:    // Display the array's contents
015:    for (int i = 0; i < triangular.length; i++) {
016:      for (int j = 0; j < triangular[i].length; j++)
017:        System.out.print(" \t" + triangular[i][j]);
018:      System.out.println();
019:    }
020:  }
021: }
```

Running Triangle.java displays the following output (the values are randomized and so are probably different for you):

```
35
79  89
50  35  42
21  64  88  15
70  93  18  86  56
56  45  79  32  1   97
74  12  71  97  36  65  15
95  37  34  24  51  2   1   80
```

That looks like one of those point-to-point mileage charts on a map. It is a very efficient structure of a category generally known as a *sparse array* because the unused positions are given no memory space, as they would if this were a common multidimensional array in which all rows are the same size.

Because of the potential for array sizes to be variable, when programming with multidimensional arrays, it is especially important to respect the length field. The for loops at lines 010 and 011, for example, show how to peruse a triangular array's elements:

```
for (int i = 0; i < triangular.length; i++)
  for (int j = 0; j < triangular[i].length; j++) ...
```

The expression triangular.length equals the number of variable-sized arrays — that is, the number of rows — in triangular. The expression triangular[i].length equals the number of elements for the row at the specified index. For extra safety, these statements probably should be in a `try-catch` block, but to save room here, I omitted this detail.

Array Initializations

As I mentioned, you may assign values to array elements using expressions such as

```
myArray[i] = 3.14159;
```

That assigns a floating point value to one of `myArray`'s elements (assuming the array is a floating point type). Another way to initialize array elements is to assign them literal values. For example, the following statement declares and initializes an array of `int` values named `fibonacci`:

```
int[] fibonacci = {1, 2, 3, 5, 8, 13, 21, 32};
```

The array is constructed at runtime as if you used the `new` operator and a `for` loop or other statements to fill the array with these values. But it is often convenient to specify the initial values using constants as shown here. This is especially so for arrays of strings, such as

```
String[] text =
  {"Humpty", "Dumpty", "sat", "on", "a", "wall"};
```

To print out the individual strings, use a loop such as

```
for (int i = 0; i < text.length; i++)
  System.out.println(text[i]);
```

Of course, the strings may be of a more mundane nature such as the names of the months or days of the week.

Arrays of Objects

When you have a lot of objects of the same class to create, it might be good to store them in an array. To demonstrate, Listing 10-3, ObjectArray.java, creates an array of `StringClass` objects, a class that the program declares.

Listing 10-3: ObjectArray.java

```
001: class StringClass {
002:   private String s;
003:   // Constructor
004:   StringClass(String s) {
005:     this.s = s;
006:   }
```

```
007:  void ShowString() {
008:    System.out.println(s);
009:  }
010: }
011:
012: class ObjectArray {
013:  public static void main(String args[]) {
014:    // Construct an array of class objects
015:    StringClass WeekDays[] = {
016:      new StringClass("Domingo"),
017:      new StringClass("Lunes"),
018:      new StringClass("Martes"),
019:      new StringClass("Miercoles"),
020:      new StringClass("Jueves"),
021:      new StringClass("Viernes"),
022:      new StringClass("Sabado")
023:    };
024:    // Call a method for each arrayed object
025:    System.out.println("Weekdays in Spanish");
026:    for (int i = 0; i < WeekDays.length; i++)
027:      WeekDays[i].ShowString();
028:  }
029: }
```

Running the program displays the names of the weekdays in Spanish. The program's StringClass (see lines 001-010) is just for demonstration purposes — you could more easily create an array of String objects. The demonstration class simply saves a string passed to its constructor and provides a method, ShowString(), that displays the saved string value.

Line 005 in Listing 10-3 shows a neat trick for avoiding a name conflict when a constructor's parameter is named the same as a class instance variable. In this statement, the expression this.s refers to the instance variable. The other reference to s refers to the constructor's parameter.

The main program creates an array of StringClass objects using the statement at lines 015-023. Notice that this is a *single* statement that performs several operations:

◆ It declares WeekDays as an array of StringClass objects.

◆ It constructs at runtime an array containing seven objects.

◆ It initializes each object by calling the StringClass constructor.

This isn't the only way to create an array of class objects. Alternatively, instead of specifying each object in the source code as in the demonstration program, you could declare and initialize the array using statements such as

```
StringClass WeekDays[] = new StringClass[7];
WeekDays[0] = new StringClass("Domingo");
...
WeekDays[6] = new StringClass("Sabado");
```

Pay close attention to the multiple uses of new. The first use creates the array, which is initialized to hold all null references at this point. In the other statements, new initializes each individual object in the array (I deleted five of them to save space).

Copying Arrays

Java provides three ways to copy an array, but it's important to understand that the results are not identical. Listing 10-4, ArrayCopy.java, and its submodule Listing 10-5, TestClass.java, demonstrate the three techniques.

Listing 10-4: ArrayCopy.java

```
001: import TestClass;   // Import submodule
002:
003: class ArrayCopy {
004:   // Declare the two arrays
005:   public static int[] apples, oranges;
006:
007:   // Array copy method #1
008:   public static void CopyMethod1() {
009:     System.out.println("\nArray copy method #1");
010:     oranges = apples;
011: // oranges[0]++;     // Enable to change test
012:     TestClass.CompareArrays(apples, oranges);
013:   }
014:
015:   // Array copy method #2
016:   public static void CopyMethod2() {
017:     System.out.println("\nArray copy method #2");
018:     oranges = new int[apples.length];
019:     System.arraycopy(apples, 0, oranges, 0, apples.length);
020: // oranges[0]++;     // Enable to change test
021:     TestClass.CompareArrays(apples, oranges);
022:   }
023:
024:   // Array copy method #3
```

```
025:  public static void CopyMethod3() {
026:   System.out.println("\nArray copy method #3");
027:   oranges = (int[])apples.clone();
028: // oranges[0]++;    // Enable to change test
029:   TestClass.CompareArrays(apples, oranges);
030:  }
031:
032:  public static void main(String args[]) {
033:   // Construct and initialize the first array
034:   apples = new int[8];
035:   for (int i = 0; i < apples.length; i++)
036:    apples[i] = (int)(Math.random() * 100);
037:   // Copy three ways and test each copy
038:   CopyMethod1();
039:   CopyMethod2();
040:   CopyMethod3();
041:  }
042: }
```

 Despite the fact that this sample program is in two parts, and is larger than normal for the listings in this book, you still compile it using the single command, javac ArrayCopy.java. Run the resulting .class file by typing java ArrayCopy. You don't have to compile the submodule separately, although you may do so by typing javac TestClass.java. You can't run the submodule separately.

Listing 10-5: TestClass.java

```
001: class TestClass {
002:  public static void CompareArrays(int apples[], int oranges[])
003:  {
004:   // Display the array values
005:   int i;
006:   System.out.print("apples : ");
007:   for (i = 0; i < apples.length; i++)
008:    System.out.print(apples[i] + " \t");
009:   System.out.print("\noranges: ");
010:   for (i = 0; i < oranges.length; i++)
011:    System.out.print(oranges[i] + " \t");
012:   System.out.println();  // Start new line
013:
014:   // Test if the array references are the same
```

```
015:   if (apples == oranges)
016:    System.out.println("Array references are identical");
017:   else
018:    System.out.println("Array references are NOT identical");
019:
020:   // Test if the array contents are the same
021:   boolean identical = true;
022:   for (i = 0; i < apples.length; i++)
023:    if (apples[i] != oranges[i])
024:     identical = false;
025:   if (identical)
026:    System.out.println("Array contents are the same");
027:   else
028:    System.out.println("Array contents are NOT the same");
029:   }
030: }
```

When you run the program, it displays two arrays of integers, named apples and oranges, initialized to values selected at random. Each test looks like this (I show only the first of three reports here):

```
Array copy method #1
apples : 45   13    59    19    75    42    24    45
oranges: 45   13    59    19    75    42    24    45
Array references are identical
Array contents are the same
```

The copy method number is shown first, followed by the values in each array. Two final comments indicate whether the array references and the contents of both arrays are the same.

The first way to copy an array is the simplest — merely assign one array reference to another of the same type. For example, in Listing 10-4, line 010 assigns apples to oranges:

```
oranges = apples;
```

However, that does *not* create a copy of the array's contents. It merely causes the two variables to refer to the *same* array in memory. To prove this, and to better understand the consequences of the preceding statement, enable line 011 in Listing 10-4, ArrayCopy.java, which is commented out

```
oranges[0]++;    // Enable to change test
```

The statement alters one of the array's values after copying. But, when you compile and run the program, it reports that the first test's array references and contents are still identical. This is because, if you simply assign one array to another, any changes to the array's contents using either reference makes that change to the same value in memory.

The other two tests show how to copy an array's contents so that the array references are to different arrays in memory. The first of these techniques, demonstrated by CopyMethod2() at lines 015-022 in Listing 10-4, ArrayCopy.java, calls a System class method, arraycopy(), specifically provided to make copying arrays quick and easy. To use this technique, you must construct the destination array using new (see line 018):

```
oranges = new int[apples.length];
```

After that, call arraycopy() as follows to copy the source array's contents to the destination's:

```
System.arraycopy(apples, 0, oranges, 0, apples.length);
```

The two integer values indicate the starting index to use for each preceding array in the parameter list. Use zero to copy starting with the first element. The final value is the number of items to copy. To copy the entire array, use the length variable as shown for the source (the first) array.

Try the same test this time by enabling the increment statement in CopyMethod2() at line 020 in Listing 10-4, ArrayCopy.java. Now, when you run the program, it reports that the array references and contents are not the same:

```
Array copy method #2
apples : 38   82    91    63    28    43    13    50
oranges: 39   82    91    63    28    43    13    50
Array references are NOT identical
Array contents are NOT the same
```

Notice that the first value in each array differs as a result of the increment statement. Because the array references, apples and oranges, are different, a change to one array element does not affect the others.

The sample program demonstrates a third technique for copying an array that uses the clone() method, inherited from Object (see Listing 10-4, ArrayCopy.java, lines 024-030). Because Object.clone() returns type Object, you must use a type-cast expression as follows in order to compile the assignment statement:

```
oranges = (int[])apples.clone();
```

This method differs from the one that calls arraycopy() in that you do not have to construct the destination array. To test this copy technique, enable the increment statement at line 028 as you did twice before. Now, the report for the third copying method indicates that, after cloning, the array references and contents are not the same.

`Object.clone()` throws `CloneNotSupported` by default, but because of the way arrays implement the `Clonable` interface, it is not necessary to catch this exception. This wasn't so in earlier Java versions, but is no longer a concern because the array `clone()` method guarantees that it does *not* throw this exception. In fact, if you try to catch `CloneNotSupported`, the compiler reports an error. See Chapter 12, "Interfaces," for more about interfaces.

More About System.arraycopy()

As just explained, the `System` class provides method `arraycopy()` primarily for copying one array to another. However, this method is also valuable for moving values around within the same array — for example, in buffers of characters or bytes. The `System` class declares `arraycopy()` as follows:

```
public static void
 arraycopy(Object src, int src_position,
          Object dst, int dst_position,
          int length);
```

The method's parameters are

- `Object src` — Pass the name of the source array from which you want to copy array elements.

- `int src_position` — Pass the starting index value of the first source-array element to copy.

- `Object dst` — Pass the name of the destination array to which you want to copy array elements.

- `int dst_position` — Pass the starting index value of the first destination-array element to which you want to assign copied values.

- `int length` — Pass the number of array elements to copy.

Using `arraycopy()` on the same array — in other words, specifying the same array as the source and destination — moves the elements in the array up or down. This is a useful technique for shuffling data in buffers. For example, these statements define and initialize a 10-element array of integers, named `buffer`:

```
int buffer[] = new int[10];
for (int i = 0; i < buffer.length; i++)
 buffer[i] = i;
```

The code sets the element values in `buffer` to

```
0 1 2 3 4 5 6 7 8 9
```

To shuffle the values in `buffer`, specify the same array as the source and destination arguments using a statement such as

```
System.arraycopy(buffer, 3, buffer, 0, 7);
```

This moves seven values starting with the fourth element to the beginning (zero-index) of the array. After the preceding statement executes, the resulting buffer holds these values:

```
3 4 5 6 7 8 9 7 8 9
```

Notice that values beyond those moved are unchanged.

Array Exceptions

When using arrays, you may experience one of the following exceptions. These are extended from the `RuntimeException` class, and are therefore unchecked. You may catch these using `try-catch` blocks, but since they are considered to be unchecked errors, they are best handled by modifying the source code so the error never occurs. For example, as mentioned, instead of catching `ArrayIndexOutOfBoundsException`, it is considered to be better programming to ensure that this condition never occurs in the first place. The array exception classes are

- ◆ `NegativeArraySizeException` — Thrown if a statement attempts to construct an array with a negative size value. However, it is *not* an error to create a zero-size array.

- ◆ `IndexOutOfBoundsException` — This exception is the basis for two others, `ArrayIndexOutOfBounds` and `StringIndexOutOfBounds`. Java probably never throws a general `IndexOutOfBounds` object.

- ◆ `ArrayIndexOutOfBoundsException`: Thrown if a statement attempts to access an array element using an index value that is less than zero or greater than or equal to the array's `length` field. If you receive this exception, the fault is in the program's logic.

- ◆ `ArrayStoreException`: Thrown if a statement attempts to store the wrong type of object in an array element, using a statement (a type-cast expression, for example) that the compiler cannot catch and report as an error.

The Arrays Utility Class

Java provides a handy utility class, Arrays, with methods for sorting, searching, equality testing, and filling arrays of many types. The sorting methods are extensively optimized for top performance given most data sets. The following sections list and discuss each category of Arrays methods.

Sorting Arrays

Listing 10-6, ArraysSort.txt, shows the public sorting methods in the Arrays class. Each method is named sort(), but takes different data types. You can use these methods to sort arrays of long, int, short, char, byte, double, and float values. You can also use them to sort arrays of any class objects that can be compared.

Listing 10-6: ArraysSort.txt

```
001: // Arrays class sorting methods
002: public static void sort(long[] a);
003: public static void sort(long[] a, int fromIndex, int toIndex);
004: public static void sort(int[] a);
005: public static void sort(int[] a, int fromIndex, int toIndex);
006: public static void sort(short[] a);
007: public static void sort(short[] a, int fromIndex, int toIndex);
008: public static void sort(char[] a);
009: public static void sort(char[] a, int fromIndex, int toIndex);
010: public static void sort(byte[] a);
011: public static void sort(byte[] a, int fromIndex, int toIndex);
012: public static void sort(double[] a);
013: public static void sort(double[] a,
        int fromIndex, int toIndex);
014: public static void sort(float[] a);
015: public static void sort(float[] a, int fromIndex, int toIndex);
016: public static void sort(Object[] a);
017: public static void sort(Object[] a,
        int fromIndex, int toIndex);
018: public static void sort(Object[] a, Comparator c);
019: public static void sort(Object[] a,
        int fromIndex, int toIndex, Comparator c);
```

Listing 10-6 is for reference only and cannot be compiled and run. Unnumbered lines are those that are too long for this page — on screen, you see the unbroken lines. These notes apply for other listings in this section that end with the filename extension .txt.

Each overloaded sort() method has two forms. The first sorts an entire array. The second sorts a portion of an array using frontIndex and toIndex integer parameters. To sort arrays of simple types such as double, first import the Arrays class with this declaration at the top of the source code file:

```
import java.util.Arrays;
```

Then, construct the array and sort it with code such as

```
double doubleArray[] = new double[128};
// statements that fill the array
Arrays.sort(doubleArray);
```

The last line sorts the array in ascending order. To sort only a portion of the array, specify starting and ending index values as follows:

```
Arrays.sort(doubleArray, 10, 20);
```

That statement throws IllegalArgumentException if the indexes are reversed. It can also throw ArrayIndexOutOfBounds if either index is out of range. Don't catch these exceptions — they should be considered programming errors that should be prevented from occurring.

Use similar programming to sort arrays of other types. Sorting class objects, however, takes a little more effort. To demonstrate, Listing 10-7, SortStrings.java, shows how to use the Arrays class to sort an array of String objects.

Listing 10-7: SortStrings.java

```
001: import java.util.Arrays;
002:
003: class SortStrings {
004:  // Display an array of Strings
005:  public static void ShowStrings(String[] a, String msg) {
006:    System.out.println(msg);
007:    for (int i = 0; i < a.length; i++)
008:      System.out.println(a[i]);
009:  }
010:  // Create, sort, and display an array of StringClass objects
011:  public static void main(String args[]) {
012:    String colors[] = {
013:      "rojo", "azul", "verde", "negro", "blanco", "cafe", "gris"
014:    };
015:    ShowStrings(colors, "\nBefore sorting");
016:    Arrays.sort(colors);
017:    ShowStrings(colors, "\nAfter sorting");
018:  }
019: }
```

The program creates an array of `String` objects at lines 012-014, initialized to some color names in Spanish. Line 016 sorts the array. The programming is straightforward because `String` objects can be compared directly.

However, the same may or may not be true for other class objects. In most cases, the class must implement the `Comparable` interface (Chapter 12 goes into interfaces in more detail). If the class does not implement `Comparable`, the `sort()` method throws `ClassCastException`. As with other `sort()` exceptions, this indicates a programming logic error that should be fixed in the source code.

 It is possible, although unlikely, for `Arrays.sort()` to throw a `ClassCastException` if the array to be sorted somehow contains objects that cannot be compared — an array of `Object` references, for example, to a collection of objects of different classes.

Listing 10-8, SortObjects.java, shows how to create a class that implements `Comparable`. Because of this, the `Arrays.sort()` method can sort an array of class objects.

Listing 10–8: SortObjects.java

```
001: import java.util.Arrays;
002:
003: class StringClass implements Comparable {
004:   private String s;
005:   StringClass(String s) {
006:     this.s = s;
007:   }
008:   void ShowString() {
009:     System.out.println(s);
010:   }
011:   public int compareTo(Object other) {
012:     StringClass sc = (StringClass)other;
013:     return s.compareTo(sc.s);
014:   }
015: }
016:
017: class SortObjects {
018:
019:   // Display an array of StringClass objects
020:   public static void ShowStrings(StringClass[] a, String msg) {
021:     System.out.println(msg);
022:     for (int i = 0; i < a.length; i++)
023:       a[i].ShowString();
```

```
024:   }
025:
026:   // Create, sort, and display an array of StringClass objects
027:   public static void main(String args[]) {
028:     StringClass colors[] = {
029:       new StringClass("rojo"),
030:       new StringClass("azul"),
031:       new StringClass("verde"),
032:       new StringClass("negro"),
033:       new StringClass("blanco"),
034:       new StringClass("cafe"),
035:       new StringClass("gris")
036:     };
037:     ShowStrings(colors, "\nBefore sorting");
038:     Arrays.sort(colors);
039:     ShowStrings(colors, "\nAfter sorting");
040:   }
041: }
```

As you can see, the program is more complex than the one that merely sorts String objects. Here, the StringClass at lines 003-015 provides a method for comparing objects of this class. You saw another version of StringClass in Listing 10-3, SortObjects.java. This newer version of the class states that it implements Comparable (see line 003). This requires the class to provide a compareTo() method declared as

```
public int compareTo(Object other) {
  ...
}
```

The method is called in reference to an object of the class. The other object is the one to be compared. Because all classes extend Object, compareTo() can compare objects of any classes. In this case, we want to compare two StringClass objects as shown here at lines 012 and 013:

```
StringClass sc = (StringClass)other;
return s.compareTo(sc.s);
```

The first statement is optional. It assigns the other parameter to a local StringClass variable, sc. This requires a type-cast expression that tells the compiler that we *know* that other is really a StringClass object, so the assignment is safe. Remember that assignments such as this merely copy the object's reference. The object isn't cloned or copied in memory in any way. If other is not a StringClass object, or of an extended class, this statement throws ClassCastException.

The second statement simply passes the String class's compareTo() result as our method's return value. In other cases, you might have to write statements that do whatever is necessary to compare two objects. In any case, the result should be –1 if this object is less than other, 0 if they are equal, and +1 if this object is greater than other.

Sorting with Comparator Objects

Two other Arrays class sorting methods accept an object of type Comparator (refer back to Listing 10-6, ArraysSort.txt, lines 018-019). You can use these sort() methods in cases when it is inconvenient or impossible to create a class that implements Comparable. As an example, Listing 10-9 uses a Comparator object to sort an array of strings.

Listing 10-9: SortComparator.java

```
001: import java.util.Arrays;
002: import java.util.Comparator;
003:
004: // Class that implements the Comparator interface
005: class StringCompare implements Comparator {
006:   public int compare(Object o1, Object o2) {
007:     String s1 = (String)o1;
008:     String s2 = (String)o2;
009:     return s1.compareTo(s2);
010:   }
011: }
012:
013: class SortComparator {
014:   // Display an array of Strings
015:   public static void ShowStrings(String[] a, String msg) {
016:     System.out.println(msg);
017:     for (int i = 0; i < a.length; i++)
018:       System.out.println(a[i]);
019:   }
020:   // Create, sort, and display an array of StringClass objects
021:   public static void main(String args[]) {
022:     String colors[] = {
023:       "rojo", "azul", "verde", "negro", "blanco", "cafe", "gris"
024:     };
025:     ShowStrings(colors, "\nBefore sorting");
026:     // Construct the Comparator object
027:     StringCompare CompareObject = new StringCompare();
028:     // Sort the array using the Comparator object
029:     Arrays.sort(colors, CompareObject);
030:     ShowStrings(colors, "\nAfter sorting");
031:   }
032: }
```

Some of this program resembles others in the preceding section. What's different is the `StringCompare` class declared at line 005. This class implements `Comparator`, an interface in java.util. Line 002 imports the interface so we can implement its method. This method, `compare()`, receives two `Object` references (see line 006). In this case, we know the objects are strings, but if not, the statements at lines 007-008 might throw `ClassCastException`. Line 009 returns the result of the `String` class `compareTo()` method. In your own classes, you can do whatever is necessary to compare the two objects.

What's important in this program is the separation of the comparison method from the class of objects to be compared. The `Comparator` class doesn't contain the data to be compared, and therefore, this technique is useful for sorting arrays of class objects when, for example, the class cannot be extended to implement `Comparable` as in the preceding section.

Line 027 constructs the `Comparator` object. Line 029 passes the array of strings and the `Comparator` object to `Arrays.sort()`. As with other sorting methods, you can sort a portion of the array by passing two additional integer index values. This can throw an exception if the values are reversed or out of bounds.

Searching Arrays

The `Arrays` class provides several overloaded methods named `binarySearch()` that you can use to search arrays of `long`, `int`, `short`, `char`, `byte`, `double`, and `float` values. Listing 10-10, ArraysSearch.txt, shows these `Arrays` class methods.

Listing 10-10: ArraysSearch.txt

```
001: // Arrays class searching methods
002: public static int binarySearch(long[] a, long key);
003: public static int binarySearch(int[] a, int key);
004: public static int binarySearch(short[] a, short key);
005: public static int binarySearch(char[] a, char key);
006: public static int binarySearch(byte[] a, byte key);
007: public static int binarySearch(double[] a, double key);
008: public static int binarySearch(float[] a, float key);
009: public static int binarySearch(Object[] a, Object key);
010: public static int binarySearch(Object[] a,
        Object key, Comparator c);
```

When calling `binarySearch()`, it is your responsibility to ensure that the array is sorted in ascending order. If not, no exception is thrown, but the results of the search are not defined. The method is easy to use. Create an array:

```
int intArray[] = new int[100];
```

And then, sort it and pass it to `binarySearch()` using statements such as

```
Arrays.sort(intArray);
int k = Arrays.binarySearch(intArray, 50);
if (k >= 0)
  // .. use intArray[k]
```

Pass the array and value to find as arguments to `binarySearch()`. The method returns the index in the array at which the key value is located. If the method returns a negative value, the key is not in the array. This value is *not* necessarily –1, but might be any negative value. If there are duplicate values in the array, there is no way to predetermine which one will be found.

Lines 009-010 in Listing 10-10 show two overloaded `binarySearch()` methods that can search arrays of any types of objects. Use these methods in ways similar to that described in the preceding two sections. The objects must be of classes that implement the `Comparable` interface or, failing that, for which you can construct an object of a class that implements `Comparator`.

 Don't forget to sort your arrays before passing them to `Arrays.binarySearch()`!

Comparing Arrays

Use one of the overloaded `equals()` methods shown in Listing 10-11, ArraysEqual.txt, to compare two arrays for equality. There are methods available for all built in types, and one that can compare arrays of class objects.

Listing 10-11: ArraysEqual.txt

```
001: // Arrays class equality testing methods
002: public static boolean equals(long[] a, long[] a2);
003: public static boolean equals(int[] a, int[] a2);
004: public static boolean equals(short[] a, short a2[]);
005: public static boolean equals(char[] a, char[] a2);
006: public static boolean equals(byte[] a, byte[] a2);
007: public static boolean equals(boolean[] a, boolean[] a2);
008: public static boolean equals(double[] a, double[] a2);
009: public static boolean equals(float[] a, float[] a2);
010: public static boolean equals(Object[] a, Object[] a2);
```

Using an `Arrays` class `equals()` method is mostly straightforward. For most types, you can simply pass two arrays to the method using code such as

```
double a1[] = new double[32];
double a2[] = new double[32];
...
if Arrays.equals(a1, a2)
// ... code to execute if arrays are equal
```

The two arrays are considered to be equal if they meet one of the following conditions:

- They contain the same number of equivalent elements in the same order.

- They each refer to the same array of objects in memory.

- They are both null references.

When the two arrays contain class objects, they must be comparable using the equals() method inherited from Object. In other words, the arrayed objects are tested for *equivalence* – not merely whether the object references are to the same objects. Unlike the sorting methods in the Arrays class, the classes of arrayed objects do not have to implement Comparable. Also there is no Arrays.equals() method that uses a Comparator object to perform the comparison. These differences are because the arrayed objects are merely compared for equality, not for whether one is greater or lesser than the other.

Filling Arrays

When you create a new array, Java fills it with zero bytes. (If the array contains object references, this means they are all set to null initially.) To fill arrays with other values, call one of the fill() methods in the Arrays class, shown here in Listing 10-12, ArraysFill.txt. There are overloaded fill() methods for each native data type, as well as for objects of any class.

Listing 10-12: ArraysFill.txt

```
001: // Arrays class filling methods
002: public static void fill(long[] a, long val);
003: public static void fill(long[] a,
        int fromIndex, int toIndex, long val);
004: public static void fill(int[] a, int val);
005: public static void fill(int[] a,
        int fromIndex, int toIndex, int val);
006: public static void fill(short[] a, short val);
007: public static void fill(short[] a,
        int fromIndex, int toIndex, short val);
008: public static void fill(char[] a, char val);
009: public static void fill(char[] a,
        int fromIndex, int toIndex, char val);
```

```
010: public static void fill(byte[] a, byte val);
011: public static void fill(byte[] a,
        int fromIndex, int toIndex, byte val);
012: public static void fill(boolean[] a, boolean val);
013: public static void fill(boolean[] a,
        int fromIndex, int toIndex, boolean val);
014: public static void fill(double[] a, double val);
015: public static void fill(double[] a,
        int fromIndex, int toIndex,double val);
016: public static void fill(float[] a, float val);
017: public static void fill(float[] a,
        int fromIndex, int toIndex, float val);
018: public static void fill(Object[] a, Object val);
019: public static void fill(Object[] a,
        int fromIndex, int toIndex, Object val);
```

Each fill() method has two forms. The simpler one fills an entire array. Use it like this:

```
double fpArray[] = new double[64];
Arrays.fill(fpArray, 3.14159);
```

To fill only a portion of an array, supply starting and ending index values. For example, the preceding statement is actually implemented as

```
Arrays.fill(fpArray, 0, fpArray.length, 3.14159);
```

Notice that, despite the second index's name, toIndex, the last arrayed element to be filled is at fpArray[toIndex - 1]. This may be confusing, and good testing is called for when using the Arrays.fill() method to fill portions of arrays. As with other Arrays class methods that accept index parameters, an IllegalArgumentException is thrown if the index values are reversed. ArrayIndexOutOfBoundsException is thrown if either or both indexes are out of bounds for the array.

The last two fill() methods fill an array of objects of any class (see lines 018-019). This does *not* clone the objects nor copy them in any way. The methods simply equate val to each array element — in other words, following the fill, all array elements refer to the same object in memory. If that's not what you want, you must write your own fill method to clone the objects individually.

Arrays as Lists

Finally in the Arrays class is a miscellaneous method, asList(), that returns any array of objects as a List object. The method is useful when you have existing code that uses a List object, but your data is stored in an array. Listing 10-13, ArraysList.txt, shows the asList() method declaration. The remaining indented six lines show the List methods that are implemented for the array-as-list.

Listing 10-13: ArraysList.txt

```
001: // Arrays class List methods
002: public static List asList(Object[] a);
003:   public int size();
004:   public Object[] toArray();
005:   public Object get(int index);
006:   public Object set(int index, Object element);
007:   public int indexOf(Object o);
008:   public boolean contains(Object o);
```

No object conversions occur by calling asList(). Nothing is moved nor rearranged in memory. But after calling the method, you can use the returned value as a List object. Most important, any change to a List element affects the same element in the original array.

Chapter 14,"Introducing Collections," discusses List objects and other *collection classes.*

A simple example program demonstrates how to use an array as a List object. Listing 10-14, ArraysList.java, creates a small String array, converts it to a List, and then calls several of the methods from Listing 10-13 for the array-as-list.

Listing 10-14: ArraysList.java

```
001: import java.util.Arrays;
002: import java.util.List;
003:
004: class ArraysList {
005:   public static void main(String args[]) {
006:     // Create array of strings
007:     String fruits[] = {
008:       "apple", "banana", "cherry", "pear"
009:     };
010:     // Convert array to a List object
011:     List fruitList = Arrays.asList(fruits);
012:     // Call various List methods for the array
013:     int size = fruitList.size();
014:     System.out.println("List size = " + size);
015:     String s = (String)fruitList.get(2);
016:     System.out.println("List element #2 = " + s);
017:     if (fruitList.contains("banana"))
018:       System.out.println("fruitList contains banana");
019:   }
020: }
```

Lines 001-002 import the `Arrays` and `List` classes, both members of the `java.util` package. (See Chapter 13 for more about packages.) Lines 007-008 create the `String` array `fruits`, initialized to a few tasty objects. Line 011 shows how to convert the array to a `List` object by calling `Arrays.asList()`.

After calling that method, several statements near the end of the program call various `List` methods. For example, line 015 calls `List.get()` to obtain the element at index #2. This is the *third* string object in the list. Because `get()` returns `Object`, a type-cast expression is needed in this statement. Running the program displays:

```
List size = 4
List element #2 = cherry
fruitList contains banana
```

Summary

- An array is a composite data structure. As in most programming languages, Java arrays consist of data elements stored one after the other in memory.

- Declaring an array merely creates a variable that can refer to an array. Java arrays are allocated memory at runtime using the `new` operator. As a consequence, and a decided advantage, array sizes can be computed by program statements. Once an array is defined (allocated memory), however, its size cannot be changed.

- A multidimensional array is simply an array of arrays. There is no limit on the number of dimensions you may declare; however it is rarely useful to declare more than three levels. Unlike in most computer languages, nested arrays in Java multidimensional arrays do not have to all be of the same size.

- Arrays support exceptions. For example, indexing an array outside of its defined boundaries throws `ArrayIndexOutOfBounds`. These and other unchecked array exceptions are considered to be programming errors that are best fixed in the source code so that the errors never occur in the first place.

- You can copy an array three ways. However, simply assigning an array variable to another of the same type causes both variables to refer to the *same* arrayed objects in memory. To make a fresh copy of an array, use either the `System.arraycopy()` method, or call the `clone()` method inherited by all arrays from `Object`.

- The `Arrays` utility class in the `java.util` package provides many useful array methods, including methods for sorting, searching, equality testing, and filling arrays. There is also a method that converts an array of objects into a `List` object.

Chapter 11

Abstract Classes

IF A CLASS IS A BUILDING, then an *abstract class* is a blueprint that explains how the building should be constructed. You might call the blueprint an *abstraction* of the building that the construction crew uses to construct the real structure. In Java, *abstract classes* specify what extended classes should do — this is called the class's *contract* because it guarantees to users that the class performs as expected. A class's contract is similar to the agreement that the construction company probably has with the building's owners that, after the job is done, the elevators should go up and down when summoned, and the hot water should come out of the expected faucets.

In this chapter, you learn about abstract classes and how to use them to create class hierarchies. First, however, you need to learn how *access rules* affect the rights of access that users have to a class's members. Understanding access rules is fundamental to creating usable class abstractions and hierarchies, so let's begin there.

IN THIS CHAPTER

- ◆ Declaring class access rules

- ◆ Encapsulating and hiding data

- ◆ Understanding private, protected, and public declarations

- ◆ Creating abstract classes

- ◆ Extending abstract classes

Class Access Rules

Java provides three access rules that define the rights of access to a member of a class, including data and methods, whether static or non-static. The three access rules are

- ◆ `public` — Users who have access to the class have access to all members declared `public`.

- ◆ `protected` — Only the class's own methods, and those in any classes extended from this one, have access to `protected` members.

◆ private — Only the class's own members have access to a private member. Even an extended class cannot access a private member of a superclass.

Those definitions have a few quirks when viewed in the light of *packages,* explained in more detail in Chapter 13, "Packages." Some similar differences exist concerning *interfaces,* the topic for Chapter 12, "Interfaces." But for the purposes of understanding abstract classes, and in most programming situations, it's best to consider these three rules inviolate. I explain the quirks as appropriate throughout this and the other chapters.

Data Hiding

By using class access rules, you can provide safe and secure access to data members in class objects. This is often called *data hiding* or *encapsulation* because the data in the form of instance variables is made accessible only through calling one or more class methods. The benefits of this simple but essential object-oriented technique cannot be praised highly enough. With data hiding, you *control* access to data, and in that way, you ensure its proper use. In addition, you simplify the future modification of your programs.

A simple example demonstrates these benefits. Listing 11-1, DataHiding.java, uses the technique to create a class, TDate, for representing a date.

Listing 11-1: DataHiding.java

```
001: class TDate {
002:  private int month, day, year;
003:  public TDate(int month, int day, int year) {
004:   setDate(month, day, year);
005:  }
006:  public void setDate(int month, int day, int year) {
007:   this.month = month;
008:   this.day = day;
009:   this.year = year;
010:  }
011:  public String getDate() {
012:   return month + "/" + day + "/" + year;
013:  }
014: }
015:
016: class DataHiding {
017:  public static void main(String args[]) {
018:   TDate birthday = new TDate(8, 15, 1975);
019:   String s = birthday.getDate();
020:   System.out.println("birthday = " + s);
021:  }
022: }
```

Class `TDate` declares three private `int` variables, `month`, `day`, and `year`, at line 002. Because the instance variables are private, *only* the class's own methods may directly refer to them. The three variables are hidden inside the class, and the only way to get to them is by calling a class method.

For example, line 018 constructs a `TDate` object named `birthday`. The next statement calls the class's `public getDate()` method, which returns a string constructed from the `month`, `day`, and `year` private instance variables (see lines 011-014). The `getDate()` method may access the class's private data, but the main program may not. For example, if you insert the following statement between lines 018 and 019, the program no longer compiles:

```
birthday.year = 1990;   // ???
```

Attempting to compile the program now produces the error message:

```
X.java:19: year has private access in TDate
   birthday.year = 1990;
```

To change the date, the program is forced to call a public method such as `setDate()`, using code such as

```
birthday.setDate(8, 15, 1990);
```

A real program would need other methods to get and set each component of a date, but the concept is clear. Data hiding prevents the indiscriminate use of class data. In addition, because only the class's own methods can access private data variables, it's possible to change their types without affecting users of the class. We could, for example, decide to store the `month` and `day` variables using type `byte`, and perhaps save a little memory. Users of the class are unaffected by the change because *the class's contract has been maintained.*

Protected Members

Making every instance variable private may be too extreme a measure in many cases. Hiding data is a useful technique, but you may not want to limit access to data for *all* class users. For example, you often want an extended class to have direct access to instance variables instead of forcing the subclass to call methods in the superclass. Outside users of either class are still restricted from indiscriminately accessing the data directly.

This is what the `protected` access specifier does. By making a member `protected` (it can be an instance variable or a method), you state that the class's own methods, and any methods in extended classes, may directly access the member. Outside users (classes not extended from this one) must still call public methods to access the data. Listing 11-2, ProtectedData.java, demonstrates the basic technique of using protected data members.

Listing 11-2: ProtectedData.java

```
001: class TDate {
002:   protected int month, day, year;
003:   public TDate(int month, int day, int year) {
004:     setDate(month, day, year);
005:   }
006:   public void setDate(int month, int day, int year) {
007:     this.month = month;
008:     this.day = day;
009:     this.year = year;
010:   }
011:   public String getDate() {
012:     return month + "/" + day + "/" + year;
013:   }
014: }
015:
016: class TDateTime extends TDate {
017:   protected int hour, min;
018:   public TDateTime(int month, int day, int year,
019:     int hour, int min) {
020:     super(month, day, year);   // Call superclass constructor
021:     this.hour = hour;
022:     this.min = min;
023:   }
024:   public String getDate() {   // Override method
025:     return month + "/" + day + "/" + year +
026:       " : " + hour + ":" + min;
027:   }
028: }
029:
030: class ProtectedData {
031:   public static void main(String args[]) {
032:     TDate now = new TDateTime(3, 15, 2001, 14, 45);
033:     String s = now.getDate();
034:     System.out.println("now = " + s);
035:   }
036: }
```

The TDate class in the new program is the same as before, but its three instance variables are now declared protected instead of private (see line 002). An extended class, TDateTime (lines 016-028), adds hour and min variables to those inherited from TDate. The constructor initializes an object of the extended class by first calling the superclass constructor at line 020, and then assigning values to hour and min. This is a typical design; constructors in extended classes almost always call the superclass constructor to initialize inherited data members.

The new class also declares a `getDate()` method. Because this is the same name as the method in `TDate`, the new method is said to *override* the inherited one. Because the `month`, `day`, and `year` instance variables are protected, the extended class has direct access to them, as shown at lines 025-026, which build a string for the object's date and time information. Running the program displays

```
now = 3/15/2001 : 14:45
```

Abstractions

Abstract classes are especially useful in creating libraries to be shared by many programmers. They are also a great way to lock down a class's contract by providing a blueprint of the class's design. Abstract classes declare one or more *abstract methods* that provide the form of a method, but not its statements. A *pure abstract class* declares only abstract methods; however, an abstract class may also declare non-abstract, completely implemented methods. An abstract class may also declare instance variables, but no abstract class may be used to construct an object. To do that, another class must extend the abstract class and provide programming for all abstract methods. The purpose of an abstract class is to provide the *design* of extended classes, which may be implemented differently based on the programmer's needs.

Why Use Abstract Classes?

To understand how to create and use abstract classes, it is helpful to examine a series of classes that, although hypothetical in nature, demonstrate good object-oriented programming techniques. Consider this problem — you need to create primitive graphics objects that other code will combine to produce shapes on screen.

Right away, you can see that an abstraction of a graphics class helps simplify creating the real classes. The abstraction might specify shared characteristics such as color and location. It also stipulates the class's contract — for instance, you can reasonably assume that calling a method named `draw()` causes a shape to appear.

 Java does not enforce a class's contract — that's your job. If you program the `draw()` method to save data in a file instead of displaying a shape, you may be violating the class's contract, but Java won't care. However, just because a method is named `draw()` doesn't guarantee its purpose. In a game based in the Wild Wild West, `draw()` might have an entirely different meaning! Good documentation is the answer. Be sure to write down exactly what your class methods are supposed to do.

Creating an Abstract Class

To create an abstract class, simply preface the class declaration with the word abstract. A typical example is a class that represents a graphical shape — obviously this is an abstraction of what a real shape might be:

```
abstract class Shape {
...
}
```

Inside the class you may insert instance variables, constructors, and methods, just as you can for any other class. For example, Shape might have location and color information along with other items that all shapes share, but I'll leave these elements out to keep the sample code as simple as possible. The abstract class normally has at least one *abstract method* declared as follows:

```
abstract class Shape {
 abstract void draw();
}
```

The abstract method has no body, only a declaration. In this case, the program so far states that Shape is a class that can perform a method named draw(). This is a pure abstraction. We have not created any real shapes. All we have done is specify that a Shape is a kind of object that knows how to draw itself.

TIP When all declarations in an abstract class are abstract, it might be better to use an interface as described in Chapter 12. However, it is not an error to create pure abstract classes as shown here.

Extending an Abstract Class

It is not possible to construct an object of an abstract class. If you try, the compiler reports the error "Shape is abstract; cannot be instantiated." To use the abstract class, another class extends it and provides the actual programming for any and all abstract methods:

```
class Circle extends Shape {
 void draw() {
  // statements that draw a circle
 }
}
```

`Circle` extends the `Shape` abstract class, and implements the abstract `draw()` method. A real program might have many such extended classes — for example, `Rectangle` and `Polygon` classes that also extend `Shape`, and that provide their own unique implementations of the `draw()` method.

The importance of our illustrative class hierarchy may not yet be clear. But consider some code that refers to `Shape` objects in general. For example, you can create an array of `Shape` like this:

```
Shape shapeArray[] = new Shape[100];
```

It's okay to create an array using the abstract `Shape` class, even though `Shape` objects cannot be constructed, because the array contains only references to objects, all of which are initially set to `null`. Except for the array itself, no actual objects have yet been constructed. That might happen in other code such as

```
shapeArray[0] = new Circle();
shapeArray[1] = new Rectangle();
shapeArray[2] = new Polygon();
```

A `Circle` is a `Shape`, so is a `Rectangle` and a `Polygon`, so it's okay for the `Shape` references in the array to refer to real objects of classes that extend `Shape`. Magically, statements can call abstract methods such as `draw()` with no prior knowledge of what kind of object is involved. Here's a simple `for` loop that draws every `Shape` in the array:

```
for (int i = 0; i < shapeArray.length; i++)
 shapeArray[i].draw();  // !!!
```

That code can be written *and compiled* even before any classes extend the abstract `Shape` class. When the program executes, the `draw()` method is called for whatever real shape is in the array. You might hear this concept described as *polymorphism*.

TIP

If you are having trouble understanding abstract classes, think of them this way. The abstract class is like a tree, which is merely an abstraction, or generalization, of real trees such as oaks and maples. You can't grow a tree — you can only grow specific kinds of trees, but you still refer to them generally as trees. Similarly, in a program, you can't construct objects of an abstract class — you can instantiate only classes that extend the abstract class. But you can still refer to those objects as instances of the abstraction. `Circles` and `Rectangles` are Shapes, just as oaks and maples are trees.

Using an Abstract Class

A practical example of an abstract class will help you to better understand this important Java programming technique. In this section, you examine a working *container class* that knows how to sort data objects of an abstract class.

This is a typical use for an abstract class, and it is especially valuable in creating class libraries and for distributing work among members of a programming team. One group of programmers might design the container with no knowledge of the actual objects to be stored. Another team might create the real object classes. Because the container knows how to sort objects of a certain abstract class, the second team merely extends the abstract class in order to use the container.

Chapter 14, "Introducing Collections," describes Java's own collection container classes, which are far more sophisticated than the simple one listed here. The sample listings in this section work, but to keep them as short as practical, they lack many of the features that a real container class needs.

We start by designing the abstract class, shown in Listing 11-3, TObject.java. (These and subsequent listings in this section are in the c11/AbstractDemo directory on the CD-ROM.)

Listing 11-3: TObject.java

```
001: abstract class TObject implements Comparable {
002:   abstract public int compareTo(Object other);
003:   abstract public void show();
004: }
```

You can compile TObject.java using the command javac TObject.java, but you can't run the resulting class file. A demonstration program using TObject that you can compile and run appears later in this section.

I named the abstract class TObject to indicate it is a *type* of object. The abstract class implements the Comparable interface (more on that in Chapter 12), and it declares two abstract methods. The first method is required by Comparable— compareTo() compares the current object for which the method is called with another object passed as a parameter of the Object class. The second abstract method, show(), displays the contents of a TObject object.

That's all there is to the abstraction. TObject's contract states merely that it represents some kind of object that can be compared with another, and that it can be shown. The exact nature of those objects, and what happens when one is shown, are not part of the abstraction.

However, because TObject represents objects that can be compared, we have all we need to design the container class. Listing 11-4, TContainer.java, shows the complete code.

Listing 11–4: TContainer.java

```
001: import TObject;
002: import java.util.Arrays;
003:
004: class ContainerFullException extends Exception { };
005:
006: class TContainer {
007: // Private instance variables
008:   private int size;     // Size of objArray
009:   private int count;    // Count of objects in objArray
010:   private TObject objArray[];  // Array of objects
011:
012: // Constructor (n = array size)
013:   public TContainer(int n) {
014:     if (n <= 0) n = 1;  // Minimum allowed size
015:     size = n;
016:     count = 0;
017:     objArray = new TObject[size];
018:   }
019:
020: // Insert object into container
021:   public void putObject(TObject obj)
022:     throws ContainerFullException {
023:     if (count >= size)
024:       throw new ContainerFullException();
025:     objArray[count++] = obj;
026:   }
027:
028: // Display all objects in container
029:   public void showAllObjects(String label) {
030:     System.out.println(label);
031:     for (int i = 0; i < count; i++)
032:       objArray[i].show();
033:     System.out.println();
034:   }
035:
036: // Sort the objects in the container
037:   public void sort() {
038:     if (count > 1)
039:       Arrays.sort(objArray, 0, count);
040:   }
041: }
```

The first two lines in TContainer.java import our `TObject` abstract class and also import Java's `Arrays` class discussed in Chapter 10, "Arrays." I named the container class `TContainer` (see line 006), again using T for *type*. The class has three private instance variables. They are declared `private` because users of the class have no business directly accessing our storage methods — which might change in a future implementation. The three instance variables are

- `private int size` — This stores the size of the object array, equal to its capacity. The minimum size is 1.

- `private int count` — This stores how many objects are in the object array, and is initially zero.

- `private TObject objArray[]` — This is the actual array that stores objects of classes that extend `TObject`.

Carefully study the third variable. It is an array of objects of classes that extend `TObject`. The actual data structure could be something else such as a linked list, or even another type of container. I used an array to keep the listing simple. It is especially important to understand that the container can be used to store objects of *any* class that extends `TObject`. At this point, there are no such classes, but we can complete the container's code nonetheless.

For example, lines 012-018 implement the `TContainer()` constructor. The minimum storage size is 1, enforced by the first statement. The three instance variables are also initialized — a common task for most constructors. The last statement is the most important:

```
objArray = new TObject[size];
```

That constructs an array of `TObject`, with the capacity to store `size` objects. It's okay to create the array using the abstract `TObject` class because the array contains only *references* to objects — the actual objects are created elsewhere, presumably by code that uses the container.

Method `PutObject()` at lines 020-026 inserts a new object into the container's array. Again, since the program is working with only references to objects, it can insert them into the array with no foreknowledge of what actual kinds of objects they are. In addition, the method throws `ContainerFullException` (defined back at line 004) if the container is full. Obviously a more practically useful container would expand itself if necessary, but the minimal code used here at least makes the container safe to use. Line 025 inserts the object, of the `TObject` abstract class, into the array with this statement:

```
objArray[count++] = obj;
```

Method `showAllObjects()` at lines 028-034 demonstrates another important aspect of using abstract classes. The method uses a `for` loop to call the abstract `show()` method for each arrayed object:

```
for (int i = 0; i < count; i++)
 objArray[i].show();
```

A class that extends `TObject` must provide a working implementation of `show()`. But the container doesn't care what that method actually does — the container needs to know only that the `TObject` objects in the array support a `show()` method. Most important, this code can be *compiled* before any real `TObject` classes and objects are created. The correct `show()` method for those objects is called at runtime (you might hear this referred to as *late binding*).

Finally in the `TContainer` class is a method `sort()` that sorts the array of objects. For convenience, I use Java's `Arrays` class `sort()` method to perform the actual sorting as explained in Chapter 10 in the section "Sorting Arrays." Because our array is fixed in size and may contain `null` references if not completely full, it is necessary to pass index values to `Arrays.sort()` as shown:

```
if (count > 1)
 Arrays.sort(objArray, 0, count);
```

That's another good illustration of using abstract classes advantageously. Recall that `TObject` implements the `Comparable` interface and provides an abstraction for that interface's `compareTo()` method. The method is abstract because at this point there's no way to know what's needed to compare two real objects. However, since `TObject` is `Comparable`, objects of classes extended from `TObject` can be sorted. Powerful stuff indeed.

As mentioned, you can delay compiling and running the complete program for now. However, you might want to compile TContainer.java using the command `javac TContainer.java`. (Change to the c11/AbstractDemo directory if you haven't done so already.) Keep in mind that you just compiled a finished container that can sort objects even though at this point we have not defined the nature of those objects.

The next two listings finish the abstract-class and container example. The first missing piece is a class that extends `TObject` and provides some actual data to store in the container. Listing 11-5, TMyObject.java, declares another class `TMyObject`.

Listing 11-5: TMyObject.java

```
001: import TObject;
002:
003: class TMyObject extends TObject {
004:   private String s;
005:
006: // Constructor
007:   TMyObject(String s) {
008:     this.s = s;
009:   }
010:
011: // Implement Comparable interface method
012:   public int compareTo(Object other) {
013:     TMyObject otherObject = (TMyObject)other;
014:     return s.compareTo(otherObject.s);
015:   }
016:
017: // Implement TObject abstract method
018:   public void show() {
019:     System.out.print(s + "   ");
020:   }
021: }
```

The first line imports the TObject abstract class. Line 003 extends that class as TMyObject, which is not abstract. (It is possible to extend an abstract class into another abstract class, but at some point, a non-abstract class is needed in order to use the abstraction.)

For the demonstration, TMyObject stores a single String instance variable, declared private to the class. The class constructor initializes the object by saving a string passed as a parameter. This is a typical design. The abstract class has no constructor — it rarely needs one, since there's no way to construct objects of an abstract class. The extended class, however, must have a constructor so the program can, in this case, construct TMyObject objects. An abstract class may have a constructor if needed, in which case the extended class constructor would call it as super() with any necessary arguments.

Most important in the TMyObject class are the implementations of the two abstract methods declared by TObject. The first method, compareTo(), compares the strings in two TMyObject instances. The statement at line 013 uses a type-cast expression to convert the Object other parameter to a TMyObject reference. After that, the program simply calls the String class's compareTo() method to perform the actual comparison. In your own classes, the method should do whatever is necessary to compare two objects.

Finally in TMyObject is the implementation of the abstract show() method. The implemented method displays the object's string data by calling System.out.print().

TIP Non-abstract classes that extend an abstract class *must* provide implementations of all abstract methods. Be sure to respect the abstract class's contract—your methods should perform as closely as possible to specifications.

One more listing completes the puzzle and provides a runnable program that uses the preceding TObject, TContainer, and TMyObject classes. Listing 11-6, AbstractDemo.java, uses our container to store, sort, and display several objects.

Listing 11-6: AbstractDemo.java

```
001: import TContainer;
002: import TMyObject;
003:
004: class AbstractDemo {
005:  public static void main(String args[]) {
006:   TContainer container = new TContainer(100);
007:   try {
008:    container.putObject(new TMyObject("Peach"));
009:    container.putObject(new TMyObject("Mango"));
010:    container.putObject(new TMyObject("Lime"));
011:    container.putObject(new TMyObject("Banana"));
012:    container.putObject(new TMyObject("Kiwi"));
013:    container.putObject(new TMyObject("Grapefruit"));
014:    container.putObject(new TMyObject("Orange"));
015:    container.putObject(new TMyObject("Lemon"));
016:    container.putObject(new TMyObject("Apple"));
017:    container.showAllObjects("Before sorting");
018:    container.sort();
019:    container.showAllObjects("After sorting");
020:   } catch (ContainerFullException e) {
021:    System.out.println("Container overflow error");
022:   }
023:  }
024: }
```

You may now compile and run the demonstration. Make the c11/AbstractDemo directory current, and then enter the following two commands:

```
javac AbstractDemo.java
java AbstractDemo
```

Compiling the demonstration also compiles its submodules, TObject.java, TContainer.java, and TMyObject.java, unless these have already been compiled. The Java compiler checks the date and time of the resulting .class files, and it recompiles any modules whose .java files are newer, and thus probably modified. You may compile each module individually, but it is simpler in this case just to compile the AbstractDemo.java main program. That's the only module you can run because it is the only one that provides a main() method.

If you are following along, you should see the following text in your terminal or window:

```
Before sorting
Peach  Mango  Lime  Banana  Kiwi  Grapefruit  Orange  Lemon  Apple
After sorting
Apple  Banana  Grapefruit  Kiwi  Lemon  Lime  Mango  Orange  Peach
```

The program begins by importing the TContainer and TMyObject classes. It doesn't have to import TObject because the finished program doesn't refer to the abstract class. To create the container, the program executes the statement:

```
TContainer container = new TContainer(100);
```

We want to store some real objects in container, an action that takes place inside a try-catch block at lines 007-020. This is required because, as explained, TContainer.putObject() throws ContainerFullException. (To prove this works, change the container size to 5 at line 006, recompile, and run.) Each insertion statement is similar:

```
container.putObject(new TMyObject("Peach"));
```

That calls the putObject() method for the container object, and passes it a TMyObject object constructed by the new operator. Recall that TContainer.putObject() specifies a parameter of the abstract TObject class (refer back to Listing 11-4, line 021). Because TMyObject is a kind of TObject object—again, just as an oak is a kind of tree—it is perfectly fine to pass TMyObject objects to the method.

Lines 017-019 display, sort, and redisplay the objects in the container. Recall from before that TContainer's showAllObjects() and sort() methods were written with no foreknowledge of the type of real objects to be shown and sorted. Nevertheless, our container handles the real TMyObjects with ease. Using an abstract class, the container is completely generalized. It can display and sort *any* types of objects of classes extended from TMyObject.

Summary

♦ Java provides the three class access specifiers: `public`, `protected`, and `private`. Use them to allow and restrict access to the class's instance variables, fields, and methods.

♦ In general, it is best to declare instance variables `private` or `protected`, and to provide `public` methods for using such data. In this way, the class controls access to data, a technique called *data hiding* or *encapsulation*.

♦ Abstract classes provide blueprints from which actual classes are extended. The extended class implements the abstract class's contract. For example, a `Circle` class might implement a `draw()` method specified in an abstract `Shape` class.

♦ Abstract classes and their abstract methods provide the means to create pure abstractions of data types. In Java, you can write code to use objects of these types even before the real classes are created. For example, a program can call a `Shape` object's `draw()` method even though the real shape class such as `Circle` might not yet exist, or is being developed by another programming team.

♦ Abstract classes are particularly useful in creating general-purpose structures such as this chapter's `TContainer` class.

Chapter 12

Interfaces

AS YOU LEARNED IN CHAPTER 11, an abstract class provides a kind of blueprint from which other classes are created. An *interface* is similar in nature, but might be termed a *pure abstraction*. Every method in an interface is abstract.

As you learn in this chapter, Java provides several interfaces in its class library. You can also create your own interfaces.

IN THIS CHAPTER

- ◆ Introducing interfaces
- ◆ Extending and implementing interfaces
- ◆ Practical uses for interfaces
- ◆ Examples of Java interfaces

Introducing the Interface

While an abstract class may define abstract and non-abstract elements, interfaces are 100 percent abstract. Everything in an interface, with the exception of constants (more on that later), is abstract. An interface has no code, and its methods are mere declarations with no bodies. Furthermore, because a class can implement more than one interface at a time, interfaces provide a kind of multiple-inheritance that is otherwise lacking. Classes can extend only a single class at a time, but they may implement as many interfaces as needed.

 Because an interface has no constructors, no instance variables, no code, and it cannot be instantiated as an object, conflicts of multiple inheritance (requiring virtual base classes, for example) in languages such as C++ do not exist in Java.

An interface is particularly useful in providing the basis for a class hierarchy. For example, Java's Collection interface declares various common methods for classes like List and Set. Interfaces are useful also as *markers* that have no

229

content, but simply indicate that a class possesses a certain property. The Cloneable interface is one example. It indicates that a class's objects can be cloned, but the interface provides no details for implementing that process.

Creating an Interface

You will often use Java's existing interfaces, but you can certainly create your own. This is a valuable technique for class library designers, and also for programming teams who need to establish clear guidelines for designing classes and their applications. An interface looks similar to a class:

```
public interface MyInterface {
  void myMethod(Object obj);
}
```

This interface, because it is public, must be declared in a source code file named MyInterface.java. The word interface appears where class normally does. Inside the interface's body are one or more method declarations. These may not have bodies — interfaces never specify any implementation details. Every method in an interface is abstract, but you don't have to designate them as such using the abstract keyword.

An interface may not have instance variables, but it can specify constants in the following form:

```
public interface MyInterface {
 int maximum = 100;
...
}
```

The integer maximum is essentially like a final static declaration in a class — this must be so because an interface cannot be instantiated and therefore cannot have instance variables. The constant must be initialized as shown in its declaration, and its value can never be changed. Any constants are inherited in the interface's extensions and class implementations.

 TIP If you find the need for instance variables in an interface — for example, a value that needs to be unique for different class objects — then an abstract class is probably more appropriate than an interface.

Exceptions in Interfaces

In designing your interface, now is the time to decide whether a method should throw any exceptions. Any extensions and implementations of the interface must implement such a method to throw only its stated exceptions—you cannot, for example, throw additional exceptions in the implementing class. A typical design might look something like this:

```
class NewException extends Exception { }
interface NewInterface {
 void newMethod() throws NewException;
}
```

Any class that implements NewInterface must provide a newMethod() that throws NewException, and no additional exceptions can be thrown from the implemented method.

Extending an Interface

You may extend an interface just as you can extend a class; however, you may extend more than one interface at the same time. For example, if you are going to implement Java's Cloneable and Comparable interfaces, for convenience you can extend them both into a new interface:

```
interface CloneComp
 extends Cloneable, Comparable {
}
```

The CloneComp interface is an amalgam of the two interfaces that it extends. A class that implements CloneComp is expected to provide real methods for all those declared Cloneable and Comparable (in this case, there is a total of only one such method).

TIP   If the sample CloneComp interface were specified to be public, it would have to be stored in a file named CloneComp.java. Compiling that file produces a new file named CloneComp.class, which can be imported, extended, and implemented in other modules. If you are creating and implementing interfaces in the same file, you may omit the public key word, but in most cases, interfaces should be public and stored in source code files named the same and ending in .java.

Having multiple extensions of an interface brings the danger of name conflicts. In this case, no conflict occurs, but if Cloneable and Comparable each declare a method with the same name, the eventual class that implements the interface would have to refer to the methods by qualification with the interface names— Cloneable.someMethod() for instance. (Some Java technical books go into these issues of name conflicts in detail, but they are of more interest to language design-ers than to application developers.)

An interface may also contain nested interface declarations:

```
public interface MyInterface {
void myMethod(Object obj);
 public interface MyNest {
  void nestEgg(); // Nested interface method
 }
}
```

Any implementation of the interface would have to provide implementations for each level of nesting, using nested classes. As with nested classes, nested interfaces can result in confusing code, so don't use nesting unless you have excellent reasons.

Implementing an Interface

A class implements one or more interfaces, similar to the way a class extends an abstract class. The implementing class must provide bodies for all methods declared in the interface. In fact, the only significant difference between an interface and a purely abstract class is that a class can implement more than one interface — it can extend only one abstract class. For example, you might create a class that imple-ments Cloneable and Comparable like this:

```
public class MyClass
 implements Cloneable, Comparable {
...
}
```

The implementing class must provide implementations of any methods that the interfaces declare. At this stage, it should help your understanding to take a look at an arbitrary sample program that wraps up the preceding code samples into a working program. (In the next section, you examine a more practical example.) Listing 12-1, TheInterface.java, shows some important details in creating and implementing an interface.

Listing 12-1: TheInterface.java

```
001: class MyException extends Exception { }
002:
003: // Declare the interface (normally would be public)
004: interface MyInterface {
005:  void myMethod() throws MyException;
006: }
007:
008: // Implement the interface
```

```
009: class MyImplementation
010:  implements MyInterface {
011:  public void myMethod() throws MyException {
012:   System.out.println("in myMethod()");
013:   throw new MyException();
014:  }
015: }
016:
017: // Main program class
018: class TheInterface {
019:  public static void main(String args[]) {
020:   MyImplementation m = new MyImplementation();
021:   try {
022:    m.myMethod();  // Exception always thrown
023:   } catch (MyException e) {
024:    System.out.println("MyException caught");
025:   }
026:  }
027: }
```

Running the sample program displays a message and a note that it has caught an exception:

```
in myMethod()
MyException caught
```

The first message is displayed in the implemented interface method, myMethod() at lines 011-014. The exception on the second line is intentional. Lines 004-006 declare the interface, MyInterface, with a single method that throws MyException. As mentioned, this is the time to think carefully about the exceptions your methods might need to throw — you can't add them later to the implementing class.

The sample interface shown here is not designated public since this entire program is in one source code file. In most cases, interfaces are declared public and stored separately.

Lines 009-015 implement the interface — notice the word implements on line 010. Inside the implementing class, all methods in the interface must be implemented, and the method declarations must state that they throw any exceptions specified in the interface. At this point, the method is also made public. For illustration, the sample method's implementation displays a message, and then throws an exception.

That exception is caught in the main program at line 023. Notice also how an object of MyImplementation is created at line 020—you use the implementing class as you do any other class, typically as shown here, to construct an object for which you call one or more methods (see line 022).

Developing with Interfaces

A practical example shows how to put interfaces to work in Java programs. In Chapter 11, you examined a container class that uses an abstract class to provide an abstraction of data that you might need to store, sort, and display. The container itself is a good candidate for conversion to an interface so that, for example, programmers might change how the container stores information without affecting the use of the container.

 Java's own Collection interface is far more sophisticated than the simple interface presented here. See Chapter 14, "Introducing Collections," for more information on Collection and its implementations.

The next three listings make up the demonstration. You can compile each one, but only the last one runs as an application. All three listings are in the c12/InterfaceDemo directory on the CD-ROM. Listing 12-2, TContainerInterface.java, shows the declaration of the program's interface.

Listing 12-2: TContainerInterface.java

```
001: class ContainerFullException extends Exception { }
002: class NoSuchObjectException extends Exception { }
003:
004: public interface TContainerInterface {
005:   void putObject(Object obj)
006:     throws ContainerFullException;
007:   Object getObject(int n)
008:     throws NoSuchObjectException;
009:   int getCount();
010:   void sort();
011: }
```

TContainerInterface declares four methods, two of which throw the exceptions declared at lines 001-002. Method putObject() inserts an object into a container, getObject() gets an object identified by an integer index, getCount() returns the number of objects in the container, and sort() sorts the objects according to their rules of comparison. Notice that the first two methods specify the exceptions they are expected to throw.

The interface contains no code, only method declarations. (As mentioned, it could declare constants, but we don't need any here.) TContainerInterface differs from the TContainer class in the last chapter in a few subtle, but important ways:

♦ The storage mechanism to be used (an array, for example) is not specified. Interfaces cannot have any real data structures or variables.

♦ The interface also does not specify any count or size variables, even though it might seem these would be needed by all implementations. For data, interfaces can have only static final fields. If you need variables in an interface's design, you can use an abstract class, but you give up the advantages of multiple inheritance.

♦ The interface's methods are by default public. By convention, the public preface is omitted from all method declarations. However, it is not an error to include it.

♦ The putObject() method (see line 005) declares its parameter as type Object. Likewise, getObject() returns Object. In the Chapter 11's container class, which did not have a getObject() method, the abstract TObject was used in the container's methods. The interface version here is far more general because it can store any object of any class, since all Java classes are descendants of Object.

♦ As mentioned, the interface is usually declared public (see line 004), and it must therefore be in a source code file named TContainerInterface.java.

Compiling TContainerInterface.java (you can postpone that step for now) produces a class file named TContainerInterface.class, which can then be loaded by an import declaration. Listing 12-3, TContainer.java, begins by doing exactly that.

Listing 12-3: TContainer.java

```
001: import TContainerInterface;
002: import java.util.Arrays;
003:
004: class TContainer implements TContainerInterface {
005:   int count;          // Number of strings in array
006:   String strArray[];  // The array of strings
007:
008: // Constructor (not declared in the interface)
009:   TContainer(int n) {
010:     if (n <= 0) n = 1;
011:     count = 0;
012:     strArray = new String[n];
013:   }
014:
015: // Put an object into the container
016:   public void putObject(Object obj)
```

```
017:    throws ContainerFullException {
018:    if (count >= strArray.length)
019:     throw new ContainerFullException();
020:    strArray[count++] = (String)obj;
021:   }
022:
023: // Return object n from the container
024:   public Object getObject(int n)
025:    throws NoSuchObjectException {
026:    if (n < 0 || n >= count)
027:     throw new NoSuchObjectException();
028:    return strArray[n];
029:   }
030:
031: // Return number of objects in container
032:   public int getCount() {
033:    return count;
034:   }
035:
036: // Sort objects in the container
037:   public void sort() {
038:    if (count > 1)
039:     Arrays.sort(strArray, 0, count);
040:   }
041: }
```

TContainer.java fully implements TContainerInterface. The module imports the interface and also java.util.Arrays. Line 004 shows how to implement an interface as a class, in this case named TContainer. Two important and typical details begin the implementation—the declaration of instance variables count and strArray, and a constructor. Of course, your own classes provide whatever content is required, but it is highly typical for the implementing class to define some data elements and at least one constructor. These items cannot be specified in the interface; they must by supplied by the implementing class.

In this example, I designed the implementing TContainer class to store an array of String objects. The class could, however, store any type of objects. The constructor, as is typical, initializes the class's instance variables (see lines 008-013).

The other four methods in the class provide implementations of the methods specified in the interface. The first two of these, putObject() and getObject(), list the same exceptions as in the interface. As mentioned, this is not optional. Your implementations are required to satisfy the contract that the interface makes with its users. This may seem overly restrictive, but as a result, any module that uses TContainerInterface is assured that its methods throw only the stated exceptions, providing a simple but effective way to catch any and all errors that might occur.

Line 039 calls Arrays.sort() to sort the container's String array. This is possible because String implements the Comparable interface, and therefore, String objects can be compared. This is another good example of how, using interfaces and object-oriented techniques, the resulting code is greatly simplified. Instead of writing yet another sorting method, the program simply calls the one that Java provides in the Arrays class.

Listing 12-4, InterfaceDemo.java, uses the implemented interface to create a container object, insert some data into it, and then sort and display the results.

Listing 12-4: InterfaceDemo.java

```
001: import TContainerInterface;
002: import TContainer;
003:
004: class InterfaceDemo {
005:
006: // Show objects in container
007:   public static void showAllObjects(
008:     TContainerInterface c, String label) {
009:     System.out.println(label);
010:     try {
011:       for (int i = 0; i <= c.getCount() - 1; i++)
012:         System.out.print(c.getObject(i) + "  ");
013:       System.out.println();
014:     } catch (NoSuchObjectException e) {
015:       // Should never execute
016:       System.out.println("\n *** Error in for loop!");
017:     }
018:   }
019:
020: // Main program demonstrates using the container
021:   public static void main(String args[]) {
022:     TContainer container = new TContainer(100);
023:     try {
024:       container.putObject("Mexico");
025:       container.putObject("Canada");
026:       container.putObject("United States");
027:       container.putObject("Honduras");
028:       container.putObject("Bahamas");
029:       container.putObject("England");
030:       container.putObject("Germany");
031:       container.putObject("France");
032:       ShowAllObjects(container, "Before sorting");
033:       container.sort();
034:       ShowAllObjects(container, "After sorting");
035:     } catch (ContainerFullException e) {
036:       System.out.println("Container overflow error");
037:     }
038:   }
039: }
```

You may now compile and run the demonstration. Change to the c12/InterfaceDemo directory, and enter the following two commands:

```
javac InterfaceDemo.java
java InterfaceDemo
```

On screen, you see the following report (shortened here to save space):

```
Before sorting
Mexico  Canada  United States  Bahamas  England  Germany
After sorting
Bahamas  Canada  England  Germany  Mexico  United States
```

The program begins by importing the interface and implementing class. The interface is needed by method showAllObjects(), which deserves a close inspection. It is declared as

```
public static void showAllObjects(
  TContainerInterface c, String label) {...
```

The first parameter c is an object of type TContainerInterface. As you know, the interface itself cannot be instantiated as an object, but an object of the implementing class is *assignment compatible* with this reference. As such, showAllObjects() works with *any* container that implements TContainerInterface. The method doesn't care or need to know anything about the container's content; only that its implementing class satisfies the rules and regulations specified by the interface. For example, take a look at the method's for loop at lines 011-012:

```
for (int i = 0; i <= c.getCount() - 1; i++)
  System.out.print(c.getObject(i) + "  ");
```

Methods getCount() and getObject() are declared in TContainerInterface, and so, we can write statements that assume any objects of an implementing class provide real code for these methods. However, there is one wrinkle—the output statement assumes that whatever type of object is in this container, it can be converted to a string. Fortunately, this is true of all classes because Object provides a toString() method.

 TIP Object.toString() provides a default implementation that returns an object's class name and hash code (more on that in Chapter 14). Your own classes should probably override toString() to provide a more sensible string representation of any objects, but that's up to you.

Notice also that in `ShowAllObjects()`, because `GetObject()` throws `NoSuchObjectException`, the `for` loop must be in a `try-catch` block. This is a good example of a checked exception – one that Java checks is properly specified and caught. Any such exception indicates a programming error because, in this case, there can never be an instance when the loop requests a non-existent object. But, although the exception is never actually thrown, it must still be caught. Perhaps this might seem excessively rigorous, but it is far better for code to be overly robust than the opposite.

You might rightly wonder whether an interface is even needed in the preceding examples. However, consider that other modules might need to refer to container objects *as abstractions* and not as real objects. For example, a module could create an array of containers, using code such as

```
TContainerInterface cArray[] = new TContainerInterface[10];
```

Other code might create objects of various TContainerInterface implementations:

```
cArray[0] = new TContainer(100);
cArray[1] = new TGraphicsContainer(50);
cArray[2] = new TAccountContainer(25);
```

That assumes `TContainer`, `TGraphicsContainer` and `TAccountContainer` are each classes that implement `TContainerInterface`. As such, objects of those classes can be assigned to positions in the array – they are all assignment compatible to `TContainerInterface` references. Using the `showAllObjects()` method from the demonstration program, all objects in the array's dissimilar containers are easily shown using a simple loop:

```
for (int i = 0; i < 3; i++)
  showAllObjects(cArray[i], "Container # " + i);
```

This is somewhat hypothetical, but the code demonstrates how the complete abstraction of an interface leads to simple programming that can handle a wide variety of real data.

Java Interfaces – Some Examples

Java provides several useful interfaces introduced in this section. Because some of these require an understanding of techniques not yet introduced, some of the following discussions are necessarily brief. It is useful, however, to be aware of the existence of at least the following interfaces.

Cloneable Interface

As mentioned in this chapter, `Cloneable` is an example of a *marker interface,* one that has no content. Java declares `Cloneable` simply as

```
public interface Cloneable {
}
```

Classes implement `Cloneable` to indicate that their objects can be cloned by calling `Object.clone()`. They also usually implement that method, even though the `Object` class provides a default native implementation. You might think that cloning objects is a simple task, but it can be complicated by a variety of factors, and it is vital to think carefully about how exactly you want your objects to be cloned in any class that implements `Cloneable`.

 Earlier Java releases misspelled `Cloneable` as `Clonable`. **Always use the** newer, correct spelling, `Cloneable`.

An example illustrates how easy it is to get into cloning trouble. Listing 12-5, CloneDemo.java, shows the right and wrong ways to implement the `Cloneable` interface and override `Object.clone()`.

Listing 12-5: CloneDemo.java

```
001: // A simple string container class
002: class IntContainer implements Cloneable {
003:   private int size;  // Size (capacity) of array
004:   private int intArray[];
005:   public IntContainer(int n) {
006:     intArray = new int[n];
007:     size = n;
008:   }
009:   public int getValue(int n) {
010:     return intArray[n];
011:   }
012:   public void putValue(int index, int value) {
013:     intArray[index] = value;
014:   }
015:   public int size() {
016:     return size;
017:   }
018: /*
019: // The WRONG way to clone
```

```
020:  public Object clone() throws CloneNotSupportedException {
021:    return super.clone();   // ???
022:  }
023: */
024: // The RIGHT way to clone
025:  public Object clone() throws CloneNotSupportedException {
026:    IntContainer temp = (IntContainer)super.clone();
027:    temp.intArray = (int[])intArray.clone();
028:    return temp;
029:  }
030: }
031:
032: // Main program class
033: class CloneDemo {
034:
035:  // Display values in two containers side-by-side
036:  public static void showContainers(String msg,
037:    IntContainer c1, IntContainer c2) {
038:    System.out.println("\n" + msg);
039:    for (int i = 0; i < c1.size(); i++) {
040:      System.out.print(i + " : " + c1.getValue(i) + "    \t");
041:      System.out.println(c2.getValue(i));
042:    }
043:  }
044:
045:  public static void main(String args[]) {
046:    // Construct a container and randomize its content
047:    IntContainer original = new IntContainer(10);
048:    for (int i = 0; i < original.size(); i++)
049:      original.putValue(i, (int)(Math.random() * 100));
050:    try {
051:      // Clone the container
052:      IntContainer clone = (IntContainer)original.clone();
053:      showContainers("Before change", original, clone);
054:      // Modify a value in the clone at index 1
055:      clone.putValue(1, clone.getValue(1) * 2);
056:      showContainers("After change", original, clone);
057:    } catch (CloneNotSupportedException e) {
058:      System.out.println(e.getMessage());
059:    }
060:  }
061: }
```

Before examining the program, take a look at how Object declares the clone()
method:

```
protected native Object clone()
 throws CloneNotSupportedException;
```

Because clone() is protected, only Object itself and any extended classes can call clone(). This is a safety mechanism that helps prevent the improper use of the method. Class A can call its own inherited clone() method, since an extended class has access to all public and protected members inherited from its superclass. However, another class B that is not derived from A cannot call A's clone(). B is not a subclass of A, and therefore, it is denied access to A's protected and private members. This restriction generally forces programmers to override Object.clone() in order to designate it as public, and therefore, callable for objects of the class. This doesn't ensure that you write the method correctly, but it at least encourages you to think about what the method should do.

To demonstrate good and bad ways to write a clone() method, the sample program declares a simple integer container class at lines 002-030. The class declares an array of int values, and it provides methods to get and put values in the array. Lines 018-023, commented out in the program, show the *wrong* way to clone. Don't do this:

```
public Object clone() throws CloneNotSupportedException {
 return super.clone();   // ???
}
```

This simply converts the inherited protected method to public and returns the default clone()'s result. However, the overridden method fails to work correctly because the default implementation simply copies one object to a new one; it doesn't clone any *contents* in the original. The effects of this can be seen by enabling the commented out clone() method in the demonstration program, and running. The program constructs an original container and initializes it to values at random (lines 047-049). It then clones original by calling clone():

```
IntContainer clone = (IntContainer)original.clone();
```

After that, the program changes one of the values in the cloned container at index position 1:

```
clone.putValue(1, clone.getValue(1) * 2);
```

Despite that change, running the program shows that the two arrays still contain the same values at the same index positions:

```
Before change
0 : 32          32
1 : 38          38
...
```

```
After change
0 : 32          32
1 : 76          76
```

Obviously, changing a value in clone (right) resulted in a like change to original (left). Although the containers were cloned, they appear to address the same array of values in memory, a very bad error that must be avoided.

A proper clone() ensures that not only the cloned object, but also its contents, are uniquely copied. To illustrate, the sample container class implements a correct version of clone(). It's important to understand each step in the correct method, so here it is again for close inspection:

```
public Object clone() throws CloneNotSupportedException {
  IntContainer temp = (IntContainer)super.clone();
  temp.intArray = (int[])intArray.clone();
  return temp;
}
```

As in the bad method, the first statement calls super.clone(), the default implementation provided by Object. This step creates what you might call a *raw clone,* assigned here to an object, temp, using a type-cast expression to indicate the real type of object being cloned. Although the raw clone is a unique object, any instance variables in that object are simply byte-for-byte copies of those in the original. This is adequate for variables of simple types like int and double. But if any such instance variables are object references—including arrays—they must each be cloned separately. In this case, the second statement in the correct clone() method calls the int array's clone() method and assigns the result to the temporary object's intArray instance variable. Java arrays implement the Cloneable interface, so we can be sure that this step creates a fresh copy of the array and its contents. Finally, the properly initialized and cloned temp object is returned as the method's result.

If you are following along, enable the correct clone() method, compile, and run. Now, after changing a value in the cloned container, the arrays properly show different values at index position 1 after the change to the cloned container (right):

```
Before change
0 : 18          18
1 : 28          28
...
After change
0 : 18          18
1 : 28          56
```

You may not always be able to pass on cloning responsibility as I do here by calling a method such `intArray.clone()`. In your own classes, you must do whatever is necessary to create a fresh copy of any object references in the class — for example, by calling `new` to create fresh objects.

Comparable Interface

You've seen an example of the `Comparable` interface in Chapter 11 (Listing 11-3, TObject.java). Another interface can extend `Comparable`, or a class can implement it, to indicate that objects of the class can be compared by calling the `compareTo()` method. In general, a class implements `Comparable` like this:

```
class AnyClass implements Comparable {
 public int compareTo(Object other) { ... }
 // ... Other class declarations
}
```

The public `compareTo()` method must be declared as shown. However, it may be designated `abstract` if this is an abstract class, as in the last chapter's TObject class. The method is called in reference to an object, call it *A*. The other `Object` parameter passed to the method is to be compared to *A;* call this one *B*. The method is expected to return –1 if *A < B,* 0 if *A = B,* and +1 if *A > B.* In many cases, you can pass this responsibility to another class. For example, if your class declares a `String` instance variable s, you can write `compareTo()` as follows:

```
public int compareTo(Object other) {
 String otherS = (String)other;
 return s.compareTo(otherS);
}
```

No data is copied in the first statement — it merely casts the generic `Object` other parameter to a `String` reference, `otherS`. The `String` class's `compareTo()` method result is then returned for this object's string variable s compared to `otherS`.

Runnable Interface

Java's `Runnable` interface provides a single method, `run()`, used in writing threaded code. `Runnable` is declared as

```
interface Runnable {
 public abstract void run();
}
```

I discuss threads and the Runnable interface in Chapter 19, "Threaded Code," so I won't go into it in detail here. However, Runnable is used generally in designing a class for object methods that execute in a thread, but when you don't need the extra effort required to extend the Thread class.

Collection Interface

The Collection interface, in the java.util package, is the basis for all Java collection classes such as List and Set. (Collection classes are also sometimes referred to as container classes.) This interface is relatively new to Java, first appearing in JDK 1.2, and it provides a common abstraction that all collections share — as all good interfaces should do. For example, the Collection interface declares methods such as isEmpty() and contains().

Chapter 14 discusses Collection and container classes in detail, so I won't describe this interface further here. You might, however, want to look at its source code in the jdk1.3/src/java/util directory, assuming you installed the source code files as suggested in Chapter 3, "Getting Started with Java 2." Collection is a good example of a relatively complex interface.

 TIP If you want to create your own container class, implement Collection and provide working methods for all those declared in the interface. You can then pass objects of your container class to methods in other modules that accept a Collection interface parameter. Furthermore, your class objects are entirely replacement-compatible with other Java Collection implementations such as List and Vector.

Summary

◆ Interfaces are pure abstractions. They are particularly useful in providing the basis for class hierarchies and for specifying the characteristics to be shared among related classes. For example, Java's Collection class is the basis for the language's container class library.

◆ Interfaces provide a kind of multiple inheritance for Java. Other interfaces can extend multiple interfaces, and classes can implement more than one interface at a time. Conversely, classes can extend only one class at a time.

◆ An interface may declare only constant fields and methods. An interface may not have instance variables, nor constructors. It is never possible to create an instance of an interface. All methods in an interface are by default abstract and public.

◆ Interfaces can be nested. However, the results may be confusing, and this technique should be used only for good reasons.

◆ Marker interfaces contain no content, but they indicate that a class possesses a certain property. For instance, a class that implements the Cloneable interface states that objects of the class can be cloned by calling Object.clone(). However, it is still your responsibility to provide a correctly written clone() method. Simply implementing Cloneable is not enough to ensure correct cloning.

◆ Java provides several useful interfaces. Some of them are introduced in this chapter — Cloneable, Comparable, Runnable, and Collection.

Chapter 13

Packages

PROBABLY THE MOST INCONSISTENT FEATURE among the world's collection of programming languages is the concept of a module. One language might use object code files to modularize programs, another might use libraries of some kind, another uses units, and some still rely on that old standard, the lowly include file.

Java provides its own unique embodiment of a module — the *package*. All of Java's classes are members of one or another package, as are the classes you create. A package provides modularity to Java programs, and it also helps avoid naming conflicts in a sensible way. Any program larger than a breadbox will benefit from modularization using packages. In this chapter, you learn how to create your own packages, and you take a look at some of the more useful packages that Java provides.

IN THIS CHAPTER

- ◆ Introducing packages

- ◆ Importing Java packages

- ◆ Packages and access rules

- ◆ Creating and naming packages

- ◆ Java's standard packages

Introducing Java Packages

A package is simply a group of related classes (it could have just one, but usually provides several). For example, a set of graphics classes might be grouped into a package named graphics. To use the classes, one or more modules in a program can import the entire package with a declaration such as

```
import graphics.*;
```

The asterisk indicates to the compiler that it should import all classes in the graphics package. To import just one class, use a declaration such as

```
import graphics.Rectangle;
```

It is not correct to import the package itself. You can import only classes and interfaces, not packages. For example, this causes a "cannot resolve symbol" compiler error:

```
import graphics;  // ???
```

Packages may include interfaces, abstract classes, and public classes. For this chapter, I generally discuss classes only, but the same information here applies to interfaces and abstract classes.

Importing Java Packages

Every Java source code file imports the java.lang package as though the file begins with the declaration

```
import java.lang.*;
```

It's not an error to do that, but it is never necessary. Java also provides a number of standard packages, some of which you have already seen, that are not automatically loaded. For instance, sample programs in the previous two chapters import the Arrays class with the declaration

```
import java.util.Arrays;
```

If you want, you can import the entire java.util package with the declaration

```
import java.util.*;
```

It is generally better to import only those classes and interfaces that are actually used in the source code module. But because any one class might import several others, you may still end up importing the entire package.

Some packages provide one or more *subpackages,* such as java.util.jar, a subpackage of java.util. Importing a package does not import any subpackages. You must do that explicitly using statements like these:

```
import java.util.*;
import java.util.jar.*;
```

The first statement imports classes and other modules from java.util. The second statement imports classes and modules from java.util.jar.

> **TIP**
> To find what classes belong to which Java packages, install the source code files as suggested in Chapter 3, "Getting Started with Java 2." You can then browse the jdk1.3/src/java directory in which you find all of Java's standard packages. Each package is stored in a subdirectory. Each class in each package is stored in a separate .java file named the same as the class.

The import Declaration

As you have seen in many of this book's sample programs, to use a class or an interface declared in a package often requires an `import` declaration. Actually, however, this isn't the whole story: `import` declarations are an optional convenience, and they are technically not required. For example, to use the `Stack` class in the `java.util` package, a module can import the class using the declaration

```
import java.util.Stack;
```

That tells the compiler to load the declaration for the class and make it available to statements such as the following, which constructs a `Stack` object:

```
Stack storage = new Stack();
```

Alternatively, you may specify the full package and class name *without* using an `import` statement. For example, the following statement fully qualifies the `Stack` class, telling the compiler in which package it is located:

```
java.util.Stack storage = new java.util.Stack();
```

Using fully qualified expressions is more work, of course, but it eliminates the need for an `import` statement. The long form is possibly useful for debugging — for example, to use a temporary test version of a class. An `import` statement, though, is preferred in most cases.

Some Java documentation and books indicate that you can import all packages with the declaration

```
import java.*;  // ???
```

However, because that doesn't import any subpackages such as java.util or java.awt, and because the java package contains only subpackages, the preceding statement has no practical value.

Packages and Access Rules

As you learned at the beginning of Chapter 11, "Abstract Classes," the class access rules, public, protected, and private, define the rights of access to class members. However, because related classes often need direct access to one another's members, Java relaxes its access rules for classes within the same package. Qualified for classes in packages, the revised access rules are

◆ public — Users who have access to the class have access to all members declared public. Public classes in the same package have access to all public declarations in other public classes.

◆ protected — The class's own methods, and those in any classes extended from this one, have access to protected members. Protected members are also accessible to all classes within the same package. The classes do not have to be related through inheritance.

◆ private — Only the class's own members have access to a private member. Even an extended class cannot access a private member of a superclass. Classes in the same package do not have access to other classes' private declarations.

◆ none — Declarations not declared public, protected, or private are said to be friendly. (This is not a Java reserved word.) Friendly declarations are accessible to the class itself, to an extended class, and to any statements in classes within the same package. Friendly declarations are private outside of the package.

 The revised access rules apply also to classes defined in the same compilation unit — that is, the same source code file. Of course, the class itself has access to all of its own members no matter how they are declared.

The revised rules make it a little easier for classes in the same package to communicate. For instance, if public classes A and B are in the same package, objects of type B may directly access A's public, protected, and friendly declarations, even if B is not a subclass of A. But if A and B are in different packages, then B would have access to A's public and protected members only if B extends A. Otherwise, only A's public members are accessible to B.

A small demonstration that you can type and compile helps clarify these concepts. This is just throw-away code, so it's not on the CD-ROM. Create a fresh directory, and in it save the following class in a file named A.java:

```
// A.java
public class A {
```

```
  int x = 123;
}
```

You may compile the class with the command `javac A.java`. The integer instance variable is friendly (it has no explicit access specifier). As a result, another class can import A, and access the friendly variable for an object of type A. Type in and save another class in a file B.java in the same directory:

```
// B.java
import A;
public class B {
 public void f(A a) {
  int q = a.x;
 }
}
```

Compile the class with the command `javac B.java`. B's public method `f()` can access its parameter object's friendly variable x because A and B are in the same package — namely, the application itself.

 An application's classes are members of an *unnamed package*. Thus every class in a Java application is a member of some package.

Referring back to A.java, if you declare x to be `private`, class B no longer compiles. The declaration could be `public` or `protected`, and the program would work. But if classes A and B are in *different* packages, then the friendly declaration in A would no longer be accessible to B.

The next section presents a more detailed example of these access rules and their effect on packaged classes, and also explains how to create your own named packages.

Programming with Packages

Creating your own packages is a great way to preserve useful classes that you construct during the course of writing an application. I like to call them *named packages* to distinguish them from Java's standard packages and from those provided by third-party vendors. By organizing your program's classes into your own named packages, you make classes more readily available to future applications, and a little thought now in collecting generally useful classes into packages will go a long way in the future.

Package Names

You can name your own packages whatever you like. However, there is the obvious and very real danger that your package names will conflict with those from another source. To help prevent class name conflicts, Sun recommends using your URL or domain name in reverse as a preface to all of your packages. Employing this idea, if I have a package named graphics, I'd name it as follows:

```
package com.tomswan.graphics;
```

This isn't foolproof — I can't prevent somebody from using my name. But the convention ought to work well enough in most cases. Don't have a URL? Use your e-mail address:

```
package com.hotmail.yourname.graphics;
```

 TIP By convention, package names should be in lowercase. This isn't required, but due to differences in file system naming conventions, using all lowercase is highly recommended for package names.

How to Create a Package

Creating a named package is easy. Simply use a declaration such as

```
package stuff;
```

That must come before any other declarations or statements except comments in the source code file. A package declaration states that subsequent classes in the file are to be collected within the named package — stuff in this case — and as such, the .class files are to be found in a subdirectory of that same name. The source code files in a package may declare any classes, and they may import other classes, either of your own design or from Java's standard library. As I've mentioned, it's usually best to declare one class per file named the same — you must do so if the class is public, as it usually is.

 TIP Classes within the same package automatically import all other classes in that package. You don't have to use an import declaration to access classes in the same package, although you may do so for documentation purposes.

Demonstration Package

The following four listings demonstrate packages and show how to create their files and directories. While describing each file, I'll point out several important details concerning access rules among the classes. Java uses the directories to locate the packaged classes, so it's important that each file be stored where the compiler can find it. In this case, the main directory is named packageTest (on the CD, this is in the c13 subdirectory). Inside packageTest is a subdirectory named stuff, corresponding with the package name. Listing 13-1, TClass1.java, shows the first class in the stuff package.

Listing 13–1: Stuff/TClass1.java

```
001: package stuff;
002:
003: public class TClass1 {
004:   String name;  // Friendly instance variable
005:   public TClass1(String name) {
006:     this.name = name;
007:   }
008:   public String getName() {
009:     return name;
010:   }
011: }
```

 As always in this book, and as shown in your Web browser if you are viewing listings online, a slash is used as the pathname separator. If you are using Windows, remember to change this to a backslash for typing commands at a DOS prompt.

The file begins with the package declaration and as is the usual case, provides one public class named the same as the file, TClass1. The demonstration class declares a friendly instance variable, a String object name. The class constructor initializes name to a parameter passed by a statement (an example follows in a moment) that creates a TClass1 object. Method getName() returns this name. The class method has access to name because the method and instance variable are members of the same class.

Listing 13-2, TClass2.java, is another class in the same stuff package. It too is stored in the PackageTest/stuff directory.

Listing 13-2: Stuff/TClass2.java

```
001: package stuff;
002:
003: public class TClass2 {
004:   public String returnName(TClass1 obj) {
005:     return obj.name;  // Access friendly variable in TClass1
006:   }
007: }
```

Again, the source file begins with the package name, followed by a public class declaration, in this case, TClass2. This second class in the stuff package declares a single public method, returnName(). In addition, that method declares a parameter object of type TClass1. It can do this because a package imports all of the classes in that same package, so no import declaration is needed for the new class to use TClass1.

The method's return statement at line 005 shows that TClass2 may access TClass1's friendly name instance variable. This is because of the rule that all classes in the same package may access other classes' public, protected, and friendly members.

 All classes and interfaces in a package must declare the same package name, and that name must reflect the directory in which the modules exist. Thus in this example, TClass1 and TClass2 must each declare themselves to be members of package stuff, and their files must be in a directory named stuff.

A third test class in Listing 13-3, TClass3.java, shows how to create another package. This file is stored on the CD in the PackageTest/morestuff subdirectory.

Listing 13-3: MoreStuff/TClass3.java

```
001: package morestuff;
002:
003: public class TClass3 {
004:   private String name;
005:   public TClass3(String name) {
006:     this.name = name;
007:   }
008:   public String myName() {
009:     return name;
010:   }
011: }
```

The source code file begins with a package declaration that creates a second package, morestuff. TClass3 resembles the first class, TClass1, in the stuff package. However, this time the class's name instance variable is made private to the class (see line 004). This means that users of this class *must* call a member function such as myName() at line 008 to access the instance variable. No class, whether in the same package or not, has access to another class's private declarations.

To compile all classes in a package, change to its directory and enter the command javac *.java.

I'll explain more about access rules among packaged classes in a bit. First, however, we need a test program that uses the three preceding classes. Listing 13-4, PackageTest.java, imports the packaged classes and creates objects of each one. This file is stored in the PackageTest directory.

Listing 13-4: PackageTest.java

```
001: import stuff.*;
002: import morestuff.TClass3;
003:
004: class PackageTest {
005:   public static void main(String args[]) {
006:     TClass1 x = new TClass1("Message 1");
007:     System.out.println("via TClass1: " + x.getName());
008:     TClass2 y = new TClass2();
009:     System.out.println("via TClass2: " + y.returnName(x));
010:     TClass3 z = new TClass3("Message 2");
011:     System.out.println("via TClass3: " + z.myName());
012:   }
013: }
```

If you have trouble compiling PackageTest.java, review Chapter 3's installation instructions. In order for the compiler to locate the stuff and morestuff packages, the CLASSPATH variable must be set to include the current directory, represented in DOS, Linux, and UNIX as a single period.

You may now compile and run the program using the two commands shown here in bold. Following those commands is the program's output:

```
javac PackageTest.java
java PackageTest
via TClass1: Message 1
via TClass2: Message 1
via TClass3: Message 2
```

 TIP Compiling a program that uses classes in packages also compiles the packaged class source code files if necessary. You may, however, compile each class and any host programs separately if you want.

The test program constructs three objects, x, y, and z, which refer to the three packaged classes. The first two lines in the program show two different ways to import the classes from their named packages — using an asterisk to import all classes and specifying an individual class by name. These are the same techniques used to import Java's standard packages.

Some small tests and modifications to the preceding four listings help clarify access rules among packaged classes. Suppose you decide to extend the stuff package's TClass1 class. Doing this in the main program (Listing 13-4, PackageTest.java) as follows does *not* work:

```
class TDerived extends TClass1 {
 public TDerived(String name) {
  super(name);
 }
 public void f() {
  System.out.println(name);  // ???
 }
}
```

The derived class must have a constructor as shown with a String parameter because TClass1 does not declare a default constructor (one with no parameters). The derived class method f(), however, does not compile because it attempts to access the friendly name instance variable inherited from TClass1. This produces the compiler error:

```
PackageTest.java:13: name is not public in stuff.TClass1;
cannot be accessed from outside package
```

If you change TClass1.name to protected status, then the program compiles. This is because extended classes have access to public and protected members inherited from their superclasses. Classes within the same package have similar access. However, friendly declarations are accessible to other classes *only* in the same package or compilation unit.

A common misconception is that friendly members are equivalent to protected members. This is not the case. A friendly member is accessible throughout the same package or compilation unit, but is otherwise private.

If you change TClass1.name to private access, then the program doesn't compile at all. Even though TClass2 is in the same package as TClass1, it has no access to any private declarations in other classes, whether they are in the same package or not. The preceding TDerived class also has no access to inherited private members. In Java, private means private!

One more test clarifies access rules among classes in separate packages. Refer back to Listing 13-3, TClass3.java, which declares the morestuff package and the test class TClass3. Suppose that you want the TClass3 class to import the classes in the stuff package with the following declaration added to TClass3.java:

```
// Add to TClass3.java
import stuff.*;
```

That's perfectly fine — a package may certainly import the classes in other packages. However, TClass3 does *not* have access to any friendly declarations in the other package's classes. An attempt to add a new method as follows to TClass3 produces a compilation error that says the name symbol cannot be resolved:

```
// Add to TClass3
public String f(TClass1 obj) {
  return obj.name;  // ???
 }
```

The TClass1.name instance variable is friendly, but only to classes within the same package. This time, changing that instance variable's access to protected still does not allow the program to compile because TClass3 is not a subclass of TClass1. The only way that a TClass3 member can access TClass1.name is if that instance variable is made public (not recommended), or by calling a method in TClass1 (best solution).

Java's Standard Packages

Java provides a treasure house of standard packages, some of which you have already met such as java.util and java.lang. The rest of this book describes many of the classes in these and other packages (browse the jdk1.3/src/java directory to find the source code files for these packages and their numerous classes):

◆ `java.applet` — This package provides the means to create Java applets that run under the control of a Web browser and are typically downloaded over the Internet. Chapter 20, "AWT Applets and Applications," explains how to create Java applets using this package.

◆ `java.awt` — In this package are the many classes that make up Java's *Abstract Window Toolkit* (AWT). This extensive package provides a class-based graphical user interface with windows, buttons, dialog boxes, and other controls for applet and application programming. Chapter 15, "List Collections," describes how to use many of the classes in this package.

◆ `java.awt.*` — Within `java.awt` are numerous subpackages such as `java.awt.color`, `java.awt.font`, and `java.awt.image`. These packages group related classes that supplement AWT's main classes.

◆ `java.beans` — This package provides the basic elements for JavaBeans — components that support the concept of design-time *property editors*. You won't find useable JavaBeans in this package. Real beans provided by third-party vendors base their designs on the `java.beans` package to ensure that the components are useable in all Java visual development systems such as JBuilder and Visual Café.

◆ `java.io` — Classes in this package provide input and output services for reading and writing file data, for accessing keyboard input, and for printing. Chapter 24, "Input and Output Techniques," explains how to use many of this package's classes.

◆ `java.lang` — This package provides wrapper classes such as `Character`, `Integer`, and `Double`. It also provides system-standard classes such as `String` and `StringBuffer`. The Java compiler always loads all of these packages. You never need to explicitly import any classes from `java.lang`. Many of the classes in this package are described throughout this book.

◆ `java.math` — There are only a few classes in this package, which is primarily of interest to hard-core mathematics programmers. Applications probably won't use any of these classes, such as `BigInteger` and `BitSieve` (a prime number generator). Don't confuse this package with the `java.lang.Math` class, described in Chapter 9, "Numeric Classes."

◆ `java.net` — This package provides network, socket handler, and Internet utility classes.

◆ `java.rmi` — Classes in this *Remote Method Invocation* package provide support for distributed code controlled by a remote interface. With the help of the classes in this package, you can create Java applications that run in pieces distributed over different systems.

◆ java.security — Use the classes in this package, and its several subpackages, to implement security tools such as digital signatures, encryption keys, and certificates.

◆ java.sql — This package provides an implementation of *Structured Query Language* database field types and methods. Depending on your system, this package's classes may be implemented in terms of a specific database system, or as by default, as a direct mapping of the ODBC (open database connectivity) standard.

There is some controversy over what SQL stands for. Many Java documents claim it means "System Query Language." This book's technical editor votes for "Standard Query Language," while the development editor and I believe "Structured Query Language" is correct. By the way, a lot of people pronounce SQL as "sequel," but some say each individual letter.

◆ java.text — Classes in this package provide parsers and formatters — for example, the DateFormat class, which can format date strings according to the current locale.

◆ java.util — Every Java application and applet probably uses at least one class from this miscellaneous package. You have seen several examples of this package's classes in preceding chapters — for example, the Random class (Chapter 9, "Numeric Classes") and the Comparator class (Chapter 10, "Arrays"). In addition, java.util provides the Collection interface and its implemented container classes such as List and Set. Chapter 14, "Introducing Collections," explains how to use the java.util package's container classes.

◆ java.util.jar — This subpackage, contained within the java.util package, provides Java's own data compression system for creating and using .jar files. This format has replaced the older .zip compression that Java formerly used for making compiled classes available to Web browsers. However, many browsers and operating systems still use the .zip file format.

◆ java.util.zip — This subpackage supports the .zip file compression format, which, as mentioned in the preceding paragraph, is replaced by the newer .jar format.

Summary

◆ Packages modularize Java classes by grouping related classes. For example, a graphics package might provide classes that perform graphics operations.

◆ Java provides many standard packages in its class library. You can also create named packages to modularize programs and to create class libraries. A package may contain interfaces, abstract classes, and public classes.

◆ To avoid name conflicts between your packages and those from other sources, Sun recommends using your URL or domain name in reverse as a preface to the package name. If you don't have a URL, use your e-mail address.

◆ Import a package's classes using an `import` declaration. Use an asterisk to import all classes, or specify only the individual class you need. Classes within the same package automatically import all other classes in that package.

◆ Java's class access rules are relaxed for the classes within the same package. Public members are available to all users of the class. Protected members are available to all classes within the same package whether or not those classes are related through inheritance. Private members are never accessible outside of a class, even for classes in the same package.

◆ Friendly class declarations — those that do not specify `public`, `protected`, or `private` — are accessible to all classes within the same package. Outside of the package, friendly declarations are private. These same rules apply to non-public classes in the same compilation unit (as in many of this book's sample programs).

Part III

Collections

Chapter 14

Introducing Collections

THE JAVA.UTIL PACKAGE provides a grab bag full of *collection container classes* and related interfaces from which you can construct containers for storing any kind of object. Each collection container provides specific characteristics and methods related to the container's structure and intent. For example, a `TreeSet` container maintains data sorted in a tree-like structure, while the `LinkedList` container provides for super-fast insertions and removals of objects.

This chapter introduces Java's collection class library, lists its interfaces and classes, and diagrams their relationships. The rest of the chapters in Part III, "Collections," describe how to use many of these elements to store data and how to construct your own custom collection classes.

 Some texts refer to Java's container class library as *collection classes*. However, because the library contains an interface named `Collection`, from which some but not all other classes and interfaces are derived, that term can be ambiguous. For that reason, I call this group of classes Java's *collection container class library*, or just *container library*.

IN THIS CHAPTER

- ◆ Introducing collection classes
- ◆ Container interfaces
- ◆ Abstract and concrete container classes
- ◆ Interface and class diagrams
- ◆ The Collection Interface
- ◆ Creating and using containers
- ◆ Container exceptions

Class Hierarchy

A first encounter with Java's container library confuses most everybody. The library provides a seemingly jumbled set of interfaces, abstract classes, and concrete classes (ready-to-use implementations). The relationships among these elements are complex and not always obvious, but once understood they reveal the classes to be remarkably well organized and intelligently designed.

To help you learn how to use the library and understand the chapters in this part, this chapter introduces Java's container library in two ways: in table form, listing interface and class names, and diagrammatically, showing the relationships among those same elements. Some of this information won't make much sense until after you begin using the classes, so plan on referring back here as you read the rest of the chapters in this part.

The container library contains roughly four categories of declarations:

◆ *Container interfaces* – These are pure abstractions (as are all interfaces) from which all of the library's abstract classes and concrete classes are ultimately derived. The library's interfaces stipulate the most general of methods that containers are expected to support. For example, the Collection interface declares common methods such as add() and remove() that are implemented by various container classes.

◆ *Abstract container classes* – These are higher-level abstractions that provide some, but not all, implementation details for a type of container. When constructing your own container classes, it is usually easier to extend an abstract class than it is to implement a more generalized interface. For example, if you need to create a set-like container class, you can save some effort by extending the AbstractSet class rather than implementing the more generalized Set interface from scratch.

◆ *Concrete container classes* – These are completely implemented container classes, ready for use. Each concrete class is non-abstract, extends an abstract class, and implements at least one interface. Unless you need to write your own container classes, you can probably select a concrete class and just use it. For example, to create a linked list, simply construct an object of the concrete LinkedList class.

◆ *Other container classes* – The container library provides a few other interfaces and classes that are used in container programming, but are not otherwise related to the library's hierarchy. For example, the Iterator interface stands alone, but it is used extensively in Collection-based containers. I also include the BitSet class in this group, although some other texts consider this to be a general utility class and not part of the container library.

The entire container library of interfaces and classes is found in the `java.util` package. This adds more confusion because `java.util` provides many other classes such as `Arrays` and `Calendar` that have nothing to do with collection containers. Ideally, the container library would be in its own package, but for historical reasons it remains in `java.util` (see "Legacy Containers" in Chapter 18, "Utilities and Legacy Classes," for other classes in `java.util` that are still supported, but replaced by the newer collection classes described here).

Container Interfaces

Table 14-1 lists the container library's interfaces, which as mentioned, represent the highest level of container abstractions. Some interfaces are extended from others, as shown in the table's second column.

TABLE 14-1 CONTAINER INTERFACES

Interface	Extends
Collection	none
Iterator	none
ListIterator	Iterator
List	Collection
Map	none
Set	Collection
SortedMap	Map
SortedSet	Set

Abstract Container Classes

The library's abstract classes represent the next level of abstractions, one step up from the container interfaces. Abstract classes implement some, but not necessarily all, methods stipulated by an interface. For that reason, when creating your own container classes, you may want to extend one of the library's abstract classes rather than implement a more general interface. Table 14-2 lists the container library's abstract classes.

TABLE 14-2 CONTAINER ABSTRACT CLASSES

Abstract Class	Extends	Implements
AbstractCollection	none	Collection
AbstractList	AbstractCollection	List
AbstractMap	none	Map
AbstractSequentialList	AbstractList	none
AbstractSet	AbstractCollection	Set

AbstractSequentialList implements the List interface indirectly by being extended from AbstractList.

Concrete Container Classes

When you need a container, you can probably construct an object of one of the concrete classes listed in Table 14-3. Each is a ready-to-use container class that extends from one of the library's abstract classes, and also implements at least one interface as shown in the table.

TABLE 14-3 CONTAINER CONCRETE CLASSES

Concrete Class	Extends	Implements
ArrayList	AbstractList	List
HashMap	AbstractMap	Map
HashSet	AbstractSet	Set
LinkedList	AbstractSequentialList	List
TreeMap	AbstractMap	SortedMap
TreeSet	AbstractSet	SortedSet
WeakHashMap	AbstractMap	Map

Except for WeakHashMap, all concrete classes in the table also implement the Cloneable and java.io.Serializable interfaces.

When creating your own container classes based on one of the library's abstract classes, a good place to begin is by examining the source code file for one of the concrete classes in Table 14-3. This will provide useful guidelines for extending the abstract class and implementing interface methods. See instructions in Chapter 3, "Getting Started with Java 2," for getting and installing Java's source code files.

Other Container Classes

Table 14-4 lists two other classes in the container library that are used in container programming, but are not part of the interface and class hierarchy. As mentioned, I include the BitSet class as a member of the container library, but some other texts refer to it as a utility class. Both classes in the table are concrete implementations, ready to use.

TABLE 14-4 OTHER CONTAINER CLASSES

Class	Implements
BitSet	Cloneable, java.io.Serializable
Collections	none

Don't confuse the Collections (plural) class with the Collection (singular) interface. The Collections class provides utility methods such as sort() and binarySearch() to which you can pass container objects. The Collections class cannot be instantiated as an object — all of its public methods are static and are called in relation to the class name.

Interface and Class Diagrams

Because of the interrelationships among the container library's interfaces and classes, it's important to know which items descend from which others. This way, you can consult Java's sources and documentation for all of the methods available to a particular container. Following, then, are several figures that illustrate the relationships among the container library's interfaces and classes listed in the preceding sections.

Figure 14-1 shows a small legend for reference. In class diagrams, a single-line arrow shows that B extends A, which might be an interface or a class. A double-line arrow shows that B implements interface A. Note carefully the direction of the arrow — just because an interface or class appears physically higher in a diagram does not indicate its place in the hierarchy.

B extends A   B implements A

Figure 14-1: Container diagram legend

Figure 14-2, the most extensive of the container diagrams in this chapter, shows the interfaces and classes that descend from the Collection interface. Circled classes are concrete, ready-to-use implementations. Classes marked with an asterisk (all the concrete ones in this case) implement the two interfaces Cloneable and java.io.Serializable, as well as those shown in the diagram.

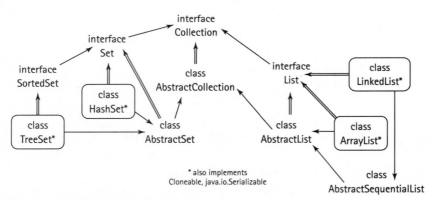

Figure 14-2: Collection interfaces and classes

From Figure 14-2, you can quickly tell that ArrayList (circled near the right side) implements the List interface (double-line arrow) and extends AbstractList (single-line arrow). Arrows always point toward a superclass or superinterface.

Notice also that Collection stands at the top of all other interfaces and classes. Two other interfaces, Set and List, extend Collection. Except for AbstractCollection, all other interfaces and classes descend from Set and List. This makes better sense when you realize that the words "set" and "list" are used in the most general way. A set is any unique collection of objects, not necessarily a mathematical set. A list is any group of objects stored or linked together in some way. A list could be a linked list data structure, but it might also be an array of objects.

> Not shown in Figure 14-2 is the Vector class, which you may find while browsing the java.util package. Although Vector extends AbstractList and implements List, the Vector and ArrayList classes are operationally the same. However, Vector methods are synchronized and can be used in threaded code; ArrayList is not thread-safe. Vector is one of Java's *legacy containers* (see that section in Chapter 18). New programs should use ArrayList in place of Vector.

Figure 14-3 shows the relationships of what you might consider to be the "other half" of the container library's interfaces and classes. All of the classes and one interface in this diagram are based on the Map interface.

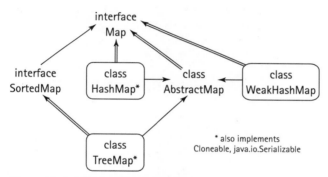

Figure 14–3: Map interfaces and classes

A Map is sometimes called an *association* because it maps keys to values. A SortedMap's values are maintained in key order. Most such containers are constructed from the concrete HashMap class. This creates a highly efficient storage device that uses hash values to search rapidly for keys, and to make quick insertions and deletions. If you need a sorted map, use the TreeMap class.

The WeakHashMap class provides a kind of caching ability in which objects can be inserted into a container and garbage collected. For example, a large number of picture objects or, perhaps, Web pages might be stored as weak references in a WeakHashMap. As such, they are subject to garbage collection provided the container's references to them are unique. By definition, weak references cannot be copied or preserved, and therefore WeakHashMap does not implement the Cloneable and java.io.Serializable interfaces.

Finally in this section, Figure 14-4 illustrates the relationships among Iterator interfaces and the container library's miscellaneous classes. Iterator objects are used to traverse containers. ListIterator objects are used with list-based container classes. The Collections and BitSet classes stand alone, and they are not related to any other interfaces or classes in the library.

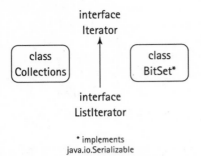

Figure 14–4: Iterator interfaces and other classes

The Collection Interface

All container classes implement one of two interfaces, Collection and Map (see Figures 14-2 and 14-3 in the preceding section). Listing 14-1, Collection.txt, shows the method declarations in the Collection interface. Chapter 17, "Map Collections," introduces the Map interface and related classes.

Listing 14–1: Collection.txt

```
001: // Collection interface methods
002: int size();
003: boolean isEmpty();
004: boolean contains(Object o);
005: Iterator iterator();
006: Object[] toArray();
007: Object[] toArray(Object a[]);
008: boolean add(Object o);
009: boolean remove(Object o);
010: boolean containsAll(Collection c);
011: boolean addAll(Collection c);
012: boolean removeAll(Collection c);
013: boolean retainAll(Collection c);
014: void clear();
015: boolean equals(Object o);
016: int hashCode();
```

Most Collection methods have obvious purposes (listings in other chapters in this part demonstrate many of them). For instance, as you probably realize without my help, the isEmpty() method returns true if the container has no objects. But other methods might not be so obvious. The iterator() method returns an Iterator object — see Chapter 15, "List Collections," for how to use one.

Two overloaded toArray() methods convert a container to an array of Object. The non-parameterized toArray() at line 006 always creates a new array. The second method lets you pass an existing array as an argument. If the container can be inserted into your array, it is used and returned; otherwise, a new array is created. The second method is more memory-efficient because it lets you reuse the same array for multiple array-conversion operations. Converting a container to an array does *not* clone the contained objects. References in the array refer to the original objects so, if you change an object's value in an array, the original container object also changes.

The `add()` and `remove()` methods provide the most basic ways to add and remove objects in a container. Concrete classes such as `ArrayList` and `HashMap` provide other techniques, as I discuss at the appropriate times.

The `addAll()` method adds all of another container's objects to this one in the same order as specified by the argument container's iterator. The `removeAll()` method removes all methods in this container equal to the ones in the argument passed to the method. The `retainAll()` method keeps all objects in this container that are the same as those in the container passed as an argument. Method `clear()` removes all objects from a container.

Two methods are inherited from `Object`, which provides default native implementations. Method `equals()` by default is true if this container equals the object argument (just the container reference, *not* its contents). However, certain classes such as `AbstractSet` override this method to return true only if the two containers are both of the same type, the same size, and have the same contents. If you are creating your own container classes, whether and how to implement `equals()` are important considerations. Method `hashCode()` returns a hash value for the container, enabling hashed containers to store other containers. This method also has a default implementation provided via `Object`, but you may override it to create a unique hash value for your objects' classes. See "Hash Tables" in Chapter 16, "Set Collections," for more information on the `hashCode()` method.

TIP For the full story on what a container offers, remember to examine its concrete class, the abstract class that it extends, and any interfaces that it implements.

Containers in Action

Now let's take a look at some simple but illustrative examples of a container in action. You'll then be ready to tackle each container class described in the coming chapters.

NOTE Containers are not synchronized for use in multi-threaded code. For instructions on how to create synchronized containers, and related issues, see Chapter 19, "Threaded Code."

Creating a Container

Creating a container object is easy. Just import the container class you want, create the object using new, and then call methods to insert and retrieve data objects. Listing 14-2, ContainerDemo.java, imports the ArrayList class and uses it to construct a container of string objects.

Listing 14-2: ContainerDemo.java

```
001: import java.util.ArrayList;
002:
003: class ContainerDemo {
004:  public static void main(String args[]) {
005:    ArrayList myList = new ArrayList(25);
006:    myList.add(new String("One"));
007:    myList.add(new String("Two"));
008:    myList.add("Buckle");
009:    String s = "My shoe";
010:    myList.add(s);
011:    System.out.println("There are " +
012:     myList.size() + " strings in myList");
013:    for (int i = 0; i < myList.size(); i++)
014:     System.out.println(myList.get(i));
015:  }
016: }
```

Line 005 constructs the container. In this case, the container's initial size is set to 25 objects. To construct a default container, omit the size argument:

```
ArrayList myList = new ArrayList();
```

All container classes have one or more similar constructors for creating containers in different ways. When using the default constructor with no arguments, the default size of an ArrayList container is 10 objects, but this number is not guaranteed. Either way, the container expands as necessary, and as memory allows, to accommodate more objects. Not all container constructors support an initial size argument — for example, the LinkedList class provides no means to reserve room for objects because, by nature, a linked list data structure expands and shrinks for each insertion and removal operation.

Using a Container

The ContainerDemo.java program in Listing 14-2 shows three typical ways to add objects to a list. The following statement, for example, uses new to construct a String object and add it to myList:

```
myList.add(new String("One"));
```

String could be an object of any class. The container is not restricted to holding objects of any particular kind – in fact, the same container can hold objects of different types. However, some operations such as sorting and searching might require those objects to be comparable, or a ClassCastException is thrown. So, extra care is called for when storing different objects in the same container.

For string containers, you can also add literal values using a statement such as

```
myList.add("Buckle");
```

Finally, you can construct an object and pass it to add(). This is probably the most common way to add new objects to a container:

```
String s = "My shoe";
myList.add(s);
```

Call size() as in the demonstration program to find out how many objects the container holds. Call get() to retrieve an object at a specified index. Because get() returns Object, you often have to use a type-cast expression to tell the compiler what type of object is retrieved:

```
String s = (String)myList.get(2);
```

One way to avoid having to use a type-cast expression is to declare an Object variable. Because every class extends Object, any object reference can be assigned to an Object variable. For example, the program could execute this statement:

```
Object obj = myList.get(1);
```

The obj object could then be passed to any method that declares an Object parameter, or it could be used in some other general way.

TIP Call the Object class's toString() method for any object to get its string representation. Override this method in your own classes to provide string representations of your data objects.

Container Exceptions

Container interfaces, abstract classes, and concrete classes are written to throw various unchecked exceptions. The following is not a complete list of all exceptions you might receive when using containers. You might receive other types thrown by methods in classes such as String, but the following are specifically documented in Java's container class library:

◆ ArrayStoreException — Thrown by a toArray() conversion method if a specified array's type is not a supertype of the classes of all objects in a container.

◆ ClassCastException — Thrown by various methods if two objects are incompatible for a specified operation such as a comparison during a sorting operation.

◆ IllegalArgumentException — Thrown by various methods to indicate a problem with arguments passed to the methods — for example, two index values in reverse order.

◆ IndexOutOfBoundsException — Thrown by various methods to indicate an index value is out of bounds for the container's size.

◆ UnsupportedOperationException — Thrown by various methods to indicate that, despite the method's presence in an implemented interface, the container class does not support that method. Many methods in the library's abstract classes intentionally throw this exception so that the subclass can safely choose not to implement selected methods.

The exceptions listed here are not used exclusively by container classes. Other Java classes may throw these same types of exceptions.

The last exception, UnsupportedOperationException, is a safety device that helps ensure the proper use of a container class. For example, if you create your own container from scratch, you might choose not to implement an inappropriate interface method — for example, inserting an object into the middle of a stack. Your abstract class simply throws the exception for all unneeded methods specified in the interface. The concrete class can then implement only the methods it needs.

All of the exceptions listed here are unchecked, meaning you do not have to call methods in try-catch blocks, nor do you have to specify that your own methods throw them. If you receive one of these exceptions, it should be considered a programming error to be fixed in the source code so the problem never occurs in the first place.

Summary

◆ Java's collection container class library provides a well-organized set of interfaces, abstract classes, and concrete classes from which you can construct containers for storing any kinds of objects.

◆ All containers are based on the `Collection` and `Map` interfaces. Abstract classes implement some, but not all, methods specified in an interface. Concrete classes implement one or more interfaces, and extend an abstract class.

◆ Most of the time, you can simply choose a concrete container class and use it as supplied. You may, however, create your own container classes. In that case, it is usually easier to extend an abstract class than it is to implement an interface from scratch.

◆ This chapter lists the container class library in table and diagram forms. Use the tables to understand the library's contents. Use the diagrams to find the relationships among the interfaces, abstract classes, and concrete classes.

◆ Using a concrete container class is easy. Just select a class such as `ArrayList` and use `new` to construct the container object. You can then call `Collection` methods such as `add()` and `remove()`.

◆ You may store any type of object in a container. You may also store objects of different types in the same container, but you might receive a `ClassCastException` error for certain operations unless the objects are mutually comparable.

◆ Container class methods throw unchecked exceptions for a variety of errors such as calling an unsupported method, or passing an out of bounds index value to a container method. These exceptions should be considered programming errors to be fixed in the source code so that the problem never occurs in the first place.

Chapter 15

List Collections

THE DIAGRAMS IN CHAPTER 14, "Introducing Collections," reveal that all collection containers stem from one of three interfaces — List, Set, and Map. Chapters 16 and 17 explain Set and Map collections. This chapter explores the List interface and its descendants.

 The word "list" here is used in a very general way to describe any container that might contain a list of items, as opposed to, say, an associative set. Thus a "list" might be an array (also called a *vector*), but it might also be a linked list.

IN THIS CHAPTER

- ◆ Implementing the List interface
- ◆ ArrayList containers
- ◆ LinkedList containers
- ◆ Searching List-based containers
- ◆ Building custom List containers

The List Interface

The List interface inherits and re-declares all methods from Collection (refer back to Listing 14-1). All interfaces and classes that descend from List include Collection's members plus those shown here in Listing 15-1, List.txt.

Listing 15-1: List.txt

```
001: // List interface methods not also in Collection
002: boolean addAll(int index, Collection c);
003: Object get(int index);
004: Object set(int index, Object element);
005: void add(int index, Object element);
006: Object remove(int index);
007: int indexOf(Object o);
008: int lastIndexOf(Object o);
```

```
009: ListIterator listIterator();
010: ListIterator listIterator(int index);
011: List subList(int fromIndex, int toIndex);
```

The List interface stipulates methods that are appropriate for list-like containers. Method addAll() overloads Collection addAll(), adding an integer index parameter. The index represents the insertion point at which the first object is added. Methods get() and set() retrieve and replace an object in a container. Method remove(), which overloads Collection remove(), removes an object at the specified index.

Two *index-of* methods find the index of a specified object in a container. The methods return –1 if no such object is found. The indexOf() method at line 007 finds the first occurrence of the specified object; lastIndexOf() finds the last one (the one having the highest index in the case of any duplicates). There are two listIterator() methods discussed in this chapter (see "Using the Iterator Interface" and "Using the ListIterator Interface").

Finally in List is method subList(), which returns a List container for the objects located at and between the specified two index values. This and similar methods that return full or partial containers are called *view methods*. They provide a new view into a container — they do not clone the container's contents. Changes made to an object in a view are made also to the original object in the container, sometimes referred to as the *backing container*.

The ArrayList Class

The concrete ArrayList class implements the List interface, and extends AbstractList, which provides implementations of several methods from Collection and List. Listing 15-2, ArrayList.txt, shows the public methods that the class itself implements. Keep in mind that listings such as ArrayList.txt show only constructors and methods not inherited from the class's underlying abstract class and interface.

Listing 15-2: ArrayList.txt

```
001: // ArrayList methods
002: public ArrayList();
003: public ArrayList(int initialCapacity);
004: public ArrayList(Collection c);
005: public void trimToSize();
006: public void ensureCapacity(int minCapacity);
007: public Object clone();
```

To find all supported methods for a concrete container class, you must also examine the class's interface and underlying abstract class. Refer back to Figures 14-2 and 14-3 to find the names of related interfaces and classes.

All container classes are required to provide at least two constructors — a default one with no parameters and one that takes a `Collection` object as an argument. `ArrayList` provides an additional constructor, making three ways to construct this type of container (see lines 002-004). You saw the first two constructors in ContainerDemo.java (Listing 14-2) and discussion. The third constructor lets you pass any other `Collection`-based container as an argument. The constructor is useful for converting one type of container to another. For example, if `oldList` is a `LinkedList` container, you can convert it to an `ArrayList` container with a simple statement:

```
ArrayList newList = new ArrayList(oldList);
```

Call `trimToSize()` to reduce an `ArrayList` container's capacity to the exact number of objects needed to hold those in the container. Don't do this frivolously. After a call to `trimToSize()`, the next addition to the container will cause it to expand, which probably means two copies of the container existing at least temporarily in memory. Call `ensureCapacity()` to expand the container to a certain size. This is good to do when you know the program will add numerous objects, which might cause periodic expansions. Increasing the container's capacity helps ensure that it is expanded infrequently, or at best, only once.

The LinkedList Class

Listing 15-3 shows another `List`-based container, `LinkedList`. This concrete class implements the `List` interface (Listing 15-1), and extends the `AbstractSequentialList` abstract class. Because `List` extends `Collection`, the `LinkedList` class also provides implementations of `Collection` methods. Shown here are only the constructors and public methods that `LinkedList` directly implements.

Listing 15-3: LinkedList.txt

```
001: // LinkedList methods
002: public LinkedList();
003: public LinkedList(Collection c);
004: public Object getFirst();
005: public Object getLast();
006: public Object removeFirst();
007: public Object removeLast();
008: public void addFirst(Object o);
009: public void addLast(Object o);
```

In this class, there are two constructors — the minimum required for `Collection`-based containers. There is no way to preset a `LinkedList`'s size. That would be senseless anyway because a linked-list data structure is composed entirely of objects linked together by memory references. Create a `LinkedList` container with a statement such as

```
LinkedList myList = new LinkedList();
```

Or, you can pass an existing `Collection` container as an argument. For example, the following statement converts a container `myArray` of type `ArrayList` to a `LinkedList`:

```
LinkedList myList = new LinkedList(myArray);
```

The `LinkedList` class provides three pairs of related methods for retrieving, removing, and adding objects to the container. Call `getFirst()` to return the object at the head of the list; call `getLast()` for the last object. These methods are fast because the container maintains references to its first and last objects. Likewise, `removeFirst()` and `removeLast()` quickly remove the first and last objects in the list respectively. When removing an object, if you don't save its reference, it may be subject to garbage collection if no other references to the object exist. These methods throw `NoSuchElementException` if the list is empty, so you might want to use code such as

```
if (!myList.isEmpty())
  myList.removeLast();
```

The `isEmpty()` method is inherited from `Collection` along with others. To erase a list entirely, call the inherited `clear()` method:

```
myList.clear();
```

To add new objects, call `addFirst()` and `addLast()`. As their names suggest, they add new objects to the head or tail of a `LinkedList` container. If your object class is named `YourClass`, use statements such as the following to insert new objects:

```
LinkedList yourList = new LinkedList();
yourList.addFirst(new YourClass());
YourClass obj = new YourClass();
yourList.addLast(obj);
```

In addition to the methods shown in Listing 15-3, `LinkedList` supports others for finding, removing, and adding objects. For example, you can call the `List` interface `get()` method to retrieve an indexed object from the container:

```
YourClass obj = (YourClass)yourList.get(2):
```

Be careful with code like that. If the index is out of bounds, the container throws `IndexOutOfBoundsException`. Also, because `get()` returns `Object`, a type-cast expression is usually necessary. However, the expression throws `ClassCastException` if the returned object is not of the specified class or subclass. To find an object's index in a `LinkedList`, call `indexOf()` like this:

```
int index = yourList.indexOf(obj);
```

It might seem odd to use integer indexes with `LinkedList` containers — classic linked lists rarely provide similar random-access capabilities. However, the `LinkedList` class implements both the `List` and `Collection` interfaces, and it therefore provides alternate ways to access objects. You might also find it odd that `LinkedList` provides no methods for traversing listed objects — but actually, it does, in the form of a `ListIterator` object as explained later in this chapter under "Using LinkedList Containers."

 Linked lists are particularly good for containers that need to conserve memory. Only the objects in the container occupy space — there are no empty spots in a linked list. Search operations such as `contains()`, however, are slower than when performed on a hashed container or a tree structure because the list has to be traversed sequentially. If you need speedy searches, an `ArrayList` or `TreeSet` container might be a better choice than a `LinkedList`.

Using ArrayList Containers

You saw a simple example of an `ArrayList` container in Chapter 14. That program (Listing 14-2, ContainerDemo.java) stored `String` objects in an `ArrayList`. More commonly you will need to store collections of objects of your own classes. To demonstrate some of the required techniques and associated problems you might run into, Listing 15-4, Chart.java, declares a `Chart` class for creating a database of objects to be stored in containers.

Listing 15–4: ArrayListDemo/Chart.java

```
001: public class Chart implements Comparable {
002:   public int number;
003:   public String name;
004:   public long scale;
005:   public Chart(int number, String name, long scale) {
006:     this.number = number;
007:     this.name = name;
008:     this.scale = scale;
009:   }
010:   public int compareTo(Object o) {
011:     Chart other = (Chart)o;
012:     return name.compareTo(other.name);
013:   }
```

```
014:  public String toString() {
015:    return number + "   " + name + "  1:" + scale;
016:  }
017: }
```

Among other information, nautical charts are identified by number and name, and they list their scale as a ratio — for example, 1:10,000. This makes a good example of a class that serves as a kind of database record. However, to keep the Chart class simple, I declared its three data members to be public (lines 002-004). These would normally be made private, and the class would provide access methods to read and write their values. The class constructor (lines 005-009) initializes a Chart object using instances of the three data types.

The Chart class implements Comparable and provides an implementation for that interface's compareTo() method (lines 010-013). Most objects in containers should similarly be comparable so that you can search and sort them. When comparing string data, it is easiest just to pass on the result of that data's class compareTo() method. As shown here, line 012 calls the String class's compareTo() method to compare the name fields in two Chart objects.

TIP A more fully implemented class might also override Object.equals(), and it might implement Cloneable and provide a clone() method. These methods are optional, however, and you don't need to provide them for use with containers.

The class also overrides toString() (lines 014-017), which returns a string representation of a Chart object's instance variables. It is almost always a good idea to override toString() unless the default Object implementation is adequate for your needs. By default, an object's string representation equals its class name and memory reference — not the kind of information you'd want your program's users to see.

Listing 15-5, ArrayListDemo.java, creates an ArrayList container and inserts several objects of the Chart class.

Listing 15-5: ArrayListDemo.java

```
001: import java.util.List;
002: import java.util.ArrayList;
003: import java.util.Collections;  // plural!
004: import Chart;
005:
006: class ArrayListDemo {
007:
008: // Display a List of objects
```

```
009:   public static void showContainer(List c) {
010:     for (int i = 0; i < c.size(); i++)
011:       System.out.println(c.get(i).toString());
012:   }
013:
014:   public static void main(String args[]) {
015: // Construct the container
016:     ArrayList charts = new ArrayList();
017:
018: // Insert some Data objects
019:     charts.add(new Chart(11013, "Morehead City Hrbr ", 12500));
020:     charts.add(new Chart(11552, "Neuse River        ", 40000));
021:     charts.add(new Chart(11428, "Dry Tortugas       ", 30000));
022:     charts.add(new Chart(11420, "Havana to Tampa Bay", 470940));
023:     charts.add(new Chart(25641, "Virgin Islands     ", 100000));
024:     charts.add(new Chart(26341, "Bermuda Islands    ", 50000));
025:
026: // Sort and display container
027:     Collections.sort(charts);
028:     showContainer(charts);
029:   }
030: }
```

The demonstration program begins by importing several interfaces and classes, including the Chart class (lines 001-004). Method showContainer() at lines 008-012 shows the object-oriented way to access objects in a List container. Notice that ShowContainer()'s parameter is an object of the List interface, not the ArrayList class. As a result, the method can operate on any container object of a class that implements List. However, the method assumes that the objects in the container provide a toString() method, as our Chart class does.

When declaring method parameters, it is usually best to specify the most general type possible. For example, instead of requiring an ArrayList object to be passed to a method such as ShowContainer(), specifying an object of the more general type List means that any object of a class that implements List can be passed to the method as an argument. This also simplifies replacing a program's container with another type — in this case, for example, any collection class that implements List.

The sample program constructs an ArrayList container at line 016 of a default size. Lines 019-024 show how to construct and add Chart objects to the container by calling the Collection class's add() method. Although this method returns a boolean true result if successful, the sample program throws out the returned values. However, in your own code, to confirm that an insertion worked, you can check that add() returns true.

Line 027 sorts the container by calling the sort() method in class Collections. Notice that this class name is plural — Collections is a utility class that provides various common methods such as sort(). (I introduce other Collections methods in the next chapter, and also in Chapter 18, "Utilities and Legacy Classes.") Objects are sorted by virtue of the Chart.compareTo() method, which compares only name fields. If this method is not provided, and if Chart does not implement Comparable, a ClassCastException is thrown.

> **TIP**
>
> If you receive a ClassCastException, especially for any container operations that sort or search objects, your class probably needs to implement a required interface such as Cloneable or Comparable and provide implementations for one or more interface methods.

After sorting, Line 028 passes the charts container to ShowContainer(), which displays the results on screen:

```
26341   Bermuda Islands       1:50000
11428   Dry Tortugas          1:30000
11420   Havana to Tampa Bay   1:470940
11013   Morehead City Hrbr    1:12500
11552   Neuse River           1:40000
25641   Virgin Islands        1:100000
```

Using Comparators and ArrayList

As mentioned earlier, the objects in a container can be compared, and therefore sorted, if the objects' class implements the Comparable interface and provides a compareTo() method. But what if you want to sort the objects on other fields — in Chart.scale order, for example? In that case, a good solution is to use a Comparator object to perform the comparison. This section explains how to write a Comparator object for the Chart class and use it in an ArrayList container, but the information applies generally to other object types and containers.

Comparator is an interface in the java.util package. One good way to implement this interface is to create a private, nested class (also called an *inner class)* that belongs strictly to your data object's outer class. In addition, the outer class provides *factory methods* that construct various Comparator objects for use in other code such as the Collections class sort() method, which lets you pass it a Comparator object to perform object comparisons.

Listing 15-6 shows a new version of the Chart class that demonstrates how to create Comparator objects using a private inner class. To save room here, I cut out lines that duplicate those in Listing 15-4 — if you are viewing the listing on screen, you see the complete text. The file is in the c15/ComparatorDemo directory on the CD-ROM.

Listing 15–6: ComparatorDemo/Chart.java

```
001: import java.util.Comparator;
002:
003: public class Chart implements Comparable {
004: // Constants
005:   final static int BYNUMBER = 1;
006:   final static int BYNAME = 2;
007:   final static int BYSCALE = 3;
...
025: // Comparator "factory" methods
026:   public static final Comparator byNumber() {
027:     return new ChartComparator(BYNUMBER);
028:   }
029:   public static final Comparator byName() {
030:     return new ChartComparator(BYNAME);
031:   }
032:   public static final Comparator byScale() {
033:     return new ChartComparator(BYSCALE);
034:   }
035:
036: // Private inner Comparator class
037:   private static class ChartComparator implements Comparator {
038:
039:     private int compType;  // Type of comparison to perform
040:
041:     // Constructor saves comparison type identifier
042:     ChartComparator(int compType) {
043:       this.compType = compType;  // BYNUMBER, BYNAME, or BYSCALE
044:     }
045:
046:     // Implement the Comparator interface's method
047:     public int compare(Object o1, Object o2) {
048:       Chart c1 = (Chart)o1;  // Type cast objects to Charts
049:       Chart c2 = (Chart)o2;
050:       switch (compType) {
051:        case BYNUMBER:
052:          return (c1.number < c2.number ? -1 :
053:          (c1.number == c2.number ? 0 : 1));
054:        case BYNAME:
055:          return c1.name.compareTo(c2.name);
056:        case BYSCALE:
```

```
057:        return (c1.scale < c2.scale ? -1 :
058:         (c1.scale == c2.scale ? 0 : 1));
059:      default:
060:       return 0;  // Satisfy compiler; can't happen
061:     }
062:    }
063:  } // private inner class
064: } // Chart class
```

The new Chart class imports java.util.Comparator (line 001), but the class itself does not implement this interface. Instead, Chart declares an inner class beginning at line 037. The class, which I named ChartComparator (it could have any name) is made private and static to the Chart class. This has two effects. One, because it is private, the inner class is available only to Chart methods. Two, because it is static, references to the inner class are made in reference to the Chart class, not to any specific Chart object. This provides other code access to the inner class's method for *all* Chart objects, not just for one specific instance.

ChartComparator implements the Comparator interface (see line 037), which stipulates two methods: compare() and equals(). Most of the time, you can implement only compare(). You do not have to provide an equals() method because Object provides a default implementation. In this example, lines 047-061 implement compare(), which receives two Object references, o1 and o2, to be compared. The method returns –1 if o1 < o2, 0 if o1 = o2, and +1 if o1 > o2.

The default Object.equals() compares only object references, not object contents. To do that, your class should override equals() and provide a suitable implementation.

In writing a Comparable class, the meaning of less, greater, and equals is up to you. Here, I use an integer value, compType, to indicate which type of comparison to make. For clarity, I also created three constants, BYNUMBER, BYNAME, and BYSCALE (see lines 005-007). In the compare() method, the first step is to cast the Object references to the real type of object being compared, namely a Chart (see lines 048-049). A switch statement then performs one of three comparisons based on compType. The default value at lines 059-060 merely satisfies the compiler's requirement that all methods return values of their declared types (except void). The default statement is never executed.

Three factory methods at lines 025-034, byNumber(), byName(), and byScale(), construct Comparator objects of each of the three types. These methods return type Comparator, *not* ChartComparator, which is private to the class and cannot be referred to by outsiders. Only the Chart class "knows" the actual type of the Comparator object. As far as Chart users are concerned, the factory methods return objects that can be passed to any other method that declares a Comparator object as a parameter.

Listing 15-7, ComparatorDemo.java, shows how to use the new `Chart` class and its `Comparator` factory methods to sort an `ArrayList` container three different ways. Again, I cut out a few lines that duplicate those in the similar ArrayList.java demonstration (Listing 15-5).

Listing 15-7: ComparatorDemo.java

```
...
006: class ComparatorDemo {
...
026:   // Sort and display container three ways:
027:     Collections.sort(charts, Chart.byNumber());
028:     System.out.println("\nBy number:");
029:     showContainer(charts);
030:
031:     Collections.sort(charts, Chart.byName());
032:     System.out.println("\nBy name:");
033:     showContainer(charts);
034:
035:     Collections.sort(charts, Chart.byScale());
036:     System.out.println("\nBy scale:");
037:     showContainer(charts);
038:   }
039: }
```

Three sets of three statements sort and display the container's objects. In each case, the `sort()` method in the `Collections` class is passed the `charts` container and a `Comparator` object, returned by calling one of the `Chart` class's factory methods. The `sort()` method uses the `Comparator` object to compare `Chart` objects, and in that way, to sort them according to whatever variables or other criteria are needed.

TIP To use a `Comparator` object to sort in reverse order, you can program its `compare()` method for objects A and B to return −1 if A > B, 0 if A = B, and +1 if A < B. But also see the discussion of the `Collections` class for another way to create a reverse `Comparator` in Chapter 18.

Using the Iterator Interface

When you need to access all objects in a `Collection`, it is often convenient to use an *iterator object*. The `Iterator` interface is used by containers to provide iterator objects that "know" how to traverse the container's data structure. The result is a more general way to access objects than by calling a container method such as

List.get(). The technique works for any container of a class that extends Collection. However, the order in which the objects are delivered is not defined unless the container itself imposes an ordering on them (for example, one that implements the SortedSet interface, described in the next chapter). Listing 15-8 shows the Iterator interface's methods.

Listing 15-8: Iterator.txt

```
001: // Iterator interface methods
002: boolean hasNext();
003: Object next();
004: void remove();
```

Although it might seem to be a lightweight among heavier interfaces, the Iterator interface's three methods provide well-defined access and removal rules for objects in containers. Method hasNext() returns true if there is another object in the container not yet accessed. Method next() returns the next object in the container. Method remove() deletes the object most recently returned by next(). Although these methods may seem intuitively simple, they must be used correctly to prevent an exception. When using Iterator objects, it's important to obey these rules:

◆ If there is no next object in the container, next() throws NoSuchElementException. To prevent that exception, *always* call hasNext() before calling next().

◆ The remove() method throws UnsupportedOperationException if removal via an Iterator object is unsupported by the implementing class. The only remedy is to not call remove() for this container's Iterator.

◆ The remove() method throws IllegalStateException if called improperly – typically by failing to first call next(). To prevent this exception, always call remove() *only* after calling hasNext() and next(), in that order.

◆ An Iterator object is not guaranteed to remain stable if the container is modified in any way *except* by calling the Iterator's remove() method.

In older Java collection classes, the Enumeration interface resembled Iterator. New code should always use Iterator objects. See Chapter 18 for more information on Enumeration and other "legacy classes."

Another demonstration of the Chart class shows how to use Iterator objects to access a container's contents, and also to remove objects. The important difference between this demonstration and the others in this chapter is that the techniques work the same for all container classes based on the Collection interface. (Using an Iterator with Map-based containers also works, but requires creating a Set view of the container, as explained in Chapter 17.)

Listing 15-9, IteratorDemo.java, shows how to use an Iterator with an ArrayList container. As with some other listings in this chapter, I deleted duplicate lines to show only the new code added to the program.

Listing 15-9: IteratorDemo.java

```
001: import java.util.Iterator;
002: import java.util.Collection;
003: import java.util.ArrayList;
004: import Chart;
005:
006: class IteratorDemo {
007:
008: // Display a Collection using an Iterator
009:  public static void showContainer(Collection c) {
010:   Chart achart;
011:   Iterator I = c.iterator();  // Get Iterator for Collection
012:   while (I.hasNext()) {        // Always call hasNext()
013:    achart = (Chart)I.next();  //  before calling next()
014:     System.out.println(achart.toString());
015:   }
016:  }
...
033:    // Erase first object
034:    Iterator I = charts.iterator();  // Get an Iterator object
035:    if (I.hasNext()) {               // Always call hasNext() and
036:     Chart c = (Chart)I.next();      //  next() before
037:     I.remove();                     //  calling remove()
038:    }
039:    System.out.println("\nAfter removing first object");
040:    showContainer(charts);
041:
042:    // Use Iterator to remove all objects
043:    I = charts.iterator();  // Get a fresh Iterator
044:    while (I.hasNext()) {
045:     I.next();     // Don't need to save returned object
046:     I.remove();   // Removes object last returned by next()
047:    }
048:    System.out.println("\nAfter removing all objects");
049:    System.out.println("Container size = " + charts.size());
050:  }
051: }
```

The new program imports the Iterator and Collection interfaces, along with ArrayList and Chart (lines 001-004). (A copy of the Chart.java file is in the c15/IteratorDemo directory for convenience.) Lines 008-016 implement the ShowContainer() method using an Iterator. It is useful to compare the listing's new method with the one from earlier demonstrations, repeated here:

```
public static void showContainer(List c) {
  for (int i = 0; i < c.size(); i++)
    System.out.println(c.get(i).toString());
}
```

Of key importance is the change from a List to a Collection parameter (see line 009). This makes the method more general because it can now work with any Collection container, not only those that implement List. Line 010 defines a Chart object, named achart, for use in accessing each container object. The next statement creates the Iterator:

```
Iterator I = c.iterator();
```

Because Collection declares the iterator() method, the statement can call it for any container class (except, as mentioned, for Map containers).

TIP   The Iterator interface is capitalized. The iterator() method in Collection is spelled in all lowercase.

After getting an Iterator object, simply named I in this case, use it as shown at lines 012-015 to access all objects in a container. A generic form of the same while loop looks something like this:

```
while (I.hasNext()) {
  YourClass obj = (YourClass)I.next();
  // Do something with obj
}
```

The code satisfies the rule that hasNext() must be called before every call to next(). The type-cast expression is usually needed because I.next() returns Object. Cast that to your own class, and then do whatever you want with the resulting object. If the object is not of the specified class, or a subclass, the cast throws the runtime error ClassCastException.

To remove an object from a container, use statements such as these (similar to those in the demonstration at lines 035-038):

```
if (I.hasNext()) {
 YourClass obj = (YourClass)I.next();
 I.remove();
}
```

If all you want to do is remove an object, you don't need to save its reference. In that case, the preceding code simplifies to

```
if (I.hasNext()) {
 I.next();
 I.remove();
}
```

The statement order ensures that remove() does not throw an exception. However, it might still throw UnsupportedOperationException if the container does not support removal using an Iterator. Similar code at lines 044-047 shows how to use an Iterator to safely remove all objects from any Collection container, but you could more easily call the container's clear() method.

Using LinkedList Containers

Like ArrayList, the LinkedList class (refer back to Listing 15-3) is based on the Collection interface, and many of the same techniques already discussed work the same for LinkedList containers. However, unlike an ArrayList, a LinkedList has no initial capacity. A LinkedList grows for each object inserted, and it shrinks for each one removed.

In a LinkedList container, objects are linked together by references. This provides for fast insertions and removals. With an ArrayList, those same operations might require shifting objects up and down, a time-costly maneuver for objects in the middle of a big container. The general rule is that, if you need fast insertions and removals, use a LinkedList. But if you need fast random access to objects, use an ArrayList.

 For very large containers, insertions in a LinkedList might avoid a wasteful garbage collection that may be needed to acquire enough memory to expand an ArrayList.

To demonstrate how to create and use a LinkedList container, Listing 15-10, LinkedListDemo.java, shows another version of the chart display program. (For convenience, a copy of the Chart.java listing is in the c15/LinkedListDemo directory.)

Listing 15-10: LinkedListDemo.java

```
001: import java.util.List;
002: import java.util.LinkedList;
003: import java.util.ListIterator;
004: import java.util.Collections;
005: import Chart;
006:
007: class LinkedListDemo {
008:
009:  static final boolean FORWARD = true;
010:  static final boolean REVERSE = false;
011:
012: // Display a LinkedList using a ListIterator
013: //  in forward or reverse order
014:  public static void showContainer(List c, boolean forward) {
015:   Chart achart;
016:   if (forward) {
017:    // Show in forward order
018:    ListIterator I = c.listIterator();
019:    while (I.hasNext()) {
020:     achart = (Chart)I.next();
021:     System.out.println(achart.toString());
022:    }
023:   } else {
024:    // Show in reverse order
025:    ListIterator I = c.listIterator(c.size());
026:    while (I.hasPrevious()) {
027:     achart = (Chart)I.previous();
028:     System.out.println(achart.toString());
029:    }
030:   }
031:  }
032:
033:  public static void main(String args[]) {
034: // Construct the container
035:   LinkedList charts = new LinkedList();  // Can't specify size
036:   Chart achart;  // For accessing the container's objects
037:
038: // Insert some Data objects
039:   charts.add(new Chart(11013, "Morehead City Hrbr ", 12500));
...
046:   // Sort the LinkedList container
047:   Collections.sort(charts);
048:
049:   // Display head and tail objects
```

```
050:    System.out.println("\nHead object is:");
051:    achart = (Chart)charts.getFirst();
052:    System.out.println(achart.toString());
053:    System.out.println("\nTail object is:");
054:    achart = (Chart)charts.getLast();
055:    System.out.println(achart.toString());
056:
057:    // Show list in forward and reverse order
058:    System.out.println("\nList in forward order");
059:    showContainer(charts, FORWARD);
060:    System.out.println("\nList in reverse order");
061:    showContainer(charts, REVERSE);
062:    }
063: }
```

Much of the new program resembles others in this chapter. To create a LinkedList container, the program executes this statement at line 035:

```
LinkedList charts = new LinkedList();
```

The only significant difference here is that, unlike with an ArrayList object, there's no reason to specify an initial size for the LinkedList container — in fact, it is not possible to do so. The program calls add() as before to insert a few Chart objects into the container (lines 037-044, some of which are deleted to save space). This demonstrates that, because LinkedList is based on the Collection interface, a program can call interface methods such as add() just as it can for other Collection containers.

The next two sections discuss a few more techniques demonstrated in the sample program.

Sorting LinkedList Containers

Listing 15-10 shows how to sort a LinkedList container. The easiest method is to simply call the Collections (plural) class method, sort(), as shown at line 047. This works the same as for ArrayList containers because both classes implement the List interface.

Calling sort() as shown here sorts the objects in their natural order — in this case using the compareTo() method implemented by Chart. Alternatively, you could use Comparator-object factory methods as demonstrated earlier in this chapter (see Listing 15-6). In terms of sorting, ArrayList and LinkedList containers operate identically.

Swapping two objects in a LinkedList means adjusting four references, since each object is linked to its next and previous objects (if any). Swapping two objects in an ArrayList container means exchanging only two object references. So, sorting an ArrayList may be faster than for the same data in a LinkedList. In any event, for either container, no objects are actually moved by sorting. Only references are moved.

Using the ListIterator Interface

For most LinkedList containers, you will probably use a ListIterator object to access the container's contents. Although you can also call Collection and List interface methods – the LinkedList class implements both interfaces – using a ListIterator makes it easy to move through the container's objects in forward or reverse order. The LinkedList class also provides methods to get and remove a list's head and tail objects. They are particularly useful in creating containers that implement *stack* and *queue* data structures. Listing 15-11, ListIterator.txt, shows the ListIterator interface's methods.

Listing 15–11: ListIterator.txt

```
001: // Inherited Iterator methods
002: boolean hasNext();
003: Object next();
004: void remove();
005: // ListIterator interface methods
006: boolean hasPrevious();
007: Object previous();
008: int nextIndex();
009: int previousIndex();
010: void set(Object o);
011: void add(Object o);
```

The ListIterator interface extends Iterator (see Listing 15-8), and its first three methods, hasNext(), next(), and remove(), are simply inherited and redeclared. These methods work the same as described earlier under "Using the Iterator Interface." In addition, ListIterator provides two similar methods to move through objects in reverse order. Method hasPrevious() returns true if there is a previous object. Method previous() returns that object. As with hasNext() and next(), you must call hasPrevious() before calling previous(), or you risk a NoSuchElementException. After calling previous(), you may call remove() to delete the returned object.

Two integer methods, nextIndex() and previousIndex(), return the index value of the next or previous object that would be returned by calling next() or previous(). Method nextIndex() returns the container's size if the iterator is at the end of the list (that is, if `hasNext()` would return `false`). Method `previousIndex()` returns –1 if the iterator is at the head of the list (if `hasPrevious()` would return `false`).

Using integer indexes might seem more appropriate for an array-like structure than for a linked list, but the `nextIndex()` and `previousIndex()` methods provide handy ways to obtain index values for passing to methods such as the `List` interface's `remove(int index)`. However, be extremely careful with this technique — any operations that change, insert, or delete any objects in the container may invalidate the `ListIterator` or `Iterator` object. Only the `Iterator` interface's `remove()` method, and the `ListIterator` interface's `remove()`, `set()`, and `add()` methods, are guaranteed not to invalidate the iterator object.

> **TIP** After changing any objects in a container — for example, by calling a container class's `add()` method — always get a fresh `Iterator` or `ListIterator` object for traversing the container.

The demonstration program's `ShowContainer()` method (refer back to Listing 15-10, lines 014-031) shows how to use a `ListIterator` object to traverse a `LinkedList` container in forward or reverse order. Moving forward is similar to using a plain `Iterator` object, shown here in generic form:

```
ListIterator I = c.listIterator();
while (I.hasNext()) {
 obj = (YourClass)I.next();
 // Do something with obj
}
```

As shown on the first line, call the `listIterator()` method, declared by the `List` interface and implemented in `LinkedList`, to obtain a `ListIterator` object. (The interface is capitalized; the method is not.) You can then call the `ListIterator`'s `hasNext()` and `next()` methods to walk through all objects in the list in forward order. Unlike for plain `Iterator` objects, which do not guarantee in what order objects are returned, `ListIterator` objects always return the objects in the same order as they were inserted into the list.

Moving backwards through a linked list is almost the same, but for one additional parameter passed to the `listIterator()` method:

```
ListIterator I = c.listIterator(c.size());
while (I.hasPrevious()) {
 obj = (YourClass)I.previous();
 // Do something with obj
}
```

Specify the container's size as shown on the first line to obtain a `ListIterator` object that initially refers to the tail of the list. Without this parameter, the first call to `hasPrevious()` would return `false`, and no objects would be returned.

 Although of little practical value, it is interesting to note that calling the `ListIterator` interface's `next()` and `previous()` methods repeatedly return the same object from a `LinkedList` container without throwing an exception.

Finally in the `ListIterator` interface are two methods that you can use to change an object in a `LinkedList` container, and to add a new one (see Listing 15-11, lines 010 and 011). Use `set()` to change an object's value. Use the `add()` method to insert a new object into a `LinkedList` container. Though seemingly simple, the methods are a little tricky to use. For best results, follow these guidelines:

◆ Always call `next()` or `previous()` before calling `set()`, or you receive an `IllegalStateException`. This rule implies that you also call `hasNext()` or `hasPrevious()` as previously mentioned.

◆ In calling `add()` or `remove()`, you must call `next()` or `previous()` before calling `set()`, or you risk the same type of exception. Again, this implies that you also call `hasNext()` or `hasPrevious()`.

◆ You may call `add()` at any time, even for an empty list. The new object is inserted between the object that would be returned by a call to `next()` and `previous()`, or at the list's head or tail as appropriate.

◆ The `add()` and `set()` methods throw `UnsupportedOperationException` if the methods are not implemented by this `ListIterator` object, `ClassCastException` if the object is incompatible in some way, and `IllegalArgumentException` for any other errors (however, I can find no evidence that this last exception is ever thrown for a `ListIterator`).

Use `add()` to insert a new object ahead of the one that would be returned by `next()`, or at the end of the list. For example, you can add the following statements to the LinkedListDemo.java program in Listing 15-10 to add a new `Chart` object to the container:

```
ListIterator I = charts.listIterator();
I.add(new Chart(26262, "Grand Turk Island  ", 25000));
showContainer(charts, FORWARD);
```

Because the `ListIterator` is freshly created, the new object is inserted at the head of the `LinkedList`. It is safe to call `add()` this way without first calling next() or previous(), but in many cases, add() and set() are called in loops that search a container. For example, you could replace an existing Chart with a new one by calling set(), but as mentioned, this method requires careful use. First, we need a few variables:

```
boolean found = false;
Chart c;
ListIterator I = charts.listIterator();
```

The ListIterator is freshly created, and so the list is ready for perusing from head to tail. A while loop seems to be a good choice for the search:

```
while (!found && I.hasNext()) {
 c = (Chart)I.next();
 if (c.number == 11552) {
  I.set(new Chart(26262, "Grand Turk Island  ", 25000));
  found = true; // End search
 }
}
```

The loop iterates while found is false and I.hasNext() returns true, indicating we haven't yet reached the end of the list. In the loop, next() returns the next Chart object to inspect. If its number field equals the one we want, 11552 in this example, method set() replaces that object with a new one.

If you simply want to update an object's information, you don't have to call set(). For instance, to change the object's name variable, you can simply write code such as the following:

```
if (c.number == 11552) {
 c.name = "New chart name";
 found = true; // End search
}
```

Searching List Containers

One way to search a container is to use an Iterator or ListIterator as described in the preceding section. This section discusses a few other search methods you can use with Collection- and List-based containers.

Collection Search Methods

If you just want to know whether a Collection container contains an object, call the contains() method, which returns true or false. For example, if obj is the object to find, and C is any Collection-based container, this statement tests whether C contains obj:

```
if (C.contains(obj))
  System.out.println("Found object!");
```

That may seem simple enough, but there are two facts about `contains()` to keep in mind. One, if `obj` is `null`, the `contains()` method returns true only if the container holds at least one object reference that is `null`. Two, and most important, `contains()` relies on `Object.equals()` to compare objects. Override this method in your own class to perform a comparison of your objects' content; otherwise, `equals()` returns true only if two object *references* are the same. In other words, if your class has a `String name` instance variable, `Object.equals()` returns false for two objects A and B even if `A.name` holds the same string as `B.name`. To compare `name` instance variables for two objects, assuming that's your intention, the objects' class must override and provide an `equals()` method.

TIP Any container may contain a `null` object reference, even a `LinkedList`. You might insert a `null` reference into a container as a sentinel and use it like a bookmark.

A related `Collection` interface method, `containsAll()`, compares two containers by calling `Collection.contains()` for all of their objects. In the following statement, the method returns `true` only if container A contains all the same objects as B (again, your class probably needs to provide an `equals()` method to compare the objects' contents):

```
if (A.contains(B))
  System.out.println("The containers are equivalent");
```

List Search Methods

For searching containers based on the `List` interface (for example, instances of the classes `ArrayList` and `LinkedList`), you can use the `indexOf()` and `lastIndexOf()` methods. These methods perform a linear search of a `List` container in forward and reverse order respectively, internally using a `ListIterator` object. If `obj` is the object to find, and C is a `List` container, the following code finds the index of the first such object:

```
int index = C.indexOf(obj);
if (index < 0)
  System.out.println("Object not found");
```

The method returns –1 if the object is not found. Call `lastIndexOf()` to find the index of the last matching occurrence:

```
int index = C.lastIndexOf(obj);
if (index >= 0)
 System.out.println("Highest index = " + index);
```

As with `indexOf()`, `lastIndexOf()` returns −1 if the object isn't found. The method performs its search using a `ListIterator` in reverse order, and it returns the highest index of the target object.

> **TIP** If the `List` container has duplicate objects, `indexOf()` finds the first such object; `lastIndexOf()` finds the last one. The container does not need to be sorted before calling these methods.

Binary Search Method

Another powerful technique for searching containers is provided by the `Collections` class's `binarySearch()` methods. In general terms, the *binary search algorithm* works by looking for an object in one half of a sorted container. If the sought object is greater than the examined object, the next comparison is made in the next half of the container. By continually dividing the search region this way, the object is more quickly located in most cases than it would be by a straight sequential search of the container from one end to the other.

Before calling `binarySearch()`, you must remember to sort the container in ascending order using any of the techniques described in this chapter. There are two overloaded versions of the method:

```
int binarySearch(List list, Object key);
int binarySearch(List list, Object key, Comparator c);
```

To the first version, pass any `List`-based container and the object that you want to find. This method requires that the `key` object's class implements the `Comparable` interface and provides a `compareTo()` method (for help doing that, refer to Listing 15-4, ArrayListDemo/Chart.java). Alternatively, call the second `binarySearch()` method and pass a third `Comparator` argument to be used in comparing the container's objects. In that case, the `key` object's class does not need to implement `Comparable` (it may do so, however). Instead, the class can provide a factory method that returns a `Comparator` object to be used in performing the binary search (refer to Listing 15-6, ComparatorDemo/Chart.java for an example).

> **TIP** If the container is not sorted, the results of calling `binarySearch()` are not defined. Always sort the container before calling `binarySearch()`!

A typical container holds objects that you may need to search for based on various object values. For example, in a database, you might need to perform searches for name, city, state, and zip code information. To demonstrate how to use `binarySearch()` to solve this type of problem, Listing 15-12, BinaryDemo.java, uses the `Chart` class from Listing 15-6. As already explained, this class provides factory methods that return `Comparator` objects. The demonstration program uses one of these methods to search a list of `Chart` objects by number. The program resembles other demonstrations in this chapter — to save space, I deleted duplicate lines (on screen you see the entire listing).

Listing 15-12: BinaryDemo.java

```
001: import java.util.List;
002: import java.util.Comparator;
003: import java.util.ArrayList;
004: import java.util.Collections;
005: import Chart;
006:
007: class BinaryDemo {
...
015:  public static void main(String args[]) {
016: // Construct the container
017:    ArrayList charts = new ArrayList();
...
027: // Display all objects if none requested
028:    if (args.length == 0) {
029:     System.out.println("\nContainer contents:");
030:     showContainer(charts);
031:     System.out.println("\nEnter a chart number to find");
032:     System.out.println("ex. java BinaryDemo 11428");
033:    } else {
034:
035: // Search container using Collections.binarySearch()
036:     try {
037: // Preparations for a binarySearch();
038:       int num = Integer.parseInt(args[0]); // Get chart number
039:       Comparator comp = Chart.byNumber();  // Create Comparator
040:       Chart key = new Chart(num, "", 0);   // Create search key
041:       Collections.sort(charts, comp);      // Sort container
042:
043: // Search the container for the key object
044:       int index = Collections.binarySearch(charts, key, comp);
045:       if (index < 0)
046:        System.out.println("Chart #" + args[0] + " not found");
047:       else
048:        System.out.println(charts.get(index)); // Show chart
```

```
049:     }
050:     catch (NumberFormatException e) {
051:     System.out.println("Error in argument " + e.getMessage());
052:     }
053:   }
054:   }
055: }
```

Compile and run the program to display a list of the container's Chart objects and to print brief instructions. Type the following lines shown in bold:

```
javac BinaryDemo.java
java BinaryDemo
Container contents:
11013  Morehead City Hrbr   1:12500
...
26341  Bermuda Islands      1:50000
Enter a chart number to find
ex. java BinaryDemo 11428
```

To activate the binarySearch() method, enter a chart number to find:

```
java BinaryDemo 25641
25641  Virgin Islands  1:100000
```

If you enter a number for a chart that's not in the container, the program reports this fact with the message:

```
java BinaryDemo 11542
Chart #11542 not found
```

Finally, if you enter a non-integer argument, the program catches the resulting exception and reports the error:

```
java BinaryDemo Bermuda
Error in argument Bermuda
```

All of these actions are demonstrative of the kinds of programming you may need when calling binarySearch(). In the program's listing, lines 038-041 show the preparations typically needed before starting a search. The first statement converts the command-line argument from a string to an integer:

```
int num = Integer.parseInt(args[0]);
```

This might throw `NumberFormatException`, and must be executed in a `try-catch` block as shown in the listing. The next statement creates the `Comparator` object to be used in sorting and searching the container:

```
Comparator comp = Chart.byNumber();
```

You could call another factory method such as `byScale()` to create a different `Comparator` object for searching on alternate fields. However, because the `Comparator` object compares `Chart` *objects,* not merely individual fields, we also need a full `Chart` object to serve as the search key:

```
Chart key = new Chart(num, "", 0);
```

You might think that only `num` is needed for the key, since in this example the program searches for a chart by number. However, an `int` value is not an object, and there is no way to pass it to `binarySearch()`. A good solution, as demonstrated here, is to create a full object with only the necessary field initialized to the search key. In this case, a new `Chart` object is created with the requested number, but the other fields are set to meaningless values. (Another way to do this is to have the class provide alternate constructors that would, for instance, create a `Chart` object given only a chart's number.)

The final preparation step sorts the container, using the `Comparator` object just created, and then calls `binarySearch()`:

```
Collections.sort(charts, comp);
int index = Collections.binarySearch(charts, key, comp);
```

The same `Comparator` object is used in sorting and searching the `charts` container for the `key` object. If the method returns –1, the search failed. Otherwise, `index` identifies the matching `Chart`. In this example, the program prints the object by calling the `List` interface's `get()` method:

```
System.out.println(charts.get(index));
```

Behind the scenes, `println()` calls the `Chart` class's `toString()` method for a string representation of the found object. Because `toString()` is inherited from `Object`, no type-cast expression is needed here. But if you want to save a reference to the saved object, use code such as the following:

```
Chart t = (Chart)charts.get(index);
String s = t.toString();
System.out.println(s);
```

The first statement requires a type-cast expression to tell the compiler that `get()`, which returns `Object`, actually returns a `Chart` object. This throws

`ClassCastException` if the object is not a `Chart`, or of an extended class, so be careful with code like this. The second statement calls `Chart.toString()` for a string representation of the found object.

The `binarySearch()` methods throw `ClassCastException` if the objects in the container cannot be compared. This typically happens because the objects' class fails to implement the `Comparable` interface and provide a `compareTo()` method. However, it can also happen if the same container holds objects of different classes that are not mutually comparable. If you run into this trouble, you might create a class with instance variables of the dissimilar types to store in the container, and then provide a `Comparator` factory method along with a `compareTo()` method that performs the necessary comparison for two objects of the class.

Building Custom Lists

Creating a custom `List`-based container from scratch means implementing the `List` interface and extending one of its descendant abstract classes such as `AbstractSequentialList`. But in many cases, you don't have to work so hard. Consider instead simply extending an existing concrete class and add the new capabilities you need. After all, that's what classes are for — don't start over from scratch when you can more simply attach new code onto an existing class.

Writing a Stack Class

To demonstrate how to create a custom `List` class, and at the same time to illustrate how to implement an algorithmic data structure using a Java container, I wrote a `Stack` class that extends `LinkedList`. The result is Listing 15-13, Stack.java. (This file is in the c15/StackDemo directory.)

Listing 15-13: StackDemo/Stack.java

```
001: import java.util.Collection;
002: import java.util.LinkedList;
003:
004: class StackEmptyException extends Exception {
005:   StackEmptyException(String s) { super(s); }
006: }
007:
008: public class Stack extends LinkedList {
009: // Constructors
010:   public Stack() { super(); }
```

```
011:   public Stack(Collection c) { super(c); }
012: // Public methods
013:   public void push(Object o) {
014:    addLast(o);
015:   }
016:   public Object pop() throws StackEmptyException {
017:    if (size() == 0)
018:     throw new StackEmptyException("pop on empty stack");
019:    return removeLast();
020:   }
021:   public Object peek() throws StackEmptyException {
022:    if (size() == 0)
023:     throw new StackEmptyException("peek on empty stack");
024:    return getLast();
025:   }
026: // Unsupported methods (incomplete -- see text)
027:   public final Object removeFirst() {
028:    throw new UnsupportedOperationException();
029:   }
030:   public final void addFirst(Object o) {
031:    throw new UnsupportedOperationException();
032:   }
033: }
```

 The java.util package provides its own Stack class. However, this is an older legacy class that is best not used in new code.

The Stack class shown in the listing implements a classic stack data structure with methods for pushing new objects onto a stack and popping off existing ones. A classic stack is a last-in-first-out (LIFO) data structure. Only the object at the top of the stack is available for use – like plates in a spring-loaded dish bin. However, Stack provides a method to peek at the top item without removing it.

The source code begins by importing the Collection interface and the LinkedList class. It also declares an exception class, StackEmptyException, for illegal operations such as attempting to pop an object off an empty stack. Stack extends the concrete class, LinkedList (see line 008).

Two constructors at lines 010-011 provide the means to construct Stack containers. As mentioned, the Collection interface specifies that all containers provide at least two ways to construct container objects – a default constructor, and one that takes a Collection object argument. In this case, there's nothing new to initialize in either constructor, so the Stack constructors simply pass on their duties to the LinkedList constructors by calling super().

Further into the `Stack` class, three public methods at lines 013-025 – `push()`, `pop()`, and `peek()` – implement the classic stack algorithm's operations. The methods simply call `LinkedList` methods to do their jobs – `addLast()`, `removeLast()`, and `getLast()`. Two of the methods, `pop()` and `peek()`, throw `StackEmptyException` if called for an empty stack. These are checked exceptions, requiring the methods to be called in a `try-catch` block.

 If the `Stack` class methods didn't throw an exception for illegal operations, the underlying `LinkedList` methods would throw the unchecked `NoSuchElementException`. Such an exception is considered to be a programming error that should be prevented from ever occurring. The `Stack` class shows one way to do that by effectively replacing the possibility of receiving an unchecked exception with a checked exception that can be properly handled, and most important, verified for proper use by the compiler.

Preventing Illegal Method Calls

Another concern when extending a container class is the inheritance of methods that you don't want programmers to use. For instance, in this case, because `Stack` extends `LinkedList`, inherited methods provide illegal ways to access a `Stack` data structure. There is nothing to prevent a program from executing a statement such as

```
myStack.remove(2);  // ???
```

A classic stack's contents must be accessed only by popping them off the top of the structure (but, as mentioned, peeking at the top object is allowed).

One way to prevent calling inherited methods that would cause harm in the extended class is to have them throw an exception as shown at lines 026-032. For example, to prevent `Stack` users from calling the inherited `removeFirst()` method, override it like this:

```
public final Object removeFirst() {
  throw new UnsupportedOperationException();
}
```

The `UnsupportedOperationException` class is provided by the `java.lang` package, and is therefore available to all Java code. Because the `removeFirst()` method is declared `public`, it can still be called, but it always throws the unchecked exception. Even if the user attempts to catch the exception, the method does not call its superclass method, and therefore, the new method has no effect. Additionally, the method is made `final` so that a class that extends `Stack` cannot override `removeFirst()` in a vain attempt to reactivate the illegal operation.

Using the Stack Class

Listing 15-14, StackDemo.java, demonstrates how to use the Stack class described in the preceding section.

Listing 15-14: StackDemo.java

```
001: import Stack;
002:
003: class StackDemo {
004:  public static void main(String args[]) {
005:    String s;
006:    try {
007:      Stack fruitStack = new Stack();
008:      fruitStack.push("Apples");
009:      fruitStack.push("Peaches");
010:      fruitStack.push("Pumpkin");
011: // Enable following to force an unchecked exception
012: //    fruitStack.removeFirst();
013: // Peek at top of stack
014:      s = (String)fruitStack.peek();
015:      System.out.println("\nTop of stack = " + s);
016: // Pop all objects from stack
017:      System.out.println("\nPopping all objects:");
018:      while (!fruitStack.isEmpty()) {
019:       s = (String)fruitStack.pop();
020:       System.out.println(s);
021:      }
022: // Enable following to force a checked exception
023: //    s = (String)fruitStack.pop();
024:    } catch (StackEmptyException e) {
025:      System.out.println("*** Error: " + e.getMessage());
026:    }
027:  }
028: }
```

Line 007 creates a Stack container using the class's default constructor. After that, a few strings are pushed onto the stack by calling the Stack class's push() method. Line 014 peeks at the top object in the stack. The String objects are then popped off the stack and displayed using a while loop at lines 018-021 that executes until the Stack object is empty.

To experiment with the Stack class's exceptions, enable line 012, compile, and run to force an UnsupportedOperationException to be thrown. This happens when the enabled statement calls the illegal method, removeFirst(), that Stack inherits from LinkedList. Enable line 023 to force a checked StackEmptyException when trying to pop an empty stack.

Summary

- ◆ The `List` interface provides fundamental methods for list-like containers. The word "list" is used in a general way for any objects that might be listed together, not necessarily for a linked-list data structure.

- ◆ The `ArrayList` and `LinkedList` classes implement the `List` interface. They provide two different ways to create lists of objects.

- ◆ An `ArrayList` container is similar to an array — it stores its object references physically together in memory. The container automatically expands as needed to hold objects added to it. You may specify an initial size for an `ArrayList` container, and you may expand it in advance of insertions. An `ArrayList` container provides rapid, random access to objects using index values.

- ◆ The `LinkedList` class links its objects together using references. This type of container grows and shrinks for every insertion or deletion and is potentially more memory-efficient than `ArrayList`. Insertions and removals from a `LinkedList` are also potentially faster than for similar operations in an `ArrayList`, especially for objects in the middle of the container.

- ◆ The `Collection` and `List` interfaces provide methods such as `contains()` and `indexOf()` that you can use to search `List`-based containers. The `Collections` class provides a `binarySearch()` method that performs fast and versatile searches for any `List`-based container, but you must remember to sort the container before calling this method.

- ◆ To build a custom `List` container, you could implement the `List` interface and extend an abstract class such as `AbstractList`. However, it is often easier to simply extend a concrete class such as `ArrayList` and add the new programming you need. The `Stack` class in this chapter demonstrates this technique and also shows how to throw an exception that prevents calls to inherited methods that are inappropriate or harmful.

Chapter 16

Set Collections

IN JAVA'S CONTAINER LIBRARY, a *set* is a container that stores a unique collection of objects. No duplications are permitted in a set, making this type of container suitable for databases of unique values – such as a set of programming-language reserved words or a set of network login names.

This chapter explores the library's two set interfaces, Set and SortedSet, on which two concrete classes are based, HashSet and TreeSet. I also point out some related Collections class utility methods that you can use to operate on sets.

IN THIS CHAPTER

◆ Using the Set and SortedSet interfaces

◆ Programming with hash tables

◆ The TreeSet class

◆ Parsing text with TreeSet

◆ Set-based utilities

Set Interfaces

Listing 16-1, Set.txt, shows the Set interface's methods. The interface is especially interesting because Set extends Collection (refer back to Figure 14-2). However, Set adds nothing to Collection, and in fact, both interfaces are identical. So you don't have to flip pages, the method declarations are repeated here.

The Set Interface

Listing 16-1, Set.txt, illustrates the methods of the Set interface.

Listing 16-1: Set.txt

```
001: // Set interface methods
002: int size();
003: boolean isEmpty();
004: boolean contains(Object o);
005: Iterator iterator();
006: Object[] toArray();
```

309

```
007: Object[] toArray(Object a[]);
008: boolean add(Object o);
009: boolean remove(Object o);
010: boolean containsAll(Collection c);
011: boolean addAll(Collection c);
012: boolean retainAll(Collection c);
013: boolean removeAll(Collection c);
014: void clear();
015: boolean equals(Object o);
016: int hashCode();
```

You might wonder, if Set is identical to Collection, why does the library bother creating it? It does so to separate the *contracts* of Set- and List-based containers, the major difference being that sets contain unique objects, but lists allow duplications. Also, from Figure 14-2, because Set and List extend Collection, they are *siblings,* but they are not otherwise directly related. (Think of it this way: a sister is not an extension of her brother, but both children are extensions of their parents.)

Because Set and Collection provide the same methods, you already know a lot about how to use Set-based classes. But keep the following key points in mind:

◆ The word "set" in Java's container library refers generally to any collection of unique objects, not necessarily a *mathematical* set.

◆ Changes to any object in a set that make that object equal to another object in the same set cause the set to behave in unpredictable ways. You are not prevented from modifying a set's objects, but the consequences of doing so are your responsibility.

◆ A container class based on Set (HashSet for example) is expected to provide at least two constructors: a default no-parameter constructor, and one that accepts a Collection container. If that container has any duplicate objects, they are not added multiple times to the set, but no error results. Set-based container classes may declare additional constructors as needed.

◆ A Set may be empty or it may be composed of a single object (a *singleton* set). See "Set Utilities" in this chapter for more on these subjects.

◆ A Set may contain one, and only one, null reference — objects in sets must all be unique, including the null reference.

◆ A Set may not contain itself.

◆ A Set does not define any ordering on its contained objects. If you need to maintain a Set in sorted order, see the SortedSet interface described in the next section.

◆ Call the iterator() method as explained in Chapter 15, "List Collections" (see line 005 in Listing 16-1), and use the resulting object to access all of a Set container's objects. Remember, however, that the order in which you receive each object is not defined.

The SortedSet Interface

The SortedSet interface, shown here in Listing 16-2, SortedSet.txt, extends Set and provides some additional methods. As the interface's name implies, a SortedSet container defines an ordering for its objects. Specifically, objects inserted into a SortedSet container must be of classes that implement the Comparable interface and provide a compareTo() method. As with Set containers, SortedSet containers are collections of unique objects. No duplications are permitted in a SortedSet container.

Listing 16-2: SortedSet.txt

```
001: // SortedSet interface methods
002: Comparator comparator();
003: SortedSet subSet(Object fromElement, Object toElement);
004: SortedSet headSet(Object toElement);
005: SortedSet tailSet(Object fromElement);
006: Object first();
007: Object last();
```

A class that implements SortedSet (TreeSet for example) is expected to provide at least four constructors:

◆ A no-parameter default constructor

◆ A constructor that accepts a Comparator object to be used in maintaining the set objects' order

◆ A constructor that accepts a Collection container whose objects are all added to the set, minus any duplicates

◆ A constructor that accepts a SortedSet container, resulting in a new set containing all the original set's objects in the same order

The TreeSet, discussed later in this chapter, provides all four constructors. You should do the same if you are creating a custom SortedSet container class. However, because interfaces cannot declare constructors, the compiler does not enforce these rules.

If you construct a SortedSet container by passing its constructor a Comparator object, you may call the comparator() method to receive that object's reference. For example, using the Chart class from Chapter 15, you can create a TreeSet container using the statement

```
TreeSet T = new TreeSet(Chart.byScale());
```

The resulting SortedSet-based container is maintained in the order defined by the Comparator object—in this example, by scale fields in the Chart objects. An iteration over the container's objects would return them sorted by those fields. If it's not convenient to maintain a copy of the Comparator object, after executing the preceding statement, you can obtain it by calling comparator() like this:

```
Comparator C = T.comparator();
System.out.println(C);
```

When I tried that, my system printed

```
Chart$ChartComparator@5d87b2
```

This is the Comparator object's default name, as provided by the native toString() implementation inherited from Object. The string is composed of the Chart and its inner ChartComparator class names, plus the object's reference address. If the SortedSet is created without using a Comparator object, then the comparator() method returns null:

```
TreeSet T = new TreeSet();  // Default constructor
Comparator C = T.comparator();
System.out.println(C);
```

That prints null on screen. You might use the comparator() method to determine whether a set is maintained by a Comparator object. After obtaining that object, if it is not null, you can pass to other methods—for example, to a Collections class sort() method to be called for a SortedSet container that has been converted to a List-based container.

If you construct a SortedSet container using another SortedSet container, the new container uses the same Comparator object, if any, in the original set. However, if you build a SortedSet container from any other Collection container, then the resulting set's Comparator is set to null, and the objects in the set must be of classes that implement the Comparable interface and provide a compareTo() method. Receiving a ClassCastException is a good indication that you have violated this rule—for example, in attempting to convert a list of non-comparable objects into a SortedSet.

The SortedSet interface provides the means to create non-inclusive subsets (see line 003 in Listing 16-2). Specify the two objects A and B from which to create the new set, which contains all objects from A up to but *not* including B. If A equals B, the resulting set is the empty set. The following hypothetical code creates a subset of objects from A to the predecessor of B:

```
TreeSet original = new TreeSet();
original.add(...);  // Add objects to set
TreeSet subset = original.SubSet(A, B);
```

The meaning of "the predecessor of B" is not strictly defined, which presents the problem of how to create an inclusive set from A up to and including B. If your class provides a method successorOf(X) that returns the successor object of X, the preceding statement could be written as

```
TreeSet subset = original.SubSet(A, YourClass.successorOf(B));
```

TIP See "TreeSet Subsets" in this chapter for another way to write a general successorOf() method and to create an inclusive subset of objects in a SortedSet container.

Two other SortedSet interface methods, headSet() and tailSet() (see lines 004-005 in Listing 16-2), also create subsets. The headSet() method returns a subset equal to the first object up to but not including the object passed to the method. The tailSet() method returns a subset from the specified object to the last object in the set.

The SortedSet interface's subSet(), headSet(), and tailSet() methods return a view of the set, which is called the *backing set*. This means that any changes to objects in the resulting subset are made also to the same objects in the original set. In addition, any attempts to insert a new object into the subset outside of the subset's specified range throw IllegalArgumentException.

Finally in the SortedSet interface are two methods, first() and last(), that (as you can probably guess) return the first and last objects in a SortedSet container. These methods throw NoSuchElementException if called on an empty set, so you should probably call isEmpty() beforehand like this:

```
TreeSet T = new TreeSet();
...
if (!T.isEmpty()) {
 YourClass firstObject = (YourClass)T.first();
 YourClass lastObject = (YourClass)T.last();
 ...
}
```

Set Containers

Two concrete classes provide two different ways to create Set-based containers. The first class, HashSet, stores and retrieves objects using their *hash values*. The second, TreeSet, stores and retrieves objects in a tree-like structure. Each container is used similarly, but in general, HashSet containers often provide the fastest lookup times. TreeSet containers provide somewhat slower lookup speeds, but maintain objects in sorted order. Using an Iterator with a HashSet returns the container's objects in an unspecified order. Using an Iterator with a TreeSet returns objects in sorted order.

 Due to the nature of sets, an Iterator applied to a HashSet or TreeSet container does not necessarily return objects in the same order they were inserted.

Hash Tables

If you are unfamiliar with how hashing works, a brief explanation will help you understand how to use the HashSet class and others that use hash values to store and retrieve objects. In general, these types of containers are known as *hash tables*. Objects in hash tables are stored and retrieved using *hash values* to compute indexes for storing object references, typically in arrays.

Those arrays are additionally organized into *buckets* that store groups of object references. Hash tables usually allocate a certain number of buckets above the minimum required to hold a certain number of objects. Generally, leaving some extra room in a hash table improves performance, at least up to a point. To do that, when creating hash tables, you typically specify two values — an *initial capacity,* and a *load factor.* The initial capacity is the table's starting size. The load factor determines when the hash table is expanded. For example, a load factor of 0.80 means the table is expanded when it becomes about 80 percent full.

 Java hash table containers, HashSet and HashMap, define a default capacity of 11 objects and a load factor of 0.75.

In Java programming, all objects have hash values as computed by Object.hashCode(). You may rely on that default implementation, inherited by all Java classes, or you can override the method in your own class and compute a hash value based on your objects' contents. Ideally, each object should return a unique hash value. Two objects that are the same (as defined by their class's equals()

method) *must* return the same hash value. Two objects that are not the same are not required to return different hash values, but they should do so if possible.

The default hash value that `Object.hashCode()` returns is typically the object's address in memory, although Java does not dictate this to implementers. If you override the method, you need to figure out some clever way to create a unique integer value for your class—for example, adding all character Unicode values in an object's string variable, perhaps limited to some arbitrary maximum.

If your class overrides `Object.equals()`—for example, to compare two objects based on their contents—then the class should probably also override `Object.hashCode()`. This is necessary because two distinct objects with identical content have different references, but if it's your intention to consider them to be equal, they should generate the same hash value. In this case, the default `Object.hashCode()` would incorrectly return different hash values for the equal objects.

A hash table uses an object's hash value to determine where to store a reference to that object. Thus, given the object's hash value, locating the object requires only a single indexing operation, nearly guaranteeing high-speed searches. (Many parsers in compilers use hash tables for looking up a programming language's reserved words.) If two objects produce the same hash value, the result is a *clash*. This is handled by storing the object at the next available position. Clashes reduce hash table lookup speeds and are best avoided if possible by making the hash table reasonably large.

To test the worst-case performance of a hash table, override `Object.hashCode()` and have it return the same value for all objects. In writing custom hash table containers, this is also a good test procedure to be sure that your container correctly handles hash-value clashes.

The HashSet Class

The `HashSet` class implements a classic hash table based on the `Set` interface. The objects in a `HashSet` container are stored (and returned by an iterator) in no particular order. Listing 16-3, HashSet.txt, shows the class's constructors. The class also provides a `clone()` method that you can call to clone a `HashSet` container. Because `HashSet` implements the `Set` interface, you may also call the methods stipulated in the `Set` interface (refer back to Listing 16-1).

Listing 16-3: HashSet.txt

```
001: // HashSet constructors
002: public HashSet();
003: public HashSet(Collection c);
004: public HashSet(int initialCapacity, float loadFactor);
005: public HashSet(int initialCapacity);
```

Create a default `HashSet` container using the statement

```
HashSet myset = new HashSet();
```

However, if you know or can calculate approximately how many objects you will store in the container, it is usually better to specify an initial capacity larger than the default of 11. If `Num` specifies the number of objects to be stored in the container, it is reasonable to specify an initial capacity of twice that value:

```
HashSet myset = new HashSet(2 * Num, 0.60);
```

That also specifies a load factor of 0.60 — in other words, the container will be expanded when it becomes about 60 percent full. To use the default load factor of 0.75, specify an initial capacity alone:

```
HashSet myset = new HashSet(2 * Num);
```

As a general rule, a large initial capacity and a small load factor improve hash table performance, but with diminishing returns. It is often necessary to experiment with different values to achieve optimum performance.

You may also convert any `Collection`-based container to a `HashSet` by passing it to the constructor shown at line 003. For example, the following code converts a `LinkedList` container to a `HashSet`:

```
LinkedList mylist = new LinkedList();
// add objects to mylist
HashSet myset = new HashSet(mylist);
```

 TIP Because all objects in `Set`-based containers are unique, to remove duplicate objects from another type container, simply convert it to a `HashSet` or `TreeSet` container.

To add objects to a `HashSet` container, call the `add()` method. To remove an object, call `remove()`. To erase the container, call `clear()`. These are the same `Collection` methods you have seen in other examples, and which are also stipulated by the `Set` interface (see Listing 16-1).

Parsing Text with HashSet

As mentioned, parsers often use hash tables for fast searches. To demonstrate some of the code needed to parse a text file's words, and also to show how to use a `HashSet` container, Listing 16-4, ParseWords.java, reads a file Quote.txt (also in the c16/ParseWords directory). The program uses a `HashSet` container to collect and count all of the unique words in the file.

Listing 16–4: ParseWords.java

```
001: import java.util.*;
002: import java.io.*;
003:
004: class ParseWords {
005:  public static void main(String args[]) {
006: // Variables
007:    int i;
008:    char c;
009:    StringBuffer sbuf = new StringBuffer();
010:    HashSet hashTable = new HashSet(100);
011:
012: // Read and parse words from Quote.txt
013:    System.out.println();
014:    try {
015:     FileReader f = new FileReader("Quote.txt");
016:     while ((i = f.read()) >= 0) {
017:      c = (char)i;
018:      System.out.print(c);
019:      c = Character.toLowerCase(c);
020:      if (Character.isWhitespace(c)) {
021:       if (sbuf.length() > 0)
022:        hashTable.add(sbuf.toString());
023:       sbuf.setLength(0);
024:      } else
025:       if (Character.isLetter(c))
026:        sbuf.append(c);
027:     }
028:     if (sbuf.length() > 0)
029:      hashTable.add(sbuf.toString());
030:    } catch (IOException e) {
031:     System.out.println("*** I/O error!");
032:    }
033:
034: // Display hash table count and contents
035:    System.out.println("\n");
036:    Iterator I = hashTable.iterator();
037:    String s;
038:    System.out.println("There are " + hashTable.size()
039:     + " unique words in the file");
040:    while (I.hasNext()) {
041:     s = (String)I.next();
042:     System.out.println(s);
043:    }
044:  }
045: }
```

Running the program displays the following information (changed in format slightly to save a little room):

```
"Not everything that can be counted counts, and not everything
that counts can be counted." - Albert Einstein (1879-1955)

There are 10 unique words in the file
einstein albert not everything can
be counted and that counts
```

After displaying the text in Quote.txt, the program reports how many unique words the text contains, and then lists the words in the file. (Chapter 24, "Input and Output Techniques," discusses file handling—I don't explain those statements here.) Lines 009 and 010 create a StringBuffer sbuf and a HashSet container, hashTable, with an initial capacity of 100. I use a StringBuffer object instead of a string because the program builds each word in the file one character at a time by calling the class's append() method (see line 026). Lines 021-022 add each completed word to the hashTable container with the statements

```
if (sbuf.length() > 0)
  hashTable.add(sbuf.toString());
```

This is repeated at lines 028-029 in case a word is left in the buffer upon reaching the end of the file. To display the number of words in the container, the program simply calls the size() method, stipulated by the Set interface:

```
System.out.println("There are " + hashTable.size()
 + " unique words in the file");
```

Finally, to display the words in the container, the program obtains an Iterator object, and then uses a while loop to get each object as a String:

```
Iterator I = hashTable.iterator();
String s;
...
while (I.hasNext()) {
 s = (String)I.next();
 System.out.println(s);
}
```

SortedSet Containers

There is only one SortedSet container in the library, TreeSet, described in this and the following sections.

The TreeSet Class

The TreeSet class, shown in Listing 16-5, TreeSet.txt, implements the SortedSet interface (Listing 16-2). Because SortedSet extends Set, TreeSet also has all of the methods in the Set interface (Listing 16-1). The listing here shows only the TreeSet constructors. See the other mentioned listings and discussions for methods you can call for TreeSet containers. Like HashSet, TreeSet also implements the Cloneable interface and provides a clone() method that you can call to clone a TreeSet container.

Listing 16–5: TreeSet.txt

```
001: // TreeSet constructors
002: public TreeSet();
003: public TreeSet(Comparator c);
004: public TreeSet(Collection c);
005: public TreeSet(SortedSet s);
```

You can construct a TreeSet container four ways. Specify no argument to the constructor to create a default object:

```
TreeSet myTree = new TreeSet();
```

You can also specify another SortedSet container, or any Collection-based object. This lets you convert another type of container to a TreeSet (minus any duplicate objects in the original). For instance, to convert an ArrayList container to a TreeSet, use code such as

```
ArrayList myList = new ArrayList();
// ... add objects to myList
TreeSet myTree = new TreeSet(myList);
```

Alternatively, you can specify a Comparator object to be used in maintaining the container's objects in sorted order. Using the Chart class from the preceding chapter, the following constructs a TreeSet container for storing Chart objects in scale order:

```
TreeSet myTree = new TreeSet(Chart.byScale());
```

When creating a TreeSet container that way, any objects added to the container must be of the appropriate class (Chart in this case), or you receive a ClassCastException error. The following statement correctly adds a Chart object to the container:

```
myTree.add(new Chart(12245, "Hampton Roads", 20000));
```

But the following attempt to add a `String` object to the same container now throws the exception:

```
myTree.add(new String("This doesn't work"));  // ???
...
Exception in thread "main" java.lang.ClassCastException:
java.lang.String
  at Chart$ChartComparator.compare(Chart.java:59)
```

Of course normally, `TreeSet` containers (and all others) can store `String` and other kinds of objects. However, because this container was created using a `Chart Comparator` object, objects added to the container must be `Chart` objects or those of a class that extends `Chart`.

Parsing Text with TreeSet

`TreeSet` and `HashSet` containers are used similarly. However, there are significant differences between the two classes, including the following:

◆ There is no way, nor any need, to specify an initial size of a `TreeSet` container as there is for a `HashSet`. `TreeSet` containers expand and shrink for every addition and removal operation.

◆ A `TreeSet` container maintains its objects in sorted order, either by virtue of the objects' class `compareTo()` method (the class must implement the `Comparable` interface), or by using a `Comparator` object. A `HashSet` container does not maintain its objects in any particular order.

◆ A `TreeSet` container provides methods stipulated in the `SortedSet` interface such as `subSet()`, `headSet()`, and `tailSet()`. Also provided are `first()` and `last()` methods. These methods are not available to `HashSet` containers or any others that implement the `Set` interface.

◆ Call the `TreeSet` class's `comparator()` method, stipulated in the `SortedSet` interface, to determine whether a `Comparator` object is being used to maintain the set's object order. If `comparator()` returns `null`, then no `Comparator` object is in use. `HashSet` and other `Set`-based containers do not use `Comparator` objects.

Aside from those observations, a `TreeSet` differs from a `HashSet` only in keeping its contained objects in sorted order. Because those objects are internally linked in a tree-like structure, insertions and removals from a `TreeSet` are fast, but in most cases not equally as fast as in `HashSets`.

To demonstrate how to use a `TreeSet`, Listing 16-6, ParseTree.java, is the same demonstration as in Listing 16-4, ParseWords.java, but replaces `HashSet` with `TreeSet`. Because the programs are nearly identical, I cut out most duplicated lines to save room here. The only real difference between the two programs is that when the `hashTable` container is created at line 010, no initial capacity is specified as was done in Listing 16-4.

Listing 16–6: ParseTree.java

```
001: import java.util.*;
002: import java.io.*;
003:
004: class ParseTree {
005:   public static void main(String args[]) {
...
010:     TreeSet hashTable = new TreeSet();
...
044:   }
045: }
```

TreeSet Subsets

Using the `TreeSet` class's `subSet()`, `headSet()`, and `tailSet()` methods to obtain subsets of `SortedSet` containers can be a little tricky. Review the methods' declarations (see also the `SortedSet` interface, Listing 16-2):

```
public SortedSet subSet(Object fromElement, Object toElement);
public SortedSet headSet(Object toElement);
public SortedSet tailSet(Object fromElement);
```

Each method returns a `SortedSet` object, which might be any container of a class that implements `SortedSet` (`TreeSet` most likely). To `subSet()`, pass the first and last object for which you want to create the subset. The resulting set contains the objects starting with `fromElement` up to *but not including* `toElement`. And therein lies the tricky part.

A subset is just a view of the original set. It is not a clone. Technically speaking, subsets are *backed* by the original set, meaning that any changes to objects in the subset, including any additions, are made also to the original set of objects. Additions outside of the subset's initial range throw an `IllegalArgumentException`.

To obtain a subset of a `SortedSet` container that includes objects from a starting element up to *and including* the end element requires that you be able to calculate or find the successor of the final object. But that is often not so easily done. To demonstrate the problem, and one possible solution, Listing 16-7, SubTree.java, creates a `TreeSet` of strings, and then attempts to obtain an inclusive subset of those entries.

Listing 16-7: SubTree.java

```
001: import java.util.*;
002: import java.io.*;
003:
004: class SubTree {
005: // Display contents of a SortedSet container
006:   static void showSet(SortedSet S, String msg) {
007:    System.out.println("\n" + msg);
008:    Iterator I = S.iterator();
009:    while (I.hasNext())
010:     System.out.print("  " + I.next());
011:   }
012:
013:   public static void main(String args[]) {
014: // Create the TreeSet container and add some objects to it
015:    TreeSet myTree = new TreeSet();
016:    myTree.add("Peach");
017:    myTree.add("Banana");
018:    myTree.add("Cherry");
019:    myTree.add("Apple");
020:    myTree.add("Pear");
021:    myTree.add("Kiwi");
022:    myTree.add("Grapefruit");
023:
024: // Get a non-inclusive subset of the tree
025:    TreeSet subTree =
026:     (TreeSet)myTree.subSet("Cherry", "Peach");
027: // Get an inclusive subset of the tree
028: //   TreeSet subTree =
029: //    (TreeSet)myTree.subSet("Cherry", "Peach\0");
030:
031: // Display both trees
032:    showSet(myTree, "Full TreeSet container:");
033:    showSet(subTree, "Subset of container:");
034:   }
035: }
```

Running the program displays the following text:

```
Full TreeSet container:
  Apple  Banana  Cherry  Grapefruit  Kiwi  Peach  Pear
Subset of container:
  Cherry  Grapefruit  Kiwi
```

Lines 015-022 construct the `TreeSet` container, `myTree`, and add some fruit names as `String` objects. To obtain a subset of `myTree`, the program executes the statement at lines 025-026 repeated here for reference:

```
TreeSet subTree =
  (TreeSet)myTree.subSet("Cherry", "Peach");
```

A type-cast expression is necessary to satisfy the compiler that this is a `TreeSet`, which is needed because `subSet()` returns the more general `SortedSet` interface type. Because `subSet()` returns a non-inclusive subset, the result (as you can see from the program's printout) includes all strings from `"Cherry"` up to but not including `"Peach"`. To obtain an inclusive subset that includes that string, you must specify the successor to `"Peach"` when creating the subset. For `String` objects, this is easily done with a little trick. Delete or comment-out lines 025-026 and enable lines 028-029, repeated here:

```
TreeSet subTree =
  (TreeSet)myTree.subSet("Cherry", "Peach\0");
```

That's the same statement except for the string `"\0"` (a null character) appended to `"Peach"`. It may not be intuitively obvious that this creates the successor to `"Peach"`, but it does exactly that because, if the container has any other strings, the next one *must* be alphabetically greater than `"Peach"` plus a null character. As I said, tricky.

But what do you do if your container has objects that are not strings? The answer depends on your objects' class. If that class can somehow calculate the successor of an object, say by providing a static `successor()` method, you might obtain an inclusive subset of a `TreeSet` container for two objects, `obj1` and `obj2`, using code such as

```
TreeSet subTree =
  (TreeSet)myTree.subSet(obj1, YourClass.successor(obj2));
```

That may not always be possible, in which case you need another way to find an object's `TreeSet` successor. There may be several possible solutions to this problem, but the one shown here should work for objects of most classes. Listing 16-8, Successor.java, duplicates the preceding program, but it uses a method to find a string's successor in a `TreeSet` container.

Listing 16-8: Successor.java

```
001: import java.util.*;
002: import java.io.*;
003:
004: class Successor {
005:
```

```
006: // Return the successor of a SortedSet object or null if none
007:   static Object successorOf(SortedSet s, Object o) {
008:     SortedSet t = s.tailSet(o);
009:     if (t.size() < 2) return null;
010:     Iterator I = t.iterator();
011:     I.hasNext(); I.next(); I.hasNext();
012:     return I.next();
013:   }
014:
015: // Return the inclusive set of SortedSet objects o1 through o2
016:   static SortedSet inclusiveSet(
017:     SortedSet s, Object o1, Object o2) {
018:     if (!s.contains(o1) || !s.contains(o2))
019:       throw new NoSuchElementException();
020:     Comparable c1 = (Comparable)o1;
021:     Comparable c2 = (Comparable)o2;
022:     if (c1.compareTo(c2) > 0)
023:       throw new IllegalArgumentException();
024:     Object successor = successorOf(s, o2);
025:     if (successor == null)
026:       return s.tailSet(o1);
027:     else
028:       return s.subSet(o1, successor);
029:   }
...
039:   public static void main(String args[]) {
040: // Create the TreeSet container and add some objects to it
041:     TreeSet myTree = new TreeSet();
042:     myTree.add("Peach");
...
050: // Get a non-inclusive subset of the tree
051:     TreeSet subTree1 =
052:       (TreeSet)myTree.subSet("Cherry", "Peach");
053:
054:     TreeSet subTree2 =
055:       (TreeSet)inclusiveSet(myTree, "Cherry", "Peach");
056:
057: // Display all tree sets
058:     showSet(myTree, "Full TreeSet container:");
059:     showSet(subTree1, "Non-inclusive subset:");
060:     showSet(subTree2, "Inclusive subset:");
061:   }
062: }
```

Two methods in the sample program find the successor of a SortedSet container object, and return an inclusive subset of objects from one element up to and including another. The first method, successorOf(), is declared at line 007 as

```
static Object successorOf(SortedSet s, Object o);
```

Pass any SortedSet container (a TreeSet for example) and an object. The method returns the next object in the container, or null if the container is empty or no successor object exists. That might happen, for instance, if the specified object is the last one in the container, or if it doesn't exist. The method creates a tailSet() of the specified set with the statement:

```
SortedSet t = s.tailSet(o);
```

Remember that subsets are only views of the original set, not clones. Speaking hypothetically, in this case, if the set contains ABCDEFG, and if the object specified is E, the resulting tailSet() equals EFG. If the resulting subset has fewer than two elements, there is no successor object and the method returns null. Otherwise, it uses an Iterator object to find the next element after the first in the tailSet(). This is the object returned.

Method inclusiveSet() declared at lines 016-017 calls successorOf() and returns an inclusive TreeSet subset. The method is declared as

```
static SortedSet inclusiveSet(
  SortedSet s, Object o1, Object o2);
```

Two exceptions are explicitly thrown: IllegalArgumentException if o1 > o2, and NoSuchElementException if one or both objects are not in the set. A ClassCastException is also thrown if the objects' class is not Comparable. After detecting these conditions and throwing any necessary exceptions, the rest of the method shows a good example of the SortedSet interface's tailSet() and subSet() methods:

```
Object successor = successorOf(s, o2);
if (successor == null)
  return s.tailSet(o1);
else
  return s.subSet(o1, successor);
```

If the successor of the specified object in the set is null, inclusiveSet() reverts to returning the container's tailSet(). Otherwise, it calls the SortedSet interface's subSet() method to return the non-inclusive set of the "from" object to the successor of the "to" object. Thus the result contains the "to" object.

Not shown here is the `headSet()` method, which works similarly but returns the first object up to but not including the second. You can use the `successorOf()` method described here to create a `headSet()` that returns an inclusive subset.

Set Utilities

The `Collections` utility class in the `java.util` package provides four utility methods that are useful for working with `Set` and `SortedSet` containers. The methods return `Set` and `SortedSet` references, not object references of concrete classes such as `TreeSet` and `HashSet`. They are therefore useful when a generalized view of a set is needed.

The first two methods return an unmodifiable view of a `Set` and `SortedSet`. They are declared as

```
public static Set unmodifiableSet(Set s);
public static SortedSet unmodifiableSortedSet(SortedSet s);
```

Simply pass any `Set` or `SortedSet` container to the appropriate method and save the result. For example, to construct an unmodifiable view of the `myTree` set from the preceding sample program, you can use the statement:

```
SortedSet fixedSet = Collections.unmodifiableSortedSet(myTree);
```

The resulting set must be saved as a `SortedSet` reference, *not* a reference to a `TreeSet` or another concrete class. Attempts to modify the resulting set throw `UnsupportedOperationException`:

```
fixedSet.add("Lime");  // ??? Throws exception
```

Empty sets are sometimes needed in algorithms that use set operations. For convenience, the `Collections` class provides a static `Set` container, `EMPTY_SET`, that, as its name implies, is always empty:

```
public static final Set EMPTY_SET;
```

Any attempts to add an object to the set result in an exception. You could use this container in a comparison to test whether another set is equivalently empty. For example, the following code erases `myTree` and then compares it with `EMPTY_SET`:

```
myTree.clear();
if (Collections.EMPTY_SET.equals(myTree))
  System.out.println("myTree is the empty set");
```

Finally in `Collections` is a method that returns a `Set` container with exactly one object, the so-called *singleton set*. The method is declared as

```
public static Set singleton(Object o);
```

Pass any object to the method and save the result in a `Set` reference. For instance, this creates a `Set` containing a single string:

```
Set oneSet = Collections.singleton("Oak");
```

A singleton set is limited to having one element. Any attempt to change that fact leads to an `UnsupportedOperationException`:

```
oneSet.add("Pine");   // ??? Throws exception
```

 See also Chapter 19, "Threaded Code," for information on creating synchronized (that is, thread-safe) sets and other containers.

Summary

- `Set` containers hold unique collections of objects. No duplicate objects are permitted in set containers; however, adding a duplicate object is simply ignored and is not considered to be an error.

- The `Set` interface stipulates the basic methods required of `Set` containers. Although `Set` extends `Collection`, its methods are identical, and the purpose of the `Set` interface is therefore largely organizational.

- The `SortedSet` interface extends `Set` and provides additional methods for unique collections of objects maintained in sorted order. The `SortedSet` interface also provides methods for obtaining subsets of `SortedSet` containers.

- Two concrete classes, `HashSet` and `TreeSet`, implement the `Set` and `SortedSet` interfaces. `HashSet` containers make rapid searches possible, but they require a little extra space to maintain performance. `TreeSet` containers are memory efficient, but searches are not as fast as with a `HashSet`.

- The `HashSet` class stores objects by way of their hash values, as returned by `Object.hashCode()`. The default implementation of that method equals the object's memory reference, however, Java does not guarantee that as a fact. You may override the hashCode() method in your own class to compute a different hash value.

◆ The TreeSet class stores objects in their natural sorted order, as provided by their class's compareTo() method. The class must implement the Comparable interface. When that is not convenient, you may alternatively construct a TreeSet container using a Comparator object, in which case the objects' class need not be Comparable.

◆ This chapter shows how to parse a text file's words and store them in a HashSet or TreeSet container. The chapter also explains techniques for obtaining subsets of SortedSet containers, which can be tricky, especially when you need an inclusive set of objects.

◆ Finally in this chapter are explanations of some utility methods provided by the Collections class in the java.util package. Two methods provide unmodifiable views of a Set or SortedSet container. The Collections class also provides method singleton() for obtaining a set containing only one item (a singleton set), and the declaration EMPTY_SET containing the empty or null set.

Chapter 17

Map Collections

IN THE JAVA CONTAINER LIBRARY, a *map* is a set of unique key-value entries that resembles a dictionary of words and definitions. The keys in a map must all be unique, and in that regard, a map resembles a set as described in Chapter 16, "Set Collections." A map's key is used to locate its associated values and to enter new key-value pairs into the container. This makes a map ideal for a container that stores *associations* — for example, value-string relationships that form a database of object properties.

This chapter explores the Map and SortedMap interfaces and the three concrete classes that implement them — HashMap, WeakHashMap, and TreeMap. This part of the container library tree stands alone — none of its interfaces or classes is based on the Collection class. For reference, look back to Figure 14-3, which shows the relationship of this branch of the container library tree. As that figure shows, all three concrete classes extend AbstractMap, which implements the Map interface.

IN THIS CHAPTER

- ◆ The Map and SortedMap interfaces
- ◆ Map containers
- ◆ Understanding Map views
- ◆ A look at the WeakHashMap class
- ◆ SortedMap containers
- ◆ Creating a TreeSet dictionary

Map Interfaces

There are two map interfaces in the collection library — Map and SortedMap, discussed in the following two sections.

The Map Interface

The Map interface stipulates the most basic of methods that related interfaces, abstract classes (there is only one, AbstractMap), and concrete classes share. Map does *not* extend Collection; it is a new interface that defines ground-zero methods for map containers. Additionally, a Map does not maintain or return objects in any defined order. See the SortedMap interface in the next section if you need that capability. Listing 17-1, Map.txt, shows the Map interface's declarations.

Listing 17-1: Map.txt

```
001: // Map interface declarations
002: int size();
003: boolean isEmpty();
004: boolean containsKey(Object key);
005: boolean containsValue(Object value);
006: Object get(Object key);
007: Object put(Object key, Object value);
008: Object remove(Object key);
009: void putAll(Map t);
010: void clear();
011: public Set keySet();
012: public Collection values();
013: public Set entrySet();
014: boolean equals(Object o);
015: int hashCode();
```

Some of the Map interface methods resemble those in Collection. For example, size() returns the number of key-value pairs in a container, and isEmpty() returns true if the container has no objects. Also, clear(), equals(), and hashCode() work as described for other containers in the preceding chapters.

Most other methods work with keys, values, or key-value pairs. Call containsKey() to determine whether a key is in a Map collection, or call containsValue() to determine whether a value is held without having to know its key.

 In a classic associative data structure, a key is often required to perform a search of values. Not so with Java Map containers — given a value, you can locate its associated key.

Call the get() method to return an object's value, given its key. The method returns null if the key is not found. This has the ambiguous characteristic that, if the container holds a value equal to null, get() returns that value. Therefore, just because get() returns null does *not* indicate whether an object is actually returned. If that causes you trouble, use containsValue(null) to determine whether null is actually a member of the container. That method is programmed in AbstractMap to search for null as an object in the container.

Call put() to insert a new key-value element into a Map container. If the key is already present, calling put() replaces that key's current value with the newly specified one. If necessary, the container expands to hold additional values — such expansion, however, depends on the internal storage device used in implementing the Map interface. Call remove() to delete a key-value element from the container given only its key.

The putAll() method inserts all of another Map's elements into a container. Use it to transfer one type of Map container's contents to another — from a TreeMap to a HashMap for example.

Three other methods provide Set and Collection *views* of a Map container. Call keySet() to return a Set container of the Map's key values. Call values() for a Collection container of all values held in a Map, minus their keys. Call entrySet() for a Set of the Map container's Map.Entry elements. Map.Entry is an inner, nested interface, declared inside the Map interface (the Map.Entry interface is discussed later in this chapter). The three methods provide different ways to view any Map container:

◆ As a Set of keys (call keySet())

◆ As a Collection of values (call values())

◆ As a Set of Map.Entry objects (call entrySet())

Keep in mind that these alternate views are backed by the Map container, meaning that any changes made to a key via keySet(), to a value via values(), or to a key or value via entrySet() are also made to the original key or value in the Map container. Also be aware that it is your responsibility to ensure that all Map container keys remain unique. If a change to a key causes it to duplicate another key already in the container, the results are unpredictable and are likely to cause serious problems with other operations.

> **TIP** The AbstractMap class implements the Map interface and provides many method implementations for the three concrete classes, HashMap, TreeMap, and WeakHashMap. When building your own custom Map container classes, it is generally easier to extend AbstractMap than it is to start from scratch by implementing the Map interface.

The SortedMap Interface

The SortedMap interface extends Map and provides some additional methods that apply to associative containers sorted by key values. A SortedMap container always maintains its objects in key order. At present, there is only one such concrete class in the library, TreeMap. Listing 17-2, SortedMap.txt, shows the SortedMap interface's method declarations.

Listing 17-2: SortedMap.txt

```
001: // SortedMap interface declarations
002: Comparator comparator();
003: SortedMap subMap(Object fromKey, Object toKey);
004: SortedMap headMap(Object toKey);
005: SortedMap tailMap(Object fromKey);
006: Object firstKey();
007: Object lastKey();
```

Remember that, because SortedMap extends Map, containers based on SortedMap implement all of the methods listed here plus those for the Map interface shown in Listing 17-1. The new methods are for use only with containers maintained in key order.

Call the comparator() method to retrieve the Comparator object used in comparing two SortedMap container entries. If no Comparator is in use for the container, then this method returns null. A Comparator is used only if specified when constructing the SortedMap container. For an example, see "The TreeMap Class" in this chapter. (For help using Comparator objects, see the section "Using Comparators and ArrayList" in Chapter 15, "List Collections.")

Three methods return type SortedMap and provide the means to obtain subset views of any SortedMap container. Call subMap() for a subset of a container's entries from a specified fromKey value up to *but not including* a toKey value. Call headMap() for a subset of entries from the first one in the container up to *but not including* the specified toKey value. Call tailMap() for a subset of entries from a specified fromKey value to the last one in the container.

To obtain an inclusive subset of a SortedMap container's objects requires being able to calculate a toKey value's successor. Similar programming discussed under "TreeSet Subsets" in Chapter 16 can be used to find a key value's successor.

Lastly in the SortedMap interface are two handy methods. Call firstKey() to find the first key value in the container. Call lastKey() to find the last one. These methods are particularly useful in determining the range of keys held in a SortedMap container.

Map Containers

Two concrete classes, HashMap and WeakHashMap, implement the methods stipulated in the basic Map interface in Listing 17-1. The classes also extend the AbstractMap class, which provides most of the common method implementations stipulated by the interface. (As with all abstract classes in the container library, no new methods are added over the declarations inherited from the interface.)

Both concrete classes use the concept of a hash table to store, retrieve, and remove key-value entries in the container. This means that the key-value class must provide a hashCode() method; however, the default method inherited by all classes from Object is probably suitable in most cases. If not, you may override the method and provide a custom hash value. For more help with hash tables, hash values, and the hashCode() method, see "Hash Tables" in Chapter 16.

Listing 17-3, HashMap.txt, shows the HashMap class's constructors and one method, clone(), which is not specified in the Map interface. In addition to these constructors and method, all methods from the Map interface in Listing 17-1 are also available to HashMap containers.

The HashMap Class

Listing 17-3: HashMap.txt

```
001: // HashMap constructors and method
002: public HashMap();
003: public HashMap(Map t);
004: public HashMap(int initialCapacity);
005: public HashMap(int initialCapacity, float loadFactor);
006: public Object clone();
```

There are four ways to construct a HashMap() container. The first and simplest technique specifies no arguments. Use this method to create a container with a default initial capacity (11) and hash-table load factor (0.75):

```
HashMap myMap = new HashMap();
```

As with other hash-table container classes such as HashSet, you might want to specify an initial size for the container. This is particularly wise if you know the program will insert numerous objects, causing an expansion to occur. If Num equals the number of object to be inserted, the following statement creates a HashMap container with a capacity of twice that value:

```
HashMap myMap = new HashMap(2 * Num);
```

Always set aside additional room in a HashMap container — hash-table performance generally improves by maintaining some extra space, at least up to a point. You can also specify a load factor as a second argument to the constructor:

```
HashMap myMap = new HashMap(2 * Num, 0.60);
```

Constructed that way, the container will be expanded when it becomes about 60 percent full. The default load factor of 0.75 is probably adequate for most uses.

However, as with all hash-tables, trial and error is the only reliable way to determine optimal initial-capacity and load-factor values.

Finally, you can construct a HashMap container out of any other container of a class that implements Map. This is sometimes useful for converting one type of Map container into another. For example, you can convert a TreeMap container into a HashMap using code such as this:

```
TreeMap symbols = new TreeMap();
// insert key-value entries into symbols
HashMap hashSymbols = new HashMap(symbols);
```

The first line constructs a TreeMap container, symbols. The last line converts the entries in symbols into a new HashMap container, hashSymbols. Even though TreeMap implements the SortedMap interface, this code is perfectly acceptable because SortedMap extends Map — in other words, a TreeMap container is most generally referred to as a Map.

Building HashMap Containers

One typical use for a HashMap container is to store associations — for example, a set of values and their descriptions. To demonstrate how to build a HashMap container for this purpose, Listing 17-4, SymbolMap.java, creates a small database of a few symbol values and their names. I selected values typically used in Web page design to insert special symbols. For instance, 169 represents the copyright symbol, entered in text as &#169. Although in order to save space here, the sample program's database is incomplete, you could add additional symbols to make a useful utility. When you come across a cryptic symbol value, run the program and enter it to see its name.

Listing 17-4: SymbolMap.java

```
001: import java.util.*;
002: import java.io.*;
003:
004: class SymbolMap {
005:
006: // Display a Map container's keys and values
007:  public static void showMap(Map m) {
008:    Iterator I = m.entrySet().iterator();
009:    while (I.hasNext()) {
010: // Get next Map.Entry object
011:     Map.Entry entry = (Map.Entry)I.next();
012:     System.out.println(
013:      entry.getKey() + "\t:: " + entry.getValue());
014:    }
015:  }
```

```
016:
017:   public static void main(String args[]) {
018: // Create a HashMap container and insert some associations
019:    HashMap symbols = new HashMap();
020:    symbols.put(new Integer( 34), "Double quote");
021:    symbols.put(new Integer( 37), "Percent");
022:    symbols.put(new Integer( 38), "Ampersand");
023:    symbols.put(new Integer( 60), "Less than");
024:    symbols.put(new Integer( 62), "Greater than");
025:    symbols.put(new Integer(162), "Cent");
026:    symbols.put(new Integer(163), "Pound");
027:    symbols.put(new Integer(169), "Copyright");
028:    symbols.put(new Integer(247), "Divide");
029:
030: // Print database or search for requested key
031:    if (args.length == 0) {
032:      showMap(symbols);
033:    } else {
034:      int key = Integer.parseInt(args[0]);
035:      String value = (String)symbols.get(new Integer(key));
036:      if (value == null)
037:        System.out.println(key + " not in symbols");
038:      else
039:        System.out.println(key + " == " + value);
040:    }
041:  }
042: }
```

Run the program with no arguments for a complete list of symbols and descriptions. Run it with a key value to search the database:

```
java SymbolMap 169
169 == Copyright
```

Line 019 creates the HashMap container, using Java's default values. As mentioned, you could specify an initial capacity and load factor by changing the statement to something like this:

```
HashMap symbols = new HashMap(50, 0.65);
```

Lines 020-028 add entries to the container by calling the Map interface's put() method. This requires two arguments – a key and its associated value. The key's associated value, in this example, is a string. Notice that you cannot simply pass an integer value as the key because an integer is not an object. So, to use integer keys, the program creates instances of the Integer wrapper class with the specified values. (Chapter 9, "Numeric Classes," covers the Integer and other wrapper classes.)

Keys and associated values can be any objects of any classes, but the key's class must provide a `hashCode()` method. As mentioned, `Object` provides a default method, but you may override it and provide your own if you want.

To search for entries by key, call the `Map` interface `get()` method as shown here on line 035. You might have to use a type-cast expression, as in the sample program, because `get()` returns `Object`:

```
String value = (String)symbols.get(new Integer(key));
```

The `get()` method returns `null` if the key is not found — but be careful. If `null` is inserted as a key, then `get()` returns it. In most cases, however, if you are sure that a `null` key has not been inserted into the container, you can consider a `null` result from `get()` as an indication that the key is not in the container; otherwise, call `containsKey()` before calling `get()`.

Changing Keys and Values

Because `Map` containers require all keys to be unique, changing a key's value is a simple matter of calling `put()` to insert the new entry. This effectively replaces the old association with the new one. For example, to change the value of key 37 from "Percent" to "Percent sign," the program in Listing 17-4 could execute the statement

```
symbols.put(new Integer(37), "Percent sign");
```

If the key exists in the database, its value is replaced; otherwise, a new key-value object is added to the container.

Map Views

One way to access keys and associated values in a `Map` container is to obtain a `Set` of its keys and then use an `Iterator` object to locate each key-value pair. For example, building on Listing 17-4, use a statement such as the following to get a set of keys from the `symbols` container:

```
Set keys = symbols.keySet();
```

That calls the `Map` interface `keySet()` method, which returns a `Set` of the container's keys.

Some programmers new to Java consider the preceding statement to be in conflict with the rule that interfaces, such as Set, cannot be instantiated as objects. That's true, but an object of a class that implements Set can be accessed via a Set reference. Internally, the HashMap class creates a customized instance of the AbstractSet class by implementing that abstract class's methods. This is the real container object that is returned by keySet(); however, outsiders may use that container only as stipulated by the Set interface. This provides for highly controlled access to the container, which can be used by calling only the well-defined methods stipulated by the Set interface, and that are actually implemented internally.

Use the keys container returned by keySet() as you do any other Set-based container, as described in Chapter 16. First, obtain an Iterator object:

```
Iterator I = keys.iterator();
```

You can then call the Iterator object's hasNext() and next() methods to browse the HashMap container's key-value associations:

```
while (I.hasNext()) {
  Integer key = (Integer)I.next();
  String value = (String)symbols.get(key);
  System.out.println(key + " :: " + value);
}
```

Because the Iterator accesses the set of keys, I.next() returns each key in succession. In this case, we know the keys are Integer objects, but the type cast throws ClassCastException if the actual type of object is not Integer. To obtain each associated value, the program calls the get() method for the symbols container. Again, a type-cast expression is used to indicate to the compiler that values in this container are String objects.

The preceding technique works well enough, but it illustrates just one of countless ways to access Map containers using differing views — for example, as a Set of keys. A more sophisticated method provides direct access to the key-value entry objects actually stored in the container. The next section describes how this works.

Map.Entry Iterators

HashMap containers store keys and associated values as objects of a private, inner class. The class, to which HashMap users have no direct access, implements the Entry interface, shown here in Listing 17-5, Map.Entry.txt. This interface is also an inner, nested declaration in HashMap and for that reason is fully named

Map.Entry. The interface is public, and therefore it provides a controlled means for HashMap users to access key-value objects in the container.

Listing 17-5: Map.Entry.txt

```
001: // Map.Entry·interface
002: public interface Entry {
003:   Object getKey();
004:   Object getValue();
005:   Object setValue(Object value);
006:   boolean equals(Object o);
007:   int hashCode();
008: }
```

There are five methods in the Map.Entry interface, the first three of which provide access to a HashMap entry's key and associated value and change the value associated with a key. The equals() and hashCode() methods do their usual jobs. No method is provided to change a key value itself because of the danger that doing so might destabilize the container by making two keys equivalent.

TIP

To change a key in a Map container, remove it by calling remove(key) and then insert a new key-value pair by calling put(). This is safer than merely attempting to change the key directly.

Refer back to Listing 17-4, lines 007-015, for a typical way to use the Map.Entry interface to access a HashMap container's contents. I repeat some of that code here for easy reference. Assuming m refers to any Map-based container, first, obtain an Iterator using the statement

```
Iterator I = m.entrySet().iterator();
```

That calls the Map interface entrySet() method, which returns type Set (see Listing 17-1). The Iterator object is not provided by Map but rather by the Set interface's iterator() method. Use that Iterator in the usual way, but with a slight twist:

```
while (I.hasNext()) {
 Map.Entry entry = (Map.Entry)I.next();
 System.out.println(
   entry.getKey() + "\t:: " + entry.getValue());
}
```

While I.hasNext() returns true, there is at least one more key-value entry in the container. To get a reference to that object, call the Iterator object's next()

method. However, use a type-cast expression as shown on the second line to tell the compiler that this is actually a Map.Entry object. Save the result in a Map.Entry reference variable, here named entry. Because the Map.Entry interface is declared public in HashMap, the type cast enables the program to call its methods (see Listing 17-5). For example, entry.getKey() returns the entry's key object, and entry.getValue() returns its associated value object. Although not used here, entry.setValue() changes the current entry's value.

TIP As usual with Iterator objects, always call hasNext() before calling next() to obtain the next Map.Entry object from a HashMap container to avoid a NoSuchElementException.

The WeakHashMap Class

The WeakHashMap class stores *weak references* to keys that are subject to garbage collection. Although many Java programmers understandably shy away from using any class with the word "weak" in it, like most concepts, weak references are less mysterious when you understand them. Especially important is a weak reference's relationship to Java's garbage collector.

First, however, consider the nature of a *strong reference*. This is the kind in use for most class object variables. When a program creates an object as follows, the reference to it is of the strong variety:

```
String s = new String("I am very strong!");
```

As long as the variable s remains in use — that is, as long as it is in scope — it is untouchable by the garbage collector. However, if that variable is declared local to a method, when that method returns, the reference is deleted, and the object to which it refers is subject to garbage collection. The object actually remains in memory until the garbage collector decides it needs to clean house, usually in response to a lack of available memory.

Weak references work a little differently. They are references to objects of the WeakReference class, provided in the java.lang.ref package, that, from birth, are subject to garbage collection. You can create a weak reference with code such as

```
import java.lang.ref.WeakReference;
...
Object weak = new WeakReference(new String("I am very weak!"));
```

I don't recommend actually writing a statement like that — it merely shows the WeakReference class in use. Because it is weak, the reference is subject to garbage collection. In other words, if the garbage collector needs more memory than it can obtain with a normal sweep of unused objects, it may dispose of any weak references it can find. It will do so, however, *only* if the weak reference is the only one to an object. Weak object references have no guaranteed lifespan – they are subject to garbage collection at any time, and so you must check them before use.

Those facts make weak references suitable for large objects that might be cached in memory, but reloaded as needed. Your Web browser uses a similar technique to cache recently visited pages, or at least to store local copies of some of the items on those pages. When you return to a page, the browser checks whether it has already downloaded an item such as a large picture, and if so, it uses the local copy. This increases the apparent speed of the network connection while using memory as efficiently as possible.

A `WeakHashMap` container stores key values as objects of an internal, private class named `WeakKey` that extends `WeakReference`. Key-value objects in a `WeakHashMap` container are therefore subject to garbage collection at any time, and they might be discarded between the time you insert them and the time you next go looking for a particular key.

Although there isn't room here to provide a complete sample listing (`WeakHashMaps` are practical only in large applications with tremendous memory requirements), as a hypothetical example, consider using this type of container to store photographic images. As with other hash-table containers, you have the option of specifying an initial capacity and load factor:

```
WeakHashMap pix = new WeakHashMap(500, 0.65);
```

You can then insert photographic images, perhaps by loading them from disk by way of a hypothetical `Photo` class constructor:

```
pix.add(filename, new Photo(filename));
```

The `filename` serves as the entry's key, and the `Photo` object, the actual image, is the value inserted into the `WeakHashMap` container. Loading numerous objects might cause the garbage collector to throw out some weak references to make room, so it's important to check whether an object still exists before using it. The following statements are in a presumed method that returns a `Photo` object:

```
Photo p = (Photo)pix.get(filename);
if (p == null) {
 p = new Photo(filename);  // Load or reload
 if (p != null)
  pix.add(filename, p);    // Cache
}
return p;
```

Again, all of that is hypothetical, but it shows the basic idea. If `get()` returns `null`, you can assume that the photo image defined by `filename` either was never inserted into the container or it has been garbage collected. Either way, the program reloads the photo, adds it to the cache, and returns the result (which might still be `null` if the file fails to load for some reason).

SortedMap Containers

Like `Map`, the `SortedMap` interface stipulates methods for storing unique key-value associations. `SortedMap` differs from `Map` in only one significant way — it guarantees that objects are maintained in key order. This means that objects inserted as keys into a `SortedMap` container must be of classes that implement the `Comparable` interface and provide a `compareTo()` method. If that's not possible, however, the container can use a `Comparator` object to compare two keys. Because `SortedMap` extends `Map`, a `SortedMap` container class provides implementations for both interfaces' methods (refer back to Listings 17-1 and 17-2 for a complete list).

The TreeMap Class

Only one concrete class in the library implements the `SortedMap` interface, `TreeMap`, shown here in Listing 17-6, TreeMap.txt. The class adds only constructors to the method declarations it receives from the `Map` and `SortedMap` interfaces.

Listing 17-6: TreeMap.txt

```
001: // TreeMap constructors
002: public TreeMap();
003: public TreeMap(Comparator c);
004: public TreeMap(Map m);
005: public TreeMap(SortedMap m);
```

You can construct a `TreeMap` container four ways. For a default container, specify no arguments to the constructor:

```
TreeMap myTree = new TreeMap();
```

Because a `TreeMap` container stores its object keys in a tree-like, reference-linked data structure, there is no way nor any need to specify an initial capacity, as there is for a `HashMap` container. (Except for the `TreeMap` object itself, the newly constructed container is completely empty and it uses no other memory.)

If the object keys to be inserted are of classes that do not implement `Comparable`, you must use the alternate constructor at line 003 to create the container. The `Comparator` is typically returned by a `static` method in the key's class, resulting in hypothetical code such as the following:

```
TreeMap myTree = new TreeMap(KeyClass.byType());
```

`KeyClass` represents the class that provides a `Comparator` method, `byType()`, which constructs the actual `Comparator` to be used in comparing two `KeyClass` objects.

TIP For help in writing an actual `Comparator` object method, see the several `Chart` class listings and related discussions in Chapter 15, especially the section titled "Using Comparators and `ArrayList`."

Two other `TreeMap` constructors provide the means to create a new container given an existing `Map` or `SortedMap` object. For example, you might use the following code to convert a `HashMap` container to a `TreeMap`, and in that way sort the hash table by its keys:

```
HashMap myMap = new HashMap();
...
TreeMap myTree = new TreeMap(myMap);
```

Creating a TreeMap Dictionary

One typical use for a `TreeMap` container is to create a dictionary of words and definitions. The words are the keys; the definitions are the associated values. Because the `TreeMap` class is based on the `SortedMap` interface, the dictionary is automatically maintained in alphabetical order. Creating a simple container of this kind is easy — just construct a `TreeMap` container and add word and definition strings by calling `put()`. Find definitions of words (the keys) by calling `get()`.

But in a real dictionary, words have multiple definitions. Since a `Map` or `SortedMap` container is limited to unique keys, how can you associate them with multiple entries? One answer is to create a *nested container* — in other words, a container that holds another container as an object. The end result is like a multidimensional array but is far more versatile and, depending on the choice of container classes, may use memory more efficiently.

To demonstrate how to create a nested container, the next program creates a small dictionary of words and definitions using `TreeMap` and `LinkedList` containers. The complete program is shown here in Listing 17-7, Dictionary.java.

Listing 17-7: Dictionary.java

```
001: import java.util.*;
002: import java.io.*;
003:
004: class Dictionary {
005:
006: // Construct TreeMap dictionary container
007:   static TreeMap dict = new TreeMap();
008:
009: // Lookup and show definition for the specified word (key)
010:   static void showDefinition(String word) {
011:     LinkedList defs = (LinkedList)dict.get(word);
```

```
012:    if (defs == null) return;  // Ignore if not there
013:    ListIterator L = defs.listIterator();
014:    int count = 1;  // Definition counter
015:    System.out.println("\n" + word);
016:    while (L.hasNext()) {
017:      String definition = (String)L.next();
018:      System.out.println(count++ + ". " + definition);
019:    }
020:  }
021:
022: // Display entire dictionary
023:  static void showDictionary() {
024:    Iterator I = dict.keySet().iterator();
025:    while (I.hasNext())
026:      showDefinition((String)I.next());
027:  }
028:
029: // Add a new word and/or definition
030:  static void addWord(String word, String definition) {
031:    if (dict.containsKey(word)) {
032:      LinkedList defs = (LinkedList)dict.get(word);
033:      defs.add(definition);  // Add new definition only
034:    } else {
035:      LinkedList defs = new LinkedList();  // New list
036:      defs.add(definition);  // Add definition to new list
037:      dict.put(word, defs);  // Add word and defs association
038:    }
039:  }
040:
041:  public static void main(String args[]) {
042:
043: // Read words and definitions into the container
044:    try {
045:      FileReader fr = new FileReader("Dictionary.txt");
046:      BufferedReader br = new BufferedReader(fr);
047:      String word = br.readLine();
048:      while (word != null) {
049:       addWord(word, br.readLine());  // Add word and definition
050:       br.readLine();          // Skip blank line
051:       word = br.readLine();  // Read next word
052:      }
053:    } catch (FileNotFoundException e) {
054:      System.out.println("File not found: " + e.getMessage());
055:    } catch (IOException e) {
056:      System.out.println("I/O error: " + e.getMessage());
```

```
057:   }
058:
059: // Look up one word or show entire dictionary
060:   if (args.length == 0)
061:     showDictionary();          // Show all
062:   else
063:     showDefinition(args[0]);   // Show selection
064:
065:   }   // main
066: }  // class
```

Compile and run the program. If you enter no arguments, it prints the entire dictionary. Enter a word to find its definition:

```
java Dictionary ingenuous
ingenuous
1. artless
2. frank
```

For a source of words and definitions, on disk is a file, Dictionary.txt (also in the c17/Dictionary directory) that contains entries such as

```
extant
still existing

ingenuous
artless

supercilious
haughtily disdainful

ingenuous
frank
```

In the source text, each word is associated with only one definition. A blank line separates the string pairs. This simple format makes it easy to add new words without concern that they are already in the list — simply add them to the end of the file and rerun the program. Some words have only one definition; others have several. The words come from a personal list that I've been adding to for years every time I run into a word that I don't know or that I want to know better (only a small sampling of the full list is on disk — the real list still uses old-fashioned technology: file cards and a rubber band).

The program begins by reading the source text into a `TreeMap` container (lines 043-057). The container, `dict`, of type `TreeMap`, is declared and initialized at line 007. Each word and definition is added to the container by calling a local method, `addWord()` (lines 030-039). First, the word is checked by calling `containsKey()` to see if it is already in the container. If so, the statements at lines 032-033 call the `Map` interface `get()` method to obtain the value associated with this word. The result is cast to a `LinkedList` — the nested container held by each `TreeMap` entry.

If the word is not already in the container, line 035 creates a new `LinkedList` container named `defs`. The definition string is added to this container, which is then inserted into the `dict` `TreeMap` at line 037. Notice especially that the `word` string is the key and the `defs` `LinkedList` container is the key's associated value. Thus each word is associated with a container that might hold one or several definition strings for each key. With nested containers, you can create some interesting and complex data structures with a minimum of programming.

Other methods in the program display a single word and list of definitions (`showDefinition()` at lines 010-020) and display the entire dictionary (`showDictionary()` at lines 023-027). The programming in these methods uses `Iterator` and `ListIterator` objects to search the `TreeMap`'s keys and the `LinkedList`'s string entries. Although the program is a little more complex looking than other examples you have seen in this part, there's nothing new here except that, instead of simple values, each key is associated with another container.

Summary

- ◆ A map, or associative container, stores unique keys and their associated values.

- ◆ The `Map` interface stipulates the most common methods of associative containers. The `SortedMap` interface extends `Map` and provides additional methods suitable for an associative container maintained in key order.

- ◆ Two concrete classes implement the `Map` interface: `HashMap` and `WeakHashMap`. Each uses hash values to store keys and their associated values. `HashMap` is an excellent choice of containers when the order of objects is not important.

- ◆ The `WeakHashMap` class stores weak references to keys and associated values that are subject to garbage collection from the time they are inserted into the container. This makes `WeakHashMap` containers suitable for use as memory caches — for example, to maintain a database of photos but permit the garbage collector to delete some references if necessary to make room.

◆ The concrete class `TreeMap` implements the `SortedMap` interface. This container maintains its entries sorted by keys and is suitable for containers such as dictionaries.

◆ As this chapter's `Dictionary` program demonstrates, a container can be nested in another — for example, using a `LinkedList` as the value associated with a key in a `TreeMap` container. Storing containers as objects in other containers is a powerful technique that can create complex data structures with a minimum of programming.

Chapter 18

Utilities and Legacy Classes

As mentioned throughout the preceding chapters, the Collections utility class provides numerous methods and a few other items that are invaluable for container library programming. In the preceding chapters, you already met some of this class's methods such as sort() and binarySearch(). This chapter lists all Collections declarations and explains how to use many of them.

Covered also in this chapter are the BitSet class and other Java *legacy container classes,* which are still supported but no longer recommended for use in new code. Although some texts consider BitSet to be a legacy container, you may find it useful especially because no other Java class provides similar bit-twiddling capabilities. Also, the Vector legacy class is still in popular use.

IN THIS CHAPTER

- ◆ Putting the Collections class to use
- ◆ Seaching and sorting with Collections
- ◆ Creating thread-safe containers
- ◆ Legacy containers and their replacements
- ◆ Manipulating bit values with the BitSet class

The Collections Class

The Collections class provides numerous utility methods that operate on containers based on the Collection interface. Listing 18-1, Collections.txt, shows all of the class's public declarations. Keep in mind that the Collections class is plural — the Collection interface is singular.

Listing 18-1: Collections.txt

```
001: // Sorting and searching methods
002: public static void sort(List list);
003: public static void sort(List list, Comparator c);
004: public static int binarySearch(List list, Object key);
```

```
005: public static int binarySearch(List list,
       Object key, Comparator c);
006:
007: // Unmodifiable wrappers
008: public static Collection unmodifiableCollection(Collection c);
009: public static Set unmodifiableSet(Set s);
010: public static SortedSet unmodifiableSortedSet(SortedSet s);
011: public static List unmodifiableList(List list);
012: public static Map unmodifiableMap(Map m);
013: public static SortedMap unmodifiableSortedMap(SortedMap m);
014:
015: // Synchronized wrappers
016: public static Collection synchronizedCollection(Collection c);
017: public static Set synchronizedSet(Set s);
018: public static SortedSet synchronizedSortedSet(SortedSet s);
019: public static List synchronizedList(List list);
020: public static Map synchronizedMap(Map m);
021: public static SortedMap synchronizedSortedMap(SortedMap m);
022:
023: // Miscellaneous operations
024: public static void reverse(List l);
025: public static void shuffle(List list);
026: public static void shuffle(List list, Random rnd);
027: public static void fill(List list, Object o);
028: public static void copy (List dest, List src);
029: public static Object min(Collection coll);
030: public static Object min(Collection coll, Comparator comp);
031: public static Object max(Collection coll);
032: public static Object max(Collection coll, Comparator comp);
033:
034: // Other declarations
035: public static final Set EMPTY_SET;
036: public static final List EMPTY_LIST;
037: public static final Map EMPTY_MAP;
038: public static Set singleton(Object o);
039: public static List singletonList(Object o);
040: public static Map singletonMap(Object key, Object value);
041: public static List nCopies(int n, Object o);
042: public static Comparator reverseOrder();
043: public static Enumeration enumeration(final Collection c);
```

Line numbers mentioned in the following five sections refer to Listing 18-1.

Searching and Sorting Methods

The two sort() and binarySearch() methods (lines 002-005) sort and search List-based containers. For more information on these methods, see Chapter 15, "List Collections," in the sections "Sorting LinkedList Containers" and "Binary Search Method."

Sorting and searching methods are not needed for other types of containers because classes based on SortedSet and SortedMap interfaces automatically maintain their objects in sorted order. However, if you need to sort another type of container for some reason, you can convert it to a List and pass it to one of the Collections sort() methods. You could then also call binarySearch() to search the container's objects.

Unmodifiable Wrappers

Containers normally provide read and write access to their objects. But in some cases, especially in class library code, it might be necessary to provide read-only containers. For instance, a class in a library might return a list of internal settings for reference purposes but disallow modifications to that list.

To create a read-only container, use one of the unmodifiable wrapper methods shown at lines 008-013. There's one method for each interface: Collection, Set, SortedSet, List, Map, and SortedMap. Each method returns an unmodifiable view of a container referenced by its interface type.

To use one of these methods, first create the normal container, and add objects to it. As an example, the following constructs a HashSet container and then inserts some programming words from the Pascal programming language:

```
HashSet hashtable = new HashSet(100, 0.65f);
hashtable.add("begin");
hashtable.add("end");
hashtable.add("procedure");
hashtable.add("function");
```

The program might allow users to view the list of words, but not add new ones or make any other changes. To ensure its proper use, the program creates an unmodifiable Set using code such as

```
Set readonly = Collections.unmodifiableSet(hashtable);
readonly.add("dowhile");  // ???
```

The readonly set offers a new view of the original container's contents—the objects are not cloned—but the new container cannot be modified in any way. Attempts to do so as shown here by calling add() throw UnsupportedOperationException. Methods such as contains() that do not modify the container work normally. Users are also prevented from casting the unmodifiable set back to one that can be changed. The following throws ClassCastException:

```
HashSet cheater = (HashSet)readonly;  // ???
```

It is possible to use an unmodifiable container to create a new one that can be modified. Passing the unmodifiable container to a container class constructor may seem to subvert the read-only restriction:

```
HashSet cheater = new HashSet(readonly);
cheater.add("goto");  // !!!
```

However, the original readonly container remains unchanged and unmodifiable, although the new cheater container can be modified.

Synchronized Wrappers

Lines 016–021 show the Collections class's synchronized wrappers. Normally, containers are not *thread-safe*—that is, statements in threaded code cannot use them safely. Wrapping a container using one of Collections's synchronized methods results in a container that is thread-safe.

Chapter 19, "Threaded Code," discusses in more detail how to write threaded Java programs. In such programs, to use one of the synchronized methods, first construct the container and add some objects to it:

```
TreeSet myTree = new TreeSet();
myTree.add("Apple");
myTree.add("Banana");
myTree.add("Cherry");
```

The myTree container is not thread-safe. To make it so, pass it to one of the Collections class's synchronized methods:

```
Collection safe = Collections.synchronizedCollection(myTree);
```

Note carefully the spellings—the safe reference variable is of the Collection (singular) interface type. The method is called in reference to the Collections (plural) utility class. You may now use the safe reference in synchronized code. For example, the following uses an Iterator to pass each object in the container to a method f() (not shown):

```
Collection safe = Collections.synchronizedCollection(myTree);
synchronized(safe) {
 Iterator I = safe.iterator();
 while (I.hasNext())
  f(I.next());
}
```

When using synchronized containers, there are two important details to keep in mind. One, iterations such as in the preceding example *must* be executed in a synchronized block. Two, the original container used to create the synchronized view must never be used. It might be okay to perform read-only operations on the original container, but as a general rule, after constructing the synchronized view, in threaded code, the program should use only the synchronized view to gain access to the container's objects.

Miscellaneous Operations

The Collections class provides a number of miscellaneous List and Collection operations that might be useful from time to time (see lines 024–032). It's a good idea to at least be aware of these methods so you don't waste time duplicating them needlessly.

As mentioned in Chapter 15, List-based containers maintain their objects in the order in which they are inserted. To reverse that order, call the reverse() method as follows:

```
LinkedList myList = new LinkedList();
// add object to myList
Collections.sort(myList);
Collections.reverse(myList);
```

As shown here, the container is typically sorted before calling reverse() in order to obtain a reverse ordering of the container's objects.

To scramble a List container's objects, call one of two shuffle() methods. The first takes a single List argument; the second adds a Random parameter to perform the shuffling. (See Chapter 9, "Numeric Classes," for how to use the Random class.) The following programming fragment uses the second method to shuffle a LinkedList container:

```
import java.util.Random;
...
LinkedList myList = new LinkedList();
// add objects to myList
Collections.shuffle(myList, new Random());
```

You might call a shuffle() method to test a sorting algorithm's performance, or to prepare test data for feeding to other methods. The shuffle() methods might also be handy in applet and game programming. Another useful method fills a List with objects. First construct a List container and add some objects to it:

```
LinkedList myList = new LinkedList();
myList.add("Apple");
myList.add("Banana");
myList.add("Cherry");
```

Call fill() to fill the container with any other object. For example, this sets the three string objects in myList to null:

```
Collections.fill(myList, null);
```

Calling fill() does not add new objects to a List container. It *replaces* the container's existing object references with the one specified. If the original container has three objects, then the preceding statement replaces their references with null. The resulting container still holds three objects. Following a call to fill(), you can use a ListIterator's set() method to insert new objects into the list.

TIP See the nCopies() method in the next section for a way to grow a List to a predefined size. The fill() method is not intended for that purpose.

To copy one List container to another, call the copy() method and pass it the destination and source lists in that order:

```
ArrayList L1 = new ArrayList();
ArrayList L2 = new ArrayList();
// add objects to L1 and L2
Collections.copy(L2, L1);   // L2 <-- L1
```

That copies all objects from L1 to L2. Although simple in appearance, the copy() method requires careful handling to use properly. Copied objects are not cloned; only their references are duplicated in the destination list. The destination list (L2 here) must be at least as large as the source list (L1) — the destination is *not* expanded automatically. If the destination list is larger than the source, remaining objects in the destination are undisturbed. If the destination is not large enough to hold all objects from the source, IndexOutOfBoundsException is thrown. In addition, the destination list class's ListIterator must support the set() method, or UnsupportedOperationException is thrown.

Finally in the miscellaneous category are four overloaded min() and max() methods that, as their names suggest, find the minimum and maximum objects in any Collection-based container (see lines 029-032). The collection does not need to be sorted. Each method has two versions. The first takes as a single argument the container to search:

```
if (!myList.isEmpty())
  String s = (String)Collections.min(myList);
```

Use `max()` similarly. Always check whether the container is empty because, if it is, `min()` and `max()` throw `NoSuchElementException`. Also, the type-cast expression is usually necessary because `min()` and `max()` return `Object`. In this case, the returned object must be a `String`, or a `ClassCastException` is thrown. That same exception is thrown if the container objects are not comparable. In such cases, you can pass a `Comparator` object to `min()` and `max()` to use in comparing the container objects. Again, always check first whether the container is empty to avoid an exception. Borrowing the `Chart` class from Chapter 15, the following code locates the chart having the maximum scale value:

```
if (!myList.isEmpty())
  Chart c = (Chart)Collections.max(myList, Chart.byScale());
```

For both `min()` and `max()`, in case of any duplications in an unsorted container, the one returned is the first one located in the order in which the list was created.

Other Declarations

Finally in the `Collections` utility class are several other declarations that appear to have been thrown in for good measure (see lines 035-043).

Three declarations, `EMPTY_SET`, `EMPTY_LIST`, and `EMPTY_MAP`, provide immutable `Set`, `List`, and `Map` containers respectively that have no contents. As their capitalized names suggest, these objects are `static` and `final` constants. One possible use for them is as return values from methods that return references to newly constructed containers. Instead of returning `null` in cases where the container is empty or cannot be constructed for some reason, the method can return one of the constants and in that way not require the method's callers to test for a `null` result.

Three other methods return singleton `Set`, `List`, and `Map` containers containing only one object. For example, this creates a singleton `List` with one string:

```
List L = Collections.singletonList("One and only");
```

The container is guaranteed to contain only one object — no new objects can be added to it, nor removed from it. The methods are primarily useful when you want to call a method that requires a container argument, but you have only a single object to pass to that method. In that case, wrap your object around a singleton method and use it as the argument. By the way, the `Set` method is named `singleton()`. The other two are named `singletonList()` and `singletonMap()`. There is no `singletonSet()` method.

When you need to create a `List` of a certain size, call the `nCopies()` method. Pass two arguments: an integer representing the desired list size, and the object to copy into the list. Save the result as a `List` reference:

```
List L = Collections.nCopies(10, "Place holder");
```

That constructs a `List` container with 10 references to the string `"Place holder"`. Each entry in the container refers to the *same* string or other object specified as the second argument to `nCopies()`. The objects are not duplicated. Because `nCopies()` returns type `List`, you may call that interface's methods to operate on the container. However, you probably want to treat the result as an object of a concrete class such as `LinkedList`. To do that, call the `addAll()` method to add the `List` to your container. Given the preceding statement, this creates a new `LinkedList` preset to 10 objects:

```
LinkedList copy = new LinkedList();
copy.addAll(L);
```

That's the proper way to create a `List` container of a specific size. Normally, `List` containers expand and shrink for each object added and removed. Given the preceding call to `nCopies()`, the new container, `copy`, now holds 10 references to the string "Place holder".

One obscure, but surprisingly useful, `Collections` method, `reverseOrder()`, returns a *reverse* `Comparator` object. This method exists primarily to make it easier to sort a `Collection`-based container in the reverse of its natural ordering. To do that without this method, you have to perform steps such as these:

1. Call `Collections.sort()` for the container.

2. Call `Collections.reverse()` to reverse the object order (if the container is a List), or access the objects in reverse order, or write custom code to reverse the sorted container.

The `reverseOrder()` method simplifies those steps into one. Use it like this:

```
Comparator reverse = Collections.reverseOrder();
Collections.sort(myList, reverse);
```

You don't need to save the `Comparator` object as shown here — you can pass the method's result directly to `sort()`. Although the code is seemingly simple, the use of a `Comparator` object in this fashion is unusual. Normally, as mentioned several times throughout this part of the book (especially in Chapter 15), a `Comparator` object is used when a container's objects are not directly comparable. In this case, however, the `Comparator` object that `reverseOrder()` returns imposes a reverse ordering on objects whose classes implement the `Comparable` interface and provide a compareTo() method. If the objects are not comparable, reverseOrder() throws ClassCastException.

Finally in the Collections utility class is the method enumeration() (line 043). Pass to it any Collection-based container and save the result as an Enumeration reference:

```
Enumeration E = Collections.enumeration(myList); // ???
```

The only reason to call this method is to support older code that uses one of the legacy container classes discussed in the next section. (An Enumeration is similar to an Iterator.) For example, if you must call a library method that requires an Enumeration argument, you can use this technique to obtain one for a newer Collection-based container. However, new code should use Iterator and ListIterator objects in place of Enumeration.

Because the enumeration() method requires a Collection-based container argument, it cannot be used directly with classes that implement the Map interface. If you must get an Enumeration object for a Map container, call one of the Map view methods keySet(), values(), or entrySet(), and pass the result to enumeration().

Legacy Containers

Container classes based on the Collection and Map interfaces and their derivatives are relatively new additions to Java. Past versions of the java.util package provided several similar container classes, which unlike the newer classes were not as well organized nor as versatile. The older *legacy containers* listed here should no longer be used in new code. In alphabetic order, the legacy containers and their suggested replacements are

♦ Dictionary — Use a Map container such as TreeMap

♦ Enumeration — Use an Iterator or ListIterator object

♦ Hashtable — Use the HashMap or HashSet classes

♦ Properties — Use the HashMap class

♦ Stack — Use a LinkedList or ArrayList class

♦ Vector — Use the ArrayList class

Although Java 2 continues to support these legacy containers, not all older code that uses them compiles. Some techniques that worked with the JDK 1.0 — for example, code that uses HashTableEnumerator, which no longer exists – do not work at all in Java 2. Support for legacy containers is provided because of their extensive use in existing code, but you should never use the preceding classes in new programs.

Unlike other legacy classes that are unrelated to the newer collection containers, the Vector class extends AbstractList and implements List, Cloneable, and java.io.Serializable — similar in design to the newer container class ArrayList. Vector might therefore be considered a member of the newer collection containers, but it is not synonymous with ArrayList. Most important, Vector is safe for use in threaded code because the class's methods are synchronized. The same is not true of ArrayList. To use an ArrayList container in threaded code, you must create a synchronized view of the container by calling synchronizedList() in the Collections utility class (see "Synchronized Wrappers" in this chapter).

BitSet Containers

The java.util package provides the BitSet class for storing and manipulating bit values. You might find the class handy for keeping true and false values compressed into single bits, or you might use it for bit-wise boolean-logic code. Listing 18-2, BitSet.txt, shows the declaration of the BitSet class.

Listing 18-2: BitSet.txt

```
001: // BitSet constructors
002: public BitSet();
003: public BitSet(int nbits);
004:
005: // BitSet methods
006: public int length();
007: public void set(int bitIndex);
008: public void clear(int bitIndex);
009: public void andNot(BitSet set);
010: public boolean get(int bitIndex);
011: public void and(BitSet set);
012: public void or(BitSet set);
013: public void xor(BitSet set);
014: public int hashCode();
015: public int size();
016: public boolean equals(Object obj);
017: public Object clone();
018: public String toString();
```

As mentioned, some texts include the BitSet class among Java's legacy containers (see the preceding section). However, BitSet does not extend any other legacy classes, and it provides useful techniques that are not available through any other Java classes. For that reason, I consider BitSet to be a viable utility class with plenty of life remaining. Others may disagree.

Technically, the BitSet class implements a *vector* of single bits — but it is not based on Vector or any other class. A module that uses the BitSet class can import it from the java.util package using the statement

```
import java.util.BitSet;
```

A BitSet container grows as needed to accommodate additional bits, but in most cases, you should construct the container of the size you need. Here are two ways to create a BitSet object:

```
BitSet setOfBits = new BitSet(16);
BitSet secondSet = new BitSet();
```

The first and most common form specifies the number of bits to store in the BitSet container. The second form constructs a default empty BitSet object. All bits in non-empty containers are initially set to false. Internally, BitSet containers store data in the individual bits of an array of long integer variables. Consequently, there is no practical limit on the number of bits that a BitSet container can store.

Specifying a negative size when constructing a BitSet container throws NegativeArraySizeException. When using a variable to construct BitSet containers, avoid this exception by verifying that the value is not negative.

Bits in a BitSet container are indexed starting with zero. Set a particular bit to true by calling set() like this:

```
setOfBits.set(5);   // Set bit 6 true
```

Clear a bit, setting it to false, by calling clear():

```
setOfBits.clear(3);   // Set bit 4 false
```

Calling set() or clear() with an index value greater than or equal to the BitSet's current length automatically allocates more memory to the container. IndexOutOfBoundsException is thrown if the specified index is negative. If the index is greater than the container's current size, the container is expanded. Use that fact to expand a BitSet object with a statement such as

```
secondSet.clear(64);  // Expand to 64 bits
```

There is no way to reduce the size of a BitSet except by re-creating it. To obtain the value of a particular bit, call the get() method:

```
if (setOfBits.get(5))
 System.out.println("Bit 6 is true");
```

The get() method throws IndexOutOfBoundsException if the index is negative.

You may combine BitSet containers using AND, OR, and XOR (exclusive-OR) Boolean logic. These methods are declared as follows, and they are used as their names suggest:

```
public void and(BitSet set);
public void or(BitSet set);
public void xor(BitSet set);
```

 By convention, the uppercase words, AND, OR, and XOR, and the capitalized word *Boolean* refer generally to logical operations — they are not Java programming words. The preceding three BitSet methods are spelled in all lowercase, as is the Java boolean data type.

Pass a BitSet container to one of these methods, called in reference to the destination BitSet that you want to alter according to the specific Boolean operation. Listing 18-3, BitSetDemo.java, demonstrates how to do this using the xor() method.

Listing 18-3: BitSetDemo.java

```
001: import java.util.BitSet;
002:
003: class BitSetDemo {
004:   // Display string and value of BitSet object
005:   public static void show(String s, BitSet obj) {
006:     System.out.println(s + obj.toString());
007:   }
008:   // Main program tests BitSet Boolean logic
```

```
009:   public static void main(String args[]) {
010:     // Construct two BitSets
011:     BitSet set1 = new BitSet(16);
012:     BitSet set2 = new BitSet(16);
013:     // Set bits 2, 4, and 8 in set 1
014:     set1.set(2); set1.set(4); set1.set(8);
015:     // Set all bits in set 2
016:     for (int i = 0; i < set2.size(); i++)
017:       set2.set(i);
018:     // Test Boolean logic and show results
019:     show("before XOR set1 = ", set1);
020:     set1.xor(set2);
021:     show("after XOR set1  = ", set1);
022:     set1.xor(set2);
023:     show("after XOR set1  = ", set1);
024:   }
025: }
```

The sample program constructs two 16-bit BitSet containers. It sets the first container's bits 2, 4, and 8 to true and also sets all bits in the second container using a for loop along with the BitSet size() method to determine how many bits the set contains. Two calls to the xor() method then demonstrate one of the principles of Boolean XOR logic: XORing (exclusive ORing) any bit value with 1 twice in succession returns the original value. In other words, the xor() method works as a bit toggle. The sample program's show() method proves this by displaying

```
before XOR set1 = {2, 4, 8}
after XOR set1  = {0, 1, 3, 5, 6, 7, 9, 10, 11, 12, 13, 14,
15, 16, 17, 18, 19, 20, 21, 22, 23, 24, 25, 26, 27, 28, 29,
30, 31, 32, 33, 34, 35, 36, 37, 38, 39, 40, 41, 42, 43, 44,
45, 46, 47, 48, 49, 50, 51, 52, 53, 54, 55, 56, 57, 58, 59,
60, 61, 62, 63}
after XOR set1  = {2, 4, 8}
```

The first line shows that the first set's bits 2, 4, and 8 are true. The next several lines show the results of XORing this set with another set with all bits equal to true. The final line shows that repeating the XOR operation restores the first set's original values.

To display the BitSet contents, the sample program calls the BitSet class's toString() method using this statement:

```
System.out.println(s + obj.toString());
```

This provides a handy way to display the values of any BitSet. The resulting string shows the index values of all true bits, delimited with braces.

Summary

◆ The `Collections` class provides numerous utility methods and a few other declarations that are valuable for container programming.

◆ Remember that the `Collections` class name is plural. The `Collection` interface, on which `Set` and `List` containers are based, is singular. The two names are easily confused.

◆ Java's legacy container classes are similar to the newer ones detailed in this part's chapters. Although still supported, legacy containers should not be used in new code. The legacy `Vector` class, however, remains popular and is suitable for use in threaded code. The similar `ArrayList` class is not synchronized. To use `ArrayList` in threaded code, you must call the `Collections` method `synchronizedList()` to create a thread-safe view of the container.

◆ The `BitSet` container, which some texts, but not this one, consider to be a member of the legacy group, stores bit values and provides bit-wise Boolean logic operations AND, OR, and XOR (exclusive OR).

Part IV

Applets and Applications

Chapter 19

Threaded Code

A *THREAD* IS A PROCESS that runs independently of other processes. Although you don't have to use threads in writing Java programs, threads provide advantages that are difficult to achieve in their absence. Some possible uses for threaded applications include printing in the background, implementing parallel algorithms, programming multi-user databases, and loading and displaying large graphics images and animations without disrupting user actions such as entering text into input fields.

Learning how to write threaded code requires learning some new terms and concepts. The following sections introduce threaded programming in general. After that, you learn how to apply these concepts using Java threaded-code techniques. The chapter ends with a complete demonstration of threaded programming.

IN THIS CHAPTER

- ◆ Thread concepts and terminology

- ◆ Extending the `Thread` class

- ◆ Implementing the `Runnable` interface

- ◆ Synchronizing threads with object locks

- ◆ A client-server threaded model

Concepts of Threaded Programming

If you could sew a line through the instructions of a program, the thread would follow the code's sequence of execution. A *threaded application* has two or more such lines, each identifying separately executing code sequences that weave in and out of each other like the threads and warps on a loom.

Every Java application is already threaded. The Java virtual machine executes an application in a separate thread, and the virtual machine's garbage collector, which frees memory occupied by unused objects, runs in the background in another thread. A program can also spawn multiple threads to perform operations in the background, foreground, and anywhere in between. To control relative activity among threads, you may specify a thread's *priority level*. Threads having highest priority get first crack at system resources; those with lower priorities operate in the shadows of more critical tasks.

363

Because Java code is interpreted, it can execute multiple threads by time-slicing on a single-tasking processor, or on more sophisticated hardware, by spawning tasks that are handled on the operating system and processor levels. These facts mean that threaded code can run on single-processor machines, but it can also take advantage of those with multiple processors. However, these are implementation details that are unimportant to application developers. If the Java interpreter is programmed correctly, threaded code runs similarly on any platform, from the simplest single-tasking systems to sophisticated multitasking operating environments.

A Few Good Terms

Threaded programming comes with its own terminology that you need to understand before you can make good use of the involved techniques. Following are some terms and related concepts you need to know to understand the programming examples in this chapter:

◆ *Daemon* — A daemon thread is one that does not have to die in order for the application to end. Specifically, the Java virtual machine exits when all non-daemon threads, also called *user threads,* have terminated. An executing thread cannot be changed to a daemon.

◆ *Deadlock* — This is a serious condition that occurs when two threads are waiting simultaneously to obtain a lock on each other's objects, and therefore neither thread is able to continue. The result is a hung program. Avoiding this deadly condition requires careful programming.

◆ *Lock* — All objects provide a lock that synchronized code can obtain, and in doing so, be guaranteed safe access to the object. Only the thread that owns an object's lock is allowed to access that object. Other threads that need the same object are *blocked* from continuing until the thread that owns the lock releases it.

◆ *Monitor* — This is just another term for a lock on an object. A thread that obtains a lock on an object is said to own the object's monitor.

◆ *Multitasking operating system* — This is generally defined as an operating system that can run multiple programs or other processes simultaneously. A multitasking operating system also typically provides protected memory so that errant code in one process cannot destroy the code and data in another. Java's threads do not require, but can take advantage of, an operating system's multitasking capabilities. However, this is the job of the Java virtual machine, of which there are many implementations, some better than others. In any case, because Java does not use pointers to address memory, and because all memory allocations are internally controlled, even in a single-tasking environment, it is next to impossible for a Java program to overstep its assigned memory boundaries.

◆ *Threaded application* – This refers to a program that runs two or more concurrent threads, each given a priority level that defines relative access to system resources. In Java, a thread is an object – usually an instance of the Thread class. However, it is also possible to create threads by implementing the Runnable interface. This chapter explains both techniques.

◆ *Race condition* – This is a serious problem that occurs when two or more threads make changes to the same object without obtaining a lock on that object. The result is at best the loss of information, and at worse, a seriously unstable system. Java's Thread class and Runnable interface provide the means to avoid race conditions. If you follow Java's rules for writing threaded code, you should never experience this problem.

◆ *Sleep* – This term refers to the state of a thread that is temporarily inactive. The thread awakens after a specified amount of time passes. A thread may sleep regardless of whether it owns a lock on an object. Unlike waiting, sleeping does not release the object's lock (if any). See also *Wait*.

◆ *Synchronized code* – Because of the potential for interactions among threads, it is frequently necessary to synchronize thread activity through the use of object locks. This protects data from being altered inappropriately by one thread while that same data is in use by another part of the program. Java permits specific regions, even single statements, to be synchronized, a fact that improves performance by allowing other non-critical code to run in unsynchronized fashion.

◆ *Thread* – A thread is the sequence of execution in a program's instructions. In a threaded application, each thread's individual instructions execute as though interspersed with one another. Once started, a thread can pause in its execution by sleeping or waiting. Once terminated, however, a thread cannot be restarted. When all threads that are not daemons end, the Java virtual machine exits.

◆ *Thread scheduler* – Internal to the Java virtual machine, the thread scheduler determines which threads run and for how long. Few guarantees are given concerning how the thread scheduler makes its decisions. For example, in some cases, regardless of a thread's priority, the scheduler may allow a thread to run only up to a certain maximum amount of time before it is paused and another thread is given a chance to execute.

◆ *Wait* – This term refers to the state of a thread that is waiting for notification from another thread. A thread may wait only if it owns its object's lock. While waiting, that lock is released so that other threads may have access to the object. To continue executing a waiting thread, another thread typically changes a condition such as a boolean state flag and then notifies waiting threads to wake up and check that condition. The technique of waiting in threads is essential for top performance because it avoids wasteful *polling instructions* that repeatedly test for a condition to become true, using up machine cycles that could be utilized by other tasks.

And a Few Good Classes

As with all Java techniques, programming with threads makes use of one or more classes, and one interface, most of which this chapter explores in detail. The key classes in thread programming, in rough order of importance, are

- Thread — Used to construct an individual thread. Constructing an object of this class and calling its start() method creates a separately executing thread. However, if your class does not override any Thread methods, you can more simply achieve the same results by implementing the Runnable interface.

- Runnable — Used by an implementing class to construct an individual thread, with the same results as instantiating the Thread class, but without requiring your class to extend Thread. Using the Runnable interface is appropriate when you don't need to override any Thread class methods; otherwise, building your class on Thread is necessary.

- ThreadGroup — Used to create thread sets, arranged in a tree-like hierarchy. All threads are members of a ThreadGroup. Among other services, ThreadGroup provides a strong reference to thread objects so they are not garbage-collected in case the program doesn't maintain a reference to its thread objects. ThreadGroup also provides a measure of security to applications. For example, threads may spawn new threads only within their own group; to spawn a thread in another group requires approval from a security manager object.

- ThreadDeath — This is an exception thrown by the now deprecated Thread.stop() method, which should no longer be used. The original intention of stop() and ThreadDeath was to provide an orderly way to terminate a thread; however, in practice, the technique can cause damage to objects by leaving them unprotected. There are better ways, described in this chapter, to terminate threads.

- InterruptedException — This exception is thrown for a Thread object that is waiting or sleeping and is interrupted by another thread by a call to the Thread.interrupt() method. A Runnable or Thread class must catch and respond to this exception to provide for an orderly shutdown of a thread.

- IllegalMonitorStateException — This exception is thrown if a thread attempts an operation such as waiting when the thread does not own its object's lock (monitor). The most common cause of this exception is attempting to call wait() in a run() method. See "Client-Server Threaded Code" in this chapter for examples of how to avoid receiving this exception.

◆ IllegalThreadStateException — This exception is thrown if a Thread object attempts an illegal operation — for example, attempting to start a thread that is already running, or trying to change a user thread into a daemon. If you receive this exception, revising the code is the only cure.

Programming Threaded Applications

There are two basic ways to create a threaded application, although there are many variations. The first and most common technique is to extend the Thread class, provided in the java.lang package. Here's how to begin:

```
class Background extends Thread {
 public void run() {
  // statements that do the thread's work
 }
}
```

The class also probably needs a constructor, variables, and various methods, but that's the basic design. Most important is the run() method, which performs the thread's activity. To create the thread and start it running, instantiate the class and call the start() method, inherited from Thread For example, the program's main() method (or another method) might execute statements such as

```
Background background = new Background();
background.start();
```

Calling start() prepares the thread object for running, and it hands the new thread to the virtual machine's thread scheduler. Soon after the call to start(), the thread scheduler calls the thread object's run() method, which performs the thread's activities. When run() ends, so does the thread.

 TIP   Never call run() directly for a thread object — that's the scheduler's job.

The second technique is to implement the Runnable interface. This is the simplest method if you don't need to override any methods inherited from Thread. The end results are identical; only the programming techniques differ. Design the class like this:

```
class Background implements Runnable {
 public void run() {
  // statements that do the thread's work
 }
}
```

Again, a constructor, variables, and other methods are probably needed, but that's the basic design. The run() method is the same as before, and it can do the same types of tasks. However, creating the thread object and starting it running are a little different. There are different ways to proceed. Here's one:

```
Background background = new Background();
Thread theThread = new Thread(background);
theThread.start();
```

After constructing the Background object, construct an instance of the Thread class by passing background to the Thread constructor. Call the start() method as shown for the Thread object. This prepares the new thread and instructs the thread scheduler to call the Background object's run() method. Because there's usually no reason to save the Thread object's reference, you can shorten the foregoing code by one statement:

```
Background background = new Background();
new Thread(background).start();
```

Those who relish terse code can reduce that even further to the single statement:

```
new Thread(new Background()).start();
```

 Extending the Thread class adds a lot of excess baggage to a class, and for that reason, implementing the Runnable interface is preferred. The only reason to extend Thread is to override an inherited method other than run().

The Thread Class

Before learning how to extend the Thread class and write a run() method, it's a good idea to become generally familiar with the Thread class's fields, constructors, and public methods. Listing 19-1, Thread.txt, lists Java's Thread class public declarations. The Thread class implements the Runnable interface (see "Implementing the Runnable Interface" later in this chapter).

Listing 19-1: Thread.txt

```
001: // Public fields
002: public final static int MIN_PRIORITY = 1;
003: public final static int NORM_PRIORITY = 5;
004: public final static int MAX_PRIORITY = 10;
005:
006: // Constructors
```

```
007: public Thread();
008: public Thread(Runnable target);
009: public Thread(ThreadGroup group, Runnable target);
010: public Thread(String name);
011: public Thread(ThreadGroup group, String name);
012: public Thread(Runnable target, String name);
013: public Thread(ThreadGroup group, Runnable target, String name);
014:
015: // Public methods
016: public static native Thread currentThread();
017: public static native void yield();
018: public static native void sleep(long millis);
019: public static void sleep(long millis, int nanos);
020: private void init(ThreadGroup g, Runnable target, String name);
021: public synchronized native void start();
022: public void run();
023: private void exit();
024: public void interrupt();
025: public static boolean interrupted();
026: public boolean isInterrupted();
027: public final native boolean isAlive();
028: public final void setPriority(int newPriority);
029: public final int getPriority();
030: public final void setName(String name);
031: public final String getName();
032: public final ThreadGroup getThreadGroup();
033: public static int activeCount();
034: public static int enumerate(Thread tarray[]);
035: public native int countStackFrames();
036: public final synchronized void join(long millis);
037: public final synchronized void join(long millis, int nanos);
038: public final void join();
039: public static void dumpStack();  // debugging only
040: public final void setDaemon(boolean on);
041: public final boolean isDaemon();
042: public final void checkAccess();
043: public String toString();
044: public ClassLoader getContextClassLoader();
045: public void setContextClassLoader(ClassLoader cl);
046:
047: // Deprecated methods -- DO NOT CALL!
048: public final void stop();
049: public final synchronized void stop(Throwable obj);
050: public final void suspend();
051: public final void resume();
```

As you can see, the `Thread` class provides numerous declarations. Rather than tediously describing them all, I'll briefly touch on some of the more important items here, and cover many of the others as needed to explain the chapter's sample programs.

Three `Thread` methods — `stop()` (two overloaded versions), `suspend()`, and `resume()` at lines 048-051 — have been deprecated, and Sun warns us never to call them. These methods are unsafe because they can allow threads to access objects in unprotected ways, causing information loss, or they can result in deadlock conditions. This chapter explains the correct ways to start, stop, and resume waiting and sleeping threads. *Never* call the deprecated methods. They are included in the `Thread` class strictly to support older code.

Three static fields specify the minimum, default, and maximum priority levels that a `Thread` object can have (see lines 002-004). Priorities range from 1 to 10 and are normally set in the middle at 5. You can inspect a thread's priority by calling `getPriority()`. Change a thread's level by calling `setPriority()`. Threads with higher priorities are supposed to get preferential treatment when it comes to accessing system resources, but regardless of priority, there is no guarantee that a thread will get any specific amount of operating time.

It may be dangerous to use the extreme high and low priority settings. If a thread's priority is set to the maximum, other threads may suffer in performance. If a thread's priority is too low, it may barely run. In most cases, priorities should be set to `NORM_PRIORITY` (the default), or values close to that constant (for example, `NORM_PRIORITY + 1`).

You can construct `Thread` objects in numerous ways (see lines 007-013). Sample programs in this chapter show how to use the class's constructors, some of which permit you to name the thread using a string of your choosing. To inspect a thread's name, call `getName()` (line 031). To set its name, call `setName()` (line 030).

To identify threads, you may assign them unique names at construction or by calling `setName()`. Threads are required to have string names, even though the thread scheduler makes no use of them. If you don't specify a thread's name, Java assigns one for you. The default name is probably, but not necessarily, the object's class name and reference address.

Start a `Thread` object by calling its `start()` method. This gives the thread object to the scheduler, which calls `run()` (see lines 022-023). (Don't call `run()` directly.)

Regardless of whether your class extends Thread or implements Runnable, you must call start() to start the thread running.

Put a thread to sleep for a specified amount of time by calling one of two sleep() methods (lines 018-019). You may specify the amount of sleep time in milliseconds, or in milliseconds and nanoseconds. Actual time spent sleeping may differ from the amount specified, depending on how the thread scheduler is implemented, and possibly by other system characteristics. The thread does not have to own a lock on the object for which the method that uses sleep() was called. But if the thread owns the lock, the object remains locked while the thread sleeps. In that case, the only way to wake up the thread is for another thread to call Thread.interrupt().

Never call the deprecated resume() method to wake up a sleeping thread. Like dogs, sleeping threads should be left alone.

You may tell a thread to yield to other threads by calling yield(). This might be done in time-consuming loops to make sure other threads get a chance at running. However, too many calls to yield() may indicate a poor design.

For one thread to wait for another thread to die, call one of the three join() methods (see lines 036-038). The join() method with no parameters waits forever, ensuring that the thread's run() method returns before the program or other thread continues. The others wait until run() returns, or until the specified amount of time elapses. You have the option of specifying the number of milliseconds to wait or, for more precision, the number of milliseconds and nanoseconds. (Similar parameters are available for the two sleep() methods.)

Specify that you want a thread to be a daemon by passing true to the setDaemon() method (see line 040). Pass false to create a non-daemon, user thread. If you don't call this method, the thread inherits its parent thread's daemon state. (If the main program creates the thread, it will have non-daemon status by default.) You may call setDaemon() only before calling a thread object's start() method. After a thread starts running, its daemon status may not be changed, and calling setDaemon() at any other time throws IllegalThreadStateException.

Throughout this chapter, you will find numerous references to the wait(), notify(), and notifyAll() methods. These are not Thread class declarations. They are inherited from Object, and therefore, are available to all Java classes. However, they should only be used in threaded code as explained in this chapter.

Programming with Threads

Now, let's examine a program that creates and runs threads using objects of the Thread class. Listing 19-2, ThreadDemo.java, shows how to use the Thread class to create a process that runs in the background.

Listing 19-2: ThreadDemo.java

```
001: import java.io.IOException;
002:
003: // Extend Thread class and provide a run() method
004: class Background extends Thread {
005:
006:   boolean finished;  // True when thread should die
007:
008:   // Constructor
009:   Background(String name) {
010:    super(name);
011:    finished = false;  // Initialize run-flag
012:   }
013:
014:   // Called by start() to run the thread
015:   public void run() {
016:    try {
017:     while (!finished) {    // Loop "forever"
018:      sleep(2000);
019:      System.out.println("\nHurry up!");
020:      sleep(1000);
021:      System.out.println("\nWhat's taking you so long?");
022:      sleep(1500);
023:      System.out.println("\nC'mon, press that Enter key!");
024:     }
025:    } catch (InterruptedException e) {
026:     return;  // End the thread
027:    }
028:   }
029:
030:   // Halt the thread
031:   public void halt() {
032:    finished = true;  // Cause while loop in run() to end
033:    System.out.println("Stopping thread " + getName() + "\n");
034:   }
035: }
036:
037: // Main program class demonstrates background processing
038: class ThreadDemo {
```

```
039:   public static void main(String args[]) {
040:
041: // Create the background thread
042:    Background background =
043:     new Background("Background process");
044:    System.out.println(
045:      "Starting thread. Press Enter to stop.");
046:
047: // Start running the background thread
048:    background.start();
049:
050: // Simulate foreground process: wait for Enter key
051:    try {
052:     while ((char)System.in.read() != '\n') ;
053:    } catch (IOException e) {
054:      System.out.println(e.getMessage());
055:    }
056:
057: // Stop the background thread
058:    background.halt();
059:  }
060: }
```

Compile and run the sample program, which asks you to press Enter — but don't do that. Instead, wait for a few seconds, and you soon see some messages that tell you to hurry up and press that key!

 After you press Enter, the program may continue printing warning messages before it finally ends. This "bug" is intentional — I left it in to demonstrate the independent nature of threads. Later in this section, I explain how to repair the problem.

The program's hurry-up messages are printed by a background Thread object, whose run() method executes simultaneously with a statement that waits for you to press Enter (see line 052):

```
while ((char)System.in.read() != '\n') ;
```

It is traditional to insert a single space ahead of the semicolon to indicate that the loop executes a null statement — in other words, as written here, the while statement loops "forever" until interrupted in some way. Some programmers insert a comment to make the statement's purpose perfectly clear:

```
while ((char)System.in.read() != '\n') /* wait */ ;
```

In a conventional, single-threaded program, such a statement pauses the program until the user presses Enter. However, because this program creates a background thread that runs concurrently with the main program (itself a thread), the messages are printed while the loop waits for you to press the Enter key.

The first step in creating a thread is to extend the Thread class. The sample program does that by declaring a new class, Background, like this (see line 004):

```
class Background extends Thread {
...
}
```

The extended class's constructor (see lines 009-012) performs two jobs that are typical in classes that extend Thread:

```
super(name);
finished = false;
```

Calling super() executes the Thread constructor, and this must be the first statement. It is optional to pass a String name, but usually you'll want to do this to distinguish multiple threads by giving them unique names. The second statement initializes a boolean variable to false. The run() method examines finished, often called a *state flag,* to determine when the thread should end.

Every extended Thread class *must* override run() to provide the code that the thread object is to execute. The run() method does not throw any checked exceptions. However it will almost always catch InterruptedException as shown in the listing. In general form, a run() method usually looks like this:

```
try {
 while (!finished) {
  // execute the thread's statements
 }
} catch (InterruptedException e) {
   return;
}
```

Another do "forever" while loop executes the thread's statements while finished remains false. Apparently, something must happen to cause finished to become true so that run() and the thread can end. Catching InterruptedException is necessary only if run() calls a method such as sleep() that throws it. In most cases, however, you'll want to catch this exception to provide for the thread's orderly shutdown in case it is interrupted. Otherwise, the proper way to terminate a thread is to simply return from run(). When run() ends, so does the thread, which can never be restarted.

Inside run(), your code can perform whatever actions you want the thread to take. Here, the sample program executes three pairs of statements. Here's one pair:

```
sleep(2000);
System.out.println("\nHurry up!");
```

Calling sleep() pauses the thread for the specified number of milliseconds — or about 2 seconds in this case. Sleeping *pauses* the thread, and it allows other threads to run. In this case, one other thread is the main program, which waits for you to press the Enter key.

To create the background thread, the sample program's main() method executes the statement at lines 042-043:

```
Background background =
  new Background("Background process");
```

This does not create the actual thread — it merely creates the Background class *object*, which serves as an interface to the thread. To create the actual thread and start it running, the program must also call the start() method as shown at line 048:

```
background.start();
```

This creates the thread and causes the scheduler to call the background object's run() method. You may construct as many other threads of the same class as you want, and they may have the same or different names.

After you finally press Enter, the main while loop ends. To stop the thread, the program executes the statement at line 058:

```
background.halt();
```

The halt() method is just a common one that I added to the Background class — it's not inherited from Thread, and a similar method is not required in threaded code. But even though you don't have to provide a halt() method in your own classes, you do need to provide some way to change the state of the object and thereby cause the thread to end. In this case, halt() performs that duty by setting the state flag to true:

```
finished = true;
System.out.println("Stopping thread " + getName() + "\n");
```

The method also prints a message informing you that the thread is stopping. Method getName() returns the name of the current thread object. On screen you see something like this:

```
Stopping thread Background process
C'mon, press that Enter key!
```

As mentioned, you might also see extraneous messages that continue to tell you to hurry up. This proves that our `Thread` class's `run()` method indeed executes independently of other code. Take another look at the `while` loop in `run()` to see why the extra message is printed:

```
while (!finished) {
 sleep(2000);
 System.out.println("\nHurry up!");
 ...
}
```

When `halt()` sets `finished` to `true`, there's no telling which statement in the loop is executing. Therefore, other output statements might be executed until the loop starts over from the top, and the now `true finished` flag is noticed, causing the loop, and subsequently the thread, to end. To repair the problem, you could change each output statement to something like this:

```
if (!finished) {
 sleep(2000);
 if (!finished)
  System.out.println("\nHurry up!");
}
```

As I said, I left this bug in to illustrate an important aspect of threaded code. One method might change a variable's value while another method is using it. In this small example, no harm occurs because there's only one background thread. In more sophisticated programming, as later examples in this chapter show, it is necessary to use locks to ensure the proper use of thread variables. It is also usually necessary to pause threads so they can continue when needed and shut down in a more orderly fashion than in this simple demonstration.

Implementing the Runnable Interface

The second way to create a thread is to implement the `Runnable` interface. This avoids extending the `Thread` class and inheriting its multitude of methods, most of which you probably don't need. As a side benefit, implementing `Runnable` also permits you to extend another class *and* implement the interface at the same time. If you extend `Thread`, you can't also extend another class because Java classes are limited to single inheritance. (You could extend the class, and then extend it again from `Thread`.) Listing 19-3, Runnable.txt, shows the `Runnable` interface declaration.

Listing 19-3: Runnable.txt

```
001: // The Runnable interface
002: public interface Runnable {
003:   public abstract void run();
004: }
```

As you can see, Runnable is only a simple interface with one method, run(), which some documents call the "soul of a thread." There is no difference in purpose or design between the Thread class and Runnable interface run() methods. Each method performs whatever actions you want in a separate thread.

As with Thread.run(), never directly call the Runnable interface's run() method. The thread scheduler calls run() to start the thread running.

Listing 19-4, Primes.java, demonstrates how to implement the Runnable interface. This program is becoming an old standard for Java thread demonstrations, but my version uses structured programming instead of the usual labeled-loop and break statements that appear in several other sources.

Listing 19-4: Primes.java

```
001: import java.io.IOException;
002:
003: class Background implements Runnable {
004:
005:   boolean finished = false;   // True to end run()
006:   int num = 3;                // Prime number candidates
007:   int delay;                  // Time between each output
008:
009:   // Constructor
010:   Background(int delay) {
011:     this.delay = delay;
012:   }
013:
014:   // Return true if num is a prime number
015:   public boolean isPrime(int n) {
016:     for (int i = 2; i < n; i++)
017:       if ((n % i) == 0)
018:         return false;
019:     return true;
020:   }
021:
```

```
022: // Search for prime numbers in the background
023: public void run() {
024:   try {
025:     while (!finished) {
026:       if (isPrime(num))
027:         System.out.println(num);
028:       num++;
029:       Thread.sleep(delay);
030:     } // while
031:   } catch (InterruptedException e) {
032:     return;
033:   }
034: }
035:
036: // Set flag to stop run()
037: public void halt() {
038:   finished = true;
039: }
040:
041: }
042:
043: // Compute prime numbers in the background
044: class Primes {
045:
046:   static char getChar() {
047:     char ch = '\0';
048:     try {
049:       ch = (char)System.in.read();
050:     } catch (IOException e) {
051:       System.out.println(e.getMessage());
052:     }
053:     return ch;
054:   }
055:
056:   static void waitForKey(char key) {
057:     while (getChar() != key) /* wait */ ;
058:   }
059:
060:   public static void main(String args[]) throws Exception {
061:     System.out.println("Press Enter to begin and again to quit");
062:     waitForKey('\n');
063:     // Construct and start thread
064:     Background background = new Background(50);
065:     Thread T = new Thread(background);
066:     T.setPriority(4);
```

```
067:    T.start();
068:    // Wait for Enter key while thread runs
069:    waitForKey('\n');
070:    background.halt();  // Stop the thread
071:  }
072: }
```

To create a class that executes its code in a separate thread, declare it as the sample program does at line 003:

```
class Background implements Runnable {
...
}
```

A `Runnable` class is required to provide a `run()` method, which is called when the thread starts. As when extending `Thread`, however, you probably also need a constructor, some kind of state flag such as the `boolean finished` variable used here, and various methods to perform actions while the thread runs. In this case, `Background` provides a constructor that saves a `delay` value to pause the thread between each output operation (see line 011).

The program constructs the thread a little differently than before. Take a close look at lines 064-067:

```
Background background = new Background(50);
Thread T = new Thread(background);
T.setPriority(4);
T.start();
```

After constructing the `Background` object, a `Thread` object is also created by passing `background` as an argument to the constructor. This creates the `Thread` object and connects it to our object's `run()` method. (The next section explains the third statement.) Calling `start()` for the `Thread` object causes the thread scheduler to call the `Background` object's `run()` method.

Setting a Thread's Priority

Line 066 in Listing 19-4 calls `setPriority()` to set the thread's priority to 4, one less than the median value of 5. This is not required, but I added the statement to demonstrate a common technique that can improve user-response times.

In general, code that waits for user input should run at a slightly higher priority than code that merely outputs information or performs calculations. This is especially important in programs such as this one where the user expects an immediate response to key presses. There's nothing more annoying than hitting the Escape key, or pressing a Cancel button, and having the program travel on for several more steps before recognizing the command. Setting input code priority a little higher or setting other threaded code lower helps, but does not guarantee, better responsiveness.

Implementing the run() Method

Implement the run() method to execute your code while the finished flag remains false (or until some other external condition changes). In this case, referring again to Listing 19-4, the program calculates and displays prime numbers using a while loop that inspects the finished state flag, which becomes true when the program commands the thread to end:

```
while (!finished) {
 if (isPrime(num))
  System.out.println(num);
 num++;
 Thread.sleep(delay);
}
```

The statements must be executed in a try-catch block that watches for InterruptedException, which sleep() throws if the thread is interrupted before it is done sleeping for the specified amount of time. This might happen, for example, if another thread calls Thread.interrupt(). The usual response to InterruptedException is to simply return from run(), and in that way end the thread.

In any method other than run(),different techniques may be called for. This is because when a method such as sleep() throws InterruptedException, the interrupted state of the thread is cleared. To force the thread to stay interrupted, call the interrupt() method as follows:

```
try {
...
} catch (InterruptedException e) {
 Thread.currentThread().interrupt();
}
```

You may use the same code whether your class extends Thread or implements Runnable. The static currentThread() is called in reference to the Thread class (see line 016 in Listing 19-1). That method returns a reference to the Thread object, for which you can call other methods such as interrupt(). If your class extends Thread, however, you can simply call interrupt() directly as you can other inherited methods.

In addition to run(), you'll probably also want to include a method that changes the finished flag, and thus ends the thread. The sample program does this with a simple halt() method at line 037-039:

```
public void halt() {
 finished = true;
}
```

This is the same technique used to halt a thread created using a class that extends Thread. When the program calls halt() at line 070, the thread's run() method detects the change to the state flag, and returns, terminating the thread.

Sleeping Threads

To slow the program's output, the Background thread calls sleep() at line 029 (see Listing 19-4), passing the delay value used to construct the Background object (see line 064). The only reason this program calls sleep() is to slow output to a reasonable speed.

There are two forms of sleep() (refer to lines 018-019 in Listing 19-1). The single argument sleep(M) waits for approximately M milliseconds or until the thread is woken. The two-argument sleep(M, N) waits for about M milliseconds plus N nanoseconds or until woken. Passing 0 to sleep() creates a sleeping beauty that waits "forever" until another Prince Charming thread wakes it up usually by calling Thread.interrupt(). Sleeping indefinitely is acceptable if you are sure the thread will be interrupted; otherwise, it is usually best to specify a sleep time value.

Theoretically, the statement sleep(0, 1) sleeps for the least amount of time, about 1 nanosecond. However, this assumes the system and thread scheduler are capable of controlling activity within such a small time frame.

Daemons

It is useful to comment out the statement at line 070 in Listing 19-4 and run the program:

```
// background.halt();
```

Now, even after you press Enter, the thread continues to run in the background, effectively preventing the main program from halting! After all, the main program is just another user thread, and by Java's rules, the program ends only when all user threads terminate. If you try this, to end the program, press the interrupt key, usually Ctrl+C or Ctrl+Z, depending on your operating system. (Ctrl+Break might also work.)

Obviously, this kind of runaway thread is undesirable, and you should normally prevent its occurrence by providing a means such as a halt() method and a state flag variable that cause run() to end. However, when that is not convenient — for example, you may want a thread to run independently and end on its own when the program ends — the solution is to make the thread a daemon. To make that change to the sample program, in addition to commenting out line 070, add this statement between lines 066-067 (the new line is shown here in bold):

```
T.setPriority(4);
T.setDaemon(true);   // Make thread T a daemon
T.start();
```

You must call `setDaemon()` before starting the thread. Making the thread a daemon causes it to end automatically after all other user threads end. In this case, the only user thread is the main program, so making the separate thread a daemon causes it to shut down when the program ends.

Synchronizations

When two or more threads use the same objects, the data must be protected so that one thread doesn't read the information while another is updating it, or so that both don't attempt to change the data simultaneously, which might cause one of the changes to be discarded. If the object in question is your bank balance, you certainly wouldn't want to lose a deposit because the programmers didn't properly guard the information against these kinds of problems.

With Java threads, a program uses *object locks* to ensure that only one thread at a time has access to critical data. Threads obtain locks by executing *synchronized statements*. Obtaining locks and writing synchronized statements are not difficult tasks, but it takes careful programming to ensure that the results work correctly. Following are some overviews of how locks and synchronizations work in Java. After that, I present a full demonstration of a threaded client-server application that you can use as the basis for your own threaded code.

Object Locks

Every Java object can provide a lock that is respected by synchronized code. You don't have to do anything special to create a lock — one is automatically provided for every object as needed. However, you need to know a few important points about locks to understand this section's sample programs:

◆ There is one lock available per object. All Java objects are therefore potentially *thread-safe*.

◆ A locked object may be of any class, but that class does not have to implement `Runnable` or extend `Thread`, although it may. Locks are available for *all* Java objects of *any* class.

◆ Locks are issued on a per-thread basis. When a thread has a lock on an object, no other thread may use that object in synchronized code until the first thread releases the lock.

◆ Locks may be specified for named objects (for example, instance variables in an object), or for an entire object. Another way to say this is that in Java, synchronized code can be *regional*. A single statement can be synchronized, as can entire methods.

◆ Locks are not available for non-object variables such as `int`s and `float`s. However, Java guarantees that reading and writing native data types are *atomic operations*. This means that two or more threads cannot accidentally scramble a native-type variable by writing to it simultaneously, even if the variable occupies multiple bytes. However, there is no way (unless you invent one) to specify the order in which threads read and write native variables, and for that reason, critical data that needs to be protected should always be in object form.

A lock is sometimes also called a *monitor*. When a thread obtains a lock for an object, it is said to "own the object's monitor." This is just another way of stating that a thread has locked the object for the thread's use.

Synchronized Statements

To lock an object for a thread, the program executes synchronized statements. This can take one of several different forms, but always uses the word `synchronized`. The most common way to create synchronized statements is to declare a method like this:

```
public synchronized void anyMethod(Object v) {
  anyData = v;
}
```

The assignment to `anyData` takes place only when the thread that calls the method is given a lock on the object in which `anyData` resides. The method can be `private`, `public`, or `protected`, and it can return any data type. There are no restrictions on what a synchronized method can do, but it must obey various rules as explained in this chapter in order to work correctly in threaded code.

When a thread calls `anyMethod()`, a lock is obtained for the current object. If another thread already owns that lock, `anyMethod()` is said to *block*, causing it to wait indefinitely for the lock to become available. Obviously, threads must eventually release the locks they obtain so that other blocked threads may continue. If two threads block on each other's objects, deadlock results, and the program will hang. Careful programming is the only way to avoid this problem.

Java automatically obtains object locks for synchronized statements. When those statements finish, Java automatically releases the held lock. You do not have to obtain locks nor release them in code — all you need to do is execute the synchronized statements.

When a thread calls a synchronized method, it locks the entire object for which that method was called. Another way to write a synchronized method is to encase it in a *synchronized statement block*. Here's another version of anyMethod():

```
public void anyMethod(Object v) {
 synchronized(this) {
  anyData = v;
 }
}
```

Again, the assignment to anyData takes place only when the thread can obtain a lock on the object (this) for which anyMethod() was called. There are no functional differences between this technique and the former one, but if all statements are to be synchronized — in other words, if you want the thread to own the lock on the object for the entire time the method executes — it's easier simply to declare the method to be synchronized. Use the second technique to synchronize only a portion, or region, of the method. Here's one more version of anyMethod():

```
public void anyMethod(Object v) {
 if (v == null) return;   // unsynchronized
 synchronized(this) {
  anyData = v;
 }
 // more unsynchronized statements
}
```

Outside of the synchronized statement are any statements that do not need to obtain the object's lock. Here, there is no reason to lock the object for the if statement that checks if v is null. Only the assignment to anyData needs to be protected against access from multiple threads. Using regional synchronized code this way helps improve performance by limiting the amount of time that a thread owns a lock on an object, causing other threads to block.

 TIP The more you can do to limit the time that a thread owns an object's lock, the better your program will perform. For best results, synchronize *only* the statements that read and write object data — don't synchronize other statements that, for example, merely perform a calculation or do other non-critical tasks.

You can also synchronize statements for a specific object. Using this technique, you can write the synchronized statement block in the preceding anyMethod() like this:

```
synchronized(anyData) {
 anyData = v;
}
```

Instead of synchronizing on this, which obtains a lock on the entire object, the revised code obtains a lock only for anyData. Other data in the object remains unprotected from access via other threads. Remember that anyData must be an object of a class; it cannot be a variable of a native data type such as int or double. However, it can be an object of a wrapper class such as Integer or Double (see Chapter 9, "Numeric Classes").

Synchronization and Data Hiding

As you learned way back in Chapter 6, "Object-Oriented Programming," encapsulation (data hiding) helps protect data from harm. By making data private to a class, and providing methods that read and write the data's values, the class controls access to its information. This lends better organization to the program, and it helps simplify debugging.

By using *synchronized methods* to access private data, you protect that data from being used by more than one thread at a time. Probably, the best way to do this is to make the data private to its class, and then use synchronized methods to read and write the data. This technique gives you the benefits of encapsulation and also makes the data thread-safe. Listing 19-5, SafetyClass.java, illustrates the basic class design. This is not a complete program — you may compile it, but it lacks a main() method, and it doesn't run.

Listing 19-5: SafetyClass.java

```
001: // Illustration only: not a complete program
002: public class SafetyClass {
003:
004:   private int counter;  // Private data in class
005:
006: // Thread-safe method to write data
007:   public synchronized void setCounter(int n) {
008:     counter = n;          // Assign new value to counter
009:   }
010:
011: // Thread-safe method to read data
012:   public synchronized int getCounter() {
013:     return counter;        // Return counter's current value
014:   }
015: }
```

Any threads that use the same object of the class SafetyClass obtain a lock on that object when calling the synchronized setCounter() and getCounter() methods. The lock is obtained for the entire SafetyClass object, including its private `counter` variable. As a result of the lock, it is not possible, say, for one thread to be changing `counter`'s value while another thread is reading it. The lock on the object is automatically released when the synchronized method ends.

But despite the class's protections, there is still no way to specify the order in which two or more threads call `setCounter()` and `getCounter()`, and for that and other reasons, `SafetyClass` can still be abused. For example, as written, the class does not prevent problems with *get-change-put* types of operations. This can happen if one thread calls `getCounter()`, changes the returned result, and then calls `setCounter()`. Meanwhile, another thread might be doing the same, causing one set of changes to be lost! The following code is unsafe:

```
SafetyClass obj = new SafetyClass();
...
int temp = obj.getCounter();
temp += 10;
obj.setCounter(temp);  // ???
```

The calls to `getCounter()` and `setCounter()` obtain the object's lock, but the addition of 10 to `temp` is unprotected. During that statement's execution, another thread might very well access `obj`. This illustrates that, when writing threaded code, it is always necessary to have a clear understanding that objects are protected *only* when locked for the thread that accesses the object's data. To solve the *get-change-put* problem, you could add another synchronized method to the class:

```
public synchronized addToCounter(int n) {
  counter+= n;
}
```

Now, the program's threads can safely add values to `counter` by calling the synchronized `addToCounter()` method. Even so, it is still possible for a thread to call `getCounter()` and `setCounter()` in an unsafe attempt to modify the object. Threads, locks, and synchronized code go only so far in protecting data. Writing threaded code that works correctly still takes careful planning and programming.

Class constructors cannot be synchronized, nor do they need to be since it would be senseless for two threads to attempt to construct the same object at the same time.

Synchronized Containers

As mentioned in Chapter 18, "Utilities and Legacy Classes," Java's container library of `Collection` and `Map` classes are *not* thread-safe. No methods in the container classes are synchronized, and threads that access objects in unprotected containers may risk losing information. (The legacy Vector class, however, is thread-safe.)

One solution to this problem is to encase the container in a synchronized wrapper, as provided by the Collections class. For example, if myTree is any Collection-based container such as a TreeList, the following code synchronizes the container:

```
import java.util.*;
...
Collection safe = Collections.synchronizedCollection(myTree);
```

All methods for the safe container are now synchronized, effectively preventing threads from calling them in unsafe ways. However, it is still necessary to use a synchronized block for iterations on the container's objects:

```
synchronized(safe) {
 Iterator I = safe.iterator();
 while (I.hasNext())
  f(I.next());  // pass each object to method f()
}
```

However, this solution still doesn't prevent the *get-modify-put* problem mentioned in the preceding section. If one thread gets an object from the container, changes it, and then puts the object back, there's nothing to prevent another thread from doing the same. To prevent this kind of problem, it may be best to *remove* the object, modify it, and then put it back. Or, write a synchronized method or statement block that performs the entire modification operation while the thread has a lock on the container.

A simpler solution to the problem of creating thread-safe containers is to declare the unsynchronized container as a private member of your class. The class can them also provide synchronized public methods for all operations involving the container. This is just an extension of the data-hiding illustration in the preceding section. The program listings discussed in the next sections demonstrate more about this technique.

Client–Server Threaded Code

As a demonstration of threaded code, and to provide a framework for your own programs, the next several listings create a simulated client-server model that uses multiple, concurrent threads for all operations. I am using the word "server" here in the sense of a print server—a program that queues and executes printing jobs so the client program (and its user) can go on with other tasks without waiting for each printout to finish.

Threaded code handles this type of problem perfectly. In addition to showing the design for the client-server programming, the following examples also make each job perform its actions in a separate thread. Although the programming is just a shell, to make the results interesting, each job is given a name and a random amount of time from 1 to 10 seconds, representing the amount of time that a real job, such as a printout, might require. You might want to compile and run the full program now before examining its construction. All listings are in the c19/LockDemo directory on the CD-ROM. Running the program produces output such as shown here:

```
javac LockDemo.java
java LockDemo
<<< Press Enter to end program >>>
Sleeping for 1 second(s)

Starting Job #1
Time = 3 second(s)
Sleeping for 5 second(s)

Starting Job #2
Time = 4 second(s)

Finishing Job #1
Ending thread Job@77d134

Finishing Job #2
Ending thread Job@47e553
Sleeping for 3 second(s)

Starting Job #3
Time = 5 second(s)

Finishing Job #3
Ending thread Job@20c10f
```

Each job executes for its specified amount of time, and the program also sleeps in between jobs, also for a random length of time. This simulates the client side of the program — users typically feed jobs to the server at irregular intervals. Press Enter after watching the display for a while. When you do, any unfinished jobs complete before the program ends. But pressing Ctrl+C interrupts all threads and ends the program immediately.

A Thread-Safe Queue Class

Now let's take a look at how the client-server demonstration works. First, we need a mechanism to store jobs as they are handed to the server. For this, I wrote a thread-safe Queue class, shown in Listing 19-6, Queue.java.

Listing 19-6: Queue.java

```
001: import java.util.LinkedList;
002:
003: public class Queue {
004:
005:   private LinkedList q = new LinkedList();
006:
007:   public synchronized void add(Object o) {
008:     q.add(o);
009:   }
010:
011:   public synchronized Object get()
012:     throws InterruptedException {
013:     while (q.isEmpty())
014:       wait();
015:     return q.removeFirst();
016:   }
017:
018:   public synchronized boolean isEmpty() {
019:     return q.isEmpty();
020:   }
021: }
```

A classic queue data structure inserts objects at one end of a list and takes them off the other — like a queue at a grocery store where each customer waits for a turn at the register. This is the perfect container for our server because we want to process each job in the order received.

For the actual storage device, Queue uses a LinkedList container (see line 005) imported from the java.util package. This is ideal because the container takes only as much memory as needed to store its contents, and we don't need to be concerned about the container expanding or occupying too much memory.

The Queue class declares three synchronized methods. The add() method adds an object to the queue's tail. The get() method returns the first object from the queue. The isEmpty() method returns true if the Queue contains no objects. It may be obvious that add() and get() must be synchronized so that threads calling those methods obtain a lock on the object beforehand, and in that way prevent conflicting access to the private LinkedList container. However, method isEmpty() must also be synchronized because it wouldn't do for a thread to be in the process of inserting an object, and for another thread to miss detecting that fact because isEmpty() returns true.

TIP   It does no harm to synchronize a method that doesn't need to be, but making every method synchronized might have a negative effect on performance. As mentioned, for best results, a program should synchronize as few statements as possible.

The `get()` method in the `Queue` class is particularly interesting, and it illustrates a fundamental technique in writing threaded code. Take a close look at the method's programming:

```
public synchronized Object get()
 throws InterruptedException {
 while (q.isEmpty())
  wait();
 return q.removeFirst();
}
```

First, in addition to being synchronized, `get()` throws `InterruptedException`. This exception is thrown by `wait()`, which pauses the thread that calls `get()`. The reason for throwing the exception back to `get()`'s caller is that we want that thread's `run()` method to receive the exception if thrown, and in that case, to terminate the interrupted thread gracefully.

In most all cases, as demonstrated in `get()`, a synchronized method calls `wait()` inside a loop that inspects some kind of condition involving the object. Here, the condition is whether the queue is empty. While it is, the program waits until an object is handed to the server for processing. Calling `wait()` pauses the thread and, most important, it releases the lock on the object. Thus other threads may access the queue while `get()` waits for it to receive something to store. In this case, another thread may call `add()` or `isEmpty()` while `get()` is waiting for something to come into the queue.

When `wait()` returns, the thread resumes, and the lock on the object is again obtained. This happens automatically, but it is important always to call `wait()` in a loop that inspects the associated condition. It is entirely possible for `wait()` to return and for the condition to be unchanged, thus indicating that the thread should again wait. Never write code like this:

```
if (!condition) wait();   // ???
```

When `wait()` returns, `condition` might still be false. Use a `while` or other loop as in the former example to ensure that the thread continues only when the waited-upon condition is satisfied.

A Runnable Job Class

The client-server example needs jobs to perform. For that, I created the Job class in Listing 19-7, Job.java. The class implements the Runnable interface — although not required for the model, our jobs run in separate threads. The class also demonstrates how objects can install themselves in threads with no help from the statements that create those objects.

Listing 19-7: Job.java

```
001: public class Job implements Runnable {
002:
003:   private String name;      // Name of this job
004:   private int delay;        // How long it takes to do this job
005:   private boolean ready;    // True when job is ready to be done
006:
007: // Constructor
008:   Job(String name, int delay) {
009:     this.name = name;
010:     this.delay = delay;
011:     ready = false;
012:     new Thread(this).start();  // Job runs itself in a thread!
013:   }
014:
015: // Run method called by thread scheduler
016:   public void run() {
017:     try {
018:       doWhenReady();  // Do the job when it is ready
019:     } catch (InterruptedException e) {
020:       return;
021:     }
022:   }
023:
024: // Performs the job's actual work
025: // Because this calls wait(), code cannot be in run()
026: // and it must be synchronized on this object
027:   private synchronized void doWhenReady()
028:     throws InterruptedException {
029:     while (!ready)
030:       wait();          // Wait indefinitely until ready
031: // Simulate the job by displaying messages and sleeping
032: // for the amount of time this job takes
033:     System.out.println("\nStarting " + name);
034:     System.out.println("Time = " + delay / 1000 + " second(s)");
035:     Thread.currentThread().sleep(delay);  // Simulate job runtime
036:     System.out.println("\nFinishing " + name);
037:     System.out.println("Ending thread " + toString());
```

```
038:   }
039:
040:   // Set the thread state flag to true
041:   // and notify all threads of the change
042:   public synchronized void doJob() {
043:     ready = true;
044:     notifyAll();
045:   }
046: }
```

The Job class declares three private instance variables. Two, name and delay, represent the name of the Job object and the time it takes to complete. (The delay merely simulates the time a real job, such as a printout, would take.) The third instance variable, finished, serves as an object state-flag that indicates whether this Job's thread should end.

The Job class constructor at lines 008-013 initializes its instance variables, and then uses an interesting technique that starts the job running in a separate thread. This is done by executing the statement

```
new Thread(this).start();
```

Creating a Thread object, passing it this — a reference to the Runnable Job object under construction — and then calling start() causes the thread scheduler to call the Job.run() method for this object. The object starts itself running in a separate thread almost immediately after the object is constructed. To use this technique, the class must implement the Runnable interface, or it must extend Thread.

 The method shown here is the proper way to have an object install itself in a separate thread, but be careful when using this technique. If another class extends Job, the thread is started *before* finishing the initialization of the extended class object, and this may cause the thread to access uninitialized instance variables declared in the extended class.

The Job class's run() method, stipulated by the Runnable interface, shows another typical technique used in writing threaded code. Here is the run() method again for reference:

```
public void run() {
  try {
  doWhenReady();   // Do the job when it is ready
  } catch (InterruptedException e) {
  return;
  }
}
```

This is the usual way to program run(). The reason for calling another private synchronized method, doWhenReady() in this case, is because the thread probably needs to call wait() at some point. However, run() cannot do that because wait() may *only* be called when the thread owns the object's lock. This is not possible here because run() may not be synchronized. In addition to being synchronized, the doWhenReady() method is declared private because we don't want outsiders to call it.

The Job class's doWhenReady() method shows another typical example of threaded code. The method throws InterruptedException so that its caller, run(), can shut down the thread gracefully in the event it is interrupted for some reason. The first part of doWhenReady() immediately calls wait():

```
public synchronized void doWhenReady()
 throws InterruptedException {
 while (!ready)
  wait();          // Wait indefinitely until ready
...
```

Consider the effect of this code. When a Job object is constructed, its constructor installs itself in a separate thread. This causes the scheduler to call the run() method for the new Job object. That method in turn calls doWhenReady(), which inspects the boolean ready state flag, initialized to false, and then calls wait() while that condition remains false. Thus, the object starts running and then almost immediately pauses, waiting for permission to proceed.

The thread is *poised* on the brink of action, but it uses no CPU cycles. It just sits there waiting for a signal to go ahead. When it receives that signal – in other words, when wait() returns and the ready flag is found to be true – the rest of the doWhenReady() method executes. Because this is just a simulation, the statements at this stage simply print some messages and then call sleep() to simulate the amount of time that a real job takes:

```
Thread.currentThread().sleep(delay);
```

 Unlike with wait(), calling sleep() does not require the thread to own the object's lock. But if it does, as in this case, sleep() does *not* release the lock as wait() does. While sleeping, no other threads may access this object.

You might wonder at this point exactly how it is that wait() knows when to resume the thread. This happens when another thread sends a *notification* that a condition has changed, affecting one or more threads that are currently waiting. The method that performs this magic for the Job class is crucial to the success of the program:

```
public synchronized void doJob() {
 ready = true;
 notifyAll();
}
```

When another thread wants a Job object to execute its tasks, it calls doJob(). This gives the green light for the Job to go ahead by setting the ready state-flag to true. However, at this time, doWhenReady() has probably called wait(), releasing the lock on the object. So that wait() returns, and so the thread regains that lock, the program calls notifyAll(). This sends a message to all waiting threads that they should check the conditions on which they are waiting.

It should now be clear why you must always call wait() in a loop that inspects the condition causing the thread to wait. When a thread calls notifyAll(), *all* waiting threads are woken up (that is, all calls to wait() return), but only one or more selected conditions may have changed. Other conditions for other waiting threads may be unchanged, in which cases the threads should again call wait().

The notifyAll() method is inherited by all Java objects from the Object class, and it can be called from any class method. A similar method, notify(), also inherited from Object, notifies only one thread to wake up (that is, to return from a wait() operation). However, notifyAll() is usually safer because notify() wakes up at most a single thread, and there's no way to specify which one is nudged back to life. If you are absolutely positive that only one thread is waiting for a signal to proceed, you may call notify(). But it is always okay, and usually preferred, to call notifyAll().

A Server Class

So far, the client-server model has a storage device (Queue) and some objects to store (Job). It's now time to look at the server that receives Job objects, stores them in a Queue, and executes them. To best understand the code, shown in Listing 19-8, Server.java, keep in mind the idea of a print server that receives printing jobs and sends them to the printer.

Listing 19-8: Server.java

```
001: import Queue;
002: import Job;
003:
004: class Server implements Runnable {
005:
006:   Queue q = new Queue();   // Construct our Queue object
007:
008:   public void run() {
```

```
009:    try {
010:      doWhenReady();  // Do the server's activities
011:    } catch (InterruptedException e) {
012:      return;
013:    }
014:  }
015:
016: // Perform server activities until shutdown
017:  private synchronized void doWhenReady()
018:    throws InterruptedException {
019:    for (;;) {                  // Do "forever" loop
020:      while (q.isEmpty())       // Wait until there is a job in
021:        wait();                 //  the queue
022:      Job j = (Job)q.get();     // Get the job
023:      j.doJob();                // Do the job
024:    } // for
025:  }
026:
027: // Add a new job to the server's queue
028: // This returns immediately; the job is not performed
029: // until the server thread detects the queue is no longer
030: // empty.
031:  public synchronized void add(Job j) {
032:    q.add(j);
033:    notifyAll();
034:  }
035: }
```

The Server class is surprisingly similar to the Job class. Like Job, it implements the Runnable interface because we want the server to run in a separate thread. This allows clients that send jobs to the server to go on to other tasks without waiting for each job to finish.

The Server class declares a single instance variable, q, as an object of the Queue class. This provides the storage container for keeping Job objects. As in Job, the Server's run() method calls another private method doWhenReady() for the same reasons discussed for Job, namely because run() cannot be synchronized and the server needs to call wait() to wait for jobs to come into the queue.

That happens in doWhenReady() inside a do-forever for loop at lines 019-024. You'll see this kind of statement often in threaded code:

```
for (;;) {
...
}
```

Such a loop executes "forever," until that is, it is interrupted somehow. This action is appropriate for the server because we want it to run continuously in the background, and to be ready at any time that a new job needs doing. Inside the do-forever loop, a `while` loop calls `wait()`:

```
while (q.isEmpty())
  wait();
```

This pauses the server's thread while the `Queue` container is empty. As mentioned, `wait()` releases the lock on the object so that other threads can call other synchronized methods such as, in this case, `add()` (see lines 031-033). A client does that to hand a new `Job` object to the server. After adding the `Job` to the queue at line 032, line 033 calls `notifyAll()` to indicate to waiting threads that a condition has changed. Here, this causes `wait()` at line 021 to return, at which time the loop inspects `q.isEmpty()`, and on finding an object in the queue, removes the job, and executes it with the statements:

```
Job j = (Job)q.get();
j.doJob();
```

The first statement removes a `Job` from the queue. The second statement calls that `Job` object's `doJob()` method. Recall that this method simply allows the `Job` thread to continue – in other words, `doJob()` returns almost immediately. At that time, the server's do-forever loop again waits for another `Job` object to enter the queue. You can see these actions when running the program. Sometimes, new jobs come in while others have yet to finish – and many jobs might be executing all at once. This is not exactly analogous to a print server, which can probably print only one job at a time – unless, of course, the server has access to multiple printers. But it is similar to other real-world threaded code, such as the display of multiple objects on a graphics page, where numerous operations execute independently while new ones are being queued.

A Client Class

Reviewing the client-server simulation program so far, we have

- The `Queue` class, providing a thread-safe storage mechanism

- The `Job` class, providing a simulation of a job's activity running in a separate thread

- The `Server` class, whose task is to collect jobs, remove them from the queue in the order received, and execute them

We now need a client program that creates jobs and passes them to the server. This wouldn't have to run in a separate thread, but since that's what this chapter is all about, I chose to have the `Client` class implement the `Runnable` interface. Listing 19-9, Client.java, shows the programming for the `Client` class.

Listing 19-9: Client.java

```
001: import java.util.Random;
002: import Job;
003: import Server;
004:
005: class Client implements Runnable {
006:
007:   Random rand = new Random();
008:   boolean finished = false;
009:   int jobcount = 0;
010:
011: // Utility method creates a new numbered job with
012: // a random time delay to simulate how long the job takes
013:   private Job getAJob() {
014:     String name = "Job #" + ++jobcount;
015:     int delay = 1000 + rand.nextInt(9000);   // 1 .. 10 seconds
016:     Job j = new Job(name, delay);
017:     return j;
018:   }
019:
020:   public void run() {
021:
022: // Create the server daemon thread
023:     Server server = new Server();
024:     Thread T = new Thread(server);
025:     T.setDaemon(true);  // Server is a daemon!
026:     T.start();          // Start the server thread running
027:
028: // Main run() actions
029:     try {
030:      while (!finished) {
031:
032:      // Create a job and pass it to the server
033:        Job j = getAJob();  // Create simulated job object
034:        server.add(j);      // Returns immediately
035:
036:      // Simulate user activity by sleeping a random time
037:        int time = 1000 + rand.nextInt(5000);
038:        System.out.println("Sleeping for " +
039:         time / 1000 + " second(s)");
040:        Thread.currentThread().sleep(time);
041:
042:      }
043:     } catch (InterruptedException e) {
044:      return;
```

```
045:    }
046:  }
047:
048: // Halt the client
049: // However, all job threads finish to completion!
050:  public synchronized void halt() {
051:    finished = true;
052:    notifyAll();
053:  }
054: }
```

In its basic design, the Client class resembles the Primes.java program (Listing 19-4). To give the simulation something to do, Client provides the getAJob() method at lines 013-018. The method creates a new Job object, assigns it a name (Job#1, Job#2, and so on), and assigns it a delay time at random from about 1 to 10 seconds, in milliseconds.

Because it is Runnable, the Client class's activity takes place, as always, in a run() method. This time, however, run() does not call wait(), and so there is no need to call another private method to perform the thread's actions. Instead, all of the Client's activity takes place directly in run(), mostly in a large try-catch block at lines 029-045. But some interesting code takes place just before that block. Examine these statements closely:

```
Server server = new Server();
Thread T = new Thread(server);
T.setDaemon(true);
T.start();
```

This is where the Server object, named server in lowercase, is constructed. In addition, a new Thread is created and it is told to become a daemon before calling the thread's start() method, and in that way, starting the server. We want the server to be a daemon for two good reasons:

◆ The server needs to run in the background as long as the client thread is alive so that all jobs created by the client are properly handled.

◆ As explained earlier in the chapter, the Server class executes in a do-forever loop, and it provides no normal way to shut down the thread except by interrupting it. For this reason, the server thread *must* be a daemon so that it is terminated after all other user threads die—including, by the way, any Job class threads that are still not finished executing.

The code in the Client class is not otherwise interesting in terms of threaded programming. All Client does is call getAJob() to construct a new Job object, j, and then hand it to the server by executing the statement:

```
server.add(j);
```

The program then calls `sleep()` at line 040, again for a randomly selected amount of time, in order to simulate irregular user activity. Having each `Job` execute for a random length of time, and also delaying the creation of new jobs at random, provides a good test of the model's threaded code.

Testing the Client-Server Model

All that remains is a test program that puts the `Queue`, `Job`, `Server`, and `Client` threads into motion. The result is Listing 19-10, LockDemo.java. This is the program to compile and run if you haven't done so already.

Listing 19-10: LockDemo.java

```
001: import java.io.IOException;
002: import java.util.*;
003: import Client;
004:
005: class LockDemo {
006:
007: // Get a character from keyboard
008:  static char getChar() {
009:    char ch = '\0';
010:    try {
011:      ch = (char)System.in.read();
012:    } catch (IOException e) {
013:      System.out.println(e.getMessage());
014:    }
015:    return ch;
016:  }
017:
018: // Wait for user to press a specified key
019:  static void waitForKey(char key) {
020:    while (getChar() != key) /* wait */ ;
021:  }
022:
023:  public static void main(String args[]) {
024:
025: // Construct and start the client (job creator) thread
026:    Client client = new Client();
027:    new Thread(client).start();
028:
029: // Wait for Enter key so threads can run
030:    System.out.println("\n<<< Press Enter to end program >>>\n");
031:    waitForKey('\n');  // All threads run while waiting
032:
033: // Halt the client thread; sever daemon also ends
034: // However, any remaining job threads finish to completion!
```

```
035:    client.halt();
036:  }
037: }
```

There's not much to the demonstration program — most of the program's activity takes place in its Runnable classes. The main program begins by constructing a Client object and starting its thread:

```
Client client = new Client();
new Thread(client).start();
```

As previously explained, this also starts the server as a daemon thread, but the main program doesn't need to be aware of that fact. After printing a message, the program waits for you to press the Enter key (see line 031). The only reason for doing this is to keep the main program running so the threads have a chance to carry out the simulation. After you press Enter, line 035 halts the client thread by executing the statement:

```
client.halt();
```

However, because there might be Job objects waiting to be finished, the program probably does not immediately end. It will do so only after the last Job thread terminates. Also, as mentioned, the server daemon thread ends only after all user threads terminate — including any Jobs, the Client, and the program's main() method. Thus the server is the last thread to go, ensuring that all jobs are finished before the program ends.

Summary

◆ A thread represents a program's sequence of execution. Java programs can start multiple threads, all of which run as though their statements were interleaved. Threads with higher priorities get first crack at system resources; those with lower priorities operate more in the background.

◆ The thread scheduler determines which threads run and for how long. Because the thread scheduler is part of the Java virtual machine, it is implemented differently on various systems. However, threaded code runs similarly on all supported platforms.

◆ Every Java program is already threaded. The program itself executes in a thread, while the Java garbage collector executes in a separate thread of its own. You may create as many other threads as you need to run concurrent tasks such as printing in the background and loading graphics images, perhaps for an animation, while other operations take place.

◆ You can create a thread two ways. A class can extend the `Thread` class, or it can implement the `Runnable` interface. In either case, the class must provide a `run()` method that performs the thread's activity. Never call `run()` directly. The thread scheduler calls it when the program starts the thread by calling `Thread.start()`.

◆ The only reason to extend `Thread` is to override one of the class's methods. However, because extending `Thread` causes all methods to be inherited by the subclass, it is easier and more efficient for a class to implement `Runnable`.

◆ Every Java object has an associated lock that a thread may obtain in order to have exclusive access to the object. A lock is obtained by executing synchronized methods or statements. Locks are also sometimes called monitors. A lock is available for objects of any class, regardless of whether that class extends `Thread` or implements `Runnable`.

◆ A thread typically calls `wait()` to pause the thread and to allow other threads to access the object. Calling `wait()` requires the thread to own the object's lock, and it releases that lock while the thread lies dormant. The `wait()` method returns when another thread calls `notify()` or `notifyAll()`, usually after changing some condition upon which threads might be waiting. The code that calls `wait()` should always do so in a loop that inspects the waited-upon condition. This is because all threads might be woken up, but only one or some conditions might have changed.

◆ A thread may also call `sleep()` to pause for a certain length of time. It is not necessary for a thread to own the object's lock before calling `sleep()`, but if it does, that lock is *not* released. A thread can call `yield()` to allow other threads some time to run – during lengthy calculations, for example.

Chapter 20

AWT Applets and Applications

JAVA'S *ABSTRACT WINDOWING TOOLKIT* (**AWT**) provides an extensive set of classes for writing a graphical user interface, more commonly known by the sticky acronym *GUI*. Although the AWT has been around since Java's beginnings, it has undergone several radical changes from the time of its initial release in the JDK 1.0. For that reason, it is not enough merely to learn AWT's classes; you also need to understand a little about the toolkit's history and especially its different models for supporting *event handlers* — the code that is executed, for example, when a user clicks a GUI button in a window.

This chapter introduces many of the AWT's classes and discusses some the toolkit's pros and cons. You learn how to use the AWT to construct applets for execution in a Web browser, and also for stand-alone graphical applications. This information also forms the foundation for the newest GUI toolkit on the block, Java's Swing components, covered in Chapter 21, "Swing Applets and Applications." As the following sections suggest, choosing between AWT and Swing requires careful consideration of the advantages and disadvantages of each.

IN THIS CHAPTER

- ◆ Introducing the Abstract Windowing Toolkit
- ◆ Programming AWT applets
- ◆ Programming AWT stand-alone applications
- ◆ AWT event-handling models
- ◆ About events and listeners
- ◆ Using adapters and anonymous classes
- ◆ Significant AWT classes

Introducing the AWT

Often irreverently termed the "oh no, not *Another Windowing Toolkit*," the AWT provides several key features for writing GUI applets and applications. Among these are AWT's main characteristics:

◆ The AWT is a peer-based set of classes, meaning that it serves largely as an application programming interface, or API, to existing windowing capabilities provided by the operating system. For example, in Windows, an AWT button is actually a Windows button. In Linux and UNIX, a button might be provided by the KDE or Gnome desktop systems running X*.

X, which is sometimes incorrectly called X Windows, provides low-level, networked, graphical windowing software for Linux, Solaris, and other UNIX-type systems.

◆ Using the AWT, Java applets and applications display the same GUI elements used by native programs.

◆ The AWT provides two models for handling asynchronous events such as those that occur when a user drags the mouse or clicks on a GUI button. These are the *inheritance model* (sometimes also called the hierarchical model) and the *delegation model.* The second and newer delegation model is recommended for new programs. Java 2 still supports the old inheritance model, but many of its methods are now deprecated.

◆ The AWT provides *containers* and *components* that simplify the construction of GUI applets and applications. There are many classes for creating windows, dialog boxes, applets, buttons, check boxes, pull-down menus, and other elements familiar to GUI users all over the world. This chapter lists and demonstrates some, but not all, AWT classes. Full coverage of the AWT could easily fill a book of this size.

◆ The AWT provides *layout managers* that position a GUI's graphical elements according to various organizational plans. Because Java code, especially applets, might run on any type of computer system from PCs to Macs to full-blown UNIX networks, exact positioning of GUI components is rarely practical. Layout managers help ensure that AWT applets and applications look similar across widely differing operating environments and screen resolutions. (Swing can also use the AWT's layout managers.)

◆ The AWT provides numerous non-component supporting classes for 2D graphics and sound, and also for commonly needed items such as foreground and background color values. Even if you plan to move up to the newer Swing components as described in the Chapter 21, you'll still use many of AWT's non-component classes in your applets and applications.

There are two types of AWT programs: applets and applications. To introduce AWT, and to show how to compile and run Java programs that use this toolkit, the following two sections introduce both types.

Creating AWT Applets

What's the difference between an applet and an application? Answer: five letters and two syllables. Actually, there aren't many significant differences, except that an applet runs under control of a Web browser such as Netscape or Internet Explorer. An application runs as a stand-alone program under control of the Java runtime environment, and it therefore requires a main() method. Applets do not have a main() method; instead, they typically use an init() method to get started.

For security reasons, applets executed in a browser over the Internet are not permitted full access to system resources such as reading and writing files. Applications have no such restrictions.

Listing 20-1, AppletADay.java, demonstrates the rudiments of programming Java applets with AWT. Instructions for compiling and running the demonstration follow the listing.

Listing 20-1: AppletADay.java

```
001: import java.applet.Applet;
002: import java.awt.Color;
003: import java.awt.TextArea;
004:
005: public class AppletADay extends Applet {
006: // This method initializes the Applet
007:   public void init() {
008:     setBackground(Color.gray);
009:     String s = "An Applet a Day Keeps the Debugger Away!";
010:     add(new TextArea(s, 4, s.length()));
011:   }
012: }
```

You compile an applet from a command-line prompt the same way you do any other Java program. For example, to compile AppletADay, enter this command:

```
javac AppletADay.java
```

To run the resulting AppletADay.class file, you have two choices. One method is to use the appletviewer utility provided with the Java 2 development system. Specify an HTML file that loads the applet with a standard <applet> tag. In this case, do that by entering the command

```
appletviewer AppletADay.html
```

Figure 20-1 shows the AppletADay applet running in appletviewer.

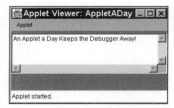

Figure 20-1: AppletADay running
in Java's appletviewer utility

The AppletADay.html file is in the same directory as the listing. In this case, the HTML file is just a minimal shell that you can use to test any applet. It contains the following <applet> tag:

```
<applet code = AppletADay width = 300 height = 200>
</applet>
```

For simple applets, the preceding code should work fine — simply change AppletADay to your applet's class filename. However, you might need to adjust the width and height parameters.

Another, and perhaps easier, way to run an applet is to open its associated HTML file using your Web browser. Or, use a directory utility such as Windows Explorer or, in Linux, a KDE or Gnome directory window to open AppletADay.html. This should bring up your browser and load the applet. If the browser is already running, you can instead use the File|Open command to open the HTML file. Figure 20-2 shows AppletADay running in Internet Explorer. Depending on your browser and operating system, the results on your screen might differ slightly from those shown here.

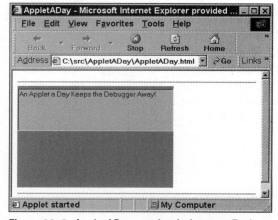

Figure 20-2: AppletADay running in Internet Explorer
under Windows

I prefer running applets in a browser because this shows how the applet appears to users over the Internet. However, the appletviewer utility provides menu commands that you can use to inspect an applet's properties such as its <applet> tag settings and other information that might be useful for debugging.

The sample applet's code begins in the usual way by importing the packages and classes it needs. In this case, I imported only the specific classes used in the program. Most of the time, you can begin your applets like this:

```
import java.applet.Applet;
import java.awt.*;
```

The first line imports only the Applet class — other classes in the java.applet package are not often needed. The second line imports all AWT classes. Remember, however, this does not import any classes in AWT subpackages such as java.awt.color and java.awt.event. To import those packages requires additional import statements. After these steps, extend the Applet class as a new public subclass named the same as its .java source code file:

```
public class AppletADay extends Applet {
...
}
```

All AWT applets have that same general form. Inside the class, this method starts the applet's ball rolling:

```
public void init() {
...
}
```

The browser calls the init() method to start the applet after its class file has been loaded, usually from the Web server over the Internet into the user's browser. Inside init(), insert the statements you want the applet to perform. Here, the program sets the background display color to gray (a standard applet convention) and creates a String object. The last statement shows an important aspect of applet programming:

```
add(new TextArea(s, 4, s.length()));
```

Applets are actually specialized containers to which you can add GUI components such as text and buttons. You don't have to specify exactly where the objects appear. Instead, as explained more fully in Chapter 21, a layout manager determines the objects' relative locations. In this case, the program simply adds a new TextArea object (one of AWT's many classes), displaying the object's text.

Creating AWT Applications

You can also write AWT applications that display GUI elements in a stand-alone window. The programming techniques are the same for applets and applications (except for the security restrictions already mentioned), but applications always run on their own. They don't require a Web browser or the appletviewer utility.

Listing 20-2, SimpleApp.java, shows a rudimentary stand-alone AWT application. As in the preceding applet, the stand-alone program merely displays a string in a window. Figure 20-3 shows the application window running under Microsoft Windows 98. As with applets, your display may differ from the one shown here depending on your operating system and GUI desktop.

Figure 20-3: SimpleApp is a stand-alone AWT application running here under Microsoft Windows 98.

Listing 20-2: SimpleApp.java

```
001: import java.awt.*;
002:
003: public class SimpleApp {
004:   public static void main(String args[]) {
005:     System.out.println("Creating application window...");
006:     Frame f = new Frame("Application Frame Window");
007:     String s = "Press Ctrl+C to close this window!";
008:     f.add(new TextArea(s, 4, s.length()));
009:     f.pack();
010:     f.show();
011:   }
012: }
```

Compile and run stand-alone AWT applications the same way you do those that run in a text terminal or a terminal window. For example, in this case, enter the following two commands at a terminal command-line prompt:

```
javac SimpleApp.java
java SimpleApp
```

When you do this, you will notice that you cannot close the resulting window by clicking its close button. This is because the program provides no code that responds to events, and therefore the only way to end the program is to switch back to the terminal window from which you started it and press Ctrl+C. (If that doesn't work, try Crtl+Z, Ctrl+X, or Ctrl+Break.)

Obviously, not being able to close a stand-alone application's window is a serious bug. I didn't include the necessary code to do that, however, because to understand how to write that code, you first need to examine the AWT's two event-handling models as explained in the upcoming section, "Event Models."

The SimpleApp program demonstrates a few important aspects of AWT application programming. Like text-based Java applications, the main public class, SimpleApp, which is named the same as the source code file, SimpleApp.java, provides a main() method. The first statement shows that, even though this is a GUI program, it can still write strings such as *Creating application window...* to the terminal window. This is often a useful debugging device for displaying the values of variables at strategic locations.

To create a graphical window, the program instantiates the AWT Frame class, using the statement

```
Frame f = new Frame("Application Frame Window");
```

That doesn't cause the window to appear. It merely creates the necessary container for holding other components. In this case, the program adds only one such component by calling the Frame class's add() method using the statement

```
f.add(new TextArea(s, 4, s.length()));
```

As in the applet demonstration, the only component here is a TextArea object, to which the program passes a string for display. Still, nothing is actually shown on screen until two more statements are executed:

```
f.pack();
f.show();
```

Calling pack() causes the frame window to be sized according to the rules of its current layout manager. The manager considers the sizes of any components in the frame, and it sizes the window to be large enough to display its contents, in this case, the TextArea component and string. After this step, calling the Frame class's show() method displays the window along with its components.

To Swing or Not to Swing?

Sun Microsystems now recommends that applets and applications use the newer Swing classes in place of AWT components. If you are skeptical about this recommendation, you are in good company. Even though it appears that Swing is destined to become the more popular choice, Sun isn't the first software company to introduce a new technology and then recommend that everybody suddenly start using it! To help you choose between AWT and Swing, following are a few pros and cons of each.

Let's start with AWT's negatives. Over time, one of AWT's main features has proven to be one of its major pitfalls – namely its reliance on the operating system's GUI elements. Originally, this seemed like a good idea, but in practice this approach has led to several problems:

♦ Operating system windows and components are *heavyweight objects* in the sense that they consume system resources that are interfaced through Java objects. Using AWT, not only does a program own an operating system GUI object such as a button, but the program also must maintain an associated Java object to interface that GUI element. AWT components are not very efficient in terms of system resources.

♦ Small differences between native GUI elements can add up to big problems for applets and applications. For example, a pop-up menu under the KDE desktop may differ in appearance from one on a Macintosh display or in Windows. It turns out to be very difficult for developers to allow for these and other minor differences, causing minor but embarrassing display quirks that are almost impossible to eradicate.

♦ AWT supports two event models, leading to much confusion among developers. Although the newer delegation model was introduced for AWT long before Swing became available, Swing uses *only* the newer model, and, therefore, using Swing might help ensure more consistent code development and, potentially, result in fewer bugs.

♦ AWT tends not to be as easily extended as Swing, which limits certain advances that are becoming more and more important, especially as the Internet expands. For example, Swing supports the concept of *assistive technologies* – those that, for instance, might be used to provide alternative computer input devices for people who for physical reasons cannot use a mouse or keyboard. Assistive technologies might include voice-activated commands for the blind or alternative display-selection methods that don't require hands and fingers. AWT as well as most other GUI APIs and development systems provide no similar assistive support techniques.

Given those considerations, many developers are shunning the AWT in favor of Swing. Although Swing offers similar tools as the AWT, the toolkits differ primarily in the following ways. The following points are considered to be Swing's key advantages:

♦ Swing uses no native operating system code. A Swing button is provided for entirely by Swing's own classes and is not merely an interface to an operating system GUI element. For this reason, Swing objects are said to be *lightweight,* and they are more efficient in terms of system resources.

◆ Swing makes it possible to completely separate the GUI from the application's content. In AWT programming, the application's code tends to be closely tied to its interface. There isn't anything wrong with this approach, but in many cases, separating the interface from the application helps reduce complexity and therefore may simplify development and debugging.

◆ Swing is more easily extended than AWT. Because Swing uses no native GUI code, a button and other components can be easily programmed to display graphics and text even if the operating system provides no such capabilities. This flexibility also promotes some interesting new GUI techniques such as support for HTML tags in button and text labels.

◆ As mentioned, Swing provides for assistive technologies such as voice command-driven and other alternative input and output systems. In the near future, this may become one of the most important considerations for using Swing.

◆ Swing provides common look-and-feel interfaces for popular systems such as Windows and Motif. You and your programs' users may select among these appearances regardless of the local operating system. Frankly, I hesitate to join those who list this Swing feature as a key advantage, but I seem to be in the minority among this issue's voices. You decide.

◆ Swing is especially attractive for X and Solaris systems because these use a networked client-server model for their graphical interfaces. Because Swing eliminates the use of native operating system GUI elements, programs that use Swing on these systems should run more smoothly than AWT applications, which may lead to relatively increased network traffic. This is not much of a consideration, however, with single-user PCs and Macs, including single-user Linux systems that run X.

 Although I have come across obscure notes and references that suggest it may be possible to combine heavyweight AWT and lightweight Swing components, this is probably never a good idea and will almost certainly lead to display problems. For this reason, it is even more important to carefully consider your choice of tools. After basing your program on one toolkit, switching to the other may mean completely rewriting your program from scratch!

Despite Swing's allure, this newer toolkit is not without its criticisms, and there are some drawbacks to using Swing that you should consider before abandoning AWT. Be aware of the following facts before deciding to become a Swinger:

◆ Early browsers do not support Swing components. In addition, to run Swing applets, users must install the Java 2 plug-in, available for free from Sun (see Chapter 21). Browsers that support only the JDK 1.0 cannot use Swing applets. Likewise, systems with only JDK 1.0 runtime support cannot run Swing applications.

◆ HTML `<applet>` tags cannot directly load Swing applets, even in browsers in which the Java 2 plug-in is properly installed. Sun provides a free conversion utility to convert `<applet>` tags for use with Swing applets (again, see Chapter 21 for details). This utility is easy to use, but it means an extra step in Web page development.

◆ For experienced Java and AWT programmers, Swing means learning yet another new set of classes and programming techniques. Because Swing is especially intended for large-scale projects, if you already know your way around AWT, you might consider continuing to use it for moderately sized applets and applications. Many existing programs use AWT, and you can save a lot of time and effort basing new code on source code files found on the Internet. Because Swing is only now core to Java 2, there aren't as many Swing sources available as there are for AWT.

◆ Using native GUI elements, while potentially leading to minor display anomalies, is not a *bad* idea. It is reassuring to know that your Java programs' users will see GUI objects that are familiar to them. As I mentioned, I am unconvinced that providing users with a choice of look-and-feel appearances is necessarily an improvement in the use of GUI operating systems. However, it's good to keep in mind that Swing lightweight components use system resources more efficiently than do AWT heavyweight components.

If you still can't decide, I suggest you learn how to use AWT (concentrating especially on this chapter's information on the newer delegation event model, which Swing also uses). Compile and run the examples in this chapter, and then compare them with the similar examples in Chapter 21. This will help you choose the toolkit that makes the best sense for your application.

Finally, don't be concerned that AWT will suddenly "go away." There are too many existing applets and applications based on AWT for that to happen anytime soon. Although if you examine Java 2's source code and online documentation, you will come across numerous "deprecated" AWT class methods, these are almost entirely related to the older inheritance event model. If you use the newer delegation model, your AWT code should be supported well into the future. Besides, a lot of Swing is based on non-component classes in the AWT, and most Swing applications therefore import both AWT and Swing packages. So, even if you decide to move to Swing, you'll still use many of the AWT classes described here.

Event Models

One of the key features of a GUI is its asynchronously interactive nature. GUIs are busy environments, posting and responding to all sorts of *events* that indicate activities such as windows that need repainting and buttons that users have clicked. Numerous programming systems have been available for writing this code – generally know as *event handlers* – and Java is no different.

However, unlike other systems, Java's AWT provides two very different event handling models. The older and original model, which dates back to the JDK 1.0, is called the *inheritance model*. The newer model, which was introduced in JDK 1.1 and remains the preferred choice today, is called the *delegation model*. Both models are still fully supported in Java 2, but you should use the delegation model in new code. Many of the inheritance model's methods have been deprecated. However, if you have code that uses the old model, this is no cause for alarm. It is highly unlikely that Java will drop support for the older event handling techniques.

The following sections introduce each of the AWT's event handling models. Readers who plan to use Swing as explained in Chapter 21 should read "The Delegation Model" following the next section because this is the model that all Swing programs use.

The Inheritance Model

As its name suggests, the inheritance model relies on subclassing to provide event handlers. With this technique, a program extends an existing AWT class and provides one or more methods for responding to specific events. For example, the Button class provides a method, mouseDown( ), called when the mouse cursor is clicked inside the button object. To respond to that and other events, you simply extend the Button class and override the appropriate method.

 If you are skipping around in this book, be aware that this section describes the older event handling model in the AWT. All such methods such as mouseDown( ), inherited from Component, are now deprecated, and these methods should not be used in new code.

The main drawback to methods such as mouseDown( ), although intuitive to use, is that they *require* programs to extend a class in order to use a GUI element. This tends to lead to more classes than the program would otherwise need. Consequently, most Java programmers don't use methods like mouseDown( ). Instead, the more typical approach is to implement either an action( ) or handleEvent( ) method as found, for example, in the Applet class. This allows the program to receive all events for specific objects – but it also requires the program to pass along other events that it doesn't process so as to not interrupt the GUI's other activities.

To demonstrate this approach, which is typical of other non-Java GUI programming systems, Listing 20-3, BackColor.java, is a small applet. Run it as you did AppletADay earlier in this chapter by opening the BackColor.html file in your Web browser. Or, you can load BackColor.html into the appletviewer utility. Click the button in the window to change the background color at random.

Listing 20-3: BackColor.java

```
001: import java.applet.Applet;
002: import java.awt.*;
003: import java.util.Random;
004:
005: public class BackColor extends Applet {
006:   Random gen;  // Random number generator for color selction
007:   String buttonLabel = "Click Me!";
008:
009:   // Initialize applet
010:   public void init() {
011:    gen = new Random();
012:    Button colorButton = new Button(buttonLabel);
013:    add(colorButton);  // Added to Applet container
014:   }
015:
016:   // Respond to button click
017:   public boolean action(Event evt, Object what) {
018:    Color c;
019:    if (buttonLabel.equals(what)) {  // Is it our button?
020:     do {
021:      c = new Color(gen.nextInt());
022:     } while (c == getBackground());
023:     setBackground(c);
024:     repaint();
025:    }
026:    return true;  // Kill event
027:   }
028: }
```

Compiling the demonstration program with the command `javac BackColor.java` produces a "deprecation" warning. Use the command-line option `-deprecation` to show that this happens because of the deprecated `action()` method. The program still compiles correctly, and it runs harmlessly, but the compiler warns you that it uses the old-style inheritance event model.

The BackColor class extends Applet (see 005) and declares two variables. One is a Random generator for selecting background colors, and the other is a String for the button's label. Method init(), as in most AWT applets, initializes the applet when it is loaded into a Web browser or started by the appletviewer utility. Inside init(), the Random generator is created, after which a Button object is instantiated and added to the applet with the statements

```
Button colorButton = new Button(buttonLabel);
add(colorButton);
```

This is a typical way to add a GUI component to a window or applet. However, because we are using the older inheritance event model, we also need a separate method to perform an action when the button is selected. In this case, the program overrides the Applet class's action() method (see lines 017-027).

One problem with this approach is immediately obvious. Because action() receives *all* events intended for the applet, the program must determine which object fired the event in question. We assume here that the action is the button's selection, since there aren't any other "action" type events for buttons; however, other GUI objects might also require determining the type of event (the next example shows how to do that). Line 019 compares the button's text with that of the Object what parameter passed to action(). If it's our button, the background is repainted in a different color selected at random. (If you are uncomfortable with this technique of distinguishing the selected button, join the club. There are other ways to do this, but none is much better than the one shown here.)

The final action() statement at line 026 returns true, which tells the AWT that the event has been processed. If action() returns false, the event is propagated up the inheritance chain until it is handled. This is the source of the term *inheritance model*. The program relies on class inheritance to process GUI events.

Unfortunately, forcing programs to handle all events makes the code prone to all kinds of errors. Critical events can be too easily killed by accident, and events can be processed but allowed to percolate upwards, and be handled more than once. Bugs arising from these errors are common in older Java applets and applications. One solution is to extend the Button class and provide code for a specific event. Using this technique, the program might create a new class like this:

```
class NewButton extends Button {
 // Constructor
 NewButton(String label) {
  super(label);  // Call ancestor constructor
 }
 // Event handler
 public boolean mouseDown(Event evt, int x, int y) {
  // perform action for mouseDown event
  return true;  // Kill event
 }
}
```

Although this technique works, it tends to bloat the program with classes and methods that typically add nothing significant to the class, but merely call code written elsewhere. For example, NewButton's constructor has nothing new to perform, but it still is needed in order to call the ancestor constructor. Also, the mouseDown() method, which might perform real work, more often simply calls another method since other objects such as menu commands probably need to perform the same operations. In short, we have gone to all the trouble of creating a new class without gaining any real benefits.

For that reason, Java programmers have typically used the action() method described before, or another even more low-level method, handleEvent(). Listing 20-4, MouseXY.java, demonstrates how to use the method to intercept mouse events intended for an AWT applet. After compiling the program, run it by loading MouseXY.html into your Web browser or the appletviewer utility. When the applet window appears, move the mouse cursor inside to see its relative screen coordinates. If you move the mouse outside of the window, a message appears telling you to move it inside.

Listing 20-4: MouseXY.java

```
001: import java.applet.*;
002: import java.awt.*;
003:
004: public class MouseXY extends Applet {
005:   String location;  // String for X=0 Y=0 display
006:
007:   // Initialize applet variables and window
008:   public void init() {
009:     setBackground(Color.yellow);
010:     resize(200, 100);
011:     location = new String("Move mouse inside window");
012:   }
013:
014:   // Paint the location string inside window
015:   public void paint(Graphics g) {
016:     g.drawString(location, 10, 10);
017:   }
018:
019:   // Create the location string from x and y
020:   public void makeString(int x, int y) {
021:     location = new String(
022:       " X=" + String.valueOf(x) +
023:       " Y=" + String.valueOf(y) );
024:   }
025:
026:   // Handle all events for this applet
027:   public boolean handleEvent(Event  evt) {
```

```
028:    boolean eventHandled = false;
029:    switch (evt.id) {
030:     case Event.MOUSE_DOWN:
031:     case Event.MOUSE_UP:
032:     case Event.MOUSE_DRAG:
033:     case Event.MOUSE_ENTER:
034:     case Event.MOUSE_MOVE: {
035:      makeString(evt.x, evt.y);
036:      repaint();
037:      eventHandled = true;
038:      break;
039:     }
040:     case Event.MOUSE_EXIT: {
041:      location = new String("Move mouse inside window");
042:      repaint();
043:      eventHandled = true;
044:     }
045:    }
046:    if (eventHandled)
047:     return true;
048:    else
049:     return super.handleEvent(evt);
050:   }
051: }
```

 As with preceding sample applet, compiling this program with the command `javac MouseXY.java` produces a "deprecation" warning due to the use of the outdated `handleEvent()` method. However, the program still runs as intended.

MouseXY.java shows the most typical techniques in AWT applets and applications to handle events using the outdated inheritance model. Because the `handleEvent()` method receives all events intended for this component, it usually contains a large `switch` statement such as listed here at lines 029-045. Actually, this is a relatively small `switch` statement — in a real application, this code might go on for dozens and dozens of lines. Not only is this type of programming non-object-oriented, but it is prone to errors. How easy it is to leave out a critical event type, or to cause a hard-to-find bug by forgetting a needed `break` statement!

Nevertheless, it's a good idea to understand how `handleEvent()` works, if only to be prepared to support older code (or even better, to revise it using the newer model). Events are objects of the `Event` class, which use integer identifier values such as `MOUSE_UP` and `MOUSE_MOVE` to represent specific types of events. In this case, most mouse events are handled similarly by creating a string that shows the mouse cursor's X and Y location, and then painting that string in the applet window by calling repaint(). An exception is the MOUSE_EXIT event (see lines 040-044), which in this example changes the string to a message that tells the user to move the mouse back inside the window.

Notice that in all cases, if an event is handled, handleEvent() must return true. If an event is not handled, the method returns false. It also calls the ancestor handleEvent() method (see line 049). These critical actions ensure that all events are properly handled. But again, these requirements are easily misapplied, leading to nasty bugs.

If you absolutely must use the older inheritance event model, the preceding discussions and sample programs will at least help you get started. However, I don't want to waste any more space on outdated techniques. As the next section explains, the newer delegation model offers a far superior way to handle GUI events.

The Delegation Model

The delegation event handling model was added to the AWT starting with the JDK 1.1 and is fully supported in Java 2's newest JDK release (1.3 as of this writing). For new AWT applets and applications, you are urged to use this model over the outdated inheritance model described in the preceding section. Also, if you plan to use Swing components as described in Chapter 21, you must use the newer delegation model.

Using the delegation model, event handling is fully object-oriented. Events are objects of classes derived from AWTEvent. To handle an event, a program delegates an *event listener,* which can be any object of a class that implements the EventListener interface, a member of the java.util package. Listing 20-5, Delegate.java, demonstrates how to use the delegation event model to create two buttons in an applet window. Compile the program as usual, and then load the Delegate.html file into your browser or the appletviewer utility. Click one of the buttons to toggle it and the other button on and off.

Listing 20-5: Delegate.java

```
001: import java.awt.*;
002: import java.awt.event.*;
003: import java.applet.Applet;
004:
005: public class Delegate extends Applet {
006:
007: // Define two AWT button objects
008:   private Button button1 = new Button("Click This!");
009:   private Button button2 = new Button("Click Me!");
010:
011:   // Declare an inner class for the listener object
012:   // Toggles between the two buttons
013:   class ButtonListener implements ActionListener {
014:     public void actionPerformed(ActionEvent e) {
015:       if (e.getActionCommand().equals("button1action")) {
```

```
016:        button1.setEnabled(false);
017:        button2.setEnabled(true);
018:      } else {
019:        button1.setEnabled(true);
020:        button2.setEnabled(false);
021:      }
022:    }
023:  }
024:
025: // Applet class constructor
026:  public Delegate() {
027:    ButtonListener actionObject = new ButtonListener();
028:    button1.setActionCommand("button1action");
029:    button1.addActionListener(actionObject);
030:    button2.setActionCommand("button2action");
031:    button2.addActionListener(actionObject);
032:    button1.setEnabled(true);
033:    button2.setEnabled(false);
034:    add(button1);
035:    add(button2);
036:  }
037: }
```

The Delegate.java program's Delegate class extends Applet. Inside the class, two AWT Button objects are created. Following this, an inner class at lines 013-023 creates the code that is performed when one of the buttons is selected. This class doesn't have to be inside the extended Applet class, but it is typically placed there so it can refer to that class's members. In this case, the code calls setEnabled() to toggle the two button objects on and off.

The inner ButtonListener class implements ActionListener, one of several different types of listener interfaces that AWT provides. ActionListener specifies a single method declared as

```
public void actionPerformed(ActionEvent e);
```

To create an ActionListener object, simply define a new class such as ButtonListener in the sample program and provide the contents for that method. Inspect the ActionEvent parameter to determine facts about this event — in this case, to find out which button was selected.

The program's constructor at lines 026-036 shows how to connect a GUI object such as a Button to an event listener. First, create the listener object as shown at line 027. Then, perform two steps to define an action label and connect the GUI object to the listener:

```
button1.setActionCommand("button1action");
button1.addActionListener(actionObject);
```

When the object fires an action-type event, it sets the action command string into the `ActionEvent` object and then passes that object to the registered listener, `actionObject`. That same action object is used for both buttons, but the program is free to define as many listeners as needed. Conversely, although not shown here, any GUI object can have multiple listeners, all of which receive any events the object fires. However, unlike with the inheritance event model, each event sent to a listener is a separate and distinct object. Consequently, it is not possible for objects to communicate by modifying event fields. (If you need to do that, define a primary listener object to receive the events for all components that need to communicate with one another.)

The Delegate.java listing works well enough, but it is not the only way, nor is it necessarily the best way, to create event listeners. The next sections show other techniques that you are more likely to use in practice.

Programming with the AWT

Programming with the AWT requires mastering the concepts of the delegation event model (as introduced in the preceding section), AWT component classes, and layouts (used to organize components in windows). The following sections introduce these topics (layouts are further explained in Chapter 21). Except for component classes, much of this information applies also to Chapter 21's discussion of Swing classes.

AWT Events and Listeners

Table 20-1 shows AWT's event classes and their associated listener interfaces. Classes marked with an asterisk are not typically used in applications. Also, be aware that `AWTEvent` is a member of the `java.awt` package. All other classes and interfaces are members of `java.awt.event`.

TABLE 20-1 AWT EVENT CLASSES AND LISTENER INTERFACES

Event Class	Event Listener	Purpose
ActionEvent	ActionListener	Fired for an object's primary action such as when a button is clicked or a menu item is selected.
AdjustmentEvent	AdjustmentListener	Fired by adjustable objects such as a scroll bar when its size changes.
AWTEvent *	AWTEventListener *	Primarily used in creating event monitors, but not for general use.
ComponentEvent	ComponentListener	Fired when a GUI component moves or changes in size or visibility. Strictly for notification; AWT takes care of any painting needed in response to the change.

Event Class	Event Listener	Purpose
FocusEvent	FocusListener	Fired to indicate that a component has gained or lost the keyboard focus.
none	HierarchyBounds Listener *	Fired when an ancestor component is moved or resized. Intended strictly for notification purposes.
HierarchyEvent *	HierarchyListener *	Fired when a component or a container's hierarchy changes — for example, when a component's show() method is called. Intended strictly for notification purposes; AWT handles all necessary reactions internally.
InputEvent	InputListener	Root class for all input types of events, often used to "consume" an event such as a button selection and thus prevent it from being handled normally.
InputMethodEvent *	InputMethodListener *	Fired to indicate a change made to a text item (see TextEvent).
ItemEvent	ItemListener	Fired to indicate that an item in an object such as a List has been selected or deselected.
KeyEvent	KeyListener	Fired when a keystroke is performed for an object.
MouseEvent	MouseListener	Fired to indicate a mouse button has been clicked or released, or when the mouse cursor enters or leaves a GUI object's boundaries.
none	MouseMotionListener	Use this interface to receive mouse movement and also click-and-drag events.
TextEvent	TextListener	Fired to indicate that a text item has been changed.
WindowEvent	WindowListener	Fired when a window changes size or state.

*Not typically used in applets or applications

As you can see in Table 20-1, most listener interfaces have associated event classes, using an easily remembered naming convention. In general, the class `<Name>Event` is matched by a listener interface `<Name>Listener`. To register a listener for a GUI object, call an `add<Name>Listener()` method and pass to it an object of a class that implements the interface. For example, to respond to mouse events for a GUI object, first create a class the implements the appropriate interface:

```
class MyMouseListener implements MouseListener {
 public void MouseClicked(MouseEvent e) {
  // ... insert code to respond to mouse click
 }
 // ... other interface methods
}
```

Next, create the component object, and call the appropriate `add<Name>Listener()` method to register the listener. Often, you will do this in the class's constructor. For instance, to listen for mouse events for an applet's window, simply use this statement:

```
addMouseListener(new MyMouseListener());
```

There's usually no need to retain a reference to the constructed `MyMouseListener()` object because its sole purpose is to respond to events, and the program probably has no need to call the object's methods or use it in any other way. Or, even easier is to have the applet or other class implement a listener interface, and then register itself using a statement such as

```
addMouseListener(this);   // !!!
```

As these and future sample statements show, the delegation model is extremely flexible. A GUI component can be made to respond to its own events, or listeners can be completely separated from the objects that fire the events. Unlike with the inheritance model, with the delegation model you can write separate GUI and action classes and, in that way, simplify future visual improvements. As a current example, it is far easier to move code based on the delegation model from AWT to Swing than it is to revise an older inheritance-model application.

To illustrate the flexibility of the delegation event model, sample listings in this chapter employ several different techniques to create GUI objects and associate them with event listeners. The inconsistencies among the listings may seem confusing at first, but I wrote the examples specifically to show several different and typical techniques used with the delegation event model.

Adapters and Anonymous Classes

A drawback of using listener interfaces (refer back to Table 20-1) is that a class must supply methods for all those defined in the interface. For example, a class that implements MouseListener needs bodies for all of that interface's methods:

```
class MyMouseListener implements MouseListener {
 public void mouseClicked(MouseEvent e){ ... }
 public void mousePressed(MouseEvent e) { ... }
 public void mouseReleased(MouseEvent e) { ... }
 public void mouseEntered(MouseEvent e) { ... }
 public void mouseExited(MouseEvent e) { ... }
}
```

Most often, however, you probably need to respond to only selected events. So you don't have to implement the other unneeded methods, the AWT provides a set of abstract *adapter classes,* but only for interfaces that declare multiple methods. Table 20-2 lists the AWT's adapter classes:

TABLE 20-2 AWT ADAPTER CLASSES

Adapter Class	Implements
ComponentAdapter	ComponentListener
ContainerAdapter	ContainerListener
FocusAdapter	FocusListener
HierarchyBoundsAdapter	HierarchyBoundsListener
KeyAdapter	KeyListener
MouseAdapter	MouseListener
MouseMotionAdapter	MouseMotionListener
WindowAdapter	WindowListener

Each adapter class implements the associated interface and provides empty bodies for all defined methods. To use an adapter, extend it into a new class and override the event methods you need. Simply ignore the others. Remember that abstract adapters exist only for interfaces that declare multiple methods. Interfaces such as ActionListener that declare only one method do not have, nor do they need, associated adapter classes. In general, to use single-method interfaces, implement the interface in your listener class. To use multiple-method interfaces, extend an adapter class in your listener class *or* implement the interface and provide bodies for all declared methods.

Another useful trick of the trade uses *anonymous classes* to create listener methods. An anonymous class is constructed and programmed in line. The class has no name and there's no object reference. At first, the construction of an anonymous class looks a bit odd. Here's a stripped down sample based on the MouseAdaptor class:

```
new MouseAdapter() {
 public void mouseClicked(MouseEvent e) {
  // ... code for mouse click events
 }
}:  // Semicolon required!
```

In effect, that creates an anonymous class that extends MouseAdapter and, as such, inherits that class's members. The new nameless class overrides the inherited mouseClicked() method to respond to mouse-click events. Notice that new creates an object of the anonymous class — in other words, this is a statement, and therefore, it must end with a semicolon. Another way to create an anonymous class is to specify an interface using code such as

```
new ActionListener() {
 public void actionPerformed(ActionEvent e) {
  // ... code for action event
 }
}:  // Semicolon required!
```

That creates an anonymous class that implements the ActionListener interface and provides a body for that interface's only method, actionPerformed(). Out of context, the anonymous classes as programmed here are impractical. But when used to create an object that is passed to another method, anonymous classes are invaluable tools. For example, an applet might create a Button using the statement

```
Button clickMe = new Button("Click Me!");
```

To provide a listener for the button's action event, fired when the button is clicked, follow that statement with a call to addActionListener():

```
clickMe.addActionListener(new ActionListener() {
 public void actionPerformed(ActionEvent e) {
  // ... code for action event
 }
});
```

That's all you have to do to create an event handler for the button — simply insert your code where the comment indicates. The anonymous class implements the ActionListener interface and provides code for the actionPerformed()

method. When the user clicks the button, this code is executed directly without any need to filter out other events. However, the form of this programming may look a little strange—notice especially the punctuation on the last line that closes the anonymous class declaration with a brace and ends the method call with a closing parenthesis. Again, this is a statement, and so it must end with a semicolon.

A more complete example better illustrates anonymous classes. Listing 20-6, RandomColor.java, displays a button in an applet window. Clicking the button randomly changes the applet's background color. This is the same visual effect demonstrated earlier in this chapter's BackColor.java program (Listing 20-3) but that uses the newer delegation event model to handle button clicks. You might want to compare the two listings.

Listing 20-6: RandomColor.java

```
001: import java.applet.Applet;
002: import java.awt.*;
003: import java.awt.event.*;
004: import java.util.Random;
005:
006: public class RandomColor extends Applet {
007:
008:   // Constructor
009:   public RandomColor() {
010:     // Create GUI button object and random generator
011:     Button clickMe = new Button("Click Me!");
012:     final Random gen = new Random();
013:
014:     // Create listener using an anonymous class
015:     clickMe.addActionListener(new ActionListener() {
016:       public void actionPerformed(ActionEvent e) {
017:         Color c;
018:         do {
019:           c = new Color(gen.nextInt());
020:         } while (c == getBackground());
021:         setBackground(c);
022:         repaint();
023:       }
024:     });
025:
026:     // Add button to Applet container
027:     add(clickMe);
028:   }
029: }
```

The program's RandomColor class extends Applet, but unlike the earlier program, all of the code is contained in the class constructor. Two objects are created: clickMe of the AWT Button class, and gen, of the java.util package's Random class. An anonymous class is used to create an `ActionListener` object passed to the `clickMe` button's `addActionListener()` method (see lines 015–024).

 As mentioned, when using the anonymous class technique illustrated here, it's important to carefully match opening and closing braces and parentheses. For example, line 024 provides the closing brace that ends the anonymous `ActionListener` class created starting at line 015. The closing parenthesis and semicolon at line 024 end the statement that calls `addActionListener()` (line 015). A program editor such as the UNIX and Linux Emacs that automatically counts and matches these symbols is invaluable in this sort of programming.

The `actionPerformed()` method — the only one declared by the `ActionListener` interface — changes the applet's background color when the button is clicked. This portion of the program is the same as the earlier demonstration, but this time there is no need to examine the type of event because the button object itself provides its own event handler. This is obviously a much more object-oriented approach than is possible with the older event model.

AWT Applications

One drawback in using anonymous classes as described in the preceding section is that inner classes cannot refer to non-`final` instance variables. This is why `Random gen` is declared to be `final`. (See line 012 in Listing 20-6.) Also, an anonymous class obviously cannot have a constructor since the class has no name! Those aren't terribly serious complaints; however, many programmers find the technique demonstrated in the preceding listing to be somewhat obscure.

A more straightforward way to create an action listener for a GUI object such as a button is to have the object's container provide the action method. That container might be an applet, or it can be a `Frame` object for a stand-alone window. With this approach, it is again necessary to distinguish among multiple components that register the same listener. In fact, it is possible for this technique to degenerate to the level of the older inheritance model, at least in the sense that a single listener can be made to handle all events. This is rarely a good idea, but at least the newer model's flexibility lets you decide which technique to use.

Listing 20-7, ColorApp.java, shows this common AWT technique and also demonstrates how to create a stand-alone AWT application that uses the delegation event model. The program is similar in operation to the preceding one, but you can run it using the java interpreter.

Listing 20–7: ColorApp.java

```
001: import java.applet.Applet;
002: import java.awt.*;
```

```
003:  import java.awt.event.*;
004:  import java.util.Random;
005:
006:  public class ColorApp
007:   extends Panel
008:   implements ActionListener {
009:
010:   protected Random gen = new Random();
011:
012:   // Constructor
013:   public ColorApp() {
014:    Button clickMe = new Button("Click Me!");
015:    clickMe.addActionListener(this);
016:    add(clickMe);  // Add button to panel
017:   }
018:
019:   // The button's event handler
020:   public void actionPerformed(ActionEvent e) {
021:    Color c;
022:    do {
023:     c = new Color(gen.nextInt());
024:    } while (c == getBackground());
025:    setBackground(c);
026:    repaint();
027:   }
028:
029:   // The main program
030:   public static void main(String[] args) {
031:
032:    // Create frame and set its size
033:    Frame frame = new Frame("Color Application Demo");
034:    frame.setSize(250, 200);
035:    frame.setLocation(50, 50);
036:
037:    // End the program when the window is closed
038:    frame.addWindowListener(new WindowAdapter() {
039:     public void windowClosing(WindowEvent e) {
040:      System.exit(0);
041:     }
042:    });
043:
044:    // Add the ColorApp panel to the frame and show it
045:    frame.add(new ColorApp(), BorderLayout.CENTER);
046:    frame.show();
047:   }
048:  }
```

ColorApp.java illustrates several important AWT programming techniques. These same techniques are used also in Swing programming, as introduced in Chapter 21. The entire program takes place in a single class, `ColorApp`, declared as

```
public class ColorApp
 extends Panel
 implements ActionListener {
 ...
}
```

The class extends the AWT `Panel` class, which serves as a container for other GUI objects, in this case a single button. The class also implements the `ActionListener` interface. As already explained, this interface declares one method — `actionPerformed()` — and therefore, our extended `ColorApp` class is required to provide a body for that method. As you will see, attaching this to the button provides the code that is called when the button is clicked.

Exactly how to do that may not be immediately obvious if you haven't much experience with the delegation event model. The key is found in the class constructor, repeated here for close examination:

```
public ColorApp() {
 Button clickMe = new Button("Click Me!");
 clickMe.addActionListener(this);
 add(clickMe);  // Add button to panel
}
```

The first statement creates the `Button` object. The second calls the button's `addActionListener()` method. Passing `this` to that method registers the `ColorApp` object as the listener for the button — thus, when you click the button, the program calls `ColorApp.actionPerformed()`. Finally, the `ColorApp` constructor adds the button to the container by calling the `add()` method inherited from `Panel`.

If there were other components in the window, they too could register the `ColorApp` object (represented as `this`) for their listeners. However, as mentioned, when using this technique, the listener's `actionPerformed()` method needs to distinguish among the components to determine which one fired the event.

Of course, you also have to provide the code for the event handler itself. In this case, that requirement is satisfied in the `actionPerformed()` method at lines 020-027. This is the same code as in the preceding example program, but now that we are no longer using an anonymous inner class, the `Random gen` object does not need to be declared `final`.

Because this is a stand-alone program, not an applet, it must have a `main()` method (see lines 030-047). The first three statements in `main()` create a `Frame` object, which creates the visual window and its title bar using the string shown. Normally, the window would be only large enough to show its GUI objects — to make it large enough to be interesting, the program calls the `setSize()` and `setLocation()` methods with arbitrary parameters.

The statements at lines 038-042 show a vital technique in creating stand-alone AWT programs that use the delegation event model. Closing the program's window does not automatically end the program. To do that, you must attach a window listener to the window's frame. Carefully examine this code:

```
frame.addWindowListener(new WindowAdapter() {
 public void windowClosing(WindowEvent e) {
  System.exit(0);
 }
});
```

You might recognize the form of this programming — it's another example of an anonymous class, this time extended from the WindowAdapter abstract class. That class provides several methods that you can use to program event handlers for actions such as the window closing or being minimized. Here, we need to override only one method: windowClosing(). When this event is received, the program calls System.exit() to end the program. You may copy this code into any stand-alone AWT program, but don't use it in applets. The programming also works in Swing programming (except that the frame object is of the class JFrame — but more on that in Chapter 21).

TIP   For a list of the methods available in classes such as WindowAdapter, consult the Java source code files in the java.awt.event package. Also browse the online documentation if you downloaded and installed it.

Finally in the sample program, two statements add a ColorApp object to the frame and show it. Remember that ColorApp extends Panel. In this case, the ColorApp object is used as a surface that holds other components (a single button here). Just for the sake of being different, I added a parameter that centers the panel within the frame:

```
frame.add(new ColorApp(), BorderLayout.CENTER);
frame.show();
```

In AWT programming, it is more typical to add components such as buttons directly to a Frame object. However, using an intermediate Panel as shown here is a good way to organize multiple objects. The technique is also used extensively in Swing programming.

Some programmers question the preceding statements because they are inside the `ColorApp` class. But there is nothing wrong with a method, but not a constructor, creating an object of its own class. This technique also is popular among Swing users.

AWT Classes

There isn't room in a single chapter to describe the entire AWT toolkit — it's a huge set of classes. However, for reference and to help you locate more information about specific classes, the following tables list and describe AWT's packages and many of their significant classes. Table 20-3 lists all of AWT's packages. Most applets and applications import all classes from at least the two packages, `java.awt` and `java.awt.event`.

TABLE 20-3 AWT PACKAGES

Package Name	Purpose
`java.awt`	Main AWT classes and components. All GUI applets and applications should import this package.
`java.awt.color`	Color "space" classes mostly for photographic work, not for common color use in windows.
`java.awt.datatransfer`	Clipboard and other "transferable" data transfer tools.
`java.awt.dnd`	Drag-and-drop tools. See also the subpackage in this set, `java.awt.dnd.peer`.
`java.awt.event`	Delegation model event classes and interfaces. Most GUI applets and applications should import this package.
`java.awt.font`	Font and text support tools.
`java.awt.geom`	Geometrical tools that support and supplement Java 2D graphics.
`java.awt.im`	Input and text editing tools primarily for supporting different locales and foreign languages. See also the supporting subpackage in in this set, `java.awt.im.spi`.
`java.awt.image`	Tools for images, raster images, buffering techniques, and color models, primarily intended for photgraphic image work. See also the supporting subpackage `java.awt.image.renderable`.

Package Name	Purpose
java.awt.peer	See note *
java.awt.print	Printing tools.

*This package's classes all contain the following note: "The peer interfaces are intended only for use in porting the AWT. They are not intended for use by application developers, and developers should not implement peers nor invoke any of the peer methods directly on the peer instances."

Each of the packages in Table 20-3 provides several classes. Table 20-4 lists some of the classes from the main java.awt package that are of primary interest to applet and application developers. AWT layout classes, used in AWT and Swing programming, are described in Chapter 21.

TABLE 20–4 AWT KEY CLASSES

Class Name	Purpose
AWTEvent	Superclass for AWT event classes (refer back to Table 20-1).
Button	Selectable GUI button component.
Canvas	Blank rectangular area for drawing graphics or for representing a component's surface.
Checkbox	Selectable check box component with optional text label.
CheckboxGroup	Used as a container to group multiple check box objects.
CheckboxMenuItem	Menu item that can be toggled on and off using a check mark symbol or check box.
Choice	Pop-up menu of choices. See also PopupMenu.
Color	Various standard named colors and their RGB values.
Component	Superclass for all AWT GUI components such as buttons and scrollbars.
Container	Superclass for all AWT objects that can contain other AWT components. Applets, frames, and windows are examples of AWT containers.
Cursor	Encapsulates in a general way a GUI mouse cursor image.
Dialog	Basis for dialog windows (see also FileDialog).

Continued

TABLE 20-4 AWT KEY CLASSES *(Continued)*

Class Name	Purpose
Dimension	Utility class used to represent size information for components.
FileDialog	File-load and file-save dialog windows.
Font	General-purpose typographical font class, used also to associate characters (symbols) and their glyphs (images).
Frame	Basic window frame, typically used as the main container of a stand-alone AWT application. See also Panel and Window.
Graphics	Abstract class that serves as a graphics "context," enabling drawing operations for components and other objects, and also provides numerous graphics operations.
Graphics2D	Extends the Graphics abstract class to provide enhanced support for rendering 2D shapes and also for text objects and color management.
Image	Superclass for all AWT image classes such as found in the java.awt.image package.
Label	Single-line, static (non-editable) text label component. See also TextArea.
List	Scrollable list of selectable text items.
MediaTracker	Utility class used in preparing animations. (However, see Chapter 23, "Graphics Techniques," for better animation techniques using Swing components.)
Menu	Used for creating pull-down menus in menubars.
MenuBar	Encapsulation of a menubar typically attached to a window frame.
MenuItem	Class for representing commands in a pull-down menu.
Panel	Simple container for collecting and arranging GUI components, and which may include other panels.
Point	Utility class for representing X, Y screen coordinates.
Polygon	Encapulation of a two-dimensional region, bounded by line segments, but represented internally as a list of coordinates.
PopupMenu	Extends the Menu class to provide a pop-up version of a pull-down menu that can be displayed anywhere.
Rectangle	Represents the concept of a rectangular region (not a visible rectangle shape).

Class Name	Purpose
Robot	A new Java 2 (JDK 1.3) class for use in creating auomated test suites and self-running demonstrations.
Scrollbar	Standard vertical and horonzontal scrollbar component.
ScrollPane	Container class for implementing automatic scrolling operations for other child components.
Shape	Utility class for representing shape characteristics. Also provides operations such as determining whether two shapes intersect.
SystemColor	Represents colors symbolically as screen elements (for example, the "window border color" and the "scrollbar color") instead of using hues and color values.
TextArea	Multiline, potentially editable, text component. See also Label.
Window	Top-level window, with no border or menu. As a component container, applications typically use a Frame object, which extends the lower-level Window class.

Summary

- The AWT, Abstract Windowing Toolkit, provides numerous classes for constructing graphical interfaces in Java applets and stand-alone applications.

- AWT components are said to be heavyweight, because they serve as interfaces to native operating system GUI elements. An AWT button, for example, is merely an interface to a native button object. This approach provides Java applets and applications with a native look and feel, but in practice heavyweight GUI objects can cause display quirks that are difficult to eradicate.

- Swing, the newest GUI toolkit on the block, largely replaces AWT components. Swing components are lightweight because they use no native operating system code. Swing components are more efficient, and they are more easily extended. Swing's primary drawback is that it requires users to have a Java 2 runtime system or browser plug-in. AWT, on the other hand, is more globally supported at this time.

◆ The AWT supports two event models. The original 1.0 inheritance model filters events though a component's class hierarchy until that event is handled. The newer delegation event model registers an event listener with a component such as a button. One advantage of the newer event model is that it sends only registered events to listeners. The old model requires handling all events fired for a GUI component. Swing also uses the newer delegation model for its event handling.

◆ The AWT provides several interfaces for creating classes to be used in making event listener objects. Those interfaces that have multiple methods, such as MouseListener, have associated abstract adapter classes (MouseAdapter for example) that simplify creating listener objects. Any class may be used as an event listener by either implementing a listener interface or by extending an abstract adapter class, whichever is more convenient.

◆ For supporting the newer delegation model, Java 2 provides the concept of an anonymous class. Using an anonymous class makes it possible to create event listeners without the need to declare a named class or to retain a reference to an object. However, the code for anonymous classes might look a bit strange at first.

◆ For reference, this chapter lists AWT's numerous packages along with many of the more commonly used classes in the main java.awt package.

Chapter 21

Swing Applets and Applications

EVERY TIME A NEW GUI TOOLKIT comes out, part of me wants to celebrate and the other part wants to throw up my hands in frustration. Who needs another steep learning curve? More to the point, what's the matter with AWT that requires an entirely new set of packages and classes that, essentially, provide the same GUI components that Java programmers already have?

Those are reasonable questions, but as this chapter suggests, there are several excellent reasons to use the new Swing components in building applets and applications.

IN THIS CHAPTER

◆ Introducing Swing

◆ Programming Swing applets

◆ Programming Swing applications

◆ Converting HTML `<applet>` tags

◆ Using containers and layouts

◆ Creating menus

Even long-time AWT fans are moving to Swing, primarily for the following reasons:

◆ Swing components are lightweight, in the sense that they have no native peers in the operating system. In other words, a Swing GUI object such as a button is created entirely by Swing, not as an interface to a native object.

◆ Swing is now core to Java 2 and the JDK 1.3. It is no longer necessary to link to compiled library files, and runtime support is easy to install on all supported platforms.

◆ Swing supports the concept of "pluggable look-and-feel." This feature solves annoying display problems common with the AWT, and it offers some additional leeway in selecting among different appearances.

◆ Swing adds new capabilities such as support for assistive technologies that provide alternate input and output facilities, such as voice-driven commands and mouseless operation.

◆ Swing is more easily extended in other ways—for example, a button can now display text and graphics, or even use HTML in its text label, even if such capabilities are not provided by the native operating system.

The only significant downside to Swing is its relative newness, and consequently, its lack of global support. However, unless you are using a really old browser, you can install the free Java 2 plug-in to provide Swing support for Internet Explorer and Netscape. Free runtime environments are also available for Solaris, Linux, and Windows, so there's no reason to worry that time invested in learning Swing will be wasted.

Swing components are *Beans,* designed to JavaBean specifications, for use in visual development systems such as JBuilder and Visual Café. Beans are useful for rapid application development (RAD) because they let you design the GUI by clicking and dragging objects, and setting their properties using specialized editors, instead of writing code to perform those jobs. However, the generated Java source code ranges from pretty good to pure junk — incredibly, some systems still generate code that uses the old inheritance event model. Visual development systems have many loyal fans, and some of them are excellent products. But do yourself a favor and learn to use Swing as explained in this chapter and the next. You can then choose a RAD developer, if you decide you need one.

Introducing Swing

Because Swing is based on AWT—many Swing classes extend those in the java.awt and related packages—you can use much of what you already know about AWT programming. However, there are some new techniques to master, and in this chapter I'll concentrate on them to give you a flying start into Swing's way of doing things. Chapter 22, "Swing Components," covers a selection of Swing components. Obviously, I can't hope to cover all of Swing in two chapters. My goal here is to introduce the key concepts of Swing programming so you can dig further into this toolkit's classes more easily on your own.

I mention this tip several times throughout the book, but it bears repeating. Because Swing is so big, and there are so many classes to wade through, if you haven't done so already, download and install Java's online documentation before going any further. JavaDoc, as it is known, is an essential tool for finding your way around Swing's library. I also find the toolkit's source code files invaluable for exploring Swing declarations. If you installed them (see Chapter 3, "Getting Started with Java 2"), you'll find most of Swing's source files in the jdk1.3/src/javax/swing directory.

Swing Applets

To demonstrate Swing, this and the next section list simple applet and application programs. As with AWT, a Swing applet runs in a browser. An application stands alone and is run under the control of the Java interpreter. In past JDK incarnations, it was necessary to specify paths and library files to compile and run Swing programs. These steps are no longer required because Swing is now core to Java 2 and the JDK 1.3.

Listing 21-1, SwingApplet.java, shows a simple Swing applet. Compile it in the usual way using javac, and then load the SwingApplet.html file (it's in the same directory as the listing file) into your Web browser. Or, use the appletviewer utility to load the HTML file and run the applet.

 Your browser must have the Java 2 plug-in to load and run Swing applets. If you don't see the sample applet's text, or if you receive an error message, consult Chapter 3's instructions for downloading and installing the Java 2 plug-in. If you don't want to do that now, you can use the appletviewer utility from the JDK 1.3 to view Swing applets. Figure 21-1 shows the program's window in appletviewer running under Microsoft Windows 98:

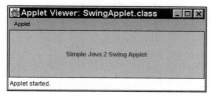

Figure 21-1: SwingApplet running in the appletviewer utility under Windows 98

Listing 21-1: SwingApplet.java

```
001: import javax.swing.*;
002: import java.awt.*;
003:
004: public class SwingApplet extends JApplet {
005:  public void init() {
006:   JLabel label =
007:    new JLabel("Simple Java 2 Swing Applet", JLabel.CENTER);
008:    label.setBorder(BorderFactory.createLineBorder(Color.black));
009:    getContentPane().add(label, BorderLayout.CENTER);
010:  }
011: }
```

The sample applet is deceptively simple looking, but it demonstrates a few key features of Swing programming. First, you must import the `javax.swing` package — note that the package name begins with `javax`, not `java`. Also, most Swing programs also import at least the `java.awt` package (many use `java.awt.event` as well). Except for components and containers, all of which are replaced by Swing classes, you will still use many AWT classes in Swing programming.

Swing classes all begin with capital J (for Java, obviously) and are often used similarly to their AWT counterparts. For example, line 004 extends the JApplet class where an AWT applet would extend Applet. As with all applets, method `init()` initializes the program when loaded into a browser. To provide a place to show some text in the window, lines 006-007 construct an object of the `JLabel` class. As you might expect, this class displays a static string. Optionally, you can supply a second parameter as shown to position the text, using the `CENTER` or other constants defined in the `JLabel` class.

Line 008 uses a handy Swing feature called a `BorderFactory`. Use this class to create various styles of borders so that, as shown here, text and other objects are surrounded by some space instead of being squished to the minimum size within their display spaces. Line 009 is, perhaps, the most important of all in this demonstration:

```
getContentPane().add(label, BorderLayout.CENTER);
```

As the previous chapter explained, AWT programs typically add components directly to a `Frame` container, which serves as the program's window and might also sport a title bar and menu. Swing requires all components to be placed on something called the *content pane*. That's not a class, but a description of a container, usually an object of type `JPanel`. To get the current content pane, call `getContentPane()` and use the result's `add()` method to insert components.

All top-level Swing containers (JFrame, JApplet, and JDialog) are guaranteed to have a valid content pane, but you can also create one of your own of any class that extends Container and add it to a top-level container by calling setContentPane().

Converting Applet HTML Tags

Not evident from the preceding listing is a minor complication concerning a Swing applet's HTML file. Unlike with AWT applets, the HTML <applet> tag cannot be used to load a Swing applet's class file. Also, the browser must have the Java 2 plug-in properly installed.

To connect the <applet> tag with the Java 2 plug in requires converting <applet> tags using a free conversion utility available from Sun. To get the converter, first log onto this Sun Web site:

```
http://java.sun.com/j2se/
```

Next, locate the Java(tm) Plug-in link under "Related Technologies." Click this link to go to the Java Plug-in 1.3 page. You can download and install the plug-in, if you haven't already done so, by clicking the link JRE 1.3 (includes Java Plug-in 1.3). After doing that, click the link Java Plug-in 1.3 HTML Converter. Because the converter is a Java application, there is only one version for all platforms. Page down until you see the link Download Java Plug-in Software 1.3 HTML Converter. Click this link and follow instructions to download and install the utility.

I installed my converter in my jdk1.3 main directory, but you can install the files anywhere you like. To run the program, from a command-line prompt, enter the following commands (or similar depending on your operating system). Windows users: type backslashes in place of the slashes:

```
cd /jdk1.3/converter/classes
java HTMLConverter
```

You should now see the converter's window (see Figure 21-2). Enter or browse to the directory containing the HTML files you want to convert, and then click the Convert button. This processes all files with the filename extensions entered into the main screen's second entry field. Notice that the program processes *all* matching files — it doesn't let you specify an individual file to convert.

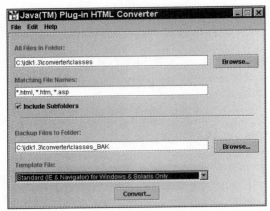

Figure 21-2: Java 2's free HTML converter utility modifies <applet> tags for Swing applets.

The HTML converter's directory browsing button didn't work correctly for me, but perhaps this problem will be repaired by the time you read this. If not, use my work-around. Create a subdirectory in jdk1.3/converter (I name mine /html). Copy all HTML files to be converted to this directory, and then enter that pathname into the converter's first entry field. Click Convert. You can then recopy the converted files to their destinations. Keep in mind that the program converts *all* matching files in *all* subdirectories. Be sure that's what you want to do before clicking Convert! Copies of converted files are stored in a backup directory, but processing the same files twice, which is easy to do by mistake, erases the original backups. (This program could use a little more design work.)

Before running the converter, try it on a test file. I have provided one for you in the c21/SwingApplet directory, named SwingApplet-html.txt. I named the file this way to prevent its accidental conversion. The original file's text looks like this:

```
<html>
<title>
SwingApplet
</title>
<body>
<h1>
SwingApplet
</h1>
```

```
<applet code = "SwingApplet.class" width = 260 height= 90>
</applet>
</body>
</html>
```

That's a standard way to load and display a Java applet in a Web page. The `<applet>` tag is shown in bold. Unfortunately, this tag can't load a Swing applet. Instead, you must convert the tag, using the free converter. Doing that changes the `<applet>` tag into an `<OBJECT>`, which looks something like this:

```
<!--"CONVERTED_APPLET"-->
<!-- CONVERTER VERSION 1.3 -->
<OBJECT classid= ...
...
</OBJECT>
```

If you examine the converted HTML text, you'll see there's a lot more to the conversion than shown here. Since you will always use the conversion utility to create this text, there's little point in trying to understand its every nuance. Frankly, the result is a bit messy, but necessary so that, if users don't have the plug-in, they can get it quickly and easily. But anyway, until Sun and the keepers of the world's Web browser protocols give us something better, you must convert all `<applet>` tags this way so they can load Swing applets.

 TIP Always keep a copy of your original HTML files before converting their `<applet>` tags for use with Swing. Because some HTML editors might have trouble displaying converted `<applet>` tags, it is probably best to edit the originals and then reconvert them for Web page development. I edit my HTML files using a text editor, so this isn't a problem for me. However, some trial runs are called for before you trust using Sun's HTML converter on your Web page files.

Swing Applications

You can also create a standalone Swing application. Listing 21-2, SwingApp.java, shows the basic design. Compile and run the program as you do any other Java program, using javac and the java runtime interpreter. Figure 21-3 shows the program's window as it appears in Windows 98.

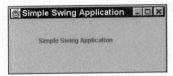

Figure 21-3: SwingApp's window running in Windows 98

Listing 21-2: SwingApp.java

```
001: import javax.swing.*;
002: import java.awt.*;
003: import java.awt.event.*;
004:
005: public class SwingApp {
006:
007: // Create application component pane as a JPanel container
008:  public static JPanel createPane() {
009:    JPanel pane = new JPanel();
010:    JLabel label = new JLabel("Simple Swing Application");
011:    pane.setBorder(
012:     BorderFactory.createEmptyBorder(30, 30, 50, 75));
013:    pane.add(label);
014:    return pane;
015:  }
016:
017:  public static void main(String[] args) {
018:    // Use system look and feel
019:    try {
020:     UIManager.setLookAndFeel(
021:      UIManager.getCrossPlatformLookAndFeelClassName());
022:    } catch (Exception e) { }
023:
024:    // Create the top-level frame and its components
025:    JFrame frame = new JFrame("Simple Swing Application");
026:    JPanel components = createPane();  // Create components pane
027:    frame.getContentPane().add(components, BorderLayout.CENTER);
028:
029:    // End program when window closes
030:    frame.addWindowListener(new WindowAdapter() {
031:     public void windowClosing(WindowEvent e) {
032:      System.exit(0);
033:     }
034:    });
035:
036:    // Engage layout manager and display window
037:    frame.pack();
```

```
038:   frame.setVisible(true);
039:   }
040: }
```

As mentioned earlier, Swing applications usually import at least three packages: `javax.swing`, `java.awt`, and `java.awt.event`. Even though you are advised never to mix Swing and AWT components, you will use classes from each toolkit, and the delegation event model is largely the same for both.

A single class encapsulates the entire program. Its first static method, `createPane()` (this can be named anything you like), constructs a `JPanel` object as a container to hold other components. In this case, the only other such object is a `JLabel` with a text string. In Swing programming, all components are usually added to one or more `JPanel` objects, not to `JFrame` containers as in AWT. As explained for the sample applet in the preceding section, `BorderFactory` provides some space around the component, a technique that is generally preferred over attempts to preset the window size. Finally, the `JLabel` object is added to the `JPanel` (see line 013), which is returned as the method's result.

You don't have to use a separate method such as `createPane()` to create a `JPanel` and its components, but this technique helps organize the program and is usually a good approach. The method is `static` in this case so it can be called in reference to the main program's class.

As with all standalone Java programs, a `main()` method is a required ingredient. Here, the first statements in `main()` select the program's look-and-feel. Almost all Swing applications begin with code similar to this:

```
try {
 UIManager.setLookAndFeel(
 UIManager.getCrossPlatformLookAndFeelClassName());
} catch (Exception e) { }
```

There are other ways to set a Swing program's look-and-feel. In this case, the third line specifies the *cross-platform look-and-feel*. This is otherwise known as the *Java look-and-feel*. (See the next section for more information on other ways to specify a look-and-feel.)

The next step in creating a standalone Swing application is to create the window frame object that contains the program's components. There are different approaches, all perfectly valid, but the following steps are most commonly used:

```
JFrame frame = new JFrame("Simple Swing Application");
JPanel components = createPane();  // Create components pane
frame.getContentPane().add(components, BorderLayout.CENTER);
```

First, create the JFrame container, specifying the window's title. The next step creates a JPanel component by calling the application class's static createPane() method. This provides a container that holds the program's GUI components. Calling getContentPane() returns the content pane for a JFrame object. As mentioned earlier, in Swing, you don't add components to a frame; you add them to the frame's content pane. As shown here, this is typically done by passing a JPanel containing the components to the content pane's add() method. Additionally, I specified the CENTER constant provided by BorderLayout. This centers the pane and its text component in the window.

TIP Another good way to organize the content pane is to have the application's class extend JFrame. The extended class constructor can then add GUI objects to the frame's content pane, and in that way greatly reduce the complexity of the main() method. See Listing 21-3, SwingMenuDemo.java, later in this chapter for an example of this technique.

Next in the sample program is code that ends the program when the window closes (see lines 030-034). This is the same code as explained in Chapter 20, "AWT Applets and Applications." Notice that the window listener is added to the frame container. It is the frame that displays the window title bar along with its usual array of sizing and close buttons, so this is the proper object to listen for the window close event, and when received, call System.exit() to end the program.

Finally, two statements complete the JFrame window and make it visible:

```
frame.pack();
frame.setVisible(true);
```

The first statement causes the layout manager for the frame to reduce all components and the frame itself to minimum or optimal sizes, depending on the manager's layout rules. (See "Containers and Layouts" later in this chapter.) Packing a frame this way before displaying it generally results in the best-looking displays. (Temporarily delete the statement to see what happens if you don't pack the frame.) Finally, call setVisible() as shown to display the frame window. Alternatively, you can replace that statement with the following line. They are functionally the same:

```
frame.show();
```

Touch Me; Feel Me

It is somewhat of a myth that Swing's *pluggable look-and-feel* (plaf) capabilities allow programs running under any operating system to duplicate the appearance of any other system's GUI. That's possible to some extent, but in practice, real-world considerations limit look-and-feel leeway. For instance, you can generally select between Java's own look-and-feel (known also as the *Metal* look) and a native appearance. However, you can't make a PC running Windows look like a Mac, nor can you do the reverse.

There are basically three choices in setting up a Swing application's look-and-feel. Your choices are

◆ Choose the Java (Metal) look-and-feel. This produces similar appearances and operation across all supported platforms, and although the results differ from the native GUI, objects and windows tend to look good regardless of the operating system in use.

◆ Choose the system's own look-and-feel. If you want your Java Swing programs to closely resemble the native GUI, use this technique.

◆ Choose a specific look-and-feel and ignore the operating system GUI. This might be called the *shoehorn approach* — you might get away with this trick, but you may also experience troubles. Currently, the Motif look-and-feel is the only one other than Java that works across all supported platforms.

 For more information about pluggable look-and-feel issues, read Java's online documentation for the `javax.swing.plaf` package.

I suggest using only the first or second techniques, but try the following suggestions if you want to experiment with Java look-and-feel capabilities. Typically, the `main()` method begins with the following `try` block:

```
try {
 UIManager.setLookAndFeel(
  UIManager.getCrossPlatformLookAndFeelClassName());
} catch (Exception e) { }
```

This goes against the general rule that catching all exceptions is unsafe; however, in this case, if a specified look-and-feel can't be selected for some reason, Swing defaults to the Java (Metal) look-and-feel. This technique, then, at least allows the program to continue.

 If you don't specify one, Swing defaults to the Java (Metal) look-and-feel. For that reason, to save space in this chapter, future examples do not include the preceding code.

The `UIManager` class provides methods for selecting a look-and-feel. Call `getCrossPlatformLookAndFeelClassName()` for the Java or Metal appearance. Use this technique if you don't care about look-and-feel issues — it generally produces good-looking results on all platforms.

Change that method to `getSystemLookAndFeelClassName()` to select the native operating system's GUI appearance. With this approach, users see GUI objects that closely resemble those used by native programs. Those objects are still lightweight, however, and they do not have peer native objects. For this reason, there may still be some minor display differences between Swing and the native GUI.

I have to wonder whether plaf's designers are attempting to win a gold medal for the longest method names. Just an idle thought.

You may also specify the exact look-and-feel that you want to use — the shoehorn approach — but be careful when using this method. To select a specific look-and-feel, pass a string to `UIManager.setLookAndFeel()`. For example, to select the Motif look-and-feel, the only available alternative to Java (Metal) supported on all platforms, use the statement

```
try {
UIManager.setLookAndFeel(
  "com.sun.java.swing.plaf.motif.MotifLookAndFeel");
} catch (Exception e) { }
```

Other strings select among the other possibilities. Use the following string to specify the Java Metal, known also as the *cross-platform* look-and-feel:

```
"javax.swing.plaf.metal.MetalLookAndFeel"
```

Since that's the default look-and-feel, you'll probably never use that string. Use the following string to force the Windows look-and-feel, but be aware that this works *only* with Microsoft Windows:

```
"com.sun.java.swing.plaf.windows.WindowsLookAndFeel"
```

Use the following string to force the Macintosh look-and-feel, but be aware that this works *only* with a Macintosh operating system:

```
"javax.swing.plaf.mac.MacLookAndFeel"
```

Be aware that users can override an application's look-and-feel by using the following command to run the program:

```
java -Dswing.defaultlaf=<string> <program>
```

Replace `<string>` with one of the aforementioned strings, minus the quote marks, and `<program>` with the application's class filename. You will be forgiven if you "accidentally" forget to include this tip in your program's documentation.

Programming with Swing

The `javax.swing` package has enough classes to fill an entire book, probably an entire shelf of books. In two chapters, I cannot do this extensive toolkit justice, but the following sections will help you get up to speed quickly with Swing components. Using the information in next several sections, and the component sample programs in Chapter 22, you should be able to figure out how to use most Swing components by reading about them in Java's online documentation.

Containers and Layouts

All Swing applets and applications are based on one of three types of containers: `JApplet`, `JDialog`, or `JFrame`. Applets that run in Web browsers are, of course, based on the `JApplet` class. Dialogs, based on `JDialog`, also called *option windows,* are interactive windows that, among other tasks, prompt for filenames, display error messages, and select program options. Standalone applications are most often built on one or more `JFrame` objects, but they might also be constructed as a `JDialog`.

All of these classes are called *top-level containers.* They serve largely as a place to insert other organizational *panes.* For example, a window's content pane, usually an object of the `JPanel` class, typically contains a Swing program's GUI objects. As mentioned, in Swing programming, you never add GUI objects to a top-level container such as a `JFrame`. Instead, you add them to a `JPanel` or other non-top-level container, and then add that object to the frame.

Creating Pull-Down Menus

Creating pull-down menus requires understanding a little more about how top-level containers are organized into panes. A `JFrame` container, for example, has two panes called the *root* and *content panes.* In general, the root pane is the behind-the-scene manager for the frame, and one of its jobs is to hold the window's pull-down menu, if any. The content pane holds other GUI objects such as buttons and text. For this chapter, you can ignore other panes, but if you consult a Swing reference, you'll come across the terms *glass panes* and *layered panes* as well as those described here.

The best way to create a pull-down menu is to call the `setJMenuBar()` method for a `JFrame` or `JApplet` container. (Dialogs don't usually have menus.) Pass to the method a menu constructed of the `JMenuBar` class. For example, if `myMenu` is the menu object, this adds it to a frame's root pane:

```
frame.setJMenuBar(myMenu);
```

Contrast that statement with the way you add components to a frame or other top-level container. For example, to add a button to a window, use code such as

```
frame.getContentPane().add(myButton, BorderLayout.CENTER);
```

The important rule to remember is that menus go with a top-level container's root pane. Other GUI objects go with the content pane. Typically, three objects are needed to create a pull-down menu:

```
JMenuBar menuBar;        // Menu bar container
JMenu menu;              // Pulldown menus (File, Edit, ...)
JMenuItem menuItem;      // Menu commands (Open, About, ...)
```

Use these objects as follows. First, create the menu bar as a `JMenuBar` object, and then insert it into the frame (you can do the same for an applet):

```
menuBar = new JMenuBar();
frame.setJMenuBar(menuBar);
```

That just creates an empty bar, ready to hold menus. Create each menu, *File, Edit, Help,* and any others, as objects of class `JMenu`. For example, this creates the typical *File* menu and adds it to the menu bar:

```
menu = new JMenu("File");
menuBar.add(menu);
```

The final step is to create the menu items — the commands. Do this by constructing `JMenuItem` objects and adding them to the menu in the order you want them to appear from top to bottom. You can also specify a mnemonic letter that, when pressed with a control key, selects the command using the keyboard (The exact control key used depends on the operating system and look-and-feel):

```
menuItem = new JMenuItem("Open");
menuItem.setMnemonic('o');
menuItem.addActionListener(this);
menu.add(menuItem);
```

You may pass an upper- or lowercase letter to setMnemonic(), as shown on the second line of the preceding sample code. The first corresponding letter in the associated menu or item, ignoring case, is underlined on screen. For example, in this case, passing either 'o' or 'O' to setMnemonic() under-lines the first letter in Open, indicating to the user that pressing the Alt (or a similarly named special key) and the letter key selects the command. You may call setMnemonic() for menus (File, Edit, and so on), and for menu items (commands). For menu items, after the menu is opened, users may press the designated key to select the command — they don't have to also press Alt.

The third statement passes this to addActionListener(), making the current container — for example, the frame or applet — the listener for the menu item's action event, fired when users select the command. This is one way to associate an action with a menu item, but it's not the only way. A slightly different approach is used in Listing 21-3, SwingMenuDemo.java. The program also shows another way to organize a standalone Swing application that results in a greatly simplified main() method.

Listing 21-3: SwingMenuDemo.java

```
001: import javax.swing.*;
002: import java.awt.*;
003: import java.awt.event.*;
004:
005: public class SwingMenuDemo extends JFrame {
006:
007: // Constructor does all the setup work
008:   public SwingMenuDemo() {
009:     JMenuBar menuBar;      // Menu bar (contains all menus)
010:     JMenu menu;            // Pulldown menus
011:     JMenuItem menuItem;    // Items inside pulldown menus
012:
013:     // End program when window closes
014:     addWindowListener(new WindowAdapter() {
015:      public void windowClosing(WindowEvent e) {
016:        System.exit(0);
017:      }
018:     });
019:
020:     // Create the menu bar, menu, and menu item
021:     menuBar = new JMenuBar();
022:     setJMenuBar(menuBar);
```

```
023:    menu = new JMenu("Demo");
024:    menuBar.add(menu);
025:    menuItem = new JMenuItem("Exit");
026:    menu.add(menuItem);
027:
028:    // Attach listener for the menu item
029:    menuItem.addActionListener(new ActionListener() {
030:      public void actionPerformed(ActionEvent e) {
031:        System.exit(0);
032:      }
033:    });
034:  }
035:
036:  // Because SwingMenuDemo is a JFrame, main() is much simpler!
037:  public static void main(String[] args) {
038:    SwingMenuDemo app = new SwingMenuDemo();
039:    app.setTitle("Swing Menu Demo");
040:    app.setSize(400, 300);
041:    app.show();
042:  }
043: }
```

Take a look first at the end of the program. Method `main()` at lines 037-042 is simpler than in earlier listings in this chapter. This is possible because the program's class, `SwingMenuDemo` (see line 005) extends `JFrame`. In this way, the application itself provides the root and content layers needed to hold a menu bar and other GUI objects. Also, since the application is its own frame, its constructor performs all the necessary setup chores that, in earlier examples, were programmed in `main()`.

Lines 014-018 in the constructor now add the window listener method for the window close event so that the frame exits the application on its own when the window closes. Likewise, the menu bar adds an `actionPerformed()` method using an anonymous class directly to the menu item instead of to the container. This way, the menu item itself responds to its selection. These techniques are more object-oriented than those shown in earlier examples.

Swing Layouts

Because Java programs run on a variety of platforms, determining how and where to position GUI objects can be a tricky task to perform. Although it is possible to position components at absolute locations (relative to their containers, that is), this is almost never a good idea. Instead, Swing and AWT use *layout managers* to arrange components according to generalized schemes. Most layout manager classes are in the `java.awt` package and are used similarly in AWT and Swing. However, Swing adds some new managers that are used only in Swing programming. Table 21-1 shows the AWT and Swing layout manager classes.

TABLE 21-1 AWT AND SWING LAYOUT MANAGER CLASSES

Class Name	Package	Purpose
BorderLayout	java.awt	Arranges components in a container using the compass headings north, south, east, and west, and also center.
BoxLayout	javax.swing	Lays out components vertically or horizontally, similar to how GridBagLayout works, but using a more flexible design that respects component constraints such as a requested minimum size.
CardLayout	java.awt	Lays out components, which are typically other containers with GUI objects, as individual panels. Cards are similar to tabbed panes or tabbed windows in some other GUI toolkits.
FlowLayout	java.awt	Lays out components in a left-to-right flow, useful for creating toolbars or simple windows.
GridBagLayout	java.awt	Lays out components in an X, Y grid of variable-size cells, as though on a checkerboard. This layout manager is tricky to use — try BoxLayout for better results.
GridLayout	java.awt	Similar to GridBagLayout, but the grid cells are all the same size.
LayoutManager	java.awt	This is the basic interface that containers implement for working with layout managers. You won't use this in application programming.
LayoutManager2	java.awt	Extends the LayoutManager interface to add the concept of constraints that components can request, such as how they would "like" to be aligned with other components. You won't use this unless you are developing your own components and layout managers.

Continued

TABLE 21-1 AWT AND SWING LAYOUT MANAGER CLASSES *(Continued)*

Class Name	Package	Purpose
OverlayLayout	javax.swing	Lays out components so that they may be placed on top of one another. Useful in creating layered panels.
ScrollPaneLayout	javax.swing	This is the layout manager used by a JscrollPane object to organize its standard components: a viewport, two scrollbars, row and column headers, and four corner objects. Applications don't use this one directly.
ViewportLayout	javax.swing	This is the default layout manager used by the JViewport container. A viewport is used to display information in windows that may change in size, most often in conjunction with a JScrollPane.

 BorderLayout is the default layout manager for frames (JFrame objects), for dialogs (JDialog objects), and for applets (JApplet objects).

To select a layout manager, you will usually create a JPanel container to hold GUI objects, and then call the setLayout() method. For example, to use the GridLayout manager, use code such as this:

```
JPanel pane = new JPanel();
pane.setLayout(new GridLayout());
```

You would then usually add the pane to the frame's or applet's content pane, as demonstrated in most of this chapter's listings. Following are five relatively simple applets that demonstrate how to use some of the layout managers in Table 21-1. Run them by opening their HTML files located in the same directories as the listings, or by using the appletviewer utility.

Listing 21-4, FlowDemo.java, demonstrates the FlowLayout manager, one of the simplest available. Use this class to lay out components in a container from left to right, wrapping to the next row if necessary. The demonstration program shows how five buttons are organized when added to the applet content pane. Figure 21-4 shows the applet in my Web browser.

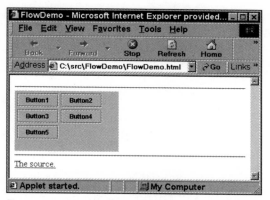

Figure 21–4: The FlowDemo applet uses the FlowLayout
manager to arrange five buttons.

Listing 21–4: FlowDemo.java

```
001: import javax.swing.*;
002: import java.applet.*;
003: import java.awt.*;
004:
005: public class FlowDemo extends JApplet {
006:   int alignment;  // Current FlowLayout alignment
007:
008:   public void init() {
009:     JPanel pane = new JPanel();
010:     alignment = FlowLayout.LEFT;
011: // alignment = FlowLayout.CENTER;
012: // alignment = FlowLayout.RIGHT;
013:     pane.setLayout(new FlowLayout(alignment));
014:     pane.add(new JButton("Button1"));
015:     pane.add(new JButton("Button2"));
016:     pane.add(new JButton("Button3"));
017:     pane.add(new JButton("Button4"));
018:     pane.add(new JButton("Button5"));
019:     getContentPane().add(pane, BorderLayout.CENTER);
020:   }
021: }
```

The main class, FlowDemo, extends JApplet, as do all Swing applets. In method
init(), the JPanel content pane is created, after which an alignment int variable
is set to the LEFT constant in the FlowLayout class. Try changing this to CENTER or
RIGHT to see the difference in how the components are arranged. Line 013 tells the
content pane to use a FlowLayout manager, after which five JButton objects are
added to the pane.

The final statement inserts the JPanel container into the applet's content pane. Notice that this uses the BorderLayout's CENTER constant to position the pane. This affects only how the content pane is arranged in the applet's container, not how individual components are placed in the pane.

Another listing shows how, by using the BorderLayout manager, you can achieve an entirely different effect. Listing 21-5, BorderDemo.java, displays five buttons as shown in Figure 21-5.

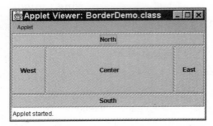

Figure 21-5: The BorderLayout manager uses compass headings to arrange components.

Listing 21-5: BorderDemo.java

```
001: import javax.swing.*;
002: import java.applet.*;
003: import java.awt.*;
004:
005: public class BorderDemo extends JApplet
006: {
007:  public void init() {
008:    JPanel pane = new JPanel();
009:    pane.setLayout(new BorderLayout());
010:    pane.add("North",  new JButton("North"));
011:    pane.add("South",  new JButton("South"));
012:    pane.add("East",   new JButton("East"));
013:    pane.add("West",   new JButton("West"));
014:    pane.add("Center", new JButton("Center"));
015:    getContentPane().add(pane, BorderLayout.CENTER);
016:  }
017: }
```

Compare the BorderDemo class with FlowDemo in the preceding listing. The programs are nearly identical, but the new program passes string positioning commands such as "North" and "Center" to the content pane's add() method. Each JButton is sized to fit neatly within the applet's window.

TIP   BorderLayout is particularly useful for arranging multiple JPanel panes, or other containers, each holding a group of GUI objects.

The BorderLayout and FlowLayout classes are useful for creating simple windows and arranging multiple panes that contain other GUI objects. However, you'll often need better control over object placement. For that, AWT and Swing provide three more sophisticated layout manager classes. The first, in the java.awt package, is GridLayout. Use this class to arrange components in a fixed-size X, Y grid, like a checkerboard. Listing 21-6, GridDemo.java, demonstrates how to use GridLayout. As Figure 21-6 shows, the result looks like a telephone touch pad.

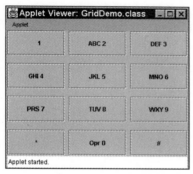

Figure 21-6: GridDemo displays a telephone touch pad using a GridLayout manager.

Listing 21-6: GridDemo.java

```
001: import javax.swing.*;
002: import java.applet.*;
003: import java.awt.*;
004:
005: public class GridDemo extends JApplet {
006:
007:   public void init() {
008:     JPanel pane = new JPanel();
009:     pane.setLayout(new GridLayout(4, 3, 8, 16));
010:     pane.add(new JButton("    1"));
011:     pane.add(new JButton("ABC 2"));
012:     pane.add(new JButton("DEF 3"));
013:     pane.add(new JButton("GHI 4"));
014:     pane.add(new JButton("JKL 5"));
015:     pane.add(new JButton("MNO 6"));
016:     pane.add(new JButton("PRS 7"));
```

```
017:    pane.add(new JButton("TUV 8"));
018:    pane.add(new JButton("WXY 9"));
019:    pane.add(new JButton("  *  "));
020:    pane.add(new JButton("Opr 0"));
021:    pane.add(new JButton("  #  "));
022:    getContentPane().add(pane, BorderLayout.CENTER);
023:  }
024: }
```

Line 009 constructs a GridLayout object, using four integer arguments representing the number of rows (4), the number of columns (3), the horizontal gap between components (8), and the vertical gap (16). Objects such as the JButtons used here are placed inside each of the grid's cells in left-to-right, top-to-bottom order. In theory, the objects are sized the same, but some strange results can occur if you mix different types of GUI components.

To similarly arrange variable-sized objects, java.awt provides the even more sophisticated GridBagLayout manager. The class is similar to GridLayout but allows component cells to vary in size. Listing 21-7, GridBagDemo.java, demonstrates how to use this layout manager. Figure 21-7 shows the results of running the program in appletviewer.

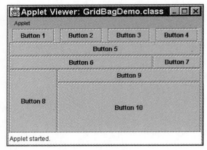

Figure 21-7: The GridBagLayout class lays out components in a grid of variable-size cells.

Listing 21-7: GridBagLayout.java

```
001: import javax.swing.*;
002: import java.applet.*;
003: import java.awt.*;
004:
005: public class GridBagDemo extends JApplet {
006:
007:   protected void makeButton(String name, GridBagLayout gridbag,
008:     GridBagConstraints c, JPanel pane)
009:   {
010:     JButton button = new JButton(name);
```

```
011:    gridbag.setConstraints(button, c);
012:    pane.add(button);
013:  }
014:
015:  // Initialize applet and GUI buttons
016:  public void init() {
017:    JPanel pane = new JPanel();  // Create content pane
018:    // Create GridBagLayout and Constraints objects
019:    GridBagLayout gridbag = new GridBagLayout();
020:    GridBagConstraints c = new GridBagConstraints();
021:    pane.setLayout(gridbag);  // Tell pane to use gridbag layout
022:
023:    // Create four "normal" buttons on the top row
024:    c.fill = GridBagConstraints.NONE;
025:    c.weightx = 1.0;
026:    makeButton("Button 1", gridbag, c, pane);
027:    makeButton("Button 2", gridbag, c, pane);
028:    makeButton("Button 3", gridbag, c, pane);
029:    c.gridwidth = GridBagConstraints.REMAINDER;
030:    makeButton("Button 4", gridbag, c, pane);
031:
032:    // Create a long button filling entire row
033:    c.fill = GridBagConstraints.BOTH;
034:    c.weightx = 0.0;
035:    makeButton("Button 5", gridbag, c, pane);
036:
037:    // Create two buttons that fill the row
038:    c.gridwidth = GridBagConstraints.RELATIVE;
039:    makeButton("Button 6", gridbag, c, pane);
040:    c.gridwidth = GridBagConstraints.REMAINDER;
041:    makeButton("Button 7", gridbag, c, pane);
042:
043:    // Create a vertical button
044:    c.gridwidth = 1;
045:    c.gridheight = 2;
046:    c.weighty = 1.0;
047:    makeButton("Button 8", gridbag, c, pane);
048:    c.weighty = 0.0;
049:
050:    // Create buttons to right of vertical Button 8
051:    c.gridwidth = GridBagConstraints.REMAINDER;
052:    c.gridheight = 1;
053:    makeButton("Button 9", gridbag, c, pane);
054:    makeButton("Button 10", gridbag, c, pane);
055:
056:    // Add content pane to applet top-level container
```

```
057:    getContentPane().add(pane, BorderLayout.CENTER);
058:    setSize(325, 250);
059:    }
060: }
```

GridBagLayout is used a little differently from other layout managers. In general, the following preparations are usually needed:

```
JPanel pane = new JPanel();
GridBagLayout gridbag = new GridBagLayout();
GridBagConstraints c = new GridBagConstraints();
pane.setLayout(gridbag);
```

First, construct the content pane to be added to the top-level container. Next, create a GridBagLayout object—this is the actual layout manager. After that, also create a GridBagConstraints object. This is used to alter GUI object placement according to various spacing rules, or constraints. Finally, pass the GridBagLayout object to the content pane's setLayout() method.

Following those steps, as shown in the sample listing, you can add GUI components to a container. To select various constraints, assign values as shown to the GridBagConstraints object. For example, to state that an object take up whatever space remains in its row, use the statement:

```
c.gridwidth = GridBagConstraints.REMAINDER;
```

Call the setConstraints() method for the GridBagLayout object, specifying also the GUI object involved. To add a JButton to the grid, follow the preceding statement with

```
JButton button = new JButton("Label");
gridbag.setConstraints(button, c);
pane.add(button);
```

You can add other objects using similar code, but be forewarned that GridBagLayout is tricky to use, and much trial and error may be needed to achieve pleasing results. Instead of this class, you might want to use the new Swing layout manager, BoxLayout. The class provides similar operations as GridBagLayout, but is far easier to use. Also, a supporting class, simply named Box, provides supporting methods that can add "glue" and "struts" for spacing components inside containers.

 The BoxLayout and Box classes are members of the javax.swing package, unlike most other layout classes, which are members of java.awt. The two layout managers are available only to Swing applets and applications, not to programs using the AWT.

Some very sophisticated GUI arrangements are possible with the BoxLayout manager, but getting started with this class may be confusing at first. You'll find more examples of BoxLayout and its associated Box class in future listings. Listing 21-8, BoxDemo.java, merely introduces the class and shows a couple of important aspects about its proper use. Figure 21-8 shows the final applet in action.

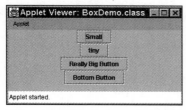

Figure 21–8: The BoxLayout manager arranges these applet buttons centered in the window.

Listing 21–8: BoxDemo.java

```
001: import javax.swing.*;
002: import java.applet.*;
003: import java.awt.*;
004:
005: public class BoxDemo extends JApplet
006: {
007:  // Add new button to pane, with center alignment
008:  protected void addButton(String label, JPanel pane) {
009:    JButton button = new JButton(label);
010:    button.setAlignmentX(Component.CENTER_ALIGNMENT);
011:    pane.add(button);
012:  }
013:
014:  public void init() {
015:    JPanel pane = new JPanel();
016:    pane.setLayout(new BoxLayout(pane, BoxLayout.Y_AXIS));
017:    addButton("Small", pane);
018:    addButton("tiny", pane);
019:    addButton("Really Big Button", pane);
020:    addButton("Bottom Button", pane);
021:    getContentPane().add(pane, BorderLayout.CENTER);
022:  }
023: }
```

Create the content pane and call setLayout() in the usual way (see lines 015-016), and also specify whether to arrange components horizontally (BoxLayout.X_AXIS) or vertically (BoxLayout.Y_AXIS):

```
JPanel pane = new JPanel();
pane.setLayout(new BoxLayout(pane, BoxLayout.Y_AXIS));
```

Because all GUI objects are arranged either in a row or column, you might think that BoxLayout is similar to FlowLayout. But this manager is far more sophisticated because it respects a component's requested alignment and sizing rules. To specify that the layout manager center a button, call setAlignmentX() for the button object as follows:

```
button.setAlignmentX(Component.CENTER_ALIGNMENT);
```

When the BoxLayout manager arranges components, it tries to respect all such requests that components make regarding positioning and size. You can similarly call setMaximumSize() and setMinimumSize() to request that objects are sized within a certain range. These methods are inherited from JComponent by all GUI component classes. One reason BoxLayout is so useful is because it tries to respect a component's constraints in arranging them in a container. Other AWT layout managers do not perform nearly as well.

TIP   Using multiple JPanel containers along with the BoxLayout manager is a good way to arrange GUI objects in groups. You might also use BoxLayout to add the panels to the top-level container's content pane.

Summary

- ◆ Sun recommends that all new applets and GUI applications now use Swing components. Programmers who are familiar with AWT may be reluctant to switch, but there are many excellent reasons for using Swing as suggested in this chapter.

- ◆ Swing components are lightweight — they have no peer objects in the native operating system. This makes Swing components more efficient, and also easier to extend.

- ◆ Swing can be used to write applets and standalone applications. However, <applet> tags in HTML files require conversion before they can load a Swing applet class file. Also, the browser must have the Java 2 plug-in. Sun offers the plug-in, and an HTML converter, free of charge for downloading over the Internet.

- ◆ Swing components are added to a top-level container's content pane, often using an object of the JPanel class. Unlike in the AWT, Swing components are never directly added to application frames or applets.

◆ Swing provides several different look-and-feel capabilities, but it's a myth that you can use this feature to duplicate any appearance on any system. The Java (or Metal) look-and-feel is used by default. That and the Motif look-and-feel work on all supported platforms. You may also specify that the native look-and-feel be used, but it may differ in minor ways compared to native GUI objects. There are also Windows and Macintosh look-and-feel settings; however, these work only on their native systems.

◆ One important aspect of Swing programming is the use of layout managers to arrange components in windows. AWT provides several managers that are used similarly in AWT and in Swing. However, Swing adds a few of its own layout managers that are more capable than those in the AWT. For example, the `BoxLayout` class is easier to use and much more flexible than AWT's tricky `GridBagLayout` manager.

Chapter 22

Swing Components

SWING OFFERS a nearly overwhelming array of classes for GUI programming. To help you learn about the classes you need, this chapter covers many of the Swing classes that are used most often. These include different types of buttons, dialogs, text objects, and lists. Also in this chapter are notes about special Swing features such as using HTML in text items and inserting graphical icons into buttons and other object. Also in this chapter are examples that show how to create pop-up menus and toolbars, and how to program event listeners to respond to user commands.

IN THIS CHAPTER

- ◆ Creating buttons and groups
- ◆ Programming dialog boxes
- ◆ Inserting text objects
- ◆ Displaying lists and combo-boxes
- ◆ Swing pop-up menus
- ◆ Action objects and toolbars

Buttons and Groups

One of the simplest Swing classes is the lowly, but ever-present, JButton. As you learned in Chapter 21, "Swing Applets and Applications," a button usually has an ActionListener event handler that performs the button's actions when selected. However, this category contains other types of buttons, including check boxes and radio buttons. Swing also provides a way to group multiple buttons so that they operate in concert. And, as the next section explains, even the simple JButton has some interesting capabilities that may not be obvious, such as its ability to display a graphical icon in addition to its usual text label.

JButton

Typically, you create a JButton object with a statement such as

```
JButton myButton = new JButton("Click Me!");
```

In addition to text, however, you can also display a graphic icon image, sometimes called a *glyph,* along with the button's text label. This was difficult, if impossible, to do using the AWT because of its reliance on native GUI objects. Because Swing objects are lightweight, and do not use any native code, it's easy to extend them. Listing 22-1 demonstrates this capability by adding image icons to two JButton objects. Figure 22-1 shows the program's window.

Figure 22–1: Two Swing buttons with image icons and text labels

Listing 22–1: ButtonIcon.java

```
001: import javax.swing.*;
002: import java.awt.*;
003: import java.awt.event.*;
004:
005: public class ButtonIcon extends JFrame {
006:
007: // Constructor does all the setup work
008:  public ButtonIcon() {
009:
010:    // Select local system look and feel
011:    try {
012:     UIManager.setLookAndFeel(
013:       UIManager.getSystemLookAndFeelClassName());
014:    } catch (Exception e) { }
015:
016:    // End program when window closes
017:    addWindowListener(new WindowAdapter() {
018:     public void windowClosing(WindowEvent e) {
019:      System.exit(0);
020:     }
021:    });
022:
023:    ImageIcon prevIcon = new ImageIcon("lefthand.gif");
024:    JButton prevButton = new JButton("Prev", prevIcon);
025:    prevButton.setToolTipText("Move to the previous page");
026:    ImageIcon nextIcon = new ImageIcon("righthand.gif");
027:    JButton nextButton = new JButton("Next", nextIcon);
028:    nextButton.setToolTipText("Move to the next page");
```

```
029:
030:    Container content = getContentPane();
031:    content.setLayout(new FlowLayout());
032:    content.add(prevButton);
033:    content.add(nextButton);
034:  }
035:
036:  public static void main(String[] args) {
037:    ButtonIcon app = new ButtonIcon();
038:    app.setTitle("Button Icon Demo");
039:    app.setSize(320, 120);
040:    app.show();
041:  }
042: }
```

Most images, whether large or small, are represented in Swing as ImageIcon objects. That class and its Icon interface are members of the javax.swing package. Lines 023-028 show how to load GIF images (Compuserve's Graphics Interchange Format) and then use them to create JButton objects. You may also use JPEG image files with ImageIcon. Because these two formats are generally supported throughout the Web, they are two you will probably use in Java programs, especially in applets. However, ImageIcon also supports the relatively new PNG (Portable Network Graphics) format. To the ImageIcon constructor, you may specify either an image filename or its URL.

 Because the JPEG format uses a "lossy" compression technique, it is more suitable for large pictures, especially when you need to reduce their file sizes for fast loading without too much degradation in quality. Use the GIF format for small images such as button and label icons, typically 16-by-16 pixels, or in multiples of 8 pixels, in size. These aren't hard and fast rules, but they generally produce the best results in Web browsers. The PNG format is relatively new and might not be supported in older browsers.

As Listing 22-1 shows, you can also add *tooltip text* to a button (or to any GUI Swing JComponent subclass). This is also sometimes called *fly-over text*. For example, the following statement adds a tooltip to the prevButton object:

```
prevButton.setToolTipText("Move to the previous page");
```

To see the text, run the program and move the mouse cursor over one of the two buttons. After about a second, the tooltip text is displayed. Tooltips may have been special features in the recent past, but they are universally expected in today's GUIs. Use them lavishly.

Not shown in the program is how to specify a frame's default button. Do that by calling the setDefaultButton() method for the frame's root pane:

```
getRootPane().setDefaultButton(nextButton);
```

Although keyboard mnemonics are not shown in the listing, you can easily set them for a button. For example, create a button using code such as

```
JButton anyButton = new JButton("Click me!");
anyButton.setMnemonic('c');
```

You may specify the mnemonic letter in upper- or lowercase, similar to the way you can set a menu item's mnemonic, as explained in Chapter 21. Pressing the current look-and-feel setting's mnemonic key (Alt for example on PC keyboards) plus the specified letter selects the button as though the user clicked it. You can use mnemonics similarly with most other selectable Swing components.

JToggleButton

Another kind of simple button is called a JToggleButton. As its name suggests, this button is used for operations that need to be toggled on and off. It is also called a *two-state button*. Click it once to toggle it on; click again to toggle it off. Create a JToggleButton the same way you do a JButton using statements such as

```
ImageIcon icon = new ImageIcon("image.gif");
JToggleButton button = new JToggleButton("Off", icon);
```

Although that works, the button uses the same image for its two states. To change the button icon and its text label to reflect the current state requires implementing a ChangeListener object. Listing 22-2, ToggleDemo.java, shows the necessary programming. As Figure 22-2 illustrates, the program displays a toggle button with a dimmed light bulb icon. Click the button to turn the light on, and to change the button's label from "Off" to "On."

Figure 22-2: Use JToggleButton to create a two-state button.

Listing 22-2: ToggleDemo.java

```
001: import javax.swing.*;
002: import javax.swing.event.*;
```

```
003: import java.awt.*;
004: import java.awt.event.*;
005:
006: public class ToggleDemo extends JFrame {
007:
008:    ImageIcon bulbOnIcon;
009:    ImageIcon bulbOffIcon;
010:    JToggleButton onOffButton;
011:
012: // Constructor does all the setup work
013:   public ToggleDemo() {
014:
...
028:    bulbOnIcon = new ImageIcon("bulbon.gif");
029:    bulbOffIcon = new ImageIcon("bulboff.gif");
030:    onOffButton = new JToggleButton("Off", bulbOffIcon);
031:    onOffButton.addChangeListener(new ChangeListener() {
032:     public void stateChanged(ChangeEvent e) {
033:      if (onOffButton.isSelected()) {
034:       onOffButton.setIcon(bulbOnIcon);
035:       onOffButton.setText("On");
036:      } else {
037:       onOffButton.setIcon(bulbOffIcon);
038:       onOffButton.setText("Off");
039:      }
040:     }
041:    });
042:
043:    Container content = getContentPane();
044:    content.setLayout(new FlowLayout());
045:    content.add(onOffButton);
046:   }
...
054: }
```

To save space in the listing, I removed statements at lines 015-027 and 047-053 that are mostly duplicated in Listing 22-1. Most other listings in this chapter are similarly shortened. However, if you are viewing the listings using this book's *Just Click!* indexes, you see the full text on screen.

   Unlike most other event listener interfaces supplied in the java.awt.event package, ChangeListener is a member of javax.swing.event, imported at line 002. The program declares three objects in the ToggleDemo class: two ImageIcon objects and one JToggleButton. The class constructor initializes these objects at lines 028-030.

To change the button's icon and label to match the button's state, the program creates an anonymous class starting at line 031 in a call to the ToggleButton's addChangeListener() method. In this class, method stateChanged() is called when the button's state changes. Call isSelected() to determine the button's current state after any change has been put into effect. As shown, calling setIcon() and setText() changes the button's appearance to match the button's current on or off state.

TIP The setLabel() method is now deprecated in Java 2. Call the setText() method instead. Both methods do the same job of changing a button's text label.

JRadioButton and ButtonGroup

Another popular type of button is called a *radio button* because it resembles the buttons on an automobile radio in which only one button can be selected at a time. Pressing another button causes the previously selected one to pop out. In GUI programming, radio buttons are useful for offering users an easy way to select one of several options. For proper operation, radio buttons should always be assigned to a ButtonGroup object. This ensures that selecting any button turns the others off, and that only one button may be selected at a time.

To demonstrate button groups and radio buttons, Listing 22-3, ButtonDemo.java, displays the window shown in Figure 22-3. The radio buttons are at left. Click one to change the color of the small square below from red, to white, to blue. (The next section explains how to create the program's check box buttons shown to the right.) The program is also a good example of how to make GUI objects that affect one another's states. For example, click the top check box to disable the radio buttons. Click the bottom check box to enable the program's Exit button.

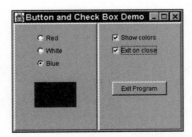

Figure 22-3: ButtonDemo demonstrates radio buttons and check boxes.

Listing 22-3: ButtonDemo.java (partial)

```
001: import javax.swing.*;
002: import javax.swing.border.*;
003: import javax.swing.event.*;
004: import java.awt.*;
005: import java.awt.event.*;
006:
007: // The main program class
008: public class ButtonDemo
009:   extends JFrame implements ActionListener {
010:
011:   // GUI objects displayed in the frame window
012:   ButtonGroup group;            // Groups radio buttons
013:   JRadioButton redButton;       // First radio button
014:   JRadioButton whiteButton;     // Second radio button
015:   JRadioButton blueButton;      // Third radio button
016:   JPanel colorBox;              // Displays selected color
...
020:
021:   // Constructor initializes the GUI objects and panels
022:   public ButtonDemo() {
023:
...
042:     // Create radio button panel and an inner pane
043:     // to help display the GUI objects neatly
044:     JPanel radioPane = new JPanel();
045:     JPanel innerRadioPane = new JPanel();
046:     radioPane.setBorder(
047:       BorderFactory.createBevelBorder(BevelBorder.RAISED));
048:     innerRadioPane.setLayout(
049:       new BoxLayout(innerRadioPane, BoxLayout.Y_AXIS));
050:     innerRadioPane.setBorder(
051:       BorderFactory.createEmptyBorder(10, 10, 10, 10));
052:
053:     // Construct the radio group and its buttons
054:     // All button events go to the program's ActionListener
055:     group       = new ButtonGroup();
056:     redButton   = new JRadioButton("Red  ");
057:     whiteButton = new JRadioButton("White");
058:     blueButton  = new JRadioButton("Blue ");
059:     whiteButton.setSelected(true); // Select one button
060:     redButton.addActionListener(this);  // See ActionPerformed()
061:     whiteButton.addActionListener(this);
062:     blueButton.addActionListener(this);
063:     group.add(redButton);   // The group ensures that when one
```

```
064:    group.add(whiteButton); // button is selected, the previously
065:    group.add(blueButton);  // selected button is turned off
066:
067:    // Construct a small panel for displaying the selected color
068:    colorBox = new JPanel();
069:    colorBox.setBackground(Color.white);
070:    colorBox.setPreferredSize(new Dimension(50, 50));
071:
072:    // Add the GUI objects to the inner radio pane
073:    innerRadioPane.add(redButton);
074:    innerRadioPane.add(whiteButton);
075:    innerRadioPane.add(blueButton);
076:    innerRadioPane.add(
077:     Box.createRigidArea(new Dimension(0, 25)));  // Spacer
078:    innerRadioPane.add(colorBox);
079:
080:    // Add the inner pane to the raised radio panel (left side)
081:    radioPane.add(innerRadioPane);
...
141:    // Add the panels and GUI objects to the frame's content pane
142:    Container content = getContentPane();
143:    content.setLayout(new GridLayout(1, 3, 2, 2));
144:    content.add(radioPane);
...
146:  }
147:
148:  // Change the colorBox background color when user
149:  // selects a radio button.
150:  public void actionPerformed(ActionEvent e) {
151:    Color c;
152:    if (redButton.isSelected()) c = Color.red;
153:    else if (whiteButton.isSelected()) c = Color.white;
154:    else c = Color.blue;
155:    colorBox.setBackground(c);
156:  }
...
166: }
```

The listing shows only the statements related to the radio buttons, their group object, the sample color box, and their event handlers. Always create a ButtonGroup object to hold related radio buttons, using code such as

```
ButtonGroup group;
JRadioButton redButton;
group = new ButtonGroup();
```

Add each radio button to the group:

```
redButton = new JRadioButton("Red");
group.add(redButton);
```

You don't have to do anything further with the group, but be sure that the group object is not local to a method, and thus subject to garbage collection. It is probably best to make the group object a `private` member of the program's `JFrame` or other container class.

To respond to a radio button's selection, the sample program uses an `actionPerformed()` method in the main class, which implements the `ActionListener` interface (see line 009). In that method (see lines 150-156), `isSelected()` determines which button is currently chosen, and the color box's background color is set to the appropriate color. Most of the time, a group of radio buttons share the same action event handler using similar code, although it is possible to program a `ChangeListener` for each individual button.

The program also demonstrates a good use of `JPanel` objects to create a pleasing, well-organized display. Each half of the program's window is created using two `JPanels`, an outer and an inner one:

```
JPanel radioPane = new JPanel();
JPanel innerRadioPane = new JPanel();
```

The outer panel, `radioPane` here, gets a beveled look using the `BorderFactory` class (see lines 046-047). After that, the inner panel gets a `BoxLayout` manager and is also designed with an invisible border to provide a little space around the panel's components. Lines 143-144 show how the frame's content pane is given a `GridLayout` manager (other managers could also be used), after which simply adding the outer `radioPanel` inserts the nested panes and their GUI objects into the program's window:

```
content.setLayout(new GridLayout(1, 3, 2, 2));
content.add(radioPane);
```

Using panels this way is much easier to manage than trying to insert multiple GUI components directly into the content pane.

TIP As a general rule, in a group of radio buttons, one button should be selected initially, although this is not a requirement. Line 059 presets the white radio button to match the color of the sample color box.

JCheckBox

Like a radio button, a *check box* is one of the more commonly used GUI button objects. Check boxes are appropriate for presenting multiple choices, such as program options, in which users might select one, two, several, or none of the choices offered. To create a Swing check box, simply construct a JCheckBox object with the text you want to display. Listing 22-3, continued from the preceding listing, shows the parts of the program related to the creation of the check boxes shown in Figure 22-3.

Listing 22-3: ButtonDemo.java (continued)

```
. . .
008: public class ButtonDemo
009:   extends JFrame implements ActionListener {
010:
011:   // GUI objects displayed in the frame window
. . .
017:   JCheckBox showColorsButton;    // First check box
018:   JCheckBox exitOnCloseButton;   // Second check box
019:   JButton exitButton;            // Plain button
020:
021:   // Constructor initializes the GUI objects and panels
022:   public ButtonDemo() {
. . .
087:     // Create check box panel and an inner panel
088:     // for a neat appearance
089:     JPanel checkPane = new JPanel();
090:     JPanel innerCheckPane = new JPanel();
091:     checkPane.setBorder(
092:      BorderFactory.createBevelBorder(BevelBorder.RAISED));
093:     innerCheckPane.setLayout(
094:      new BoxLayout(innerCheckPane, BoxLayout.Y_AXIS));
095:     innerCheckPane.setBorder(
096:      BorderFactory.createEmptyBorder(10, 10, 10, 10));
097:
098:     // Create the "show colors" check box object and
099:     // enable or disable the color radio buttons
100:     showColorsButton = new JCheckBox("Show colors");
101:     showColorsButton.setSelected(true);
102:     showColorsButton.addChangeListener(new ChangeListener() {
103:      public void stateChanged(ChangeEvent e) {
104:       boolean t = showColorsButton.isSelected();
105:       redButton.setEnabled(t);    // Enable or disable all
106:       whiteButton.setEnabled(t); // radio buttons depending on
107:       blueButton.setEnabled(t);   // state of check box
```

```
108:    }
109:   });
110:
111:   // Create the "exit on close" check box object and
112:   // enable or disable the Exit Program button
113:   exitOnCloseButton = new JCheckBox("Exit on close");
114:   exitOnCloseButton.addChangeListener(new ChangeListener() {
115:    public void stateChanged(ChangeEvent e) {
116:     boolean t = exitOnCloseButton.isSelected();
117:     exitButton.setEnabled(t);
118:    }
119:   });
120:
121:   // Create the plain "Exit Program" button
122:   // and its action event listener
123:   exitButton = new JButton("Exit Program");
124:   exitButton.setEnabled(false);  // Initially disabled
125:   exitButton.addActionListener(new ActionListener() {
126:    public void actionPerformed(ActionEvent e) {
127:     System.exit(0);
128:    }
129:   });
130:
131:   // Add the buttons to the inner pane
132:   innerCheckPane.add(showColorsButton);
133:   innerCheckPane.add(exitOnCloseButton);
134:   innerCheckPane.add(
135:    Box.createRigidArea(new Dimension(0, 50)));
136:   innerCheckPane.add(exitButton);
137:
138:   // Add the inner pane to the raised check box panel
139:   checkPane.add(innerCheckPane);
...
166: }
```

As for the radio buttons, two JPanel panes neatly arrange the check boxes along with the window's Exit button (see lines 089-096). Generally, unlike radio buttons, check boxes need to respond individually to their selection. Do that by creating a ChangeListener object, as shown at lines 102-109 and also 114-119. The first event handler shows how to disable the radio buttons when the associated check box is not selected. Likewise, the second event handler enables and disables the program's Exit button. These parts of the program demonstrate useful techniques for creating GUI objects that affect one another's states.

TIP

When using the `BoxLayout` manager, as with the `JPanel` object, `innerCheckPane`, you may need to add some "dead space" between GUI objects. To do that, lines 134-135 call the `Box` class's `createRigidArea()` method using an object of the `Dimension` class to specify a space 0 units wide by 50 high. The end effect depends on how the layout manager works, but in general this is the correct way to add additional space between components — for example, between the two check boxes and the Exit button in the sample program's window.

Dialog Boxes

Dialog boxes are generally secondary windows that present lists of options or display messages. For example, dialog boxes might be used to select configurations or to display directories of filenames. Simple dialogs might display error messages and other notes, although these kinds of dialogs offer only one-sided conversations. Typically, a dialog box provides buttons to confirm changes or entries into component fields, to cancel any changes, or to not perform an operation such as saving a file or exiting the program.

Swing offers several standard dialog boxes, discussed in the next four sections, that find wide use in GUI programming. These include simple message dialogs, interactive confirmation dialogs, file dialogs, and the sophisticated `JColorChooser`, a good-looking component that offers methods for selecting display colors.

Message Dialogs

Swing provides five types of message dialog boxes that are useful for informational, warning, and error messages. These objects are ready-to-use; you simply supply the text and select the type of dialog you want. The dialogs are *modal*, meaning the user must close them before continuing to use the program.

Listing 22-4, MessageDemo.java, displays each type of Swing message dialog. Click one of the program's buttons to select a type of dialog. Figure 22-4 shows the five types of dialogs. The program's buttons are all created the same way. To save space in the listing, I deleted all but the statements that create the Default button. The others are created using nearly identical code.

Figure 22-4: Swing's message dialogs

Listing 22-4: MessageDemo.java

```
001: import javax.swing.*;
002: import java.awt.*;
003: import java.awt.event.*;
004:
005: public class MessageDemo
006:   extends JFrame implements ActionListener {
007:
008:   final int WARNING = JOptionPane.WARNING_MESSAGE;
009:   final int ERROR = JOptionPane.ERROR_MESSAGE;
010:   final int PLAIN = JOptionPane.PLAIN_MESSAGE;
011:   final int INFO = JOptionPane.INFORMATION_MESSAGE;
012:
013:   JButton defaultButton;
...
018:
019:   public void showMessage(String s, int msgType) {
020:    if (msgType < 0)
021:     JOptionPane.showMessageDialog(this, s);
022:    else
```

```
023:      JOptionPane.showMessageDialog(this, s, "Message", msgType);
024:    }
025:
026: // Constructor does all the setup work
027:   public MessageDemo() {
...
042:    defaultButton = new JButton("Default");
...
047:    defaultButton.addActionListener(this);
...
053:    Container content = getContentPane();
054:    content.setLayout(new GridLayout(3, 2, 2, 2));
055:    content.add(defaultButton);
...
060:   }
061:
062:   public void actionPerformed(ActionEvent e) {
063:    Object source = e.getSource();   // Which button?
064:    if (source.equals(defaultButton))
065:     showMessage("Default message dialog", -1);
066:    else if (source.equals(warningButton))
067:     showMessage("Warning message dialog", WARNING);
068:    else if (source.equals(errorButton))
069:     showMessage("Error message dialog", ERROR);
070:    else if (source.equals(plainButton))
071:     showMessage("Plain message dialog", PLAIN);
072:    else if (source.equals(infoButton))
073:     showMessage("Information message dialog", INFO);
074:   }
...
082: }
```

For simplicity, the program declares and calls a method, showMessage(), that displays each type of message dialog (see lines 019-024). Class JOptionPane provides three overloaded showMessageDialog() methods that you can use to create your own messages. The simplest technique simply passes a parent component reference and a string to display

```
JOptionPane.showMessageDialog(frame, s);
```

If you don't have the parent reference (I use a JFrame object here), you may set the first argument to null. In that case, the method uses a default frame, but this might be positioned anywhere on screen (probably dead center). Specifying a frame displays the dialog over the relevant window, and this may help better direct the user's attention to the message.

You can also select a message type and window title by supplying two more arguments, a title and an integer value. For the integer, use one of the following constants defined in JOptionPane to indicate the type of message you want:

```
ERROR_MESSAGE
INFORMATION_MESSAGE
WARNING_MESSAGE
PLAIN_MESSAGE
```

For example, to display a warning message dialog, use a statement such as

```
JOptionPane.showMessageDialog(frame, "System is low on memory!",
 "Warning message", JOptionPane.WARNING_MESSAGE);
```

The first argument is the parent container to which you want the dialog window aligned (as mentioned, you can set this to null). Next is the message to display inside the window, followed by the window title. Finally, specify one of the JOptionPane type constants.

A third form of the showMessageDialog() method accepts an Icon argument. Use this form to display your own image inside the dialog, loaded as an ImageIcon object. For example, you might display a welcome dialog using code such as

```
ImageIcon welcomeIcon = new ImageIcon("welcome.gif");
JOptionPane.showMessageDialog(null, "Welcome to my program!",
 "Hello", JOptionPane.INFORMATION_MESSAGE, welcomeIcon);
```

Confirmation Dialogs

Too many Yes-No-Cancel dialogs can detract from a program's smooth operation, but too few might jeopardize its health. It takes a lot of careful planning to strike a good balance between performing operations immediately on demand and request-ing confirmation for relatively dangerous tasks. The design work is your job, but at least Swing makes it easy to create confirmation dialogs.

Forgive me for tossing in a pet peeve here (if this were an e-mail message, I'd say "Flame on"), but I just hate it when programs ask me for permission to "Throw out changes to document?" I think that's backwards. I'd rather be asked, "Save changes to document?" so that the positive response reflects the more positive action. I'd much rather save changes accidentally, and be forced to recover an original document from a backup, than to throw out my changes accidentally and have no way of getting them back. Whenever possible, try to program confirmation dialogs so that a Yes answer selects the least harmful action. I wish more programs would follow this advice. Flame off.

To request confirmation from users, call the `JOptionPane` class's `showConfirmDialog()` method. There are two forms. One displays Yes and No buttons, and another adds a Cancel button. Listing 22-5, YesNoDemo.java, shows how to use the method. Figure 22-5 shows the program's display and confirmation dialog. Click the program's single button (it occupies the entire window), and answer Yes to end the program, or No to continue running.

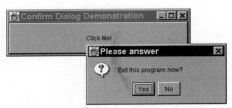

Figure 22-5: The YesNoDemo program displays a confirmation dialog with Yes and No buttons.

Listing 22-5: YesNoDemo.java

```
001: import javax.swing.*;
002: import java.awt.*;
003: import java.awt.event.*;
004:
005: public class YesNoDemo extends JFrame {
006:
007: // Constructor does all the setup work
008:   public YesNoDemo() {
...
023:    JButton optionButton = new JButton("Click Me!");
024:    optionButton.addActionListener(new ActionListener() {
025:     public void actionPerformed(ActionEvent e) {
026:      int result =
027:       JOptionPane.showConfirmDialog(null,
028:        "Exit this program now?",
029:        "Please answer",
030:        JOptionPane.YES_NO_OPTION);
031:      if (result == JOptionPane.YES_OPTION)
032:       System.exit(0);
033:     }
034:    });
035:
036:    Container content = getContentPane();
037:    content.add(optionButton);
038:   }
039:
040:   public static void main(String[] args) {
```

```
041:    YesNoDemo app = new YesNoDemo();
042:    app.setTitle("Confirm Dialog Demonstration");
043:    app.setSize(320, 240);
044:    app.show();
045:  }
046: }
```

The confirmation dialog is created inside the program's lone button action event handler, method `actionPerformed()`. Lines 026-030 call `showConfirmDialog()` and save the dialog's result in an `int` variable. This equals either `YES_OPTION` or `NO_OPTION` depending on which button the user clicked to close the dialog's window. Change the constant in that line to `YES_NO_CANCEL_OPTION` to add a Cancel button, in which case the method might also return `CANCEL_OPTION`. All of these constants are static members of `JOptionPane` and, therefore, must be used in reference to the class name.

TIP If the user closes a confirmation dialog by clicking the window's close button or by selecting the system menu's Close command, `showConfirmDialog()` returns `JOptionPane.CLOSED_OPTION`. This equals –1, the same value as `DEFAULT_OPTION`. You may use either constant. If you receive this value, depending on the dialog's purpose, you should probably treat it the same as a No or Cancel button's selection. However, this is another, and subtle, aspect of confirmation dialogs that requires careful thought to ensure against the loss of information.

File Dialogs

One of the more capable standard Swing dialogs displays directory paths and filenames. Use the `JFileChooser` class to display two types of these valuable dialogs: one to open files, and one to save them. The dialogs don't perform any file operations. That's still your job (for help with this topic, see Chapter 24, "Input and Output Techniques"). But using these dialogs helps simplify the often tedious job of building directory trees and filtering filenames for extensions such as .txt and .html. Remember too that these dialogs are cross-platform tools – they work similarly on Solaris, Linux, Macintosh, and Windows systems, despite major differences in file and path name conventions between these systems.

Listing 22-6, FileDialog.java, demonstrates how to create standard file-open and file-save dialogs. Run the program and click one of program's two buttons to display a `JFileChooser` dialog. Feel free to "open" and "save" files – the program does not read or write any real file data. However, you *can* create directories, and apparently, you can use the dialogs to modify filenames, so exercise some caution when running the demonstration. Figure 22-6 shows the program and its two dialogs.

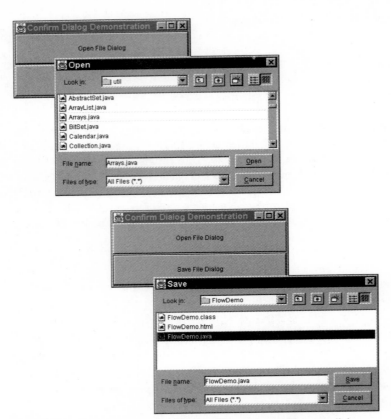

Figure 22-6: Use JFileChooser to display file-open and file-save dialogs.

Listing 22-6: FileDialog.java

```
001: import javax.swing.*;
002: import java.awt.*;
003: import java.awt.event.*;
004:
005: public class FileDialog extends JFrame {
006:
007:   private JFileChooser fDialog;
008:   JFrame frame;  // Reference to this frame object
009:
010: // Constructor does all the setup work
011:   public FileDialog() {
012:
013:     frame = this;  // So action listeners can find it
...
028:     // Construct the file chooser dialog object
```

```
029:    fDialog = new JFileChooser();
030:
031:    // Open button displays File:Open dialog
032:    JButton openButton = new JButton("Open File Dialog");
033:    openButton.addActionListener(new ActionListener() {
034:     public void actionPerformed(ActionEvent e) {
035:      String msg;
036:      int result = fDialog.showOpenDialog(frame);
037:      if (result == JFileChooser.APPROVE_OPTION) {
038:       String fname = fDialog.getName(fDialog.getSelectedFile());
039:       frame.setTitle(fname);
040:       msg = "File Open Approved";
041:      } else
042:       msg = "File Open Cancelled";
043:      JOptionPane.showMessageDialog(frame, msg);
044:     }
045:    });
046:
047:    // Save button displays File:Save dialog
048:    JButton saveButton = new JButton("Save File Dialog");
049:    saveButton.addActionListener(new ActionListener() {
050:     public void actionPerformed(ActionEvent e) {
051:      String msg;
052:      int result = fDialog.showSaveDialog(frame);
053:      if (result == JFileChooser.APPROVE_OPTION) {
054:       String fname = fDialog.getName(fDialog.getSelectedFile());
055:       frame.setTitle(fname);
056:       msg = "File Save Approved";
057:      } else
058:       msg = "File Save Cancelled";
059:      JOptionPane.showMessageDialog(frame, msg);
060:     }
061:    });
...
068:   }
...
076: }
```

It's probably best to construct a JFileChooser object as shown here at line 029 and keep that object available throughout the program's life. However, to conserve resources, you could create the dialog object each time it is needed. In the sample program, clicking one of the two buttons calls one of two action event handlers at lines 033-045 and also 049-061. These two sections show how to display and use file-open and file-save dialogs.

For the first type, call showOpenDialog() (line 036) and pass a reference to the current frame or other top-level container. Or, you can pass null to center the dialog on screen. If the method returns JFileChooser.APPROVE_OPTION, the user requested that a selected file be opened. Get its name as shown at line 038, or if you prefer, you may do the same operation in two steps:

```
File selectedFile = fDialog.getSelectedFile();
String fname = fDialog.getName(selectedFile);
```

You might use separate statements that way to inspect other aspects about the selected file using the File object returned by getSelectedFile(). For example, call getAbsolutePath() to get the file's full pathname. Look up the File class in the java.io package in Java's online documentation for a full list of this class's methods and fields.

A file-save dialog is equally easy to create. In fact, the code is nearly identical, but it calls showSaveDialog() (see line 052). JFileChooser, however, does not automatically ask whether to overwrite an existing file. You need to provide code to do that after calling showSaveDialog(), for example, by using a Yes-No confirmation dialog.

TIP Using the technique shown in the sample program, the file dialog "remembers" its previous settings. Reopening the dialog displays the most recently visited directory, and the current filename is automatically filled in. If you want a fresh start each time, simply recreate the JFileChooser object for each file-open and file-save operation.

Many times, you will need to filter these dialogs so they display specific file types based on their filename extensions. This requires a little extra work, and unfortunately it is not a native capability of the JFileChooser class. For an example of the necessary programming, locate the ExampleFileFilter class from the JDK demonstration programs. On my system, the source files are in the following directory:

```
jdk1.3/demo/jfc/FileChooserDemo/src
```

There you will find instructions and examples that show how to implement the javax.swing.FileFilter abstract class. Cut and paste this code into your program (however, you might want to name the class something other than ExampleFileFilter). You can then add filters to the fDialog JFileChooser dialog object using code such as

```
ExampleFileFilter filter = new ExampleFileFilter();
filter.addExtension("txt");
filter.addExtension("html");
```

```
filter.addExtension("java");
filter.setDescription("*.java, *.html, *.text ");
fDialog.setFileFilter(filter);
```

Beware that Java has two `FileFilter` classes, apparently a minor JDK naming error. If this causes a conflict for you in creating file filters, use the full package and class names `java.io.FileFilter` and `javax.swing.filechooser.FileFilter` to distinguish between the two classes.

JColorChooser

Finally in this section is one more standard dialog that I think is one of the best looking windows of its kind in any GUI toolkit I've used. If you like rainbows, you'll love this one. Use `JColorChooser` to give users a handy way to select colors, either by clicking samples displayed on a colorful grid; by selecting hue, saturation, and brilliance values; or by specifying Red, Green, and Blue color levels. The `JColorChooser` class also displays sample text areas to show how color selections look.

`JColorChooser` is not a dialog box, but I describe it here because its operation is usually associated with dialogs. You can install a `JColorChooser` component in any window — if you want to create a separate window for it, just add it to a `JFrame` or `JDialog` container, and then call that object's `show()` method. Figure 22-7 doesn't do justice to the `JColorChooser`'s colorful display. Listing 22-7, ColorDemo.java, shows how to use the component. To illustrate how to respond to a color selection, the program also paints a box along the top of the window. You don't usually need to add this code, however, because the `JColorChooser` class provides its own color preview area (see the bottom of the window in the figure).

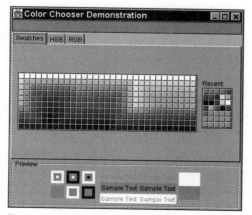

Figure 22-7: JColorChooser is a capable color-select component useful in dialogs.

Listing 22-7: ColorDemo.java

```
001: import javax.swing.*;
002: import javax.swing.event.*;
003: import java.awt.*;
004: import java.awt.event.*;
005:
006: public class ColorDemo extends JFrame {
007:
008:   private JColorChooser colorChooser;   // The Color chooser
009:   private JPanel colorBox;              // Color sample
010:   private Color selectedColor;          // Selected color
011:
012: // Constructor does all the setup work
013:   public ColorDemo() {
...
028:    // Set current color and sample panel (top)
029:    selectedColor = Color.white;
030:    colorBox = new JPanel();
031:    colorBox.setBackground(selectedColor);
032:    colorBox.setPreferredSize(new Dimension(150, 100));
033:    colorBox.setBorder(
034:      BorderFactory.createLineBorder(Color.black));
035:
036:    // Create color chooser and change event listener
037:    colorChooser = new JColorChooser(selectedColor);
038:    colorChooser.getSelectionModel().addChangeListener(
039:      new ChangeListener() {
040:        public void stateChanged(ChangeEvent e) {
041:          selectedColor = colorChooser.getColor();
042:          colorBox.setBackground(selectedColor);
043:        }
044:      }
045:    );
046:
047:    // Add the sample color pane and chooser to the frame
048:    Container content = getContentPane();
049:    content.setLayout(new BoxLayout(content, BoxLayout.Y_AXIS));
050:    content.add(colorBox);
051:    content.add(colorChooser);
052:  }
...
060: }
```

To use JColorChooser, create an object of that class and, usually, one of Color to save the current selection. Lines 008-010 in the sample program declare these variables along with a JPanel container for showing the selected color. The color chooser component is easy to create. Optionally specify an initial color value in parentheses:

```
colorChooser = new JColorChooser(Color.white);
```

To respond to the user's color selections, create a ChangeListener object as shown at lines 038-045. Because JColorChooser is built by implementing the ColorSelectionModel interface, the event handler is correctly associated with an object of that type, in this case by using an anonymous class to implement the interface. Write a ChangeListener() method as shown—it is called for every color selection. To find that selection, the demonstration calls the colorChooser object's getColor() method. Line 042 paints the sample panel's background using this choice, but if you are simply designing a color-selection dialog, you can cut out this code.

Text Objects

The simplest text class is JLabel. Of course, you can use it to display static text, but you can also add an icon for a little extra visual punch. In addition, JLabel can now display HTML-encoded text. (JButton can do the same, and other Swing components that display text labels are expected to follow suit.) Listing 22-8 demonstrates a few ways to use JLabel. Figure 22-8 shows the program's window.

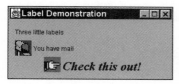

Figure 22-8: JLabel can display simple text, icons, and HTML-formatted text.

Listing 22-8: LabelDemo.java

```
001: import javax.swing.*;
002: import java.awt.*;
003: import java.awt.event.*;
004:
005: public class LabelDemo extends JFrame {
006:
007: // Constructor does all the setup work
008:   public LabelDemo() {
...
```

```
023:    // Place components in a pane for better appearance
024:    JPanel pane = new JPanel();
025:    pane.setLayout(new GridLayout(3, 1, 2, 2));
026:    pane.setBorder(BorderFactory.createEmptyBorder(10, 10, 10,
0));
027:
028:    // Create a simple label using default text
029:    JLabel titleLabel = new JLabel("Three little labels");
030:
031:    // Add an icon image to a label
032:    ImageIcon mailIcon = new ImageIcon("mailbox.gif");
033:    JLabel mailLabel = new JLabel(mailIcon, JLabel.LEADING);
034:    mailLabel.setText("You have mail");
035:
036:    // Use HTML to format a label's text font and size
037:    String s = "<html>"
038:     + "<font size=+2><b><i>Check this out!</i></b></font>"
039:     + "</html>";
040:    ImageIcon handIcon = new ImageIcon("righthand.gif");
041:    JLabel htmlLabel = new JLabel(s, handIcon, JLabel.CENTER);
042:
043:    // Add components to the pane, and the pane to content layer
044:    pane.add(titleLabel);
045:    pane.add(mailLabel);
046:    pane.add(htmlLabel);
047:    getContentPane().add(pane);
048:  }
...
056: }
```

Use the ImageIcon class to load a GIF, JPEG, or PNG file with the image to display along with a JLabel's text. Lines 032-034 show a good way to do this. When creating the JLabel object, pass the loaded ImageIcon as the first argument, followed by a JLabel constant such as LEADING to position the icon ahead of the text. Among others, you can use constants such as BOTTOM, CENTER, TOP, and TRAILING to position the icon. (For a full list of positioning constants, see Java's online documentation for JLabel.)

One of Java's prime attractions is its cross-platform support. However, that support complicates certain operations such as specifying fonts, font sizes, and other characteristics such as italic and bold text. HTML is one good answer to this problem, and now JLabel can format text using tags such as <font>. Lines 037-041 show how to use this feature to display the text *Check this out!* along with an icon (see Figure 22-8). You can pass HTML text directly to a JLabel constructor, but I like to use a String variable to prepare the text. The string should have the general form:

```
String s = "<html>text</html>";
```

As shown in the listing, between the opening and closing tags, <html> and </html>, you can insert a <font> tag, and use <b> and <i> bold and italic modifiers. You can also use other tags — consult a reference to HTML programming for all available options. For clarity and easier editing, I like to use the string concatenation operator as shown to join each element of the string, but you can type the string all on one line if you want. Apparently, the ending </html> tag is optional; however, it's probably best to include it anyway just in case it is someday required.

HTML text can include new-line control codes, \n, but these seem to work only with multiline text components such as JTextArea, not for JLabel. If you need multiline labels, it is probably best to create multiple JLabel objects, one for each line, or use JTextArea as described after the following section.

JTextField

Of course, most programs need ways to input text as well as to display it. For single-line entry fields, use a JTextField object. Listing 22-9, Password.java, demonstrates how to use JTextField to prompt users for their names. The program also shows how to use the related JPasswordField to prompt for a password, which is not displayed onscreen. Figure 22-9 shows the program's display along with a confirmation dialog that reveals the password entered. And no, that's not one of my real passwords.

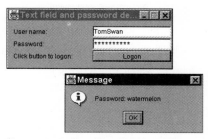

Figure 22-9: Use JTextField and JPasswordField to prompt for single-line text entries.

Listing 22-9: Password.java

```
001: import javax.swing.*;
002: import java.awt.*;
003: import java.awt.event.*;
004:
005: public class Password
006:   extends JFrame implements ActionListener {
007:
```

```
008:   JTextField username;
009:   JPasswordField password;
010:   JButton logon;
011:
012: // Constructor does all the setup work
013:   public Password() {
...
028:    // Use inner panel for a neat appearance
029:    JPanel pane = new JPanel();
030:    pane.setLayout(new GridLayout(3, 2, 2, 2));
031:    pane.setBorder(
032:     BorderFactory.createEmptyBorder(10, 10, 10, 0));
033:
034:    username = new JTextField(16);
035:    password = new JPasswordField(16);
036:    logon = new JButton("Logon");
037:    logon.addActionListener(this);
038:
039:    // Prevent user from resizing this JFrame
040:    setResizable(false);
041:
042:    // Add components to the pane, and the pane to content layer
043:    pane.add(new JLabel("User name:"));
044:    pane.add(username);
045:    pane.add(new JLabel("Password:"));
046:    pane.add(password);
047:    pane.add(new JLabel("Click button to logon:"));
048:    pane.add(logon);
049:    getContentPane().add(pane);
050:   }
051:
052:   public void actionPerformed(ActionEvent e) {
053:    Object source = e.getSource();  // Which component?
054:    if (source.equals(logon)) {
055:     // *** WARNING: SECURITY DANGER
056:     char[] ptext = password.getPassword();  // ok
057:     String s = new String(ptext);  // ???
058:     JOptionPane.showMessageDialog(this, "Password: " + s);
059:     // Erase password for safety
060:     for (int i = 0; i < ptext.length; i++)
061:      ptext[i] = 0;
062:     // *** END SECURITY DANGER
063:    }
064:   }
...
072: }
```

JTextField and its subclass JPasswordField are easy to use. Create objects as follows, specifying widths as positive integer values in parentheses:

```
JTextField username = new JTextField(16);
JPasswordField password = new JPasswordField(16);
```

The two objects scroll horizontally if necessary — the integer values merely size the component in the window. Add each component to the frame's content layer, or use a JPanel or other container as shown in the sample listing. Notice how line 040 prevents users from resizing the frame:

```
setResizable(false);
```

Because the program uses the GridLayout manager, this is necessary to prevent the entry fields from being resized ridiculously if, for example, the user expands the window to full screen. You may want to use that statement when designing dialogs that contain JTextField entry fields, or use a different layout manager such as BoxLayout to prevent components from being resized along with the window.

Lines 052-064 provide an actionPerformed() method that is registered for the sample program's "Logon" button. This demonstrates how to retrieve the text from a JPasswordField object. Calling getPassword() returns an array of char, containing the entered password. This poses a security risk, especially because Java objects cannot be explicitly disposed but are destroyed by the garbage collector at an unspecified future time. For this reason, Sun recommends that you overwrite the returned char array as shown at lines 060-061.

TIP

To obtain text entered into a JTextField object, call the getText() method inherited from JTextComponent, JTextField's immediate superclass. That method is disabled for JPasswordField. When using that class, the only way to retrieve entered text is to call getPassword().

JTextArea

For multiline text displays and entries, create a JTextArea object. Most often, you can insert that object into a JScrollPane to provide for automatic vertical and horizontal scrolling, without requiring any supporting code or event handlers. However, you may use a plain JTextArea object if you don't need scrolling. Listing 22-10, TextDemo.java, demonstrates how to use JTextArea and JScrollPane. Figure 22-10 shows the program's display after cutting and pasting some text into the window.

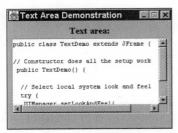

Figure 22-10: Use JTextArea and JScrollPane
to provide multiline text areas.

Listing 22-10: TextDemo.java

```
001: import javax.swing.*;
002: import java.awt.*;
003: import java.awt.event.*;
004:
005: public class TextDemo extends JFrame {
006:
007: // Constructor does all the setup work
008:  public TextDemo() {
...
023:   // Use inner panel for a neat appearance
024:   JPanel pane = new JPanel();
025:
026:   // Create text area object
027:   JTextArea theText = new JTextArea();
028:   theText.setFont(new Font("Courier", Font.PLAIN, 12));
029:   theText.setLineWrap(false);
030:
031:   // Add a scroller to the text area object
032:   JScrollPane scroller = new JScrollPane(theText);
033:   scroller.setPreferredSize(new Dimension(300, 150));
034:   scroller.setVerticalScrollBarPolicy(
035:    JScrollPane.VERTICAL_SCROLLBAR_ALWAYS);
036:
037:   // Create a label for the text area object
038:   String s = "<html>"
039:    + "<font size=+1><b>Text area:</b></font>"
040:    + "</html>";
041:   JLabel inputLabel = new JLabel(s);
042:   inputLabel.setLabelFor(theText);
043:   inputLabel.setAlignmentX(Component.LEFT_ALIGNMENT);
044:
045:   // Add all components to the content pane
046:   pane.add(inputLabel);
```

```
047:    pane.add(scroller);
048:    getContentPane().add(pane);
049:    setResizable(false);
050:  }
...
058: }
```

In addition to constructing a JTextArea object, you can also specify a font and state whether lines should wrap, as follows:

```
JTextArea theText = new JTextArea();
theText.setFont(new Font("Courier", Font.PLAIN, 12));
theText.setLineWrap(false);
```

For a different style, change PLAIN to BOLD or ITALIC (or to combine both styles, use the logical expression BOLD | ITALIC). See the Font class in the java.awt package for other constants and methods you can use. The last statement calls setLineWrap() to specify whether lines should wrap around at the component's edge (true). If line wrapping is set to false, a horizontal scroll bar appears if text extends beyond the right edge, but only if the JTextArea object is embedded in a JScrollPane. Do that as follows:

```
JScrollPane scroller = new JScrollPane(theText);
scroller.setPreferredSize(new Dimension(300, 150));
scroller.setVerticalScrollBarPolicy(
 JScrollPane.VERTICAL_SCROLLBAR_ALWAYS);
```

First, construct the JScrollPane object, passing the JTextArea object to embed. Next, although optional, call setPreferredSize() so the layout manager can properly size the components. You have to do this only for the scroll pane. Finally, call setVerticalScrollBarPolicy(), passing the JScrollPane constant shown. Or, you may change that constant to VERTICAL_SCROLLBAR_NEVER to never display a vertical scroll bar, or to VERTICAL_SCROLLBAR_ALWAYS to display one even if not needed. Call setHorizontalScrollBarPolicy() with similar constants (but change VERTICAL to HORIZONTAL) to dictate a horizontal scroll bar policy. This is usually not necessary, since horizontal scroll bars are warranted depending on whether line wrapping is enabled.

Lists

Lists are useful for — well, listing things, naturally. Swing has two basic list varieties. Use a plain JList for a fixed list of items such as the days of the week or the months of the year. Use a JComboBox for lists from which users can select entries, but can also enter new text. You can program either object to permit single or multiple selections. The following sections show examples of both of these handy components.

JList

Listing 22-11, ListDemo.java, shows how to use a `JList` object to present users with a list of fixed choices, here the days of the week. Figure 22-11 shows the program's window. If the list is larger than its window container, a vertical scrollbar appears automatically if the `JList` object is embedded in a `JScrollPane`.

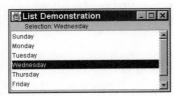

Figure 22-11: JList presents users with a fixed list of selections.

Listing 22-11: ListDemo.java

```
001: import javax.swing.*;
002: import javax.swing.event.*;
003: import java.awt.*;
004: import java.awt.event.*;
005:
006: public class ListDemo extends JFrame {
007:
008:   private JFrame frame;  // Refers to this JFrame window
009:   private JLabel label;  // Shows current selection
010:
011: // Constructor does all the setup work
012:   public ListDemo() {
...
027:     frame = this;  // So event handler can find our window
028:
029:     String[] items = {
030:       "Sunday", "Monday", "Tuesday", "Wednesday",
031:       "Thursday", "Friday", "Saturday"
032:     };
033:     JList dayList = new JList(items);
034:     dayList.setSelectionMode(
035:       ListSelectionModel.SINGLE_SELECTION);
036:     dayList.setAlignmentX(Component.CENTER_ALIGNMENT);
037:     JScrollPane listScroller = new JScrollPane(dayList);
038:
039:     // Respond to a list selection event
040:     dayList.addListSelectionListener(
041:       new ListSelectionListener() {
```

```
042:       public void valueChanged(ListSelectionEvent e) {
043:        JList list = (JList)e.getSource();
044:        if (!list.isSelectionEmpty()) {
045:         int i = list.getSelectedIndex();
046:         String s = (String)list.getModel().getElementAt(i);
047:         label.setText("Selection: " + s);
048:        }
049:       }
050:      }
051:     );
052:
053:     label = new JLabel("Select a day");
054:     Container content = getContentPane();
055:     content.setLayout(new BoxLayout(content, BoxLayout.Y_AXIS));
056:     content.add(label);
057:     content.add(listScroller);
058:    }
...
066: }
```

The first step in using JList is to provide the text for the list's selections. This text might come from a file or other source, but it is most easily programmed as an array of String objects as shown at lines 029-032. Pass the array to the JList constructor (see line 033). After constructing the list object, call setSelectionMode() like this:

```
yourList.setSelectionMode(
 ListSelectionModel.SINGLE_SELECTION);
```

Change SINGLE_SELECTION to SINGLE_INTERVAL_SELECTION to permit multiple contiguous selections. Or use MULTIPLE_INTERVAL_SELECTION to permit multiple selections that do not have to be contiguous. The keys that users press to make multiple selections depend on the current look-and-feel, but generally, the Shift key makes contiguous selections, and the Ctrl key non-contiguous selections, and the user may use either the keyboard arrow keys or the mouse to navigate the list.

Embed a JList object in a JScrollPane if you want a vertical scroll bar to appear automatically as needed. You can further configure the scroll pane as explained in the section on JTextArea in this chapter. Horizontal scroll bars are never displayed for JList.

Of course you also need to provide code that responds to the user's selection. To demonstrate one way to write that code, the sample program displays the current selection in a label above the list (see Figure 22-11). This capability is enacted by calling the `addListSelectionListener()` method for the `JList` object to listen for a selection event. Usually, you can create an object of an anonymous class that implements the `ListSelectionListener` interface (in the `javax.swing.event` package) as follows:

```
dayList.addListSelectionListener(
 new ListSelectionListener() {
  public void valueChanged(ListSelectionEvent e) {
   // ... handle list selection here
  }
 }
);
```

Take care to type the punctuation exactly as shown. The two closing braces end the `valueChanged()` method and the anonymous class declaration respectively. The final close parenthesis and semicolon end the call to `addListSelectionListener()`. Despite appearances, this is a statement, and so it must end with a semicolon.

 As mentioned elsewhere, a programming editor such as Emacs that automatically matches parentheses and braces goes a long way in preventing compilation errors caused by simple typing mistakes. This is especially true in Java programming in which the use of anonymous and inner classes is becoming ever more popular. Emacs is available in most UNIX and Linux installations. Its unusual name originates from its early days as a collection of "Editor Macros," but the program has evolved way beyond its humble beginnings. Incredibly, Emacs is written in Lisp. Versions of the program are available for Windows and Macintosh, but I haven't tried them. For more information and a list of supported platforms, try one of the following links:

```
http://www.gnu.org/software/emacs/
http://www.gnu.org/software/emacs/windows/ntemacs.html
```

In the method, add statements to respond to a selection from the list. First, obtain a reference to the list object:

```
JList list = (JList)e.getSource();
```

If you already have such a reference, you can skip this step, but it ensures that the correct list object is used. It is usually also a good idea to check whether no selections have been made, although this might not be strictly necessary:

```
if (!list.isSelectionEmpty()) {
 // ... get selection
}
```

Inside that statement, obtain an index to the selected item:

```
int i = list.getSelectedIndex();
```

To get the actual text requires some complex-looking code:

```
String s = (String)list.getModel().getElementAt(i);
```

The JList class is based on a *list model* that is responsible for the list object's operation. Call getModel() as shown to obtain a reference to the model, for which you can call methods such as getElementAt() to obtain the selected string.

JComboBox

JComboBox offers a different way to present users with selection lists. Unlike JList, JComboBox can present users with a static list of selections, but it can also allow users to enter new items. This is highly useful for lists such as country names that present a fixed list of selections, but must also allow users to enter alternate text not in the original list.

It is natural to consider JComboBox to be a descendant of JList, but unfortunately, that is not the case. The two classes are siblings (they are both subclasses of JComponent) but are otherwise unrelated. As a result, different techniques are required to use these two components despite their apparent similarities in operation.

Listing 22-12, ComboDemo.java, demonstrates how to use JComboBox and to respond to user selections. Run the program and select a month name from the list by clicking the component's drop-down arrow. Also try entering a new entry into the component's text-entry field. Of course, you probably wouldn't do this for a list of month names, but this shows how a JComboBox can optionally be made editable. Figure 22-12 shows a sample of the program's window.

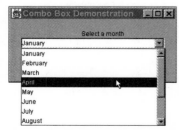

Figure 22-12: JComboBox presents an optionally editable list of selections.

Listing 22-12: ComboDemo.java

```
001: import javax.swing.*;
002: import javax.swing.event.*;
003: import java.awt.*;
004: import java.awt.event.*;
005:
006: public class ComboDemo extends JFrame {
007:
008:  private JFrame frame;  // Refers to this JFrame window
009:  private JLabel label;  // Shows current selection
010:
011: // Constructor does all the setup work
012:  public ComboDemo() {
...
027:   frame = this;  // So event handler can find our window
028:   label = new JLabel("Select a month");
029:
030:   String[] items = {
031:    "January", "February", "March", "April", "May",
032:    "June", "July", "August", "September", "October",
033:    "November", "December"
034:   };
035:   JComboBox months = new JComboBox(items);
036:   months.setSelectedIndex(0);
037:   months.setEditable(true);
038:   months.addActionListener(
039:    new ActionListener() {
040:     public void actionPerformed(ActionEvent e) {
041:      JComboBox box = (JComboBox)e.getSource();
042:      String s = (String)box.getSelectedItem();
043:      label.setText("Selection: " + s);
044:     }
045:    }
046:   );
047:
048:   JPanel pane = new JPanel();
049:   pane.setLayout(new BoxLayout(pane, BoxLayout.Y_AXIS));
050:   pane.setBorder(
051:    BorderFactory.createEmptyBorder(20, 20, 20, 20));
052:   pane.add(label);
053:   pane.add(months);
054:
055:   getContentPane().add(pane, BorderLayout.CENTER);
056:  }
...
064: }
```

Creating a `JComboBox` resembles the steps in creating a `JList`. Start with an array of `String` items to be listed in the component:

```
String[] items = {
 "January", "February", ...
};
```

Pass the `items` array to the `JComboBox` constructor:

```
JComboBox months = new JComboBox(items);
```

Next, call the following two methods to specify the initial selection and whether to permit entering a new item's text:

```
months.setSelectedIndex(0);
months.setEditable(true);
```

Always specify an initial index for the selected entry so that one item is shown in the `ComboBox` entry field by default. Of course, you may change `true` to `false` in calling `setEditable()` to disable entry of new items. The default value is `false`.

 TIP Set a combo box's first entry string to "None," and specify 0 for the initial selected index. That way, "None" is a selection like any others, neatly solving the problem of how to permit users to make no entry from a combo box's list.

Responding to a combo box's selection differs from how to do that with a `JList`. (Ideally, these classes would use identical techniques making them interchangeable. They're not.) Use an `ActionListener` object to respond to a selection in a combo box. Register the listener with the component by calling `addActionListener()` as follows:

```
months.addActionListener(
 new ActionListener() {
  public void actionPerformed(ActionEvent e) {
  }
 }
);
```

That creates an anonymous class and implements the `ActionListener` interface, which specifies the method, `actionPerformed()`. Add statements to that method to get the user's selection from the combo box. First, obtain a reference to the component using the statement:

```
JComboBox box = (JComboBox)e.getSource();
```

After that, call getSelectedItem() for the selected item's text. You can then use the string as you wish. Here it is sent to the program's label to display the current selection. This works for static and editable combo boxes:

```
String s = (String)box.getSelectedItem();
label.setText("Selection: " + s);
```

 Do not use the list-model technique shown in the preceding section for JList. That code compiles for JComboBox, but using the list model fails to handle the action event resulting from users entering new text into an editable combo box.

Special Features

Most users now expect programs to feature pop-up menus and toolbars for easier use. Swing makes creating these special and popular features quick and easy, but as the following sections explain, there are a few *gotchas* to observe so they don't *getcha*.

JPopupMenu

Creating a pop-up menu is similar to how you create a root panel's pull-down menu (see "Creating Pull-Down Menus" in Chapter 21). In fact, a pull-down menu is really just a pop-up menu that is rooted in a JMenuBar object. Listing 22-13, PopupDemo.java, demonstrates how to use Swing's JPopupMenu class to create a pop-up menu, and how to respond to item selections. Run the program and click inside the window to bring up the pop-up menu, shown in Figure 22-13. Select any command to see a message dialog confirmation (only one command, Exit, actually works).

 Usually, clicking the right mouse button brings up a pop-up menu, but this depends on the system's look-in-feel, and possibly on the mouse's configuration. Unlike with many GUI toolkits, with Java and Swing, there is no need to write code for such concerns.

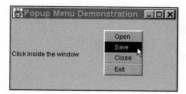

Figure 22-13: Pop-up menus are quick and
easy to create using Java's Swing library.

Listing 22-13: PopupDemo.java

```
001: import javax.swing.*;
002: import java.awt.*;
003: import java.awt.event.*;
004:
005: public class PopupDemo
006:   extends JFrame implements ActionListener {
007:
008:   // This is the popup menu object
009:   protected JPopupMenu popupMenu;
010:
011:   // These are the popup menu items
012:   protected JMenuItem openMenuItem;
013:   protected JMenuItem saveMenuItem;
014:   protected JMenuItem closeMenuItem;
015:   protected JMenuItem exitMenuItem;
016:
017:   // Inner class pops up the menu when the proper mouse
018:   // click or release is detected for the current look and feel
019:   class PopupHandler extends MouseAdapter {
020:    public void mousePressed(MouseEvent e) {
021:     if (e.isPopupTrigger())
022:      popupMenu.show(e.getComponent(), e.getX(), e.getY());
023:    }
024:    public void mouseReleased(MouseEvent e) {
025:     if (e.isPopupTrigger())
026:      popupMenu.show(e.getComponent(), e.getX(), e.getY());
027:    }
028:   }
029:
030:   // Create the popup menu and its commands
031:   private void createPopupMenu() {
032:    popupMenu = new JPopupMenu();
033:    openMenuItem = new JMenuItem("Open");
034:    openMenuItem.addActionListener(this);
035:    popupMenu.add(openMenuItem);
036:    saveMenuItem = new JMenuItem("Save");
```

```
037:    saveMenuItem.addActionListener(this);
038:    popupMenu.add(saveMenuItem);
039:    closeMenuItem = new JMenuItem("Close");
040:    closeMenuItem.addActionListener(this);
041:    popupMenu.add(closeMenuItem);
042:    popupMenu.addSeparator();
043:    exitMenuItem = new JMenuItem("Exit");
044:    exitMenuItem.addActionListener(this);
045:    popupMenu.add(exitMenuItem);
046:
047:    // Register frame listener so menu pops on the
048:    // proper mouse click depending on the look and feel
049:    addMouseListener(new PopupHandler());
050:  }
051:
052:  // Constructor
053:  public PopupDemo() {
...
068:    createPopupMenu();
069:    Container content = getContentPane();
070:    content.add(new JLabel("Click inside the window"));
071:  }
072:
073:  // All popup menu items are registered on this event handler
074:  public void actionPerformed(ActionEvent e) {
075:    JMenuItem menuItem = (JMenuItem)e.getSource();
076:
077:    // Show selected command text (just for demonstration)
078:    JOptionPane.showMessageDialog(this,
079:     "Command: " + menuItem.getText());
080:
081:    // Find out which command was selected
082:    if (menuItem.equals(openMenuItem)) {
083:     // ... do open command
084:    }
085:    if (menuItem.equals(saveMenuItem)) {
086:     // ... do save command
087:    }
088:    if (menuItem.equals(closeMenuItem)) {
089:     // ... do close command
090:    }
091:    if (menuItem.equals(exitMenuItem)) {
092:     System.exit(0);  // Only implemented command
093:    }
094:  }
...
102: }
```

The demonstration's listing is longer than many in this book, but it shows several important techniques in creating pop-up menus. First, declare a `JPopupMenu` object to serve as the menu's container:

```
protected JPopupMenu popupMenu;
```

That could be made `private` or `public` depending on your needs, but should probably be a member of the program's main class. In this case, our class extends `JFrame` and implements `ActionListener` (see lines 005-006) to provide for the pop-up menu's selections. Before writing that code, also declare `JMenuItem` objects, one for each of the menu's commands:

```
protected JMenuItem openMenuItem;
protected JMenuItem saveMenuItem;
protected JMenuItem closeMenuItem;
protected JMenuItem exitMenuItem;
```

Again, these don't have to be `protected`. It is possible to do away with these objects, but as I explain a bit later, having them simplifies the job of detecting which item was selected. Conversely, the menu items could provide their own event listeners, but it's more common to have the frame or other container do this job, and in that way make it possible to add the same `JMenuItem` objects to the frame's main window (however, the demonstration doesn't do that).

Lines 030-050 create the action menu items and add them to the pop-up menu. First create the pop-up menu object:

```
popupMenu = new JPopupMenu();
```

Then, create each `JMenuItem`. Usually, programming each such object takes at least three steps:

```
openMenuItem = new JMenuItem("Open");
openMenuItem.addActionListener(this);
popupMenu.add(openMenuItem);
```

The first statement creates the menu item object. Call `addActionListener()` to register the code that responds to the item's selection. Here, the program specifies the frame itself (`this`) as the listener, but as mentioned, you could create separate listeners for each item if you prefer. Finally, add the menu item object to the pop-up menu by calling its `add()` method. To display a separator line between items, call `addSeparator()` like this:

```
popupMenu.addSeparator();
```

After creating all menu items, create and register a mouse listener object to cause the pop-up menu to appear on demand. Because the program's class extends

JFrame, the following statement makes the frame responsible for listening for the appropriate mouse event:

```
addMouseListener(new PopupHandler());
```

PopupHandler is an inner class that provides the code to bring up the pop-up menu. The class is written as shown at lines 019-028 and is generally programmed using this form:

```
class PopupHandler extends MouseAdapter {
 public void mousePressed(MouseEvent e) {...}
 public void mouseReleased(MouseEvent e) {...}
}
```

The class extends MouseAdapter, which implements the MouseListener interface. Using MouseAdapter this way avoids having to provide bodies for all methods declared in the interface—for example, there's no need to respond to mouse movements. It is apparently necessary to provide code for mouse-pressed and mouse-released events. For instance, in Windows, a pop-up menu is displayed only after *releasing* the right mouse button; but that might not be the case across all platforms. So, for safety, it's best to program both event handlers using the following code:

```
if (e.isPopupTrigger())
 popupMenu.show(e.getComponent(), e.getX(), e.getY());
}
```

Call method isPopupTrigger() for the MouseEvent passed to the method. If this method returns true, call show() to display the pop-up menu. This should always be done at the X and Y coordinate values found in the event object. You don't need to write code to remove the pop-up menu window. It is removed automatically when the user selects a command or performs another operation such as a mouse click elsewhere in the program's window.

Lastly, provide code for responding to a menu item's selection. As mentioned, the sample program does this by having the main class implement the ActionListener interface, which declares actionPerformed(). Program that method as shown at lines 074-094, generally using the form

```
public void actionPerformed(ActionEvent e) {
 JMenuItem menuItem = (JMenuItem)e.getSource();
 // ... use menuItem
}
```

The first statement inside actionPerformed() obtains a reference to the menu item that fired the event. Because the sample program keeps references to the pop-up menu's JMenuItem objects, it's easy to compare them to the menuItem just obtained to identify the selected command. For example, this detects the Open command:

```
if (menuItem.equals(openMenuItem)) {
 // ... do open command
}
```

This is only one of many ways to program event listeners for objects such as pop-up menu commands. The next section describes another technique that you may find useful, especially in cases where multiple GUI objects perform the same operations.

Action Objects

The `javax.swing` package provides the `Action` interface to simplify programming event handlers for multiple objects. This is a typical requirement because, in most GUI programs, menu items, toolbar buttons, and pop-up menu items typically perform the same tasks. Instead of requiring listeners for each object, or forcing you to write code to use one listener for them all, Swing provides the `Action` interface and associated `AbstractAction` class.

Using `Action` and `AbstractAction` is a little different from the event-listener techniques presented so far in this chapter and Chapter 21. For each action, first declare an object, using the `Action` interface as the data type:

```
Action openAction;
```

In essence, this states that `openAction` can refer to any object of a class that implements the `Action` interface. An anonymous class that extends `AbstractAction`, which implements `Action`, is the usual way to initialize the object. For example, to create an `Action` object and assign it to `openAction`, use code such as this:

```
openAction = new AbstractAction("Open") {
 public void actionPerformed(ActionEvent e) {
  // ... do Open command
 }
};
```

That creates an `Action` object with the text string "Open." Because `Action` extends `ActionListener`, you simply provide an `actionPerformed()` method to respond to the item's selection.

All of this may seem overly complicated until you realize that the *same* `Action` object (`openAction` in this case) may be used to create a menu item, a toolbar button, or a pop-up menu item. In that way, the identical action is easily programmed for all of these GUI elements without requiring you to write more than a single actionPerformed() method. The next section shows a complete example of the technique and also demonstrates how to add icons to toolbars and pop-up menus.

JToolBar

The final example program in this chapter demonstrates how to create a toolbar of buttons and a pop-up menu, complete with graphical icons. Listing 22-14, ToolDemo.java, also shows how to use Action objects as explained in the preceding section to simplify programming event handlers for multiple GUI objects. The sample toolbar is floatable — run the program, then click and drag the toolbar to any border, or drop it inside or outside of the program's window to detach the toolbar entirely from its parent top-level container. You can disable this feature if you want, but floating toolbars require only a single line of code, and they provide an extra level of usefulness in GUI design. Figure 22-14 shows the program's display.

Figure 22-14: ToolDemo uses Action objects to program a floating toolbar and a pop-up menu.

Listing 22-14: ToolDemo.java

```
001: import javax.swing.*;
002: import java.awt.*;
003: import java.awt.event.*;
004:
005: public class ToolDemo extends JFrame {
006:
007:   // The popup menu object
008:   protected JPopupMenu popupMenu;
009:
010:   // the toolbar object
011:   protected JToolBar toolbar;
012:
013:   // Each Action object responds to a toolbar or menu selection
014:   Action openAction;
015:   Action saveAction;
016:   Action closeAction;
017:   Action exitAction;
...
032:   // Create the Action objects, one for each command in
```

```
033:   // the toolbar and popup menu
034:   protected void createActionObjects() {
035:     ImageIcon icon;  // For loading the toolbar and menu icons
036:
037:     // Create the Open command Action handler
038:     icon = new ImageIcon("openicon.gif");
039:     openAction = new AbstractAction("Open", icon) {
040:       public void actionPerformed(ActionEvent e) {
041:         // ... do Open command
042:       }
043:     };
044:
045:     // Create the Save command Action handler
046:     icon = new ImageIcon("saveicon.gif");
047:     saveAction = new AbstractAction("Save", icon) {
048:       public void actionPerformed(ActionEvent e) {
049:         // ... do Save command
050:       }
051:     };
052:
053:     // Create the Close command Action handler
054:     icon = new ImageIcon("closeicon.gif");
055:     closeAction = new AbstractAction("Close", icon) {
056:       public void actionPerformed(ActionEvent e) {
057:         // ... do Close command
058:       }
059:     };
060:
061:     // Create the Exit command Action handler
062:     icon = new ImageIcon("exiticon.gif");
063:     exitAction = new AbstractAction("Exit", icon) {
064:       public void actionPerformed(ActionEvent e) {
065:         System.exit(0);
066:       }
067:     };
068:   }
069:
070:   // Create the popup menu and its commands
071:   // Assumes all Action objects are initialized
072:   protected void createPopupMenu() {
073:     popupMenu = new JPopupMenu();
074:     popupMenu.add(openAction);
075:     popupMenu.add(saveAction);
076:     popupMenu.add(closeAction);
077:     popupMenu.addSeparator();
```

```
078:    popupMenu.add(exitAction);
079:  }
080:
081:  // Create the toolbar
082:  // Assumes all Action objects are initialized
083:  protected void createToolbar() {
084:   toolbar = new JToolBar();
085:   toolbar.add(openAction);
086:   toolbar.add(saveAction);
087:   toolbar.add(closeAction);
088:   toolbar.addSeparator();
089:   toolbar.add(exitAction);
090:  }
091:
092:  // Constructor
093:  public ToolDemo() {
094:
095:   // Select local system look and feel
096:   // One of the following two choices produces the best
097:   // looking toolbars
098:   try {
099:    UIManager.setLookAndFeel(
100:    "com.sun.java.swing.plaf.motif.MotifLookAndFeel");
101: //    "javax.swing.plaf.metal.MetalLookAndFeel");
102:   } catch (Exception e) { }
...
111:   createActionObjects();
112:   createPopupMenu();
113:   createToolbar();
114:
115:   // Register frame listener so menu pops on the
116:   // proper mouse click depending on the look and feel
117:   addMouseListener(new PopupHandler());
118:
119:   Container content = getContentPane();
120:   // BorderLayout is required for a floating toolbar
121:   content.setLayout(new BorderLayout());
122:   content.add(toolbar, BorderLayout.NORTH);
123:   toolbar.setFloatable(true);
124:   content.add(new JLabel("Click inside the window"));
125:  }
...
133: }
```

Because the listing for ToolDemo.java is one of the longest in this chapter, I cut a few sections that were duplicated in other listings. Cuts include the inner class that brings up the pop-up menu. See Listing 22-13 (lines 019-028) for that code, or view the listing online to see the complete text.

Lines 008-017 declare the main variables used in creating the pop-up menu and toolbar. The pop-up menu is of type JPopupMenu. The toolbar is of type JToolBar. Only one set of Action objects (see lines 014-017) is needed for both. Each Action object is programmed with its own event listener as explained in the preceding section. This code makes up the bulk of the listing at lines 038-068. In addition, ImageIcon is used to load GIF files for displaying icons in the toolbar and pop-up menu.

Using Action objects greatly simplifies creating the pop-up menu and toolbar. For better clarity, these jobs are handled in separate methods. For example, createPopupMenu( ) at lines 072-079 constructs the pop-up menu:

```
protected void createPopupMenu( ) {
 popupMenu = new JPopupMenu( );
 popupMenu.add( openAction );
 . . .
}
```

To add each item to a pop-up menu, simply pass an initialized Action object as shown to an instance of JPopupMenu. The other menu items are added similarly. (Use similar code to add Action objects to a frame's pull-down menu bar.) To create the toolbar, the program calls another method:

```
protected void createToolbar( ) {
 toolbar = new JToolBar( );
 toolbar.add( openAction );
 . . .
}
```

The only difference between the two methods is that one uses a JToolBar object and the other a JPopupMenu object. The same Action objects are used in both cases. Don't add the pop-up menu to the frame's content layer—as explained in the preceding section, an inner class that implements the MouseListener interface is usually the best way to bring up a pop-up menu in response to the proper mouse click. Finally, add the toolbar to the frame's content, and you are done—almost.

For best results, use the BorderLayout class for the content layer's manager. In fact, you must use BorderLayout to create a floating toolbar. In general, follow these steps:

```
Container content = getContentPane();
content.setLayout(new BorderLayout());
content.add(toolbar, BorderLayout.NORTH);
toolbar.setFloatable(true);
```

First, obtain the frame's content pane, and specify `BorderLayout` as the layout manager. You can then add your toolbar object. Specify `NORTH` as shown to show the toolbar initially under the frame's title, or below any pull-down menu. You may use a different compass heading to change the toolbar's initial location — `SOUTH` for example. Call `setFloatable()` as shown with a `true` argument to create a floatable toolbar. Set this to `false` for a toolbar that is fixed in place, or if your frame's content layer does not use the `BorderLayout` manager.

Lines 098-102 in Listing 22-14 select the Motif look-and-feel for the sample program. Even though Chapter 21 states that selecting a specific look-and-feel is the least desirable technique, the Motif and Java (Metal) settings seem to produce the best-looking toolbars and pop-up menus on all supported platforms. Try the alternate setting, commented out in the listing, to display the Java look-and-feel, another good-looking choice. Or replace this section with the code from another example (for example, Listing 22-1, lines 011-014) to select the system's native look-and-feel. Under Windows, however, I think this produces relatively poor results with toolbar buttons and menu items that are way too large, even ugly. Might these differences have anything to do with the stormy relations between Sun and Microsoft? I'd rather not speculate.

Summary

◆ Swing provides a virtual warehouse of GUI components, too many to describe in one chapter, maybe too many for an entire book. However, to give you a flying start with Swing programming, this chapter lists numerous examples of selected Swing classes. From these examples, and with the help of Java's online documentation, you should be able to figure out how to use many other classes in the library.

◆ Simple `JButton` objects can display text labels, but you can also dress them up with graphical icons and HTML-formatting tags. Other useful button classes described in this chapter include `JToggleButton`, `JRadioButton`, and `JCheckBox`. `JRadioButton` objects are usually added to a `ButtonGroup` to ensure that selecting one button turns off the others in the group.

◆ Swing provides several standard dialog boxes that you can use to display messages and to prompt users for confirmation about dangerous operations such as throwing away changes to a document. Other dialogs discussed in this chapter include JFileChooser, used to create file-open and file-save dialogs, and the great-looking JColorChooser component for selecting display colors.

◆ JLabel displays simple text items, but most programs also need ways to input text. For single-line text entry, use JTextField or its subclass JPasswordField. To prevent security problems, after obtaining a password, be sure to overwrite the text so it doesn't hang around in memory.

◆ For multiple-line text displays and entries, use a JTextArea object. To provide vertical and horizontal scrollbars for this component, you can embed a JTextArea component in a JScrollPane.

◆ Swing offers two basic kinds of lists. Use JList to present users with a static list of selections. Use JComboBox to present drop-down lists, and to optionally provide a way for users to enter items not on the original list. Both types of lists permit single or multiple contiguous and non-contiguous selections.

◆ This chapter ends with program listings that demonstrate two special features that are becoming old standards in GUI programming, pop-up menus and toolbars. One way to simplify programming responses to items in these popular elements is to create Action objects as explained in this chapter. Pop-up menus can be non-floating or floating, but floating toolbars require the parent container to use the BorderLayout manager.

Chapter 23

Graphics Techniques

MANY GUI APPLETS AND APPLICATIONS are programmed entirely using Java components and icons loaded from files. However, at some point, those and other objects must draw their graphical images and update themselves so as to maintain the illusion of a desktop full of overlapping windows. To do that, the objects use Java's graphics capabilities. Of course, the computer's display is merely a two-dimensional array of pixels. GUI objects and windows don't really overlap — it's all just an elaborately visual magic show.

Using Java's graphics classes, you can create your own magic and draw anything you want in an application or applet window. Numerous example programs in this chapter demonstrate primitive drawing methods, colors, and image handling. You also learn how to animate a series of images using threaded code for a smooth-running result that can peacefully coexist with other processes.

IN THIS CHAPTER

- ◆ Programming with `paint()`
- ◆ Adding color
- ◆ Displaying text with fonts
- ◆ Showing images
- ◆ Creating offscreen and filtered images
- ◆ Animating images using threads

Graphics Fundamentals

The extensive `Graphics` class brings a wide range of system-independent graphics capabilities to applets and applications. The newer `Graphics2D` class extends `Graphics` to provide improved geometrical methods, coordinate transformations, colors, and text features.

You never create objects of these abstract classes. Instead, you most often use a `Graphics` object passed to a `paint()` method. Thus the easy way to display graphics is simply to override `paint()` and add the statements you need. Just about every GUI object and top-level window inherit `paint()` from the `Container` class. This is true even for buttons, but in most cases, you'll override `paint()` in a class that extends `JFrame`, `JApplet`, or `JDialog`. Following are some examples of how to write a `paint()` method.

Programming with paint()

A sample application shows the most common way to use the `Graphics` class to paint graphics in a window. Figure 23-1 shows the program's display, consisting of a grid on a yellow background, with a shaded blue rounded rectangle and this book's title, *Java 2 Just Click! Solutions.* These elements demonstrate the basic graphics techniques of painting background colors, drawing lines, filling shapes, and showing text. Listing 23-1, GraphicsApp.java, shows the program's source code.

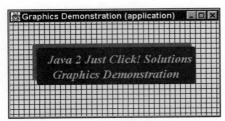

Figure 23-1: GraphicsApp shows how to draw various shapes, lines, and text in an applet's window.

Listing 23-1: GraphicsApp.java

```
001: import javax.swing.*;
002: import java.awt.*;
003: import java.awt.event.*;
004:
005: public class GraphicsApp extends JFrame {
006:
007: // Constructor
008:  public GraphicsApp() {
009:   // Select local system look and feel
010:   try {
011:    UIManager.setLookAndFeel(
012:     UIManager.getCrossPlatformLookAndFeelClassName());
013:   } catch (Exception e) { }
014:   // End program when window closes
015:   addWindowListener(new WindowAdapter() {
016:    public void windowClosing(WindowEvent e) {
017:     System.exit(0);
018:    }
019:   });
020:  }
021:
```

```
022:  public void paint(Graphics g) {
023:    // Get window size
024:    Rectangle r = getBounds(null);
025:    // Paint background yellow
026:    g.setColor(Color.yellow);
027:    g.fillRect(0, 0, r.width, r.height);
028:    // Outline window in black
029:    g.setColor(Color.black);
030:    g.drawRect(0, 0, r.width, r.height);
031:    // Draw grid inside window
032:    for (int h = 0; h < r.height; h += 10)
033:      g.drawLine(0, h, r.width, h);
034:    for (int v = 0; v < r.width; v += 10)
035:      g.drawLine(v, 0, v, r.height);
036:    // Draw overlapping round rectangles
037:    int cx = r.width / 8;
038:    int cy = r.height / 3;
039:    int w = (r.width / 4) * 3;
040:    int h = cy;
041:    g.setColor(Color.gray);
042:    g.fillRoundRect(cx - 4, cy - 4, w, h, 10, 10);
043:    g.setColor(Color.blue);
044:    g.fillRoundRect(cx + 4, cy + 4, w, h, 10, 10);
045:    // Draw text inside outer rectangle
046:    Font f = new Font("TimesRoman",
047:      Font.BOLD + Font.ITALIC, 24);
048:    g.setFont(f);
049:    g.setColor(Color.orange);
050:    g.drawString("Java 2 Just Click! Solutions", cx + 25, cy +
          36);
051:    g.drawString("Graphics Demonstration", cx + 35, cy + 66);
052:  }
053:
054:  public static void main(String[] args) {
055:    GraphicsApp app = new GraphicsApp();
056:    app.setTitle("Graphics Demonstration (application)");
057:    app.setSize(450, 280);
058:    app.show();
059:  }
060: }
```

You can use similar programming to create graphics in applets, either in a class descended from the java.awt.Applet class, or the newer (and recommended) Swing class, javax.swing.JApplet. To show as many different approaches as possible, this chapter's examples include a mix of applets and applications using the AWT and Swing component libraries.

GraphicsApp consists of a large `paint()` method that draws the program's shapes. The `paint()` method is declared in the `Container` class as

```
public void paint(Graphics g) {
...
}
```

The `Graphics` object g, often called the *graphics context,* is actually an object of a subclass provided by the browser or the Java virtual runtime system. This subclass is tailored to the system so that you can simply draw shapes without having to deal with low-level issues such as how many colors are supported and the display's resolution.

The `paint()` method is called whenever the display needs updating. For example, if the user opens or moves another window that obscures the applet, when the user returns to the browser, `paint()` is called to re-create the display. For this reason, your code must always be prepared to draw its graphics as many times as necessary. This might mean storing coordinates and other values that can be used to recreate shapes on demand.

GraphicsApp's `paint()` method begins with a statement that you will find handy in your own graphical escapades. To find the boundaries of the current window, the method executes the statement

```
Rectangle r = getBounds(null);
```

This creates and sets a `Rectangle` object, r, to the height and width of the object (the window in this case) — information that is highly useful in restricting drawing to within that region. Pass `null` to `getBounds()` to create a new instance of the `Rectangle` class. Or, if you already have a `Rectangle` object, you can pass it to `getBounds()` as follows:

```
Rectangle r = new Rectangle();
...
r = getBounds(r);
```

Doing that prevents needlessly creating a new `Rectangle` object for every call to `getBounds()`. This technique replaces the JDK 1.0 `bounds()` method, now deprecated. Use the preceding code in place of the following, which you may find in numerous published sources and listings:

```
Rectangle r = bounds();   // ??? deprecated
```

The sample program uses the `Rectangle` object obtained from `getBounds()` to position graphics relative to the window. (Try resizing the window to see how this works — the graphics always attempt to fill the window completely.) For example, to paint the window's background yellow, the program executes these statements:

```
g.setColor(Color.yellow);
g.fillRect(0, 0, r.width, r.height);
```

Notice that each statement calls a `Graphic`'s class method in reference to the `g` object received by `paint()`. The first statement sets the drawing color to `yellow`, specifying that constant in reference to the `Color` class, which I'll explain in the next section, "Using Color."

Calling `fillRect()` paints a rectangular area in the current color. The coordinate values passed to `fillRect()` use the information returned by `bounds()` to paint the applet's entire background. To outline that same region in black, the program executes these statements:

```
g.setColor(Color.black);
g.drawRect(0, 0, r.width, r.height);
```

TIP   `Graphics` class methods with "draw" in their names draw outline shapes; those with "fill" in their names draw filled shapes.

Using two `for` statements, the program next draws a grid in the current color (black) on top of the yellow background (see lines 032-035). To draw the lines of the grid, the two statements call the `drawLine()` method, which simply connects two points with a solid line in the current drawing color.

After calculating some integer variables, GraphicsApp draws two rounded rectangles by calling the `fillRoundRect()` method. The program then creates and selects a font with the following statements:

```
Font f = new Font("TimesRoman",
 Font.BOLD + Font.ITALIC, 24);
g.setFont(f);
```

The specified font is used to draw the text you see inside the outer blue rectangle. The following statements display the text at the indicated coordinates, a technique that is adequate for this program, but not as exacting as needed in many cases:

```
g.drawString("Java 2 Just Click! Solutions", cx + 25, cy + 36);
g.drawString("Graphics Demonstration", cx + 35, cy + 66);
```

NOTE   For more information on drawing text and using fonts, see "The `Font` Class" in this chapter.

Using Color

The Color class provides versatile methods and static declarations for specifying color values. In many cases, you can use this class simply by referring to one of several constant values such as Color.white and Color.red. These constants are objects of the Color class, and they can be used wherever a Color object is required. For example, in a paint() method, set the current drawing or fill color using a statement such as

```
g.setColor(Color.green);
```

Or, construct a Color object and pass it to setColor() using statements like these:

```
Color c = new Color(255, 0, 128);
g.setColor(c);
```

If you don't want to keep the Color object, create a temporary one as the method argument, and pass it directly to setColor():

```
g.setColor(new Color(0, 0, 64));
```

Any drawing, filling, or text method uses the selected color until you choose another. In some cases, it is useful to preserve the current drawing color. Do that by calling getColor()as follows:

```
Color saveColor = g.getColor();
g.setColor(Color.red);
// ... insert drawing statements here
g.setColor(saveColor);  // Restore original color
```

Internally, Color class objects store color values in a single 32-bit private integer. This integer stores individual red, green, and blue color intensities as byte values ranging from 0 to 255. To construct the Color.pink constant, for example, the Color class executes the statement

```
public final static Color pink = new Color(255, 175, 175);
```

That gives the pink object a full blob of red, with approximately two-thirds portions each of green and blue. You can similarly construct your own Color objects, and then call various methods for them. Listing 23-2, Gradient.java, uses this technique to display graduated color bands from lighter to darker shades. Figure 23-2 shows the program's display.

Figure 23-2: The Gradient program displays
bands of color from lighter to darker shades.

Listing 23-2: Gradient.java

```
001: import javax.swing.*;
002: import java.awt.*;
003: import java.awt.event.*;
004:
005: public class Gradient extends JFrame {
006:
007: // Constructor
008:   public Gradient() {
...
020:   }
021:
022:   public void paint(Graphics g) {
023:     int increment = 40;
024:     Rectangle r = getBounds(null);
025:     Color c = new Color(50, 255, 50);
026:     int x = 0;
027:     while (x < r.width) {
028:       g.setColor(c);
029:       g.fillRect(x, 0, x + increment, r.height);
030:       c = c.darker();
031:       x += increment;
032:     }
033:   }
034:
035:   public static void main(String[] args) {
...
041: }
```

As with many of this book's longer listings, I cut out lines that are mostly
duplicated from previous examples. Use this book's *Just Click!* indexes to
view the full listings on screen.

The sample program constructs a Color object as a shade of green using this statement:

```
Color c = new Color(50, 255, 50);
```

Alternatively, you can create Color objects with a single integer value, most conveniently expressed in hexadecimal. For example, the statement

```
Color c = new Color(0x00112233);
```

creates a Color object with red, green, and blue component values of 0x11, 0x22, and 0x33 respectively. The most significant byte, set to 0x00 here, is ignored.

You can also specify floating point red, green, and blue color values. Each value must be greater or equal to zero and less than 1.0. For example, the following statement constructs a color value with floating point arguments:

```
Color c = new Color(1.0f, 0.75f, 0.75f);
```

Each argument value represents a desired fraction of 255, the maximum color integer component value. In other words, the floating point argument 0.75f is equivalent to an integer component value of 191.

 Floating point constants passed to the Color constructor must be followed by the letter f to indicate that they are of type float.

The Gradient program calls the Color class's darker() method to create a color slightly darker than the current one. Because this method returns a new Color object, you'll normally assign its result to the same object for which you call the method:

```
c = c.darker();
```

Similarly call brighter() for a color slightly brighter than the current one. Again, this method returns a Color object that you'll need to assign to a variable. If you don't do this, nothing will seem to happen. For example, calling either method in the following way merely throws away the method results and produces no effects on the Color object c:

```
c.darker();    // ???
c.brighter();  // ???
```

To obtain a `Color` object's red, green, or blue component values, call methods `getRed()`, `getGreen()`, or `getBlue()`. You can also obtain a single integer representation of a `Color` object by calling `getRGB()`. This assigns to `colorInt` the 32-bit integer representation of the `Color` constant, `magenta`:

```
int colorInt = Color.magenta.getRGB();
```

The Polygon Class

The `Graphics` class provides four ways to draw outlined and filled polygons, defined as a set of coordinate points. Polygons are useful for drawing wire-frame graphics and for other complex figures. Two of the polygon methods accept integer arrays of coordinate values. These methods are defined as

```
void drawPolyline(int xPoints[], int yPoints[], int nPoints);
void fillPolygon(int xPoints[], int yPoints[], int nPoints);
```

Call `drawPolyline()` for an outlined shape; call `fillPolygon()` for one filled with the current color. Pass two arrays of integer values, representing the x and y coordinates of each polygon point. The third argument indicates the number of points in the array. More convenient are the two overloaded `Graphics` methods — named `drawPolygon()` and `fillPolygon()` — which take as arguments an object of the `Polygon` class. These methods are defined as

```
void drawPolygon(Polygon p);
void fillPolygon(Polygon p);
```

To use the class, construct a `Polygon` object using code such as

```
Polygon p = new Polygon();
```

Or, if you have arrays of integer coordinates, construct the object with this statement:

```
Polygon p = new Polygon(xints, yints, numElements);
```

To add a new point to the object, call the `addPoint()` method. For example, the following code fragment creates a triangular `Polygon` object:

```
Polygon p = new Polygon();
p.addPoint(50, 0);
p.addPoint(75, 50);
p.addPoint(25, 50);
p.addPoint(50, 0);
```

Display the resulting polygon, in a `paint()` method using statements such as these:

```
g.setColor(Color.blue);
g.drawPolygon(p);
g.setColor(Color.white);
g.fillPolygon(p);
```

Two additional methods are handy for working with `Polygon` objects. Call `getBounds()` as follows for a `Rectangle` object that outlines the polygon's points:

```
Rectangle r = p.getBounds();
g.drawRect(r.x, r.y, r.width, r.height);
```

The `getBounds()` method replaces the now deprecated `getBoundingBox()`, but this seems to be a name change only. The sample code outlines the polygon with a rectangle. Notice the order of the `Rectangle` object's parameters passed to `drawRect()`. The width is specified before the height.

The Font Class

For programming graphical text, Java provides two classes — `Font` and `FontMetrics`. The classes are typically used together to create a font and to obtain spacing information for that font's characters. By *font*, I mean not only its family — Helvetica or Times Roman, for example — but also its size and style. The `FontMetrics` class provides additional information useful for precise positioning of text.

Listing 23-3, `FontDemo.java`, displays a list of all available fonts in a `JComboBox` component. Run the program and select any font to see a sample of it in a separate window. Figure 23-3 shows a sample of the program's two windows.

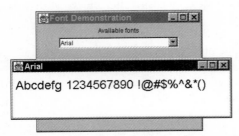

Figure 23-3: FontDemo displays available font names; select one for a sample.

Listing 23-3: FontDemo.java

```
001: import javax.swing.*;
002: import javax.swing.event.*;
003: import java.awt.*;
004: import java.awt.event.*;
005:
006: // Window frame class for showing selected font sample
007: class FontSample extends JFrame {
008:  Font font;     // Currently shown font
009:  String text;   // Sample text to display
010:
011:  // Constructor
012:  public FontSample() {
013:   super();
014:   font = null;
015:   text = "Abcdefg 1234567890 !@#$%^&*()";
016:   setDefaultCloseOperation(JFrame.HIDE_ON_CLOSE);
017:   setSize(425, 120);
018:  }
019:
020:  // Called before showing window
021:  public void changeFont(Font f) {
022:   font = f.deriveFont(24.0f);   // Resize to 24 pts
023:   setTitle(font.getFontName()); // Title = font name
024:   if (isShowing()) repaint();   // Repaint if already visible
025:  }
026:
027:  // Paint sample text using current font in window
028:  public void paint(Graphics g) {
029:   Rectangle r = getBounds(null);
030:   g.setColor(Color.white);  // Erase background to white
031:   g.fillRect(0, 0, r.width, r.height);
032:   if (font != null) {
033:    g.setFont(font);
034:    g.setColor(Color.black);
035:    g.drawString(text, 10, r.height / 2);
036:   }
037:  }
038: }
039:
040: // Main program class
041: public class FontDemo extends JFrame {
042:  final protected Font[] fonts;          // Array of fonts
043:  final protected FontSample fontSample; // Sample window
044:
045: // Constructor
```

```
046:  public FontDemo() {
...
060:    // Create child sample font window
061:    fontSample = new FontSample();
062:
063:    // Loading fonts may take a while; tell user
064:    System.out.print("Loading font names...");
065:
066:    // Get available fonts in 1pt sizes
067:    GraphicsEnvironment ge =
068:     GraphicsEnvironment.getLocalGraphicsEnvironment();
069:    fonts = ge.getAllFonts();
070:
071:    // Create a JComboBox object for listing font names
072:    JComboBox fontBox = new JComboBox();
073:    for (int i = 0; i < fonts.length; i++)
074:     fontBox.addItem(fonts[i].getFontName());
075:    fontBox.setEditable(false);
076:
077:    // Respond to item selection
078:    fontBox.addActionListener(
079:     new ActionListener() {
080:      public void actionPerformed(ActionEvent e) {
081:       JComboBox box = (JComboBox)e.getSource();
082:       int fontIndex = box.getSelectedIndex();
083:       fontSample.changeFont(fonts[fontIndex]);
084:       fontSample.show();
085:      }
086:     }
087:    );
...
102: }
```

Use the GraphicsEnvironment class as shown at lines 067-069 to obtain an array of Font objects, each one set to a size of one point. This list may take a few seconds or longer to prepare, so you might also display a message that tells users to wait for the operation to finish. After getAllFonts() returns, use any of the Font objects to display text, or to set the font for a JLabel or other component that displays text. Here, the program adds all font names to a JComboBox component from which the user can select a font name and display sample text in a child window.

In typesetting, one *point* equals a space of $1/72$ inch. However, due to imperfections in a display's pixels, this measurement may not be perfectly accurate on screen.

The sample program's `JFrame` class, `FontSample`, at lines 007-038, handles most of the program's details. The class creates the child window that displays a text sample using the selected font. The window stays visible unless the user closes it, and it is automatically closed along with its parent window. To keep the window object alive in memory even if closed, the class constructor executes the statement:

```
setDefaultCloseOperation(JFrame.HIDE_ON_CLOSE);
```

You may do the same for any `JFrame` object. Other default-close options you can specify to that method are

```
DO_NOTHING_ON_CLOSE
DISPOSE_ON_CLOSE
EXIT_ON_CLOSE
```

The child window, `FontSample`, implements a `paint()` method to display sample text using the current font. Three statements are typically required:

```
g.setFont(font);
g.setColor(Color.black);
g.drawString(text, 10, r.height / 2);
```

First, set the font into the graphic's context passed to `paint()`. Also set the color you want to use. Be sure to do this every time because the drawing color might have been changed to the background color, in which case nothing will appear. Finally, call `drawString()` to display the text at an X,Y coordinate.

Although the preceding code works just fine, in practice more precise positioning of graphically drawn text is necessary, especially in cases where the text uses a mix of fonts, sizes, and styles. For that, you can use the `FontMetrics` class, discussed next.

Listing Fonts with the `Toolkit` Class

The FontDemo program in this section shows the correct way to find all available fonts on the system using the `GraphicsEnvironment` class. Formerly, there was only one other way to do this job, but many Java books and documents, as well as many source code files, still show the older technique. This requires using the `java.awt` package's `Toolkit` class, which serves as a kind of glue between the AWT and the native tools that provide actual GUI elements.

Because Swing components use no native code, `Toolkit` is not needed in programs that use the newer component library. Also, `Toolkit` is not intended for application use — for example, even though its `createCheckBox()` method creates a native check box component, Java programs should instead instantiate an AWT or Swing class to create that and all other GUI objects.

However, you may use `Toolkit` in applets and applications to list available font names. Do that with code such as

Continued

Listing Fonts with the Toolkit **Class** *(Continued)*

```
String[] fontNames;
Toolkit tools = Toolkit.getDefaultToolkit();
fontNames = tools.getFontList();
```

Although this technique works, it is better to use the GraphicsEnvironment class as demonstrated in this chapter to obtain a list of available fonts. By the way, the Toolkit class can also load GIF and JPEG image files, although this use of the class is now also superseded by the Swing library's ImageIcon class. See "Images" later in this chapter for more information on this use of Toolkit.

The FontMetrics Class

The FontMetrics class, a member of the java.awt package, provides information about a particular font's rendering. This gives you precise information that you can use to position text precisely in a component or window. FontMetrics is an abstract class that is never directly instantiated. Instead, call a method such as getFontMetrics() in the Graphics class as shown in this section to obtain a FontMetrics object. That object is actually of a class that extends FontMetrics according to the current system. Obviously, fonts differ greatly across the platforms that Java supports, and information about a particular font rendering is available only at runtime.

Using FontMetrics isn't difficult, but it requires a good understanding of a few terms from the world of professional typesetting. These terms — *baseline, leading, ascent, descent, height,* and *advance* — represent specific elements in the spacing of characters on lines of text. (By the way, *leading* is pronounced like *sledding,* not *bleeding.* A reference to the olden days of hot-lead typesetting, leading equals the amount of space above the tallest character in a font.)

Figure 23-4 shows how the various typesetting terms apply to the spacing of text. The *Reference point* is the location of the coordinate values passed to a method such as Graphics.drawString(). This location is on the baseline at the beginning of the first character in the string. The other values are relative to the reference point.

To use the FontMetrics class, first assign a Font object by calling the Graphics method setFont(). Usually, you'll do this in a paint() method, but if you want to prepare text-positioning variables elsewhere, you can obtain a Graphics context object by calling getGraphics():

```
Graphics g = getGraphics();
```

Next, create a Font object, and assign it to the Graphics context:

```
Font f = new Font("Helvetica", Font.PLAIN, 14);
g.setFont(f);
```

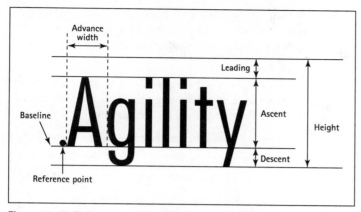

Figure 23-4: Typesetting terms exactly describe the spacing of text using a specific font.

You may skip those two steps if you want to use the default font, or if one has already been set into the Graphics object by other means. Finally, obtain a FontMetrics object for the selected font by calling getFontMetrics() in reference to the Graphics context object:

```
FontMetrics fm = g.getFontMetrics();
```

This gives you extensive information in one handy package that you can use to position text with precision. Remember that this information is accurate for only the current font. If you set a different font into the Graphics context object, you must again call getFontMetrics(). To inspect the Font referenced by a FontMetrics object, call the getFont() method. You might do that to save the current Font object using this statement:

```
Font saveFont = fm.getFont();  // Save font referenced by fm
```

The FontMetrics class provides several methods that are most commonly used to get spacing information for a specific font rendering (refer back to Figure 23-4). These methods are as follows:

- ◆ int getLeading() — Returns the standard leading, also called the *interline spacing*. Use this value to reserve space *below* the descent of a preceding line. This is not necessarily the maximum leading for all characters in the font.

- ◆ int getAscent() — Returns the standard ascent of most characters in the font, equal to the space from the average tallest character to the baseline. This is not necessarily the maximum ascent for all characters in the font.

- `int getDescent()` — Returns the standard descent of most characters in the font, equal to the space below the baseline that characters such as *g* and *y* dangle their tails. Some characters may extend beyond the space indicated by this method.

- `int getHeight()` — Returns the standard height of most characters in the font, equal to the sum of the standard leading, ascent, and descent values. Some characters may be taller than indicated by this method.

- `int getMaxAscent()` — Returns the maximum ascent of any character in the font.

- `int getMaxDescent()` — Returns the maximum descent of any character in the font.

- `int getMaxAdvance()` — Returns the maximum advance width of any character in the font, equal to the character's width plus space to the right, up to the beginning of the next character. If this value is not known, `getMaxAdvance()` returns –1.

The JDK 1.0 incorrectly spelled `getMaxDescent()` as `getMaxDecent()`, which is now deprecated. The misspelled method is still available in `FontMetrics` for backwards compatibility with older programs. Of course, you should now use the correctly spelled method.

The first four of the preceding methods return standard information that, in most cases, is probably all you need for positioning text accurately. If you use these standard values, however, some text might not be exactly spaced — a character's descent might extend a bit too low and touch another character on a line below. The other three methods return maximum values that are guaranteed not to be violated, but might produce too widely spaced text for most characters. In most cases, it is safe to use the standard values and risk an occasional spacing problem.

Six other methods in `FontMetrics` provide additional information about the width of specific characters and strings. (Refer again to Figure 23-4.) These methods are

- `int charWidth(int ch)` — Returns the advance width of the specified character code value.

- `int charWidth(char ch)` — Returns the advance width of the specified character.

- `int stringWidth(String str)` — Returns the sum of the advance widths of all characters in the specified `String` object.

- ◆ `int charsWidth(char data[], int off, int len)` — Returns the sum of the advance widths of `len` characters in the `char` array, starting with the character at `data[off]`.

- ◆ `int bytesWidth(byte data[], int off, int len)` — Returns the sum of the advance widths of `len` characters in the `byte` array (presumably holding ASCII character data), starting with the character at `data[off]`.

- ◆ `int[] getWidths()` — Returns an array of integer values equal to the advance widths of the first 256 characters in the selected font.

Images

There are two fundamental ways to load and display bit-mapped images. One technique is relatively difficult to master but works with all versions of Java 2 as early as the JDK 1.1. The second technique uses the new Swing library's `ImageIcon` class. Because not everyone is ready to move up to Swing, the following sections explain how to use the `Image` and `MediaTracker` classes to load and display GIF and JPEG image files. Only `ImageIcon` supports the newer PNG graphics file format. See "ImageIcon" later in this chapter for a discussion of the newer Swing image techniques.

Image Display methods

Although the `Graphics` class provides several overloaded `drawImage()` methods for displaying image files, and the `Applet` and `Toolkit` classes provide overloaded `getImage()` methods for loading image data, using these methods correctly takes careful programming. Loading image data — especially over the Internet using a slow dialup connection — is a time-consuming chore that must not be allowed to interfere with other processes. This is especially important when animating multiple images and when displaying large pictures. While an image is loading and forming onscreen, users expect to be able to read other text and to interact with other components. This means that calls to `getImage()` and `drawImage()` must be in one or more separate threads that run concurrently with other processes.

The following sections explain how to program applets to display static images, and also how to create animations that display multiple image files. In both cases, threaded code handles the loading and displaying of image data to ensure a smoothly running result.

The Image Class

The `java.awt` package provides the `Image` class as an object-oriented abstraction of a bit-mapped image. Using this class requires understanding four categories of images as follows:

- ◆ *Images:* These objects represent the actual image data, rendered in memory according to the requirements of the local operating system.

◆ *Image observers:* These are objects that monitor image loading and display images when they are ready. Technically, an image observer is an object of any class that implements the ImageObserver interface. The ImageObserver interface requires a method, imageUpdate(), that is called when an image, or a portion of an image, is ready for display.

◆ *Image producers:* These are objects that provide a source for image data. Think of them as conduits through which image data flows.

◆ *Image consumers:* These are objects that provide for the use or display of image data. A component such as a button that displays an image is a good example of an image consumer. Because the Applet class lists Component among its ancestors, applets can also be image consumers. The same is true for the newer Swing JApplet class.

You do not construct Image objects as you do others, even though the class has a default constructor. Instead, to construct an Image object, you commonly use one of the following two techniques:

◆ In an applet, call Applet.getImage() to load an image file. In an application, call Toolkit.getImage(). You may do the same for the Swing JApplet class, which inherits getImage() from Applet, but as mentioned, if you are programming with Swing, you may want to use the ImageIcon class to load images.

◆ Call Component.createImage() to prepare a new image, usually for creating an offscreen drawing surface.

This section focuses on the first technique — loading and displaying image files. "Offscreen Images" later in this chapter shows how to use the second technique to prepare and use offscreen Image objects.

It's important to realize that an object of the Image class is not simply a collection of graphics bits in memory. In fact, there is no defined way to access an image's actual bitmap data. An Image object is an abstraction of that data — a mere interface to the real visual image, the nature of which is necessarily system-dependent. On disk, a GIF or JPEG file is essentially a set of instructions for creating this data. In memory, the format of the image depends entirely on the operating system and hardware. In memory, a bitmap is a *rendered* image that can be shown on the system's display.

The more commonly used Image class's public methods are

◆ int getWidth(ImageObserver observer) — Returns the width of the image in pixels, or if the image is still loading and the width is therefore unknown as dictated by the ImageObserver parameter, the method returns −1.

- `int getHeight(ImageObserver observer)` — Returns the height of the image in pixels, or if the image is still loading and the height is therefore unknown as dictated by the `ImageObserver` parameter, the method returns –1.

- `ImageProducer getSource()` — Returns the producer, or in other words, the source of the image. The method is used most often with filtered images — for example, those that are cropped to a portion of a full image bitmap. (See "Filtered Images" in this chapter.)

- `Graphics getGraphics()` — Returns a `Graphics` context object for drawing to offscreen images. (See "Offscreen Images" in this chapter.)

- `Object getProperty(String name, ImageObserver observer)` — Returns a property defined for the image and labeled according to the `String` name. A commonly available property is `"comment"`, which identifies the image's author or other source. If the property is not available, or if the image is still loading as dictated by the `ImageObserver` parameter, this method returns `UndefinedProperty`, an object of the `Object` class, defined as a public member of the `Image` class.

- `void flush()` — Flushes any image-related system resources such as an in-memory cache. Calling this method resets the image to its just-loaded or just-created state. Subsequent uses of the image require reloading or reforming the image from its source.

Using the `Image` class properly requires the help of another class, `MediaTracker`, explained a bit later. As the next sample program demonstrates, `MediaTracker` simplifies the threaded aspects of loading and displaying image files, which as mentioned, must not interfere with the program's and browser's other processes. This is especially so in applets, because many users probably have slow dialup Internet connections. For that reason, the following image-display examples are programmed as applets. However, the same techniques work in stand-alone applications.

Listing 23-4, ShowPic.java, displays a JPEG image file. The same program can also display GIF files. To run the program, load the ShowPic.html file into your Web browser or the appletviewer utility. Figure 23-5 shows the program's display. The photograph shows the Space Shuttle Atlantis blasting off pad 39A early evening, February 7, 2001. (Picture source: NASA, http://spaceflight.nasa.gov/gallery/.)

Figure 23–5: ShowPic demonstrates how to load a graphics image using threaded code.

Listing 23–4: ShowPic.java

```
001: import java.applet.*;
002: import java.awt.*;
003:
004: public class ShowPic extends Applet
005:   implements Runnable {
006:
007:   // Instance variables
008:   Image pic;               // GIF image producer
009:   int picID;               // Arbitrary image ID
010:   MediaTracker tracker;    // Tracks loading of image
011:   Thread loadingThread;    // Thread for loading image
012:   String filename = "ksc-01pp-0287.jpg";   // Filename
013:
014:   // Initialize applet
015:   public void init() {
016:     // Create MediaTracker object
017:     tracker = new MediaTracker(this);
018:     // Start image loading
019:     pic = getImage(getDocumentBase(), filename);
020:     picID = 0;
021:     tracker.addImage(pic, picID);
022:     // Create thread to monitor image loading
023:     loadingThread = new Thread(this);
```

```
024:    loadingThread.start();
025:  }
026:
027:  // Run loading thread
028:  // Allows other processes to run while loading
029:  // the image data
030:  public void run() {
031:    try {
032:      tracker.waitForID(picID);
033:    } catch (InterruptedException ie) {
034:      return;
035:    }
036:    repaint();  // Cause paint() to draw loaded image
037:  }
038:
039:  // Paint window contents
040:  // Displays loading or error message until
041:  // image is ready, then shows image
042:  public void paint(Graphics g) {
043:    if (tracker.isErrorID(picID))
044:      g.drawString("Error loading " + filename, 10, 20);
045:    else if (tracker.checkID(picID))
046:      g.drawImage(pic, 0, 0, this);
047:    else
048:      g.drawString("Loading " + filename, 10, 20);
049:  }
050: }
```

You might see far simpler image-display programs in various Java tutorials, but as mentioned, doing this job correctly in a threaded environment requires more care than might be obvious. The first step is to make the Applet subclass capable of executing a threaded run() method. Be sure to add implements Runnable to the class declaration as shown here (see lines 004-005). You can do the same with Swing's JApplet class—I used Applet in this example, but the techniques are the same for AWT and Swing programming.

The applet class needs several variables for loading and displaying the image. In the sample program, these variables are declared as

```
Image pic;
int picID;
MediaTracker tracker;
Thread loadingThread;
String filename = "ksc-01pp-0287.jpg";
```

The Image pic object represents the image data and serves as a conduit for its importation from a source into memory. The integer picID is optional, but it can be used to numerically identify multiple images. The ID numbers are up to the program to assign and do not come from the images themselves. A MediaTracker object, named tracker here, operates as a kind of director that monitors image loading and allows the program to do other tasks until the image is ready for display. The single MediaTracker object can monitor the loading of an unlimited number of images, and it helps keep the program running fast while simplifying error detection. The Thread object, loadingThread, cooperates with MediaTracker to load and display one or more images concurrently with other processes. Finally, a String object represents the image's filename or URL.

The sample applet's init() method prepares the class's variables for use. After sizing the applet's window, the program creates a MediaTracker object with the statement

```
tracker = new MediaTracker(this);
```

Passing this to the MediaTracker constructor tells the object which component, or Applet subclass object, displays the images. This argument can be any object of a class extended from Component. For example, a custom component could use a MediaTracker object as shown here to load a bitmap.

The next step loads the actual image. This uses a sequence of steps that might appear a little odd:

```
pic = getImage(getDocumentBase(), filename);
picID = 0;
tracker.addImage(pic, picID);
```

Despite the method's name, getImage() does not actually load the specified image file, optionally referenced by a document base URL. Calling getImage() merely starts the process by which the image is eventually loaded, and the method returns immediately. As shown here, you can save the returned Image object in a variable (named pic, in this case) and prepare an optional ID value if needed. The final statement adds the Image object and its ID to the MediaTracker object, which monitors the image's loading in a separate thread. The program continues immediately after the call to addImage(). None of these steps actually loads any image data from disk. That happens a bit later.

By interrogating the MediaTracker object, the program can determine when an image is available for use. To allow other processes to run concurrently, it's best to call MediaTracker methods in a separate thread. The sample program's init() method starts this process by executing the statements:

```
loadingThread = new Thread(this);
loadingThread.start();
```

The first statement creates the Thread object. The second statement causes the applet's or application's run() method to be called. Meanwhile, the MediaTracker object may still be loading images. To detect when an image is ready, run() calls

MediaTracker.waitForID(), passing the image's ID value assigned by init().
This is done in a try block that catches InterruptedException, thrown if another
thread interrupts this one:

```
try {
 tracker.waitForID(picID);
} catch (InterruptedException ie) {
 return;
}
```

When the program calls waitForID(), the image begins to load into memory
from disk or over the network. Because this code is executed in a separate thread,
other processes can interrupt this one, in which case run() immediately returns.
This might happen, for example, if the user leaves the applet. When waitForID()
returns normally, run() forces a display update by executing

```
repaint();
```

Doing that eventually calls paint() to display the image and any other graphics. However, even though waitForID() returns normally, the image still might not
be ready for display. For example, its file might be missing, or a glitch might have
caused the download to fail. To detect such problems, paint() again interrogates
the MediaTracker object using this if statement:

```
if (tracker.isErrorID(picID))
 g.drawString("Error loading " + filename, 10, 20);
```

If isErrorID() returns false, an error occurred and the image cannot be displayed. To see the effect of this code, make an intentional error in the image's
filename string, and reload the applet.
    Even if no errors are detected, and despite all the preceding code, it's important
to keep in mind that image-loading is taking place in a separate thread—thus, you
still have to verify that the image is ready for display. Do this by calling a
MediaTracker method such as checkID(), which returns true only if the specified
image (or other data) is completely loaded and ready for use. The sample program
does this by following the preceding code with

```
else if (tracker.checkID(picID))
 g.drawImage(pic, 0, 0, this);
```

Only if checkID() returns true does paint() call the drawImage() method in
reference to the Graphics context object passed to paint(). The arguments passed
to drawImage() identify the Image, its relative display coordinates, and this as the
ImageObserver object responsible for the rendered image's display.
    Finally, if no errors occur, but the image is still not ready for display, paint()
shows a message stating that the image is loading:

```
else
 g.drawString("Loading " + filename, 10, 20);
```

When running the sample applet locally, you will have only a brief moment to see this message. Over a slow dialup connection to a Web site, however, this message tells users what's going on while they wait for a large image to download.

The MediaTracker Class

The sample ShowPic applet in the preceding section uses the MediaTracker class to manage the loading of image data. Although the class may seem complex, it is not difficult to use, and most methods have obvious purposes. This section explains more about how to use the class.

A MediaTracker object may be created for any Component but is often associated with an applet's object or an application's top-level frame. For example, the ShowPic applet in this chapter creates a MediaTracker object using this statement in method init():

```
tracker = new MediaTracker(this);
```

To add an Image object to this MediaTracker, call addImage():

```
tracker.addImage(pic, picID);
```

This assumes that the Image (pic here) has been constructed by some other means. The ID is useful when working with multiple images, all of which may be managed by the same MediaTracker.

After adding an image to a MediaTracker, call the class's methods to determine the image's status. There are numerous ways to proceed. For example, you can receive a status integer by calling statusID():

```
int status = tracker.statusID(picID, true);
```

This assigns to status the bitwise OR of the appropriate MediaTracker flags: ABORTED, COMPLETE, ERRORED, and LOADING. The true argument passed to statusID() tells MediaTracker to begin loading the specified image if it hasn't already done so. You might try this code, perhaps in a small loop or, better, in a thread, to retry loading in the event of an error.

Some MediaTracker methods check that all images are available. This is especially useful in animation programming when you don't want to begin displaying a sequence of images until they are all ready. Code such as the following example calls a method only if MediaTracker confirms that all images assigned by addImage() are ready for use:

```
if (tracker.checkAll(true))
 showPictures();
```

The `true` argument, which is optional, tells `MediaTracker` to begin loading the images if it hasn't already done so.

Inside an image thread, call a method such as `waitForAll()` to allow `MediaTracker` to continue loading image data without blocking other threads. This will usually be in a `run()` method, using a `try` statement to catch a thread interruption. For example, the following code gives the `MediaTracker` 50 milliseconds to load or scale its monitored images:

```
try {
 tracker.waitForAll(50);
} catch (InterruptedException ie) {
 return;
}
repaint();  // Or other method
```

The `paint()` method, or its equivalent if using other display techniques, needs to check with the `MediaTracker` to determine whether the images are ready for use.

Offscreen Images

Creating an image offscreen and then displaying the results all at once can help give a program a snappy appearance by hiding the individual steps that go into forming complex graphics. The technique also figures prominently in animation when two or more images with minor changes are kept offscreen, ready for displaying in sequence. This is sometimes called *double buffering*. There are four basic steps in creating and using an offscreen image:

1. Prepare an `Image` object in memory to serve as the drawing surface.

2. Obtain a `Graphics` context object for drawing to the offscreen image.

3. Draw onto the offscreen image using `Graphics` class methods.

4. Display the `Image` object the same way you display one loaded from a file.

Listing 23-5, `Offscreen.java`, demonstrates how to create and display an offscreen image. As with other sample applets in this chapter, the code is threaded so that, while the image is forming, other processes continue to run concurrently. Run the applet by loading the Offscreen.html file, in the same directory as the listing file, into your browser. Figure 23-6 shows the program's display of 100 colorful ovals, which are painted to an offscreen image and then displayed all at once with a single command. To see a different pattern, click the browser's Refresh button.

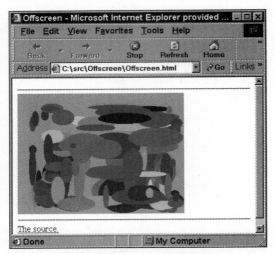

Figure 23-6: The Offscreen applet demonstrates how to paint
and display graphics using an offscreen image.

Listing 23-5: Offscreen.java

```
001: import java.applet.*;
002: import java.awt.*;
003: import java.util.Random;
004:
005: public class Offscreen extends Applet
006:   implements Runnable {
007:
008:   // Instance variables
009:   Thread drawingThread;
010:   Image offscreenImage;
011:   Graphics offscreenContext;
012:   Random gen;
013:   boolean imageReady = false;
014:   int imageW, imageH;
015:   int numOvals = 100;
016:
017:   // Initialize applet
018:   public void init() {
019:     // Size applet window
020:     imageW = 320;
021:     imageH = 240;
022:     resize(imageW, imageH);
023:     // Construct random number generator
024:     gen = new Random();
025:     // Create offscreen image and Graphics context
```

```
026:    offscreenImage = createImage(imageW, imageH);
027:    offscreenContext = offscreenImage.getGraphics();
028:  }
029:
030:  // Create and start drawing thread
031:  public void start() {
032:   drawingThread = new Thread(this);
033:   drawingThread.start();
034:  }
035:
036:  // Return positive integer at random between
037:  // low and high. Assumes low < high and are positive
038:  public int nextInt(int low, int high) {
039:   return low + (Math.abs(gen.nextInt()) % (high - low));
040:  }
041:
042:  // Create image using separate thread
043:  public void run() {
044:   // Paint image background white
045:   offscreenContext.setColor(getBackground());
046:   offscreenContext.fillRect(0, 0, imageW, imageH);
047:   // Create and paint ovals at random
048:   for (int i = 0; i < numOvals; i++) {
049:    // Select oval color at random
050:    Color c = new Color(nextInt(0, 0xffffff));
051:    offscreenContext.setColor(c);
052:    // Select oval position
053:    int x = nextInt(20, imageW - 20);
054:    int y = nextInt(20, imageH - 20);
055:    // Calculate oval width and height
056:    // so it remains inside image boundaries
057:    int w = nextInt(10, Math.min(imageW - x, x));
058:    int h = nextInt(10, Math.min(imageH - y, y));
059:    // Draw oval to offscreen image
060:    offscreenContext.fillOval(x, y, w, h);
061:    Thread.yield();
062:   }
063:   imageReady = true;
064:   repaint();
065:  }
066:
067:  // Paint window contents
068:  public void paint(Graphics g) {
069:   if (imageReady) {
070:    showStatus("Showing image...");
```

```
071:    g.drawImage(offscreenImage, 0, 0, this);
072:    } else {
073:      g.setColor(getBackground());
074:      g.fillRect(0, 0, imageW, imageH);
075:      showStatus("Preparing image...");
076:    }
077:  }
078:
079:  // Override inherited update() method
080:  // to prevent screen flicker
081:  public void update(Graphics g) {
082:    paint(g);
083:  }
084: }
```

This sample applet might seem overly complex, but as with other image code in this chapter, the extra programming — which handles image creation and display using separate threads — ensures a smooth result. Because the applet is threaded, its class implements the Runnable interface. The class also declares several instance variables, the most important of which are

```
Thread drawingThread;
Image offscreenImage;
Graphics offscreenContext;
```

The Thread object, drawingThread, forms the offscreen image using a separate thread, so that other processes can run concurrently. The Image object, offscreenImage, provides a surface for drawing offscreen. The Graphics context object, offscreenContext, is provided by the image for use in calling graphics methods such as fillOval() and directing the results to the offscreen surface.

Method init() constructs the essential objects to prepare for drawing offscreen. In this example, the two variables, imageW and imageH, are assigned the same width and height values used by the applet's window, but they could be different:

```
offscreenImage = createImage(imageW, imageH);
offscreenContext = offscreenImage.getGraphics();
```

Calling Component.createImage(), inherited by the extended Applet class, creates an Image object that you can draw to offscreen. To obtain a Graphics context object for drawing commands, call Image.getGraphics() as shown for that Image object.

To draw to the offscreen image, call Graphics class methods in reference to the associated Graphics context object obtained by calling getGraphics(). For example, fill the offscreen image's background using any color with code such as

```
offscreenContext.setColor(Color.red);
offscreenContext.fillRect(0, 0, imageW, imageH);
```

The sample applet performs similar instructions in method `run()`, which runs concurrently with other processes. For example, after creating each oval's position and size, this statement adds a new oval to the image:

```
offscreenContext.fillOval(x, y, w, h);
```

To give other processes the opportunity to run, each loop executes this statement:

```
Thread.yield();
```

When the image is finished, the thread sets the `imageReady` flag to `true`, and calls `repaint()`. This initiates an eventual call to `paint()`, which displays the off-screen image using the statement:

```
g.drawImage(offscreenImage, 0, 0, this);
```

The programming is similar to that used in this chapter's ShowPic applet to display a graphics file — in other words, the entire image appears at once. Sometimes, you might want users to see the image forming but still use offscreen drawing. To do this, simply call `repaint()` inside the loop that creates the graphics. See how this works by modifying the sample program. Insert the following two statements into the `run()` method's `for` loop, immediately after the call to `Thread.yield()` (between lines 061 and 062):

```
imageReady = true;
repaint();
```

When you run the modified program, you see each oval as it is created. Even so, the code is properly threaded, and the image is still formed offscreen — but the entire image is redisplayed to show each new oval, which is not as efficient as drawing them directly to the screen. (Click the browser's Refresh button to create a new set of shapes.)

The Offscreen applet also demonstrates a useful trick that eliminates an annoying flicker you might see when displaying multiple images. This happens because, for top-level windows such as frames, `update()` clears the drawing area by filling it with the background color. When that happens multiple times, the result is a flicker between each new drawing operation. To eliminate the background painting, override `update()` and replace it with this streamlined model:

```
public void update(Graphics g) {
 paint(g);
}
```

Filtered Images

The AWT package includes a nested package of classes that you can use to filter images. As a demonstration of these classes, the next sample applet shows how to convert a colored image into a gray-scale picture. Each pixel of the original image is filtered to an equivalent pixel of the same intensity, but lacking any color information.

This technique illustrates image producers and consumers. In general terms, a *producer* is an object that is used as a source of image data—whether that data is downloaded over a network, or is loaded from a file on disk. A *consumer* is an object that serves as a destination for image data. An applet, for example, is a consumer that can display an image. Programmatically speaking, an image producer is an object of a class that implements the ImageProducer interface. A consumer is an object of a class that implements ImageConsumer. These protocols dictate the necessary methods for obtaining and using image pixel data.

By creating your own image producer object, you can filter that pixel data as requested by an image consumer. The filtered image is formed offscreen as explained in the preceding section, and it is displayed in the usual way.

The AWT image package provides ready-to-use filters. For example, the CropImageFilter class is useful for loading portions of large graphics files. To use this filter, first import the AWT image package at the top of the source code file:

```
import java.awt.image.*;
```

Load the image file by calling getImage() as demonstrated by this chapter's ShowPic applet:

```
Image gifPic = getImage(getDocumentBase(), "filename.gif");
```

To insert a filter into the works, obtain the image's producer by calling getSource():

```
ImageProducer picSource = gifPic.getSource();
```

This provides the means to tap into the image's source of pixels. To modify those pixels, create a filter object, in this case, using the supplied CropImageFilter class:

```
CropImageFilter picFilter = new CropImageFilter(0, 0, 50, 50);
```

The arguments specify the coordinates of the portion of the image to use. Finally, create an offscreen image using a new object of the FilteredImageSource class, which takes two arguments—the image producer and filter objects:

```
pic = createImage(new FilteredImageSource(picSource, picFilter));
```

This assumes that `pic` is an object of the `Image` class, probably declared as an instance variable in an extended `Applet` or `JApplet` class. When the image is loaded via the specified producer, the filter object filters the image's pixels. In this example, the filter restricts loading pixels to those that fall within the defined coordinates. Display the filtered offscreen image in the usual way. For example, `paint()` might execute the following statement:

```
g.drawImage(pic, 0, 0, this);
```

As a more sophisticated example, Listing 23-6 shows how to extend an existing filter class to create your own filters. The applet is similar to the ShowPic sample — I used a copy of that program as a starting place — but it adds a new class and additional code to convert a color image to a gray-scale picture. This is done by filtering each pixel using the `Color` class's hue, saturation, and brightness methods. Figure 23-7 shows the program's display of a clown in black and white. Load this file (`Clown.gif` in the Filter subdirectory) into your browser or other GIF viewer to see the image in its original colors.

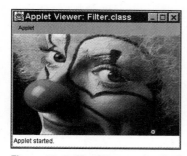

Figure 23-7: The Filter applet displays a color GIF image converted to a gray-scale image.

Listing 23-6: Filter.java

```
001: import java.applet.*;
002: import java.awt.*;
003: import java.awt.image.*;
004:
005: //===========================================================
006: // BWFilter (black and white filter) class
007: //===========================================================
008:
009: class BWFilter extends RGBImageFilter {
010:
011:   // Constructor
012:   public BWFilter() {
```

```
013:    canFilterIndexColorModel = true;
014:  }
015:
016:  // Return rgb color converted to shade of gray
017:  public int filterRGB(int x, int y, int rgb) {
018:    // Reduce rgb to hue, saturation, brightness elements
019:    Color c = new Color(rgb);
020:    float[] hsbvals = Color.RGBtoHSB(c.getRed(), c.getGreen(),
021:     c.getBlue(), null);
022:    // Return new color value of same brightness but
023:    // with hue and saturation set to zero
024:    return Color.HSBtoRGB(0.0f, 0.0f, hsbvals[2]);
025:  }
026: }
027:
028: //===========================================================
029: // Applet class
030: //===========================================================
031:
032: public class Filter extends Applet
033:  implements Runnable {
034:
035:   // Instance variables
036:   Image pic;              // GIF image producer
037:   int picID;              // Arbitrary image ID
038:   MediaTracker tracker;   // Tracks loading of image
039:   Thread loadingThread;   // Thread for loading image
040:   String filename = "Clown.gif";  // Filename
041:   boolean imageReady = false;  // Offscreen image flag
042:   Image bwPic;                 // Offscreen image object
043:
044:   // Initialize applet
045:   public void init() {
046:    // Size applet window
047:    resize(320, 200);
048:    // Create MediaTracker object
049:    tracker = new MediaTracker(this);
050:    // Start image loading
051:    pic = getImage(getDocumentBase(), filename);
052:    picID = 0;
053:    tracker.addImage(pic, picID);
054:    // Create thread to monitor image loading
055:    loadingThread = new Thread(this);
056:    loadingThread.start();
057:  }
```

```
058:
059:   // Run loading thread
060:   // Allows other processes to run while loading
061:   // the image data
062:   public void run() {
063:     try {
064:       tracker.waitForID(picID);
065:       if (tracker.checkID(picID, true)) {
066:         // Create offscreen image using loaded GIF
067:         // file filtered by our BWFilter class
068:         ImageProducer picSource = pic.getSource();
069:         BWFilter bwFilter = new BWFilter();
070:         bwPic = createImage(new
071:           FilteredImageSource(picSource, bwFilter));
072:         imageReady = true;
073:       }
074:     } catch (InterruptedException ie) {
075:       return;
076:     }
077:     repaint();  // Cause paint() to draw loaded image
078:   }
079:
080:   // Paint window contents
081:   // Displays loading or error message until
082:   // image is ready, then shows image
083:   public void paint(Graphics g) {
084:     if (tracker.isErrorID(picID))
085:       g.drawString("Error loading " + filename, 10, 20);
086:     else if (tracker.checkID(picID) && imageReady)
087:       g.drawImage(bwPic, 0, 0, this);  // Show offscreen image
088:     else
089:       g.drawString("Loading " + filename, 10, 20);
090:   }
091: }
```

BWFilter **extends an existing filter class,** RGBImageFilter, **in the** awt.image **package. This provides a filter that can modify individual pixels of an** Image **object. For faster results, the extended class's constructor sets the following flag true:**

```
canFilterIndexColorModel = true;
```

This obscurely named flag, when true, indicates that the filterRGB() method uses only its rgb color parameter and ignores its x and y integer coordinate values. This way, pixels of the same color need to be filtered only once each. If you do not set the flag true, *every* pixel of the image is sent to filterRGB() for filtering.

Needless to say, this might be a lengthy process, so unless you must examine every pixel, it's best to set the `canFilterIndexColorModel` flag `true` in your filter class's constructor.

Implement the `filterRGB()` method to return its `rgb` parameter modified however you wish. In this case, I use the `Color` class to construct gray-scale pixels. To do that, the program creates a `Color` object using the `rgb` object:

```
Color c = new Color(rgb);
```

Next, the program obtains an array of hue, saturation, and brightness floating point values by calling `Color.RGBtoHSB()`:

```
float[] hsbvals = Color.RGBtoHSB(c.getRed(), c.getGreen(),
  c.getBlue(), null);
```

It is now a simple matter to create the equivalent gray-scale pixel for any color. The final statement in the `filterRGB()` method returns an integer value with the hue and saturation levels set to zero and the brightness unchanged:

```
return Color.HSBtoRGB(0.0f, 0.0f, hsbvals[2]);
```

To display the filtered image, the rest of the program uses code similar to that in the ShowPic program. Two new variables, however, are needed:

```
boolean imageReady = false;
Image bwPic;
```

The `boolean` flag indicates when the filtered image is ready for display. The `Image` object represents the offscreen surface used to form that image.

The image file is loaded using a separate thread. (See the ShowPic sample in this chapter for a discussion of this code.) However, the `run()` method adds new statements to create the filtered image. The following obtain an `ImageProducer` object for the original color GIF image and create an object of our `BWFilter` class:

```
ImageProducer picSource = pic.getSource();
BWFilter bwFilter = new BWFilter();
bwPic = createImage(new
  FilteredImageSource(picSource, bwFilter));
imageReady = true;
```

These two objects are passed to `createImage()` to construct an offscreen image. That image's pixels are filtered by running them through `filterRGB()`. Finally, the `imageReady` flag is set to `true` so that `paint()` can display the modified image.

TIP The Filter applet holds both the original color image and its filtered gray-scale offscreen image in memory. To eliminate the original image, which you might do to conserve memory, set that `Image` object (`pic` in the sample code) to `null`. The object is eventually disposed if necessary during the next garbage collection.

ImageIcon

If you are willing to move up from AWT to Swing components, displaying image files is a lot easier. Simply use the `IconImage` class to load the image. To display it, add the icon object to another component such as `JLabel`. You'll probably also want to use `JScrollPane` to add scrollbars to the window. With this technique, there is no need to use `MediaTracker` because `IconImage` does that for you. What's more, you can use this approach to load and display GIF, JPEG, and the relatively new PNG image graphics files.

Listing 23-7, SwingPic.java, shows the fundamental techniques needed for displaying image files using Swing. Figure 23-8 shows the program in action — that's a picture of Earth taken during the Apollo 17 space flight to the moon, December 7, 1972. (Picture source: Nasa, `http://spaceflight.nasa.gov/gallery/`).

Figure 23-8: Using Swing's ImageIcon simplifies loading and displaying image files.

Listing 23-7: SwingPic.java

```
001: import javax.swing.*;
002: import java.awt.*;
003: import java.awt.event.*;
004:
005: public class SwingPic extends JFrame {
006:
007:   // Picture filename
008:   protected String filename = "AS17-148-22721.jpg";
009:   protected ImageIcon image;
...
027:   // Load image from file
028:   image = new ImageIcon(filename);
029:   int height = image.getIconHeight();
030:   int width = image.getIconWidth();
031:
032:   // Create a label to hold the image as an icon
033:   JLabel labeledPic = new JLabel(image, JLabel.CENTER);
034:   labeledPic.setText(filename);
035:
036:   // Create a scroller to hold the labeled image
037:   JScrollPane scroller = new JScrollPane(labeledPic);
038:   scroller.setPreferredSize(new Dimension(height, width));
039:
040:   // Add the scroller to the frame's content layer
041:   Container content = getContentPane();
042:   content.add(scroller);
043:   setSize(width, height);  // Sets window's initial size
044:   }
045:
046:   public static void main(String[] args) {
047:   SwingPic app = new SwingPic();
048:   app.setTitle("Swing Picture Demonstration");
049:   app.show();
050:   }
051: }
```

The program is straightforward. Lines 028-030 load the image from disk and obtain its height and width, two values used in sizing the window and scroll bar panes. You can't add an IconImage object directly to a top-level container's content pane. Instead, you must attach the image to another component such as JLabel as shown at lines 033-034. Omit the call to setText() if you want to display only the image with no label.

Lines 037-038 create a JScrollPane object, using the JLabel component and its picture to construct scroller. That object is then added to the frame's content pane (line 042). When using this technique to display images, there's no need to write a `paint()` method because the component takes care of displaying and updating the image as needed.

Animation Threads

I end this chapter with a sample applet that can animate a series of bitmap images. The program is an AWT applet, but the same methods can be used with Swing's `JApplet` class. Figure 23-9 shows the program's display, which, of course, is not animated on this page. (Wouldn't that be a neat trick?)

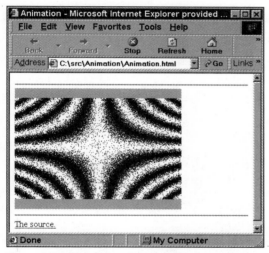

Figure 23-9: The Animation demo displays a series of bitmap images in a separate thread.

Listing 23-8, `Animation.java`, shows the sample applet's source code. The program follows standard Java techniques for loading a series of images using a separate thread so that the loading process doesn't interfere with the browser's other operations. The threaded code is what makes the program seem complex, but the actual animation is a simple process of merely displaying each image in succession. However, that too must be done in a thread so the animation does not grab all processor cycles.

Listing 23-8: Animation.java

```
001: import java.applet.*;
002: import java.awt.*;
003:
004: public class Animation extends Applet
005:   implements Runnable {
```

```
006:
007:   // Thread for loading and displaying images
008:   Thread animThread = null;
009:
010:   private final int NUM_IMAGES = 10;  // Number of image files
011:   private Image images[];             // Array of images
012:   private int currImage;              // Index of current image
013:   private int imgWidth  = 0;          // Width of all images
014:   private int imgHeight = 0;          // Height of all images
015:   private boolean allLoaded = false;  // true = all loaded
016:   private MediaTracker tracker;       // Tracks image loading
017:   private int width, height;          // Applet width and height
018:
019:   // Initialize applet
020:   public void init() {
021:    width = 320;
022:    height = 240;
023:    resize(width, height);
024:    // Create MediaTracker object. The string is
025:    // for creating the image filenames.
026:    tracker = new MediaTracker(this);
027:    String strImage;
028:    // Load all images. Method getImage() returns immediately
029:    // and all images are NOT actually loaded into memory
030:    // by this loop.
031:    images = new Image[NUM_IMAGES];  // Create image array
032:    for (int i = 1; i <= NUM_IMAGES; i++) {
033:     strImage = "images/img00" + ((i < 10) ? "0" : "")
034:      + i + ".gif";
035:     images[i-1] = getImage(getDocumentBase(),
036:      strImage);
037:     tracker.addImage(images[i-1], 0);
038:    }
039:   }
040:
041:   // Paint window contents
042:   public void paint(Graphics g)
043:   {
044:    // Draw current image
045:    if (allLoaded) {
046:     g.drawImage(images[currImage],
047:      (width - imgWidth) / 2,
048:      (height - imgHeight) / 2, null);
049:    }
050:   }
051:
```

```
052:  // Create and start animation thread
053:  public void start() {
054:   if (animThread == null) {
055:    animThread = new Thread(this);
056:    animThread.start();
057:   }
058:  }
059:
060:  // Run image load and display thread
061:  public void run() {
062:   // Load images if not already done
063:   if (!allLoaded) {
064:    showStatus("Loading images...");
065:    // Wait for images to be loaded
066:    // Other processes continue to run normally
067:    try {
068:     tracker.waitForAll();
069:    }
070:    catch (InterruptedException e) {
071:     stop();  // Stop thread if interrupted
072:     return;  // Abort loading process
073:    }
074:    // If all images are not loaded by this point,
075:    // something is wrong and we display an error
076:    // message.
077:    if (tracker.isErrorAny()) {
078:     showStatus("Error loading images!");
079:     stop();
080:     return;
081:    }
082:
083:    // All images are loaded. Set the loaded flag
084:    // and prepare image size variables
085:    allLoaded = true;
086:    imgWidth  = images[0].getWidth(this);
087:    imgHeight = images[0].getHeight(this);
088:   }
089:
090:   // Loop endlessly so animation repeats
091:   // User ends loop by leaving the page or exiting
092:   // the browser.
093:   showStatus("Displaying animation");
094:   while (true) {
095:    try {
096:     repaint();
```

```
097:      currImage++;
098:      if (currImage == NUM_IMAGES)
099:        currImage = 0;
100:      Thread.sleep(50);  // Controls animation speed
101:      }
102:      catch (InterruptedException e) {
103:        stop();
104:      }
105:    }  // end of while statement
106:  }  // end of run() method
107: }
```

Constant NUM_IMAGES indicates the number of image files, which are stored in the Images subdirectory in the form img0001.gif. The applet also declares several instance variables to control image loading and the display of individual bitmaps (see lines 008–017). The image bitmaps are stored in an array of Image objects. Variable currImage indicates which image from this array should be drawn next. A boolean variable, allLoaded, is true after all images are loaded using a MediaTracker object as explained earlier in this chapter.

That object, named tracker, greatly simplifies the process of loading multiple image files using a separate thread. It also makes error detection easier. Method init() initializes the program's instance variables and constructs the tracker object. Each image is loaded using the Applet.getImage() method and is stored in the images array. Each image is added to the tracker object by calling MediaTracker.addImage(). After the for loop ends (lines 032–038), the tracker is ready to begin loading the images from disk. It's important to realize, however, that this process continues to execute in a separate thread, and the images might not be ready for display until some time after init() ends.

 TIP If you need to modify an animation's bitmap data, use the image filtering techniques described in this chapter, and then display the resulting off-screen images instead of directly showing the image files.

The program's paint() method is simply written — a desirable characteristic in all graphics programs because, if this method takes too long to complete, other processes halt in their tracks while paint() updates the display. In this example, to keep paint() short and fast, the method's if statement first checks the boolean flag allLoaded to determine whether all images have been loaded and the animation is ready to begin:

```
if (allLoaded) {
 g.drawImage(images[currImage],
  (width - imgWidth) / 2,
```

```
(height - imgHeight) / 2, null);
}
```

If the flag is `true`, `Graphics.drawImage()` displays the current image using some optional calculations to reduce the image sizes. Notice that `paint()` draws only one image — it would be a grievous error to use a loop in `paint()` to animate the display. That would block other processes and cause the applet to perform badly. Always keep `paint()` simple, and use threaded code for carrying out lengthy graphics operations.

Key elements toward that goal are the construction of a `Thread` object, created in the applet's `start()` method:

```
animThread = new Thread(this);
```

That constructs the `Thread` object using a reference (`this`) to the applet object. As a result, the thread looks for a `run()` method in the applet (see lines 061-106). The method is a lengthy affair that demonstrates several techniques with broad application in threaded programming. An initial `if` statement checks whether the images are already loaded, in which case the method can proceed directly to its display statements. This might happen, for example, if the user switches away and then back again to the applet.

If the images are not already loaded, a `try` statement calls the `tracker`'s `waitForAll()` method, which returns only after all monitored images — as specified by `MediaTracker.addImage()` — are either loaded or an error is detected. However, if another thread interrupts the process, `waitForAll()` throws an `InterruptedException` object, caught in this statement:

```
try  {
 tracker.waitForAll();
}
catch (InterruptedException e) {
 stop();  // Stop thread if interrupted
 return;  // Abort loading process
}
```

After the `try` block ends normally, the images are either in memory, or an error has occurred. To detect any problems, `run()` executes this code:

```
if (tracker.isErrorAny()) {
 showStatus("Error loading images!");
 stop();
 return;
}
```

Method `isErrorAny()` returns `true` if any errors were detected for any of the images — even if only one file, for example, could not be found. In that case, `showStatus()` displays a message in the browser, and the program kills the image-loading thread.

Finally, if all is well, the `allLoaded` flag is set to `true` so that `paint()` can begin displaying images, and the image width and height variables are initialized using the first image referenced at index 0 in the `Image` object array:

```
allLoaded = true;
imgWidth  = images[0].getWidth(this);
imgHeight = images[0].getHeight(this);
```

The purpose of `this` as an argument passed to `getWidth()` and `getHeight()` might seem obscure. These methods require an *image observer*, an object of any class that implements the `ImageObserver` interface. This interface specifies that the implementing class should provide an `imageUpdate()` method, called when image data is ready for display. Through this protocol, the image consumer (such as a component or the applet) receives its image data via the image producer.

Following these preliminary steps — all of which are concerned with preparing the animation's multiple images — the program is ready to begin displaying each image in sequence. This is done inside `run()` using a so-called "do-forever" `while` loop that continues until another thread interrupts this one, or until the applet ends. To display each image, a `try` block executes the statements

```
repaint();
currImage++;
if (currImage == NUM_IMAGES)
 currImage = 0;
Thread.sleep(50);
```

This shows the proper way to perform potentially time-consuming graphics operations, which must not be allowed to inhibit other processes. Calling `repaint()` causes `paint()` to display a single image as specified by the `currentImage` index. So that the animation loops continuously, the index is rotated through the values 0 to `NUM_IMAGES - 1`. Finally, to give other processes time to run — and also to control the speed of the animation — a call to `Thread.sleep()` pauses in a thread-friendly way for 50 milliseconds between each image.

Summary

◆ Use `Graphics` class methods to draw outlined and filled shapes, paint text, display images, and show other kinds of graphics.

◆ Most often, you commonly use the `Graphics` context object passed to method `paint()`. However, you may create your own `Graphics` context objects by calling `Component.getGraphics()`.

◆ Loading and displaying image files requires careful threaded programming. Simply loading and displaying a GIF or JPEG image can potentially block other processes. A well-written applet or application must not allow that to happen.

◆ Use the `Color` class to create color values of red, green, and blue components. The class can also specify colors as hue, saturation, and brightness levels.

◆ Use the `Font` class to select a font family, size, and style for use with `Graphics` class methods that display text. Use the `FontMetrics` class to obtain spacing information for selected fonts.

◆ The `Image` class, which represents the source or producer of a bitmap image, is typically used in conjunction with the `MediaTracker` class to load image files. This chapter explains the threaded code needed for using these classes to smoothly load and display bitmap images.

◆ Swing's `ImageIcon` class greatly simplifies image loading and display, and it also recognizes the relatively new PNG graphics file format. `ImageIcon` uses `MediaTracker` internally.

◆ You may prepare an offscreen image and draw to it by calling `Graphics` class methods. The image is displayed using the same techniques for displaying an image loaded from a file.

◆ By obtaining an image's producer and creating an offscreen image, you can plug in an image filter that modifies the image's pixels. This chapter explains how to program a filter that converts a color GIF image to a gray-scale, black-and-white picture.

◆ Animating multiple images requires careful, threaded programming. The animation techniques in this chapter work for AWT and Swing applets and applications.

Chapter 24

Input and Output Techniques

THE JAVA.IO PACKAGE provides a rich set of input and output tools that you can use for reading and writing binary and character data. This chapter introduces several of the java.io package's classes and lists several sample programs that demonstrate how to read and write data interactively using file streams.

 For security reasons, applets cannot use the file I/O techniques described in this chapter. Only Java stand-alone programs are permitted to read and write disk files.

IN THIS CHAPTER

◆ Standard input and output files

◆ Programming with the File class

◆ Using file streams and buffers

◆ Input and output of typed data

◆ Random-access file techniques

Standard Input and Output

Java implements I/O using the concept of *streams*. Data objects in an I/O stream flow like boats down a narrow river, one after the other. To use a stream, you first need to open it. After receiving the last data object, the program should close the stream in order to release any reserved system resources such as file buffers and associated file descriptor variables.

Java has two basic kinds of streams—byte streams and character streams. Byte streams are more general and can be used to read and write any kind of information. Character streams are, of course, used only with character data.

Java also provides standard input and output classes, associated usually with the keyboard and text display, but also redirectable to use other kinds of files. Java calls its standard output streams PrintStream and PrintWriter, and the input

555

counterparts, InputStream and InputStreamReader. Most I/O classes have similarly related input and output classes.

TIP In Java I/O terms, the words "Reader" and "Writer" in a class name refer to streams intended for use with character data.

Originally, Java did not have character streams, and for that reason, its standard I/O classes are byte streams. Changing this would break too many programs, and so we are stuck with the problem. As a result, standard input and output methods usually require type-cast expressions to convert from binary to character data. Java's standard I/O objects, defined in the System class, are

```
public static PrintStream err;
public static InputStream in;
public static PrintStream out;
```

Use these static objects in reference to System, as in the following statement, which prints a message on the terminal. Similar examples are strewn throughout this book's listings:

```
System.out.println("Please enter your password:");
```

Call print() similarly if you don't want to start a new line. Another PrintStream object, System.err, represents the standard error output file. This file may not be redirected, and it is therefore guaranteed to send its output to the display. Use it to report error messages such as

```
System.err.println("Error: System has lost its marbles.");
```

Inputting data takes a little more work. The classic approach requires two variables:

```
StringBuffer str = new StringBuffer();
char ch;
```

Follow that with a while loop to read characters from the standard input (the keyboard, unless input has been redirected), and append them to the StringBuffer object:

```
while ((ch = (char)System.in.read()) != '\n')
  str.append(ch);
```

As mentioned, the type-cast expression, (char), is needed because the standard input is a byte stream. Sun and most Java programmers now suggest not using that classic approach in new code. Instead, the recommended technique uses a BufferedReader object, along with an InputStreamReader object, to read strings entered at the keyboard. Listing 24-1, ReadLine.java, demonstrates the new and improved way to input character data.

Listing 24-1: ReadLine.java

```
001: import java.io.*;
002:
003: public class ReadLine {
004:
005:   // Input a string
006:   public static String readLine()
007:     throws IOException {
008:     BufferedReader br =
009:       new BufferedReader(new InputStreamReader(System.in));
010:     return br.readLine();
011:   }
012:
013:   // Prompt for and input a string
014:   public static String readLine(String prompt)
015:     throws IOException {
016:     System.out.print(prompt);
017:     return readLine();
018:   }
019:
020:   // Main program
021:   public static void main(String args[])
022:     throws IOException {
023:     System.out.println("Enter strings when prompted.");
024:     System.out.print("Enter your first name: ");
025:     String s1 = readLine();
026:     String s2 = readLine("Enter your last name: ");
027:     System.out.println("Your name: " + s1 + " " + s2);
028:   }
029: }
```

The first step in using Java I/O is to import the java.io package, as shown in the listing at line 001. In the program's ReadLine class, the BufferedReader class creates an input character stream that buffers characters as they are entered. Calling readLine() for that object returns characters entered until the user presses Enter or Return (in other words, until a new-line symbol is detected).

Notice how InputStreamReader, a non-buffered input character string, is associated with System.in. The two overloaded readLine() methods in the sample program provide unprompted and prompted versions. The main program shows how to use these methods — simply call them and assign their results to `String` variables.

> To save space in this chapter, instead of catching exceptions, some methods simply throw them to their callers. For example, see lines 007 and 015 in Listing 24-1. For this reason, any I/O errors cause the program to end. In your own programs, it is better to use `try-catch` blocks to handle `IOExceptions` using the techniques outlined in Chapter 7, "Exception Handling."

Files and Directories

A large part of I/O programming involves accessing files and directories, but these are subjects not well covered in many Java sources. Following are notes and sample programs that demonstrate the `java.io` package's `File` class, which is useful for obtaining information about files, and also for listing directory contents.

The File Class

Java's `File` class soothes a lot of the pain that comes from writing system-independent I/O code. Use `File` to create objects that represent files and directories in system-independent ways. Keep in mind, however, that separator characters differ among operating systems. For that reason, always use these `File static` declarations in place of explicit separators:

```
static String pathSeparator;
static char pathSeparatorChar;
static String separator;
static char separatorChar;
```

Each separator has `String` and `char` forms for convenience. The `separator` and `separatorChar` objects represent the character used to separate directories in path names. For example, Windows uses a backslash as the separator; Linux and UNIX use a forward slash. The `pathSeparator` and `pathSeparatorChar` objects represent the character used in multiple-entry directory lists. In Windows, a semicolon is the path separator. Linux and UNIX use a colon.

> Among supported platforms, only Windows prefaces path names with drive letters such as C: and D:. Also, Windows filenames are not case sensitive, as they are in Linux and UNIX. Despite the `File` class's attempt to generalize file naming conventions across platforms, accommodating such differences still takes careful programming.

Create a File object using one of the class's three constructors. For example, the following statement creates a File object that refers to the Readme.txt file in the \Wizbang directory:

```
File fobj = new File("/Wizbang/Readme.txt");
```

For better cross-platform support, you may want to insert the aforementioned constants into a filename rather than type the explicit slashes used for space reasons in this chapter. Although this takes some extra work, the results work correctly on all supported platforms. For example, using a String object, the following statements construct a pathname and then use the string to create a File object:

```
String s = File.separator + "Wizbang"
 + File.separator + "Readme.txt";
File fobj = new File(s);
```

You may also construct a File object that represents a directory name using a statement such as

```
File dobj = new File("/Wizbang");
```

It doesn't matter whether the file or the directory actually exist. A File object may refer to an existing or nonexistent file, directory, or path. The File object is just an abstraction of a file, it neither creates a real file nor does it hold any file data.

Another way to construct a File object is to specify a path and filename separately:

```
File fobj = new File("/Wizbang", "Readme.txt");
```

This File construction technique is useful when the program stores pathnames and filenames in separate String variables. The proper separator is automatically inserted between the path and file strings. Finally, you may specify a path using another File object plus a filename. This fragment creates two File objects:

```
File dobj = new File("/Wizbang");
File fobj = new File(dobj, "Readme.txt");
```

The first object refers to the path string "/Wizbang". The second is created using the first object as the path and a string as the filename.

An *absolute path* is one that completely specifies a path, as opposed to a *relative path* that relates to another directory. In Linux, for example, an absolute path begins with a forward slash as in `"/usr/bin"`. In Windows, an absolute path looks like this: `"C:\Downloads\Java"`. Relative paths might use double periods `".."` to go up one level in a directory structure. A relative path in Linux, for instance, might be written as `"../../include"`. A similar path in Windows uses forward slashes as in `"..\..\include"`.

In addition to its constructors, the `File` class provides several useful methods for determining various facts about a file, directory, or path. Be aware that some of these methods — `mkdir()`, for example — can make changes to your file system's directory structures. Selected `File` `public` methods include the following:

◆ `String getName()` — Returns the name of the file or directory.

◆ `String getPath()` — Returns the full path name.

◆ `String getAbsolutePath()` — Returns the current absolute path, or if the `File` object does not represent an absolute path, returns the concatenation of the current directory, a separator character, and the object's relative path or filename.

◆ `String getParent()` — Returns the directory of the file represented by this `File` object. This is the pathname up to the separator character before the filename. If the path has no such separator character, this method returns `null`.

◆ `boolean exists()` — Returns `true` if the file or directory exists.

◆ `boolean canWrite()` — Returns `true` if a program can write to the file — for example, if it is not marked read-only.

◆ `boolean canRead()` — Returns `true` if a program can read from the file. (This method returns `false` if the file is a directory.)

◆ `boolean isFile()` — Returns `true` if the `File` object represents a disk file.

◆ `boolean isDirectory()` — Returns `true` if the `File` object represents a directory name.

◆ `native boolean isAbsolute()` — Returns `true` if the represented path is absolute (not relative to another path).

◆ `long lastModified()` — Returns the date and time of the file's most recent modification or creation. Use the `Date` class to convert the returned value to a useable form.

◆ `long length()` — Returns the length of the file in bytes.

◆ boolean mkdir() – Creates the directory represented by this File object. Any outer nested directories in the path must already exist (see also mkdirs()). Returns true if the directory was successfully created.

◆ boolean renameTo(File dest) – Renames the file represented by this File object to the name represented by the dest File object. Returns true if the filename change was successful.

◆ boolean mkdirs() – Works the same as mkdir(), but also creates any outer nested directories in the path. Returns true if all directories were successfully created.

◆ String[] list() – Returns an array of String objects representing the filenames in the directory referenced by this File object.

◆ String[] list(FilenameFilter filter) – Works the same as list(), but returns only filenames matching the specified filter (for an example, see the "File Filters" section in this chapter).

◆ boolean delete() – Deletes the file or directory referenced by this File object. Returns true if the deletion was completed successfully.

File and Directory Programming

Listing 24-2, Directory.java, demonstrates how to use the File class to list the names of files in a specified directory path. To save a little space on the page, I cut out the readLine() methods at lines 002-019 duplicated from Listing 24-1.

Listing 24–2: Directory.java

```
001: import java.io.*;
002:
003: public class Directory {
...
020:   // Construct File object for directory path
021:   public static File getFileForPath(String path)
022:     throws IOException {
023:     File dir = new File(path);
024:     if (!dir.isDirectory())
025:       throw new IOException("Not a directory");
026:     return dir;
027:   }
028:
029:   // Main program method
030:   public static void main(String args[]) {
031:
032:     String path;
033:
034:     try {
```

```
035:
036:    // Get pathname from command line or prompt user
037:    if (args.length > 0)
038:     path = args[0];
039:    else
040:     path = readLine("Path name? ");
041:
042:    // List directory
043:     File dir = getFileForPath(path);
044:     String[] filenames = dir.list();
045:     for (int i = 0; i < filenames.length; i++)
046:      System.out.println(filenames[i]);
047:    } catch (IOException e) {        // Trap exception
048:     System.err.println(e.toString());   // Display error
049:    }
050:   }
051: }
```

Compile and run the program, and then enter a path name as a command-line argument, or in response to the program's prompt (in Windows, type a backslash as the path separator):

```
javac Directory.java
java Directory /mnt/floppy

. . .

java Directory
Path name? /usr/tswan
```

After obtaining a path name, the program calls the local method getFileForPath(). This method converts the entered pathname string into a File object, created with the statement

```
File dir = new File(path);
```

The method then checks whether this object represents a directory. If the File.isDirectory() method returns false, the local method throws an object of the IOException class (see line 025). This is a good example of how file I/O programming uses exceptions to report not merely errors, but also exceptional conditions — in this case, entering the name of a file when a directory is required. To see the result of this programming, enter a filename such as

```
java Directory Directory.class
java.io.IOException: Not a directory
```

File Information

Listing 24-3, FileInfo.java, shows another way to use the File class. Compile and run the program, but this time, at the command line or when prompted, enter the name of a file. To test the program's exception handling, try entering nonexistent pathnames. Only if you enter the name of an existing file does the program report information such as the file's name, size, and last-modified date.

Listing 24-3: FileInfo.java

```
001: import java.io.*;
002: import java.util.Date;
003:
004: public class FileInfo {
...
021:   // Construct File object for named file
022:   public static File getFileForFilename(String filename)
023:     throws IOException {
024:     File fi = new File(filename);
025:     // Do not move the following statements;
026:     // order is critical
027:     if (!fi.exists())
028:       throw new IOException("File not found");
029:     if (!fi.isFile())
030:       throw new IOException("Not a file");
031:     return fi;
032:   }
033:
034:   // Show a labeled string
035:   public static void showLabel(String label, String s) {
036:     System.out.print(label);
037:     System.out.println(s);
038:   }
039:
040:   // Display information about file fi
041:   public static void showInformation(File fi) {
042:     showLabel("Path     = ", fi.getPath());
043:     showLabel("Filename = ", fi.getName());
044:     showLabel("Length   = ",
045:       new Long(fi.length()).toString());
046:     showLabel("Readable = ",
047:       new Boolean(fi.canRead()).toString());
048:     showLabel("Writable = ",
049:       new Boolean(fi.canWrite()).toString());
050:     showLabel("Modified = ",
051:       new Date(fi.lastModified()).toString());
```

```
052:   }
053:
054:   // Main program method
055:   public static void main(String args[]) {
056:     String filename;
057:     try {
058:       // Get pathname from command line or prompt user
059:       if (args.length > 0)
060:         filename = args[0];
061:       else
062:         filename = readLine("File name? ");
063:       File fi = getFileForFilename(filename);
064:       showInformation(fi);
065:     } catch (IOException e) {            // Trap exception
066:       System.err.println(e.toString());  // Display error
067:     }
068:   }
069: }
```

Line 024 creates a File object for the specified filename. After determining that the file both exists and is a file, and not a directory name, method showInformation() at lines 041-052 calls various File methods to display facts about the file.

File Filters

A filename filter uses *wildcards* to represent characters that match any pattern. For example, the filter *.* is typically used to represent any filename. The filter *.txt represents all files ending with .txt. The filter *.00? represents all files with any name, a period, two zero characters, and any final character.

I could find only scant documentation on how to use filename filters with the File class, but with a little experimentation, I was able to figure out most of the particulars. The key is to create your own class that implements the FilenameFilter interface, which specifies the single method:

```
boolean accept(File dir, String name);
```

The method returns true if the designated file, directory, or path should be included in the File.list() method's return value. Return false to exclude a file, directory, or path. Listing 24-4, FilterDir.java, demonstrates how to implement the FilenameFilter interface to list only the subdirectories in a given path. The listing is a modified copy of the Directory.java program in this chapter. Only the new statements are listed here (but the full listing is, of course, on the CD-ROM).

Listing 24-4: FilterDir.java

```
001: import java.io.*;
002:
003: // File filter class
004: class FilterClass implements FilenameFilter {
005:  public boolean accept(File dir, String name) {
006:   File f = new File(dir, name);
007:   if (f.isDirectory())
008:    return true;
009:   else
010:    return false;
011:  }
012: }
013:
014: public class FilterDir {
...
031:  // Construct File object for directory path
032:  public static File getFileForPath(String path)
033:   throws IOException {
034:   File dir = new File(path);
035:   if (!dir.isDirectory())
036:    throw new IOException("Not a directory");
037:   return dir;
038:  }
039:
040:  // Main program method
041:  public static void main(String args[]) {
042:   String path;
043:   try {
044:    // Get pathname from command line or prompt user
045:    if (args.length > 0)
046:     path = args[0];
047:    else
048:     path = readLine("Path name? ");
049:    File dir = getFileForPath(path);
050:    String[] filenames = dir.list(new FilterClass());
051:    for (int i = 0; i < filenames.length; i++)
052:     System.out.println("<DIR> " + filenames[i]);
053:   } catch (IOException e) {              // Trap exception
054:    System.err.println(e.toString());   // Display error
055:   }
056:  }
057: }
```

The program's `FilterClass` implements the `FilenameFilter` interface, which declares the method:

```
public boolean accept(File dir, String name);
```

The `File` parameter specifies the absolute or relative pathname, or directory, of the indicated file. The `String` parameter is the candidate file or directory name to be returned by `File.list()`. Only if `accept()` returns `true` is the file accepted for listing. In this case, the program simply checks whether the `name` `String` is a directory name, and in that way the program filters out all non-directories.

 The `File.list()` method does not return the current (.) or outer (..) directory names, and you don't need to write code to filter these names out.

File Streams and Buffers

A file stream is simply a sequential source of data bytes that flow from one location to another. An object-oriented file stream is a class that represents an abstraction of this concept. As the examples in the following sections show, file streams are often associated with disk files.

The FileInputStream Class

The `FileInputStream` class provides methods for accessing file stream data. You can construct `FileInputStream` objects in three ways. Pass a string representing the filename or path:

```
FileInputStream fin =
 new FileInputStream("/Wizbang/Accounts.dat");
```

You can also pass a `File` object to the constructor—useful for checking the status of the file before creating the stream. For example, the following code fragment throws an exception if the indicated file does not exist:

```
File fi = new File("/Wizbang/Accounts.dat");
if (!fi.exists())
 throw IOException("Not a file");
FileInputStream fin = new FileInputStream(fi);
```

A third way to construct a `FileInputStream` object is to pass it a `FileDescriptor` object, which serves as an interface to a file handle—a term that typically refers to the operating system's file resource. `FileDescriptor` is necessarily system dependent and is rarely used in I/O programming, but you might call the `FileInputStream` class's `getFD()` method to obtain the `FileDescriptor` object for an existing stream. You can then use this object to construct another stream—perhaps to clone a stream so that you can reference the same file data using two objects.

Selected `FileInputStream` `public` and `protected` methods are as follows:

- `int read()`—Reads a single byte from the stream.

- `int read(byte b[])`—Reads `b.length` bytes from the file into the byte array. Returns the number of bytes read, or –1 if the end of the file is reached. This method does not construct its array—you must do that before calling `read()`.

- `int read(byte b[], int off, int len)`—Similar to the preceding method, but ignores the array length. Deposits bytes from the stream starting at `b[off]` and reading up to `len` bytes or to the end of the file.

- `long skip(long n)`—Throws away the specified number of bytes from the stream, thus skipping from the current file position to a new position n bytes away. Returns the number of bytes skipped.

- `int available()`—Returns the number of bytes that can be read from the stream without blocking. This value is not necessarily the same as the file's size.

- `void close()`—Closes the input stream. It is always optional to close file streams, but this is usually a good idea because it frees system resources.

- `FileDescriptor getFD()`—Returns the system-dependent file descriptor object for this input stream. You can use this object to clone a file input stream by passing the method's return value to the `FileInputStream` constructor.

- `void finalize()`—This method is `protected`, and you cannot call it from a program. However, I list it here as a rare example of a `finalize()` method with a useful purpose—in this case, closing a file if an unreferenced `FileInputStream` object is deleted by the garbage collector.

The FileOutputStream Class

As counterpoint to the `FileInputStream` class, `FileOutputStream` represents a destination for a file stream of data bytes. Construct a `FileOutputStream` object using similar techniques described for `FileInputStream`. The `public` methods that differ from those in `FileInputStream` are as follows:

- `void write(int b)`—Writes a single byte, b, to the output stream. The data is written to disk immediately.

- ◆ void write(byte b[]) — Writes an entire array of bytes to the output stream.

- ◆ void write(byte b[], int off, int len) — Writes len bytes starting with b[off] to the output stream.

File Programming

Listing 24-5, CopyFile.java, demonstrates how to use the FileInputStream and FileOutputStream classes to copy a disk file. Because the program uses low-level data streams, it can copy a file of any type.

Listing 24–5: CopyFile.java

```
001: import java.io.*;
002:
003: public class CopyFile {
...
020:  // Construct File object for named file
021:  public static File getFileForFilename(
022:    String filename, boolean checkExistence)
023:    throws IOException {
024:    File fi = new File(filename);
025:    if (checkExistence) {
026:     // Do not move the following statements;
027:     // order is critical
028:     if (!fi.exists())
029:      throw new IOException(fi.getName() + " not found");
030:     if (!fi.isFile())
031:      throw new IOException(fi.getName() + " is not a file");
032:    }
033:    return fi;
034:  }
035:
036:  // Returns true if user answers yes to prompt
037:  public static boolean yes(String prompt)
038:    throws IOException {
039:    System.out.print(prompt);
040:    char ch = (char)System.in.read();
041:    if (ch == 'y' || ch == 'Y') {
042:     return true;
043:    }
044:    return false;
045:  }
046:
047:  // Copy an old file to a new one
```

```
048:   // Overwrites or creates the new file
049:   public static void copy(File fileOld, File fileNew)
050:     throws IOException {
051:     FileInputStream fin = new FileInputStream(fileOld);
052:     FileOutputStream fout = new FileOutputStream(fileNew);
053:     System.out.println("Copying...");
054:     int b = fin.read();
055:     while (b != -1) {
056:       fout.write(b);
057:       b = fin.read();
058:     }
059:     System.out.println("Finished");
060:   }
061:
062:   // Main program method
063:   public static void main(String args[]) {
064:     String fileOldName, fileNewName;
065:     File fileOld, fileNew;
066:     try {
067:       if (args.length >= 2) {
068:         fileOldName = args[0];
069:         fileNewName = args[1];
070:       } else {
071:         fileOldName = readLine("Copy what file? ");
072:         fileNewName = readLine("To what file? ");
073:       }
074:       fileOld = getFileForFilename(fileOldName, true);
075:       fileNew = getFileForFilename(fileNewName, false);
076:       if (fileNew.isDirectory())
077:         throw new IOException(
078:           fileNew.getName() + " is a directory");
079:       if (fileNew.exists()) {
080:         if (!yes("Overwrite file " + fileNew.getName() + "? "))
081:           throw new IOException("File not copied");
082:       } else {
083:         if (!yes("Create new " + fileNew.getPath() + "? "))
084:           throw new IOException("File not copied");
085:       }
086:       copy(fileOld, fileNew);
087:     } catch (IOException e) {          // Trap exception
088:       System.err.println(e.toString());   // Display error
089:     }
090:   }
091: }
```

Most of the sample program's code is concerned with prompting for filenames or obtaining them from the command line, checking that the source file exists, and asking for permission to overwrite an existing destination file, or to create a new one. File copying takes place in method copy(), which creates FileInputStream and FileOutputStream objects:

```
FileInputStream fin = new FileInputStream(fileOld);
FileOutputStream fout = new FileOutputStream(fileNew);
```

That creates the two stream objects using the File objects passed to copy(). At this point in the program, the files have been verified, and copying proceeds immediately using a while loop:

```
int b = fin.read();
while (b != -1) {
 fout.write(b);
 b = fin.read();
}
```

The first statement reads the first source-file byte. While that byte is not –1, the loop writes it to the destination file, and then reads the next byte. Because read() returns a 32-bit int value, only the least significant 8 bits represent valid data, leaving –1 (hexadecimal 0xffffffff) available as an end-of-file flag. As a side benefit, the copy() method and other statements in the program demonstrate how exception handling keeps the code simple while trapping all possible errors.

The BufferedInputStream Class

Plain file streams are adequate for small data files, but to maintain good performance, you'll want to use extensions of the basic file stream classes that add buffered I/O. A buffer is simply a block of memory that collects file stream data on its way to and from memory and disk. Because entire blocks of data are read and written at a time, disk accesses are kept to a minimum, which usually results in a great speed improvement. The downside of using buffers is that, if the computer is shut down prematurely, a greater amount of data is at risk. You can minimize this danger by flushing the file. (Output classes provide a flush() method for this purpose.)

The BufferedInputStream class constructs buffered input file stream objects. To use the class, you must first construct an unbuffered FileInputStream. Actually, you may use any InputStream object, but in file I/O programming, it's more common to use the FileInputStream class. For example, these statements construct and use a FileInputStream object using a File object, fi:

```
FileInputStream fin = new FileInputStream(fi);
BufferedInputStream bin = new BufferedInputStream(fin);
```

The resulting unbuffered stream object (fin) is passed to the BufferedInputStream constructor to create the buffered stream. You may optionally pass a size argument to the constructor to specify a buffer of a certain length. The following statement constructs the buffered input stream object using the file stream but increases the buffer size to 1024 bytes:

```
BufferedInputStream bin = new BufferedInputStream(fin, 1024);
```

Following are methods in the `BufferedInputStream` class that you can call:

- `int read()` — Reads a single byte from the input stream. Returns –1 if the end of file is reached.

- `int read(byte b[], int off, int len)` — Reads `len` bytes and deposits them in the `byte` array starting at `b[off]`. Returns the number of bytes actually read, or –1 if the end of the file has been reached.

- `long skip(long n)` — Throws away n bytes from the input stream starting at the current position. Returns the number of bytes actually skipped.

- `int available()` — Returns the number of bytes that can be read from the input stream without blocking. This value is not necessarily the same as the file size.

- `void mark(int readlimit)` — Sets a marker at the current position so that `reset()` can return to this position. The parameter `readLimit` equals the number of bytes that are permitted to be read before the mark becomes invalid.

- `void reset()` — Returns the file pointer to the position most recently recorded by `mark()`. The default mark is –1, which represents no valid position. Calling `reset()` without a preceding call to `mark()` throws an `IOException` error.

- `boolean markSupported()` — Returns `true` if `mark()` and `reset()` are supported by the operating system. Although the standard Java implementation always returns `true` for this method, a local installation may not support file marking, and it's a good idea to call `markSupported()` before using `mark()` and `reset()`.

The `mark()` and `reset()` methods are typically used to remember the current position and then to peek ahead to see what kind of data is coming up. Calling `reset()` repositions the file to its marked location. A parser might use these methods to look ahead for a specific character. It's important to realize, however, that reading more bytes than passed to `mark()` invalidates the mark and throws an exception if `reset()` is subsequently called. An exception is also thrown if `reset()` is called without a prior call to `mark()`. The two methods are not intended for skipping around at will in a file; if you need that capability, see the `RandomAccessFile` class described later in this chapter.

The BufferedOutputStream Class

The counterpart to the `BufferedInputStream` class is `BufferedOutputStream`. As with `BufferedInputStream`, you can construct a `BufferedOutputStream` object two ways. Each requires an existing `OutputStream` object, which in file I/O programming is typically an object of the `FileOutputStream` class. For example, the following two statements construct a `FileOutputStream` object using a `File` object, `fi`:

```
FileOutputStream fout = new FileOutputStream(fi);
BufferedOutputStream bout = new BufferedOutputStream(fout);
```

The resulting unbuffered output stream `fout` is passed to the `BufferedOutputStream` constructor to create the buffered output object. You may optionally specify a buffer size by passing an integer argument to the class constructor. The next statement creates a buffered output stream object with a buffer size of 1024 bytes:

```
BufferedOutputStream bout =
 new BufferedOutputStream(fout, 1024);
```

The `BufferedOutputStream` class provides three `public` methods:

- ◆ `void write(int b)` — Writes a single byte to the output stream. Because the stream is buffered, the data is not necessarily transferred to disk immediately.

- ◆ `void write(byte b[], int off, int len)` — Writes `len` bytes to the output stream starting with `b[off]`. As with the other form of `write()`, the actual transfer of data to disk might not occur immediately.

- ◆ `void flush()` — Flushes the current buffer, causing any data held in memory to be written to disk immediately.

Typed Input and Output

The file I/O classes and methods presented so far blindly treat file data as no more than a pool of bytes. Although that's an accurate low-level description for all files, their bits and bytes are more interestingly viewed as typed-data values such as integers and characters. For typed I/O, Java provides several useful classes described in the next sections.

The DataInputStream Class

The `DataInputStream` class can read data of any type from a file, using buffered or unbuffered streams. The class's constructor requires an `InputStream` object:

```
DataInputStream(InputStream in);
```

By constructing a `DataInputStream` object, you connect it to any type of low-level input stream object. This can be a file stream, or it can be a buffered file stream — the two most common uses. In most cases, you'll probably want to use a buffered file stream. Doing this takes three steps:

1. Construct a file stream of the `FileInputStream` class.

2. Construct a buffered file stream of the `BufferedInputStream` class using the object from Step 1.

3. Construct a `DataInputStream` object using the buffered stream from Step 2.

These steps build the data input stream in stages, starting with a plain unbuffered stream, progressing to a buffered stream, and finishing with the typed data file stream object. Here are the three steps in code:

```
FileInputStream fin = new FileInputStream(fi);
BufferedInputStream bin = new BufferedInputStream(fin);
DataInputStream din = new DataInputStream(bin);
```

The first statement constructs the unbuffered file stream object, `fin`, using a `File` class object `fi` that represents the file's path name. The resulting file stream object is passed to the `BufferedInputStream` constructor to create the buffered file object, `bin`. Finally, that object is passed to the solitary `DataInputStream` constructor, creating the finished typed data stream, `din`. That object is now ready for reading typed data from the file.

Reading Text Files

Although the preceding steps are valid for most kinds of typed-file I/O, they are no longer recommended for use with character data. For that, relatively newer classes such as `BufferedReader` provide file streams that work correctly with Unicode characters. (Remember that classes with "Reader" in their names are for use with character data.) To demonstrate this class, Listing 24-6, ReadText.java, shows how to read a file as a collection of lines of text.

Listing 24–6: ReadText.java

```
001: import java.io.*;
002:
003: public class ReadText {
...
020:    // Construct File object for named file
021:    public static File getFileForFilename(String filename)
022:      throws IOException {
```

```
023:   File fi = new File(filename);
024:   // Do not move the following statements;
025:   // order is critical
026:   if (!fi.exists())
027:    throw new IOException(fi.getName() + " not found");
028:   if (!fi.isFile())
029:    throw new IOException(fi.getName() + " is not a file");
030:   return fi;
031:  }
032:
033:  // Main program method
034:  public static void main(String args[]) {
035:   String filename;
036:   try {
037:    // Get pathname from command line or prompt user
038:    if (args.length > 0)
039:     filename = args[0];
040:    else
041:     filename = readLine("Read what text file? ");
042:    File fi = getFileForFilename(filename);
043:    FileInputStream fin = new FileInputStream(fi);
044:    BufferedReader bin =
045:     new BufferedReader(new InputStreamReader(fin));
046:    String line = bin.readLine();  // Read first line
047:    while (line != null) {         // Loop until end of file
048:     System.out.println(line);     // Print current line
049:     line = bin.readLine();        // Read next line
050:    }
051:   } catch (IOException e) {        // Trap exception
052:    System.err.println(e.toString());  // Display error
053:   }
054:  }
055: }
```

Lines 042–045 show the correct way to create a BufferedReader object for reading text files line by line. First, create the File object that represents the file. Here, local method getFileForFilename() (lines 021–031) ensures that the specified file exists and that it is a file, not a directory. After this, line 043 constructs the low-level FileInputStream object using the File object:

```
FileInputStream fin = new FileInputStream(fi);
```

Finally, that object is used to construct the BufferedReader:

```
BufferedReader bin =
 new BufferedReader(new InputStreamReader(fin));
```

Use the resulting object to read the text file line by line. A `while` loop handles the job nicely:

```
String line = bin.readLine();
while (line != null) {
 System.out.println(line);
 line = bin.readLine();
}
```

The DataOutputStream Class

As you might suppose, the counterpart to `DataInputStream` is `DataOutputStream`. Use this class to construct a typed output stream object to which you can write strings, integers, floating point values, and other typed data.

Construct a `DataOutputStream` object using the same three steps described for `DataInputStream`. The only difference is that, if the file does not exist, it is created. An existing file is overwritten by the class's output methods, some of which are described in the next section.

Typed File Programming

As an example of how to use the `DataOutputStream` class, Listing 24-7, `WriteData.java`, writes typed data to a test file named Data.bin in the current directory. The program also demonstrates an effective, though not foolproof, way to check that the file contains the expected type of data.

Listing 24-7: WriteData.java

```
001: import java.io.*;
002: import java.util.Random;
003:
004: public class WriteData {
005:
006:  // Main program method
007:  public static void main(String args[]) {
008:   // Instance variables
009:   int dataSize = 10;
010:   Random gen = new Random();
011:   try {
012:    // Create file objects
013:    FileOutputStream fout = new FileOutputStream("Data.bin");
014:    BufferedOutputStream bout = new BufferedOutputStream(fout);
015:    DataOutputStream dout = new DataOutputStream(bout);
016:    // Write data to file in this order:
017:    // 1. number of data elements
018:    // 2. elements
019:    dout.writeInt(dataSize);
```

```
020:       for (int i = 0; i < dataSize; i++) {
021:         dout.writeDouble(gen.nextDouble());
022:       }
023:       dout.flush();
024:       fout.close();
025:       System.out.println(dout.size() + " bytes written");
026:     } catch (IOException e) {              // Trap exception
027:       System.err.println(e.toString());   // Display error
028:     }
029:   }
030: }
```

The sample program constructs the typed output stream using three statements:

```
FileOutputStream fout = new FileOutputStream("Data.bin");
BufferedOutputStream bout = new BufferedOutputStream(fout);
DataOutputStream dout = new DataOutputStream(bout);
```

Rather than use a File object, as is typically done, this time the program specifies the name of a data file as a string. The buffered output file object is created from the plain stream, and finally, the DataOutputStream object, dout, is constructed using the buffered stream from the second step. It is now a simple matter to write typed data to the file. The file may contain any values, of any types, and in any order. To provide a simple verification, the program first writes the number of data elements to the file using this statement:

```
dout.writeInt(dataSize);
```

Next, a for loop writes that many double values, generated at random using an object of the Random class:

```
for (int i = 0; i < dataSize; i++) {
  dout.writeDouble(gen.nextDouble());
}
```

After this, to ensure that the buffered values are written immediately to disk, and that the stream is closed, the program executes two more statements:

```
dout.flush();
fout.close();
```

These actions are optional, but they flush any buffered data to disk and close the file, releasing any held system resources. An output statement displays the number of bytes written by calling the DataOutputStream method, size():

```
System.out.println(dout.size() + " bytes written");
```

The generated file contains two types of data: an integer that represents the number of stored values, each of which is an 8-byte double. Listing 24-8, ReadData.java, shows how to read the file data back into memory.

Listing 24-8: ReadData.java

```
001: import java.io.*;
002:
003: public class ReadData {
004:
005:   // Main program method
006:   public static void main(String args[]) {
007:     // Instance variables
008:     int dataSize;
009:     double data[];
010:     try {
011:       // Create file objects
012:       FileInputStream fin = new FileInputStream("Data.bin");
013:       BufferedInputStream bin = new BufferedInputStream(fin);
014:       DataInputStream din = new DataInputStream(bin);
015:       // Read data from file in this order:
016:       // 1. number of data elements
017:       // 2. elements
018:       dataSize = din.readInt();        // Get number of elements
019:       data = new double[dataSize];   // Create array for data
020:       // Read elements into array
021:       for (int i = 0; i < dataSize; i++) {
022:         data[i] = din.readDouble();  // Read each element
023:       }
024:       fin.close();
025:       // Display results:
026:       System.out.println("\n" + dataSize + " data elements:\n");
027:       for (int i = 0; i < dataSize; i++) {
028:         System.out.println("data[" + i + "] = " + data[i]);
029:       }
030:     } catch (EOFException eof) {        // Trap EOF exception
031:       System.err.println("File damaged or in wrong format");
032:     } catch (IOException e) {           // Trap exception
033:       System.err.println(e.toString());   // Display error
034:     }
035:   }
036: }
```

The sample program uses the same DataInputStream class explained earlier to read the integer and floating point values from the sample data file created by WriteData.java. (For convenience, a copy of the data file is in the ReadData directory on the CD-ROM.)

To hold the data loaded from disk, the program declares an array of double values:

```
double data[];
```

Because Java arrays are created at runtime, the exact size of this array can be determined after opening the file and determining how many values it contains. To do this, the program opens the data file as a buffered stream using three statements:

```
FileInputStream fin = new FileInputStream("Data.bin");
BufferedInputStream bin = new BufferedInputStream(fin);
DataInputStream din = new DataInputStream(bin);
```

These are the same three steps you have seen in other examples. After constructing the input data stream object, din, the program loads the integer stored at the head of the file that indicates how many double values follow:

```
dataSize = din.readInt();
```

The array is then constructed to hold the indicated number of elements:

```
data = new double[dataSize];
```

After this step, a simple for loop loads the double values into the array:

```
for (int i = 0; i < dataSize; i++) {
 data[i] = din.readDouble();  // Read each element
}
```

The readDouble() method reads and returns one double value from the file. The rest of the code in the sample displays these values.

Writing Text Files

Similar to the BufferedReader class, BufferedWriter provides the means to write text files using strings that represent lines. The class's newLine() method ensures that the correct new-line character terminates each line, and calling this method is preferred over writing new-line characters explicitly. Listing 24-9, WriteText.java, demonstrates how to write character data to a text file one line at a time.

Listing 24-9: WriteText.java

```
001: import java.io.*;
002:
003: public class WriteText {
004:
005:   static String[] text = {
```

```
006:    "This is a line of text",
007:    "This is the second line",
008:    "End of text" };
009:
010:    // Main program method
011:    public static void main(String args[]) {
012:      try {
013:        // Create output file object
014:        BufferedWriter tout =
015:          new BufferedWriter(new FileWriter("Data.txt"));
016:        for (int i = 0; i < text.length; i++) {
017:          tout.write(text[i]);
018:          tout.newLine();
019:        }
020:        tout.flush();
021:        tout.close();
022:        System.out.println("File created");
023:      } catch (IOException e) {          // Trap exception
024:        System.err.println(e.toString());  // Display error
025:      }
026:    }
027:  }
```

Running the program creates a file named Data.txt in the current directory with three lines of text, stored in a static array (lines 005-008). To create the text-file stream, construct a BufferedWriter object like this:

```
BufferedWriter tout =
 new BufferedWriter(new FileWriter("Filename.txt"));
```

You may instead pass any Writer object to the constructor, and in that way use a File object to represent the file. Use that method, for example, to check whether a file exists before overwriting it. After creating the BufferedWriter stream object, use it as shown at lines 016-019 to write lines of text to the file. As mentioned, instead of writing the new-line character '\n' explicitly, it's best to call newLine() in the output loop to terminate each line:

```
tout.write(text[i]);
tout.newLine();
```

When finished writing, the program flushes and closes the output stream (see lines 020-021). This simple program could skip the call to flush(). However, if you need to keep the output stream open for any length of time, call flush() every so often to ensure that any buffered text is written to the output file.

Random Access File I/O

The term *random access* is often associated with database file programming, but the term has general application in other types of file I/O. Using the RandomAccessFile class, you can access a file's data randomly at any position. For example, you can skip to a particular byte and read data of a known type at that location.

The RandomAccessFile class handles input and output using random-access techniques. This is a large class with numerous methods such as writeInt() and and readLong() that you can call to read and write typed data. To demonstrate how to use the class, Listing 24-10, ReadRandom.java, reads individual values from a copy of the Data.bin file created by the WriteData.java sample application in this chapter.

Listing 24-10: ReadRandom.java

```
001: import java.io.*;
002:
003: public class ReadRandom {
...
019:   // Main program method
020:   public static void main(String args[]) {
021:     // Instance variables
022:     int dataSize;          // Number of elements in file
023:     int rn;                // Record number
024:     double value;          // Value of requested record
025:     int sizeOfInt = 4;     // Size of int variable
026:     int sizeOfDouble = 8;  // Size of double variable
027:     boolean wantsToQuit = false;
028:     try {
029:       // Create file objects
030:       File fi = new File("Data.bin");
031:       RandomAccessFile rin = new RandomAccessFile(fi, "r");
032:       dataSize = rin.readInt();     // Get number of elements
033:       // Prompt user for element to read
034:       System.out.println("\nFile has " +
035:         dataSize + " elements\n");
036:       while (!wantsToQuit) {
037:         rn = getRecordNumber();
038:         wantsToQuit = (rn == -1);
039:         if (!wantsToQuit) {
040:           // Seek to requested record
041:           rin.seek(sizeOfInt + (rn * sizeOfDouble));
042:           // Read and display value
043:           value = rin.readDouble();
044:           System.out.println("Record " + rn + " = " + value);
045:         }
```

```
046:    }
047:    } catch (IOException e) {          // Trap exception
048:      System.err.println(e.toString());  // Display error
049:    }
050:  }
051: }
```

Compile and run the program using the following commands. Enter the record number of the data value to read. Enter –1 to end the program. Here's a small sample run:

```
javac ReadRandom.java
java ReadRandom
File has 10 elements
Record number (-1 to quit)? 4
Record 4 = 0.9635224138277356
Record number (-1 to quit)? -1
```

To access the data in the file at random, the program constructs two objects using these statements:

```
File fi = new File("Data.bin");
RandomAccessFile rin = new RandomAccessFile(fi, "r");
```

The first line creates a `File` object that refers to `Data.bin`. That object and the mode string `"r"` (for read-only access) are passed to the `RandomAccessFile` constructor. Change the mode string to `"rw"` for read and write access. (There is no write-only `"w"` mode because that would be senseless.) The resulting object, `rin`, is ready for use in randomly accessing the file's data.

In preparation for that operation, the program reads and reports the number of elements from the head of the file. After prompting you to enter a record number, which can be from zero to the number of reported elements minus one, the program positions the file pointer using `seek()`:

```
rin.seek(sizeOfInt + (rn * sizeOfDouble));
```

This statement multiplies the requested record number by the size of a record (a single `double` value). Added to the size of an integer — which accounts for the value written to the head of the file — the statement positions the file pointer to the first byte of the required record. The next statement

```
value = rin.readDouble();
```

reads that value into a `double` variable. You could use similar techniques to read data of any types — even objects of classes that might, for example, represent database records.

Summary

◆ The `java.io` package provides numerous classes for file I/O programming. However, for security reasons, you may use these classes only in a stand-alone program, not an applet running in an Internet browser.

◆ Use the `File` class to represent filenames, directories, and paths. Paths may be absolute or relative.

◆ Use the `FileInputStream` and `FileOutputStream` classes to access file data using simple unbuffered streams.

◆ Use the `BufferedInputStream` and `BufferedOutputStream` to access file data using buffered streams. This may improve the program's performance.

◆ For reading and writing typed file data, Java provides the `DataInputStream` and `DataOutputStream` classes. Use these classes to read and write data of any non-text type of data.

◆ Use `BufferedReader` and `BufferedWriter` for text file input and output. In general, stream I/O classes with "Reader" and "Writer" in their names are for use with character data.

◆ To read and write data at random locations in files, construct an object of the `RandomAccessFile` class. This class contains numerous methods for seeking a file position and then reading and writing data at that location. The class has numerous methods you can use to read and write typed and untyped file data.

Part V

Just Click! Solutions

Chapter 25

Just Click! Solutions by Name

In this chapter is a copy of the online "*Just Click!* Solutions by Name" index for use when you don't have access to your computer. To view this index online, open the byname.html file on the CD-ROM using your favorite Web browser. You can then click on any entry to go directly to that line in the listing file. For reference, the listing page numbers are also printed here and shown online. Note the line number before clicking or turning the page — this will help you locate the exact solution you need. See Chapter 2, "Using the *Just Click!* Solutions Indexes," for more information about using the by-name and by-subject indexes online.

Solutions by Name

Summary

◆ Use this printed copy of the CD-ROM's online index to find solutions to problems by name.

Chapter 26

Just Click! Solutions by Subject

In this chapter is a copy of the online "*Just Click!* Solutions by Subject" index for use when you don't have access to your computer. To view this index online, open the bysubj.html file on the CD-ROM using your favorite Web browser. You can then click on any entry to go directly to that line in the listing file. For reference, the listing page numbers are also printed here and shown online. Note the line number before clicking or turning the page – this will help you locate the exact solution you need. See Chapter 2, "Using the *Just Click!* Solutions Indexes," for more information about using the by name and by subject indexes online.

Solutions by Subject

ACCESS RULES
Accessing private data, Listing 6-5, Serial/Serial.java, Line 009, Page 91
Declaring protected instance variables, Listing 11-2, ProtectedData/ProtectedData.java, Line 001, Page 216
Extending a class with protected data, Listing 11-2, ProtectedData/ProtectedData.java, Line 016, Page 216
Hiding data using private access specifier, Listing 11-1, DataHiding/DataHiding.java, Line 001, Page 214
Private constructors, Listing 7-1, ExceptDemo/ExceptDemo.java, Line 009, Page 105
Public class method, example, Listing 6-1, DateObject/DateObject.java, Line 006, Page 81
Static private data, Listing 6-5, Serial/Serial.java, Line 002, Page 91

APPLET CLASS
Animation in applets, Listing 23-8, Animation/Animation.java, Line 004, Page 547
Applet, extending, Listing 20-1, AppletADay/AppletADay.java, Line 005, Page 405
Initializing applet in threaded code, Listing 23-8, Animation/Animation.java, Line 019, Page 547
Writing extended Applet class, Listing 20-3, BackColor/BackColor.java, Line 005, Page 414

APPLETS

ARRAYLIST CLASS

ARRAYS CLASS

ARRAYS

AWT

DAEMONS

DATE CLASS

DIALOGS

EVENTS

FILEINPUTSTREAM

FILES

FILTERS

FLOW CONTROL STATEMENTS

FONTS

GRAPHICS

HASHMAP CLASS

HASHSET CLASS

HTML

JLabel, create using HTML text, Listing 22-10, TextDemo/TextDemo.java, Line 037,
  Page 490

Use HTML to format a label, Listing 22-8, LabelDemo/LabelDemo.java, Line 036, Page 485

I/O

Construct File object for a directory path, Listing 24-2, Directory/Directory.java, Line 020,
  Page 561

Construct File object for a named file, Listing 24-3, FileInfo/FileInfo.java, Line 021,
  Page 563

Display information about a File object, Listing 24-3, FileInfo/FileInfo.java, Line 040,
  Page 563

Display integer variables, Listing 4-4, IntDemo/IntDemo.java, Line 009, Page 52

Filter filenames using FilenameFilter interface, Listing 24-4, FilterDir/FilterDir.java,
  Line 001, Page 565

Get information about a file, Listing 24-3, FileInfo/FileInfo.java, Line 001, Page 563

Keypress, method to wait for, Listing 19-4, Primes/Primes.java, Line 056, Page 377

Read typed data from a file, Listing 24-8, ReadData/ReadData.java, Line 001, Page 577

Reading a string from System.in, Listing 24-1, ReadLine/ReadLine.java, Line 001, Page 557

Reading lines from a text file, Listing 24-6, ReadText/ReadText.java, Line 001, Page 573

Reading typed data using random access, Listing 24-10, ReadRandom/ReadRandom.java,
  Line 001, Page 580

Use File class to create a filename directory, Listing 24-2, Directory/Directory.java,
  Line 001, Page 561

Use File class to list a directory, Listing 24-2, Directory/Directory.java, Line 038, Page 561

Use file streams to copy a file, Listing 24-5, CopyFile/CopyFile.java, Line 047, Page 568

Use file streams to copy a file, Listing 24-5, CopyFile/CopyFile.java, Line 001, Page 568

Write lines of text to a file, Listing 24-9, WriteText/WriteText.java, Line 001, Page 578

Writing typed data to a file, Listing 24-7, WriteData/WriteData.java, Line 001, Page 575

ICONS

Add an icon to a text label, Listing 22-8, LabelDemo/LabelDemo.java, Line 031, Page 485

Demonstrate a two-state toggle button, Listing 22-2, ToggleDemo/ToggleDemo.java,
  Line 001, Page 466

Display icon images in JButton objects, Listing 22-1, ButtonIcon/ButtonIcon.java, Line 001,
  Page 464

Load an icon image GIF file, Listing 22-1, ButtonIcon/ButtonIcon.java, Line 023, Page 464

Use HTML to format a label, Listing 22-8, LabelDemo/LabelDemo.java, Line 036, Page 485

IMAGES

Display icon images in JButton objects, Listing 22-1, ButtonIcon/ButtonIcon.java, Line 001,
  Page 464

Image filtering, color to black-and-white, Listing 23-6, Filter/Filter.java, Line 001, Page 541

ITERATOR INTERFACE

JFRAME

LAYOUTS

LINKEDLIST CLASS

LIST INTERFACE

LISTING FILES

LISTITERATOR INTERFACE

LISTS

LOCALES

MAP INTERFACE

MAP.ENTRY INTERFACE

MATH

MENUS

METHODS

OPERATORS

OUTPUT

PACKAGES

PANELS

PARAMETERS

SWING

SYNCHRONIZED

SYSTEM CLASS

TEXT

THREAD CLASS

THREADS

Summary

- ◆ Use this printed copy of the CD-ROM's online index to find solutions to problems by subject.

Appendix

What's on the CD-ROM?

THIS APPENDIX PROVIDES YOU with information on the contents of the CD-ROM that accompanies this book. See the file Readme.txt (if present) for any late-breaking instructions, corrections, and other information.

This CD-ROM contains the following elements:

- ◆ Source code to over 150 sample Java 2 programs

- ◆ Tom Swan's hyper-linked *Just Click! Solutions* indexes

- ◆ Microsoft Internet Explorer 5.5

- ◆ Netscape Communicator 4.7 for Windows and Linux

- ◆ MindSpring Internet access

System Requirements

The Java 2 runtime and JDK 1.3 software runs under Microsoft Windows 2000, NT, 98, and 95, most versions of Linux, and Sun Solaris operating systems. Following are approximate system requirements for installing and running Java 2 plus this book's source code listings and indexes on Intel-based systems:

- ◆ Pentium 166MHz or faster processor

- ◆ A minimum of 32MB RAM for GUI applications; 48MB for applets running in a Web browser using the Java 2 Plug-in; additional RAM may be required for very large applications

- ◆ 65MB available disk space to install the JDK 1.3 files and runtime software

- ◆ An additional 120MB available disk space to install the optional Java 2 documentation files

- ◆ An additional 2.5MB available disk space to install this book's *Just Click! Solutions* indexes and source code listings

Using the CD with Windows or Linux

See Chapter 2, "Using the *Just Click! Solutions* Indexes," for help with installing this book's source code listings for Windows and Linux. Also see Chapter 3, "Getting Started with Java 2," for instructions about how to obtain the Java 2 development kit and runtime systems. All source code listings are in a directory on the CD-ROM titled src. To view listings online, load the file Index.html from the src directory into any Web browser.

What's on the CD

The CD-ROM contains source code examples, applications, and an electronic version of the book. Following is a summary of the contents of the CD-ROM arranged by category.

Source Code

Every program listing printed in the book is on the CD in the folder named src. See Chapter 2, "Using the *Just Click! Solutions* Indexes," for help with installing and using these files, and for viewing listings online using Tom Swan's *Just Click! Solutions* hyperlinked indexes.

Applications

The following applications are on the CD-ROM:

BROWSERS

A browser is the client software you use to access files on the Internet or to read local HTML files.

♦ Internet Explorer: a Web browser for Windows 9*x* or later. Freeware.

For more information: www.microsoft.com

♦ Netscape Navigator: a Web browser for Windows 9*x* or later; a version is also available for Linux. Freeware.

For more information: www.netscape.com

INTERNET ACCESS

♦ MindSpring Internet Access: a package of applications designed to help you subscribe to and utilize Internet service from MindSpring. Freeware.

For more information: www.mindspring.com

Troubleshooting

If you have difficulty installing or using the CD-ROM programs, try the following solutions:

♦ **Turn off any anti-virus software that you may have running.** Installers sometimes mimic virus activity and can make your computer incorrectly believe that it is being infected by a virus. (Be sure to turn the anti-virus software back on later.)

♦ **Close all running programs.** The more programs you're running, the less memory is available to other programs. Installers also typically update files and programs; if you keep other programs running, installation may not work properly.

♦ **Mark copied files for writing.** After copying files from the CD-ROM to your hard drive, they may be marked "read-only." See the "Installing the Indexes" section in Chapter 2 for instructions about marking files for writing so you can edit and save them.

If you still have trouble with the CD, please call the Hungry Minds Customer Service phone number: (800) 762-2974. Outside the United States, call (317) 572-3993 or send e-mail to techsupdum@hungryminds.com. Hungry Minds will provide technical support only for installation and other general quality control items; for technical support on the applications themselves, consult the program's vendor or author.

Index

Hungry Minds, Inc.
End–User License Agreement

READ THIS. You should carefully read these terms and conditions before opening the software packet(s) included with this book ("Book"). This is a license agreement ("Agreement") between you and Hungry Minds, Inc. ("HMI"). By opening the accompanying software packet(s), you acknowledge that you have read and accept the following terms and conditions. If you do not agree and do not want to be bound by such terms and conditions, promptly return the Book and the unopened software packet(s) to the place you obtained them for a full refund.

1. **License Grant.** HMI grants to you (either an individual or entity) a nonexclusive license to use one copy of the enclosed software program(s) (collectively, the "Software") solely for your own personal or business purposes on a single computer (whether a standard computer or a workstation component of a multi-user network). The Software is in use on a computer when it is loaded into temporary memory (RAM) or installed into permanent memory (hard disk, CD-ROM, or other storage device). HMI reserves all rights not expressly granted herein.

2. **Ownership.** HMI is the owner of all right, title, and interest, including copyright, in and to the compilation of the Software recorded on the disk(s) or CD-ROM ("Software Media"). Copyright to the individual programs recorded on the Software Media is owned by the author or other authorized copyright owner of each program. Ownership of the Software and all proprietary rights relating thereto remain with HMI and its licensers.

3. **Restrictions On Use and Transfer.**

   (a) You may only (i) make one copy of the Software for backup or archival purposes, or (ii) transfer the Software to a single hard disk, provided that you keep the original for backup or archival purposes. You may not (i) rent or lease the Software, (ii) copy or reproduce the Software through a LAN or other network system or through any computer subscriber system or bulletin-board system, or (iii) modify, adapt, or create derivative works based on the Software.

   (b) You may not reverse engineer, decompile, or disassemble the Software. You may transfer the Software and user documentation on a permanent basis, provided that the transferee agrees to accept the terms and conditions of this Agreement and you retain no copies. If the Software is an update or has been updated, any transfer must include the most recent update and all prior versions.

4. **Restrictions on Use of Individual Programs.** You must follow the individual requirements and restrictions detailed for each individual program in the appendix of this Book. These limitations are also contained in the individual license agreements recorded on the Software Media. These limitations may include a requirement that after using the program for a specified period of time, the user must pay a registration fee or discontinue use. By opening the Software packet(s), you will be agreeing to abide by the licenses and restrictions for these individual programs that are detailed in the appendix and on the Software Media. None of the material on this Software Media or listed in this Book may ever be redistributed, in original or modified form, for commercial purposes.

5. **Limited Warranty.**

   (a) HMI warrants that the Software and Software Media are free from defects in materials and workmanship under normal use for a period of sixty (60) days from the date of purchase of this Book. If HMI receives notification within the warranty period of defects in materials or workmanship, HMI will replace the defective Software Media.

   (b) HMI AND THE AUTHOR OF THE BOOK DISCLAIM ALL OTHER WARRANTIES, EXPRESS OR IMPLIED, INCLUDING WITHOUT LIMITATION IMPLIED WARRANTIES OF MERCHANTABILITY AND FITNESS FOR A PARTICULAR PURPOSE, WITH RESPECT TO THE SOFTWARE, THE PROGRAMS, THE SOURCE CODE CONTAINED THEREIN, AND/OR THE TECHNIQUES DESCRIBED IN THIS BOOK. HMI DOES NOT WARRANT THAT THE FUNCTIONS CONTAINED IN THE SOFTWARE WILL MEET YOUR REQUIREMENTS OR THAT THE OPERATION OF THE SOFTWARE WILL BE ERROR FREE.

   (c) This limited warranty gives you specific legal rights, and you may have other rights that vary from jurisdiction to jurisdiction.

6. **Remedies.**

   (a) HMI's entire liability and your exclusive remedy for defects in materials and workmanship shall be limited to replacement of the Software Media, which may be returned to HMI with a copy of your receipt at the following address: Software Media Fulfillment Department, Attn.: *Java™ 2 Just Click! Solutions*, Hungry Minds, Inc., 10475 Crosspoint Blvd., Indianapolis, IN 46256, or call 1-800-762-2974. Please allow four to six weeks for delivery. This Limited Warranty is void if failure of the Software Media has resulted from accident, abuse, or misapplication. Any replacement Software Media will be warranted for the remainder of the original warranty period or thirty (30) days, whichever is longer.

(b) In no event shall HMI or the author be liable for any damages whatsoever (including without limitation damages for loss of business profits, business interruption, loss of business information, or any other pecuniary loss) arising from the use of or inability to use the Book or the Software, even if HMI has been advised of the possibility of such damages.

(c) Because some jurisdictions do not allow the exclusion or limitation of liability for consequential or incidental damages, the above limitation or exclusion may not apply to you.

7. **U.S. Government Restricted Rights.** Use, duplication, or disclosure of the Software for or on behalf of the United States of America, its agencies and/or instrumentalities (the "U.S. Government") is subject to restrictions as stated in paragraph (c)(1)(ii) of the Rights in Technical Data and Computer Software clause of DFARS 252.227-7013, or subparagraphs (c)(1) and (2) of the Commercial Computer Software - Restricted Rights clause at FAR 52.227-19, and in similar clauses in the NASA FAR supplement, as applicable.

8. **General.** This Agreement constitutes the entire understanding of the parties and revokes and supersedes all prior agreements, oral or written, between them and may not be modified or amended except in a writing signed by both parties hereto that specifically refers to this Agreement. This Agreement shall take precedence over any other documents that may be in conflict herewith. If any one or more provisions contained in this Agreement are held by any court or tribunal to be invalid, illegal, or otherwise unenforceable, each and every other provision shall remain in full force and effect.

CD-ROM Installation Instructions

The CD-ROM contains source code to more than 150 sample Java 2 programs, the author's hyperlinked *Just Click! Solutions* indexes, and additional browser and Internet access software.

Consult the book's appendix for additional details on the CD-ROM contents; for full, platform-specific installation instructions, see Chapter 2, "Using the *Just Click! Solutions* Indexes."